Time Management with SAP® ERP HCM

 **PRESS**

SAP PRESS is a joint initiative of SAP and Galileo Press. The know-how offered by SAP specialists combined with the expertise of the Galileo Press publishing house offers the reader expert books in the field. SAP PRESS features first-hand information and expert advice, and provides useful skills for professional decision-making.

SAP PRESS offers a variety of books on technical and business related topics for the SAP user. For further information, please visit our website: *www.sap-press.com*.

Martin Gillet
2008, 232 pp.
Integrating CATS, second edition
978-1-59229-260-8

Jeremy Master and Christos Kotsakis
Implementing Employee and Manager Self-Services
In SAP ERP HCM
2008, 431 pp.
978-1-59229-188-5

Manuel Gallardo
Configuring and Using CATS
2008, 162 pp.
978-1-59229-232-5

Martin Esch, Anja Junold
Authorizations in SAP ERP HCM
2008, 336 pp.
978-1-59229-165-6

Brian Schaer

Time Management with SAP® ERP HCM

Bonn • Boston

ISBN 978-1-59229-229-5

© 2009 by Galileo Press Inc., Boston (MA)
1st Edition 2009

Galileo Press is named after the Italian physicist, mathematician and philosopher Galileo Galilei (1564–1642). He is known as one of the founders of modern science and an advocate of our contemporary, heliocentric worldview. His words *Eppur si muove* (And yet it moves) have become legendary. The Galileo Press logo depicts Jupiter orbited by the four Galilean moons, which were discovered by Galileo in 1610.

Editor   Jenifer Niles
Copyeditor   Mike Beady
Cover Design   Jill Winitzer
Photo Credit   Photos.com
Layout Design   Vera Brauner
Production   Kelly O'Callaghan
Typesetting   Publishers' Design and Production Services, Inc.
Printed and bound in Canada

Contents at a Glance

Contents

6   Time Data Recording and Administration 153

9 Time Evaluation Without Clock Times 275

Acknowledgments

To my mother, father and brother, I thank you for all you have done over the years and for providing me the foundation to be successful in life. To my wife and children, I thank you for providing me the opportunity to take on such an endeavor and for supporting me along the way. I would also like to thank all of my past clients and colleagues from whom I've learned much over the years. Finally, I would like to thank my editor for all of her efforts during the process of writing this book.

This chapter provides you with an overview of the SAP ERP HCM Time Management functionality. You'll be introduced to the various functions, terminology, and the overall layout of the chapters within this book.

1 Human Resources (HR) Time Management

Time Management is a key functionality of the SAP ERP Human Capital Management (HCM) solution. It is the area of HR that allows you to enter, track, and calculate time-related information that will be passed to a payroll system so that employees will be compensated. Examples of captured time may include regular time for hourly employees and salary, including holidays and vacation payouts, for salaried employees. In addition, there are opportunities to track the availability of employees, schedule shifts, and interface to other SAP applications such as Materials Management (MM) and Project System (PS).

You will want to utilize Time Management, or pieces of it, if any time-related data needs to be tracked in your system. The degree to which you utilize it really depends on how much functionality your business is seeking to implement. As you approach your implementation of the system, the blueprinting of the business requirements and overall system functionality will be established and what you might need to implement will become more evident.

This book is organized to guide you through the system setup. Chapter 2 is a foundational chapter to help you understand key areas to consider when blueprinting. Chapters 3 through 14 have been established to mostly follow the Implementation Guide (IMG), which is where you configure and set up the system. The following are the chapter titles within this book.

Chapter 2 Time Management Blueprint Considerations

Chapter 3 Overview of Integrating Time Management with Other Components

Chapter 4 Time Management Master Data

Chapter 5 Work Schedules

Chapter 6 Time Data Recording and Administration

Chapter 7 Personnel Time Events

Chapter 8 Time Evaluation with Clock Times

Chapter 9 Time Evaluation Without Clock Times

Chapter 10 Evaluation and Time Management Pool

Chapter 11 Time Manager's Workplace

Chapter 12 Shift Planning

Chapter 13 Time Entry Options in SAP ERP HCM Time Management

Chapter 14 Advanced Configuration Topics

Within each chapter, you will also find references to certain appendices that are in the back of the book. The appendices have various degrees of relevance depending on which stage of the implementation you are in. At a minimum, they have been provided so that you have a quick reference guide to some common areas of the system where decisions need to be based on particular fields in the system. The following appendices have been provided, broken down by chapter.

▶ Chapter 2 — Time Management Blueprint Considerations
  ▶ Appendix A — Infotypes
  ▶ Appendix B —Program Overview
▶ Chapter 4 — Time Management Master Data
  ▶ Appendix C — Time Management Features
  ▶ Appendix D — Work Schedule Combinations
▶ Chapter 8 — Time Evaluation with Clock Times
  ▶ Appendix E — Time Evaluation Storage Tables
▶ Chapter 9 — Time Evaluation without Clock Times
  ▶ Appendix F — Time Functions
  ▶ Appendix G — Time Management Operations
  ▶ Appendix H — Personnel Calculation Rules

Throughout the chapters, you will find references to the appendices. The appendices contain supplemental data, tables, advanced topics, etc., that have been extracted from the chapters and placed into an index for ongoing reference purposes. This is useful information and as your knowledge of the system increases, may serve as an ongoing reference through all stages of a project, including production support.

What does Time Management really mean? Does it mean you are on time for meetings or have found a way to work eight days a week? Time Management of employees is the system's methodology for providing a mechanism so that the administration of time-related data is accurate and as streamlined as possible. Employees enter time codes into a timesheet so that the system can capture the data, analyze the data, and adjust the data based on pay practices, and finally compensate employees for those codes processed in the system.

Does Time Management actually pay the employees? Time Management facilitates the payment of employees by providing payroll systems the required data through integration points between the two components of functionality to accurately compensate each payroll frequency. In addition to the basic functions of calculating time, the system provides tools for administrators to maintain, track, and process the data in an efficient manner.

The following list provides a brief overview of each chapter. Certain chapters provide key management decisions that will help you in the long run for a successful implementation. In addition, you will see plenty of screens, diagrams, and tables that will help you visualize the concepts, and the overall look and feel of the system.

▶ *Chapter 2 Time Management Blueprint Considerations*
This chapter was designed to provide you an overview of the blueprint process. Because the Time Management functionality heavily utilizes the Enterprise and Personnel Structures, a special emphasis has been given to these concepts and how the various components of functionality depend on the settings and groupings established.

▶ *Chapter 3 Overview of Integrating Time Management with Other Components*
This chapter was designed to provide you an overview of the integration points to other SAP components contained within the system.

▶ *Chapter 4 Time Management Master Data*
This chapter was designed to provide you an overview of all of the time-related infotypes. There are numerous infotypes delivered in the system. You can pick and choose which ones you will utilize based on the final outcome of your

system blueprint. This chapter provides screen captures of each infotype and the field descriptions.

▶ *Chapter 5 Work Schedules*
This chapter was designed to provide you with an in-depth look at the various components of a work schedule, how a work schedule is set up and provides insight to design implications.

▶ *Chapter 6 Time Data Recording and Administration*
This chapter was designed to provide you with a detailed knowledge of the configuration that supports the entry of time-data-related information on particular infotypes.

▶ *Chapter 7 Personnel Time Events*
This chapter explains the configurations related to capturing time-related information using clock times.

▶ *Chapter 8 Time Evaluation with Clock Times*
This chapter explains the various processing areas of utilizing Time Evaluation with clock times. This functionality is utilized when clock times are entered via the SAP system or a third-party bolt on the time collection system that enters the SAP system unevaluated. Schema TM00 is broken down and explained in this chapter.

▶ *Chapter 9 Time Evaluation Without Clock Times*
Similar to Chapter 8, this chapter explains the various processing areas of utilizing Time Evaluation without clock times. These are time entries that are already evaluated meaning that duration of time is already calculated. This chapter goes into detail regarding the personnel calculation rules that support the processing schema TM04.

▶ *Chapter 10 Evaluation and Time Management Pool*
This chapter explains the various setups utilized to review Time Evaluation results in the system. In addition, the Time Management pool workbench is described providing details about the various programs and reports that are linked to the workbench.

▶ *Chapter 11 Time Manager's Workplace*
This chapter explains the time manager's workplace workbench, which is mainly used to help in the administration of time in a decentralized environment. The functionality is explained and how to customize the user interfaces.

▶ *Chapter 12 Shift Planning*
This chapter explains the shift planning component and how the tool can be set up and utilized in the management of workforce demands. Shift planning is a component that, with Time Management, allows you to alter an employee's planned working time based on your workforce demands. The shift-planning functionality provides a workbench that imports your employee's data into one location so that you can view, maintain, and resolve any schedule conflicts that might arise. The shift-planning functionality is highly integrated with attendances, absences, and work schedule rule components, such as the daily work schedule.

▶ *Chapter 13 Time Entry Options in SAP ERP HCM Time Management*
This chapter provides an overview of the dataflow that utilizes the various methodologies for entering time into SAP.

▶ *Chapter 14 Advanced Configuration Topics*
This chapter is broken into four parts:

  ▶ **Incentive Wages**
  This section briefly explains the incentive wages functionality. Incentive wages represent functionality that would enable the SAP system to compensate employees based on set criteria. This criterion, at its simplest form, would be compensation for unit of work conducted. Incentive wages can integrate with the logistics component.

  ▶ **Web Applications**
  This section briefly describes the Employee Self-Service (ESS) web applications used to enter time into the SAP system.

  ▶ **Concurrent Employment Processing**
  This section briefly explains concurrent system processing within the Time Management functionality.

  ▶ **Security and Authorizations**
  This section lists the various authorization objects related to the HR component. In addition, the various transaction codes related to the Time Management functionality are presented.

In addition to the chapters listed, it is worthwhile to mention a few other key topics to help establish baseline knowledge of some functionality. The following are a few of the topics you should understand to get the most out of this book. You may already be familiar with these topics and terms, but we've included them for those new to SAP, just starting to work with Time Management, or anyone who just needs a quick refresher.

- **Timesheet**

  The timesheet is the mechanism by which most employees enter time into the system. SAP offers timesheets through their portal via ESS or from directly within SAP. We say most because you can also leverage a third-party bolt on time-keeping systems and interface the data directly to the SAP system for subsequent processing. The term Cross-Application Time Sheet (CATS) is the name SAP's time entry screens are referenced by. The data entered into CATS either directly or through the portal or third-party time-keeping system can be interfaced with other components within the SAP system, such as Project Systems or Controlling.

- **Employee Availability**

  Employee Availability is functionality in the system that enables your business to determine which employees may or may not be available for particular shifts. The system can be set up so that it leverages other components, such as time data recording, by reviewing attendances and absences to determine how much they have worked or are potentially scheduled to work in the future. Availability processing is utilized within the shift-planning components and training and events-planning components. This functionality would be very useful in planning your resources working times or perhaps in emergencies when extra resources would be needed to satisfy the working requirements.

- **Forms Processing**

  While forms are not a specific piece of functionality within the Time Management functionality, they do provide you the opportunity to allow time-related data to be viewed by time administrators and employees. Specifically, SAP provides what is called a time statement form. This form provides specific absences and attendance-related information and any custom buckets of time onto a report that would be beneficial for employees or managers to see.

- **Reporting**

  SAP offers numerous canned reports out of the box to facilitate various reporting requirements across Time Management. Some of the report names are listed here and are broken down into various functionality groupings. There are other reports available throughout the Time Management menu path as well, but we will not be covering these in this book.

1.1   Time Management Terminology

There will be a plethora of new concepts and terminology used throughout this book, so it may be helpful to have a quick review to get you started. We will elaborate on these terms in more depth when they are covered in the applicable chapters.

- **Infotypes** — A logical grouping of screen-related information that pertains to an employee's personal data. An example might include your home address. Here, all of the information would be stored on one screen for any related address information. There are many different infotypes throughout the system that are utilized by various SAP ERP HCM components. The Time Management functionality is no exception and each infotype has been defined in detail in Chapter 4.

- **Master Data** — An employee's personnel information or employee record.

There are a few key areas that set the foundation for which most master data is associated with particular employees and processing across the various HR functions occurs. Each of these sections is elaborated on in Chapter 2. This foundation is broken down into the following sections:

- **Enterprise Structure** — The Enterprise Structure is the core foundation that, once defined, associates the employees with location-related information throughout the company. Under the Enterprise Structure you find the following key terms:

  - **Company Code** — A term that has developed into one of the highest levels within the SAP ERP Finance component in which a legal company is processed.

  - **Cost Center** — A finance component term that was developed to contain costs of particular items.

  - **Personnel Area** — An HR term that usually describes a particular location or region of your business. This might be a distribution center or an office location.

  - **Personnel Subarea** — An HR term usually defined to further describe the Personnel Area. This might be a further breakdown of the Personnel Areas, such as departments like HR, sales, etc.

- **Personnel Structure** — The Personnel Structure, similar to the Enterprise Structure, is the core HR foundation for describing employee information. Under the Enterprise Structure you will find the following key terms:

  - **Employee Group** — Established to describe a type of employee. Examples include full time, part time, etc.

  - **Employee Subgroup** — Established to further describe the Employee Group. This might include Salary, Hourly, Officer, etc.

  - **Payroll Area** — Established to group employees so that they process through payroll under the same frequency.

- **Organizational Structure** — The organizational structure is the third structure used to associated employees within the business. This structure then associates employees with Job and Positions and then associates these individuals within the organizational chart within the corporation.

One of the foundations to an employee's ability to enter time-related data and accurately process this data through the Time Management functionality is a concept called *work schedules*. At its simplest form, this is merely the dates and times an employee should report for work. From an SAP software perspective, the work schedule is a little more complex as it is comprised of different elements that, when strung together, allow the work schedule to set the foundation for conducting complex calculations in Time Evaluation and control the ways in which time is entered and processed through the SAP system. These concepts are covered in detail in Chapter 5; however, the following key terms will be introduced here. Each of these terms in the order that they are listed, builds the foundation for the next term.

- **Break Schedule** — A break schedule defines when an employee should take a break and the time frames for the break. The time can be set up to be paid or unpaid time. The break schedules, once defined, are part of the daily work schedules.

- **Daily Work Schedule** — A daily work schedule is the set times or set amount of hours that an employee should be working for a particular day. A daily work schedule can even be that the employee is not scheduled to work and has zero planned hours for the day. Break schedules are linked directly to daily work schedules.

- **Period Work Schedule** — A period work schedule is comprised of daily work schedules. You can string daily work schedules together for each period the employee works. They are typically seven-day time frames; however, you can set up the schedule to rotate for particular weeks.

▶ **Work Schedule Rule** — A work schedule rule is the final component. The period work schedule is linked to the work schedule rule. All of the underlying settings are carried forward to the work schedule rule. The rules are associated with employees directly on their master data.

An employee's ability to actually enter time-related data into the SAP system requires a structure by which they can be stored. Think of your own place of employment and how you record your time. When you take the family on vacation, or if you show up to work, how does your employer know? These concepts are covered in detail in Chapter 6, however, some of the key terms will be introduced here. These are merely codes so that employees can enter their time-related data.

▶ **Attendance Type** — The description of your attendance. Examples might include regular time, training, etc.

▶ **Absence Type** — The description of your absence. Examples might include vacation, holiday, unpaid absence, etc.

▶ **Wage Type** — A descriptive code that is established to pay employees. Examples might include bonus, salary, etc. Attendance and Absence types will eventually become Wage types. The Wage types are used by the payroll system to compensate employees.

▶ **Time Type** — A code utilized in Time Evaluation to help translate the attendance and absence types to Wage types. They are also used as reference points to make decisions from and store time-related buckets of information for processing and reporting.

One of the more complex sections of this book is on the subject of Time Evaluation. Within Time Evaluation, there will also be new concepts and terminology. Chapters 8 and 9 will go into specific details; however, the following key terms should be introduced as they are used throughout the various chapters.

▶ **Schema** — A schema is a set of processing instructions that is utilized to process specific functionality related to time calculations. It is the highest level of the terms described from Time Evaluation and contains functions, rules, and operations. The Time Evaluation schema is used by the Time Evaluation program.

- **Function** — A function is a predefined set of processing instructions that are sequenced within the schema to carry out your business requirements.

- **Personal Calculation Rule** — A rule is called by a function and is where you set up all of your particular calculations. An example might be how to compensate employees for any hours worked over 40 hours for a particular week.

- **Operation** — An operation lies within a personnel calculation rule and allows you to conduct your specific calculations per your business requirements.

1.2 Summary

Hopefully this chapter has given you an overview of the SAP ERP HCM Time Management key terminology. As you read through the book, please keep in mind that it's extremely difficult to provide every possibility of how the system can and should be set up because of the flexibility of such a system. But we have attempted to provide a great deal of real-world insight and lessons learned from previous implementations. So hopefully you will glean the information that will work for you in your own business.

In the next chapter, we'll talk about the blueprinting phase. It's my belief that there is never an adequate amount of time allowed in project plans to really determine and understand business requirements in such a way that the overall design of the system is set up to optimize most business processes. With that said, be sure that you're comfortable with the blueprinting stage and learn as much as possible about how particular decisions will impact your ability to systematically solve your business requirements.

In this chapter, you will learn about key areas to consider during the blueprinting phase of a project and how key decisions will impact the SAP ERP HCM Time Management functionality.

2   Time Management Blueprint Considerations

During the implementation of SAP software, one of the first stages of a project is to determine the business requirements for the organization. These requirements are then overlaid on top of SAP's standard business processes to expose gaps in functionality or areas of the business where processing procedures may need to be adjusted.

One of the first items on the agenda when implementing the Time Management component is to determine what the business drivers are for the software. Your project team needs to decide what functionality is going to be implemented, what is slated to be implemented in the future, and how robust the system setup needs to be to accommodate the business requirements. The answers to these questions will determine to what degree your system needs to be configured, how the groupings for the various components should be structured, and the overall scope and timeline of the various phases of the implementation.

During this phase of the implementation, there are some key decisions that will require an answer early into the process.

Key Management Decision Points— Blueprinting Decisions

The following items are key decision points for the overall success of the implementation.

▶ What components of Time Management will be implemented?

▶ How is an employee's time going to be entered into the system?

The business owners of the timekeeping processes must decide if SAP's software methodologies for capturing time will be used or if a third-party time collection system will be purchased separately and implemented in conjunction with the SAP Time Management component and project timelines.

If the business elects to use both SAP and a third-party system, you need to make decisions about which system is the real source of the data, where the calculations will be made, and where management or time administrators will maintain the key pieces of data.

► Is your business willing to maintain the accurate employee master data required to support the system to automate time and payroll business rules?

► How many time management and payroll pay practices will you need to automate in the system?

► What functionality, reporting, or interface requirements will require the time-evaluation component?

2.1 Human Resources (HR) Structures

When blueprinting SAP ERP HCM Time Management, there are a couple of key activities that will take place. One of those key activities is determining the foundational infrastructure of the HR component as a whole. All of the HR subcomponents utilize the same structure and, therefore, representation from all subteams is imperative.

Infotype 0001 Organizational Assignment is a required infotype for all employees and nonemployees in the system. This infotype contains three key areas.

► Enterprise Structure

► Personnel Structure

► Organizational Structure

2.1.1 Enterprise Structure

Enterprise Structure consists of the following key elements for time management:

▶ *Company Code*

The company code is defined in the Financial Accounting component and is used by the HR component.

▶ *Personnel Area*

The Personnel Area represents an entity within the organization. This representation is most often considered a location. The Personnel Area is linked to a company code.

▶ *Personnel Subarea*

The Personnel Subarea represents a further breakdown of the Personnel Area. This subarea further defines the Personnel Area in such a way that other subcomponents, such as Personnel Administration, Payroll, and Time Management, can utilize the logical grouping to rollout proper reporting information, process specific requirements in payroll and time management for those locations.

The Personnel Subarea is a key area for the Time Management component. A large portion of the groupings in the configuration are based on the meaning of this structure. So, when determining the values of the Enterprise Structure, you'll need to take into account collective bargaining agreements, time, and payroll calculations for particular types of locations in the organization. The final meaning of the Personnel Subarea will need to be granular enough to allow the configuration of the system to meet your business requirements.

Using the following sample Enterprise Structure, we'll explain the concept further. Let's take a very simplistic company that has two Personnel Areas for its operations. The first Personnel Area represents the east coast. The second Personnel Area represents the west coast. Both locations have hourly and salaried employees; however, the west coast also has collective bargaining units. Each of the west coast bargaining units has its own special absence codes that should not be available to any other grouping within the company. So in order to accommodate the business requirements, the collective bargaining units in this scenario would be as shown in Figure 2.1.

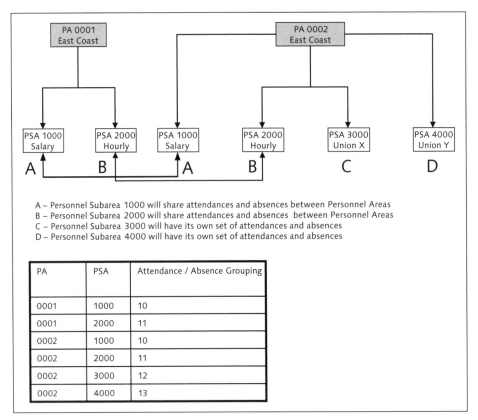

Figure 2.1 Sample Enterprise Structure

Figure 2.1 illustrates the need to have the Personnel Subarea grouping defined at such a detailed level so that each collective bargaining agreement is defined as a separate Personnel Subarea. This example only takes into account a business requirement dictating that the collective bargaining agreements have their own set of attendance and absence codes. You must look at the overall time solution in its entirely to ensure you have the correct level of granularity defined at this level.

Building on our example, let's see what happens when the company has the following business rules.

The collective bargaining agreements must have their own set of attendances and absences. One of the collective bargaining agreements (psa 3000) has two variations of contract requirements regarding work schedules:

▶ Group 1 should have one set of work schedules with no visibility to Group 2's work schedules

▶ Group 2 should also have its own set of work schedules that are not visible to Group 1.

Figure 2.2 illustrates this example.

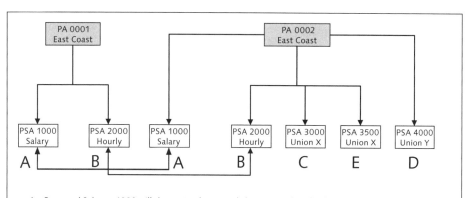

A – Personnel Subarea 1000 will share attendances and absences and work schedules between Personnel Areas
B – Personnel Subarea 2000 will share attendances and absences and work schedules between Personnel Areas
C – Personnel Subarea 3000 will have its own set of attendances and absences and work schedules
D – Personnel Subarea 4000 will have its own set of attendances and absences and work schedules
E – Personnel Subarea 3500 will share the same attendances and absences as PSA 3000, however the grouping Is granular enough to allow PSA 3000 and PSA 3500 to have its own work schedule groupings

PA	PSA	Attendance / Absence Grouping	Work Schedule Grouping
0001	1000	10	10
0001	2000	11	11
0002	1000	10	10
0002	2000	11	11
0002	3000	12	12
0002	3500	12	14
0002	4000	13	13

Figure 2.2 Displays the Layout of the Required Personnel Subarea Definitions

As you can see in Figure 2.2, Personnel Area 0002 contains additional Personnel Subareas that required their own work schedule groupings. In order to accommodate this business requirement, we would then need to associate the work schedule grouping 12, 13, and 14 to the specific Personnel Area/Subarea combination so that only those groups will be able to see their specific work schedules. You should also notice that Personnel Subareas 1000 and 2000 can share the same work schedules.

Now that you have a general understanding of the Enterprise Structure, let's take a look some of the components of the Personnel Structure.

2.1.2 Personnel Structure

Personnel Structure consists of the following key elements for Time Management:

▶ Employee Group (EG)
  The Employee Group is a definition of the type of employee. Some examples of this include:

  ▶ Full time

  ▶ Part time

  ▶ Retiree

▶ Employee Subgroup (ESG)
  The Employee Subgroup is a further breakdown of the type of employee defined in the Employee Group. Some examples include:

  ▶ Full time — Salaried, Hourly, Officer

  ▶ Part time — Salaried, Hourly, Intern

  ▶ Retiree — Salaried, Hourly, Officer

Figure 2.3 illustrates an example of the relationships between Employee Groups and Employee Subgroups.

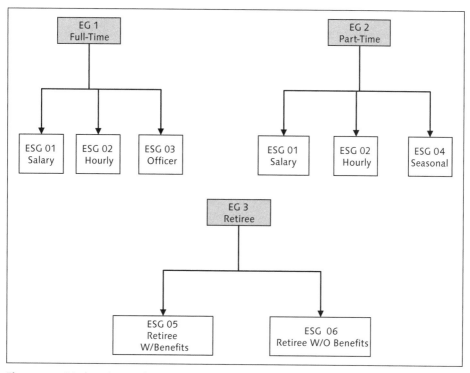

Figure 2.3   Displays the Employee Group Subgroup Example

Another key aspect of Time Management that you'll need to use is the Employee Group/Subgroup combination. When designing your Personnel Structure, this combination drives groupings associated with functionality, such as:

▶ Work Schedules

▶ Time Quotas

▶ Personnel Calculation Rules for Time Evaluation

▶ Incentive Wages

The reason you need to understand the setup of the Personnel Structure is that a lot of your decision points in time evaluation are typically built off of the value of these fields. The design of the Employee Group/Subgroup combination needs to be granular enough to take into account all of the business requirements of work schedules, quota calculation rules in the time evaluation schema, and incentive wages. If the Personnel Structure and the Enterprise Structure are set up and you are not able to identify specific populations of employees, you may not be able to deliver functionality to support the business requirements.

Let's say you have two groups of employees within the organization. Of these two groups, group 1 has very specific absence and attendance types that you don't want group 2 to be able to select. After your blueprinting sessions, the team has decided to create just one Personnel Area and one Personnel Subarea. Because the attendance and absence types are based on the Personnel Area and Personnel Subarea combination, and your team has decided to use just one, you have lost your ability to allow Group 1 to see one set of absence and attendance types and Group 2 to see a different list. Instead, both groups will be able to see all codes that are entered in the system.

2.1.3 Organizational Structure

The third area, called the Organizational Structure, consists of the following key elements for Time Management.

- Percentage
- Time Administrator
- Exempt/Nonexempt

This structure, while important, is not critical to Time Management functionality and your ability to segregate employee populations for processing.

You can use the Time Administrator to limit the employees that a time administrator needs to process by acting like a filter. Another example of the fields listed would be to use Exempt/Nonexempt as a decision point in time evaluation when determining which employees should flow through the overtime calculation rules. In this case, only the nonexempt employees are eligible for overtime.

These are a few examples of why the Personnel Structure and Enterprise Structure setup are so important to the success or your Time Management implementation. The next section of this chapter provides a matrix that will be very useful in determining what the primary keys are for the configuration tables across all Time Management functionality. How useful you say? During the blueprinting portion of the project, how can you set up the Enterprise Structure, the Personnel Structure, and the Organizational Structure if you are not familiar with all of the functionality? The following matrix outlines which functionality is based on the Personnel

Structure data, such as Employee Group/Subgroup combinations, or the Enterprise Structure data, such as the Personnel Areas and Personnel Subareas.

2.2 Time Management Groupings

This section lists the various groupings within the Time Management functionality. It is important to note that during the design of the Enterprise Structure and Personnel Structure, the various groupings within the organization should be laid out correctly to enable the Time Management functionality to meet its objectives.

The layout of the Figures 2.4 through 2.13 shows which structures are key to developing further groupings. For example, you will notice down the left side of the first page of groupings that the Employee Subgroup grouping for work schedules is determined by a combination of Employee Group and Employee Subgroup. A two-digit code is associated with the combination. In Figure 2.8 in the vertical column, at the top left, there is the line for determining the work schedule rule for availability. Following the row across, you will notice that the Employee Subgroup Grouping for Work Schedule is the driving factor for this configuration.

The intent of this section is to provide you with a quick reference during the blueprinting phase of not only the Time Management functionality, but also the Enterprise Structure and Personnel Structure. In addition, it serves as a reference when laying out all Time Management functionality in scope and to determine how the overall system can be set up. Figures 2.4 through 2.13 list the Time Management functionality and the particular structure fields that drive the processing.

In addition to the matrix of Time Management functionality groupings, Appendix A contains various screen fields and specifics pertaining to each field, such as field length. This will come in handy when building interfaces or custom reports that require specifications for particular fields. It will also come in handy when you need to map legacy field data to SAP fields for data conversion purposes.

The next section provides some sample blueprinting questions that you might think about formulating when requesting data from the business owners.

Category	EG	ESG	PA	PSA	Employee Subgroup Group for Work Schedules	PSA for Daily Work Schedules	Holiday Calendars	PSA Groupings for Substitutions	PSA Grouping for Attendances & Absences	Employee Subgroup Grouping for Time Quotas	PSA Grouping for Time Quotas	PSA Grouping for Availability	PSA Grouping for Time Recording	PSA Grouping for Leave Types	Groupings for Subsystems	Notes
Employee Subgroup Groupings for Work Schedule	YES	YES	NO	NO	NO	NO	NO	NO	NO	NO	NO	NO	NO	NO	NO	
Work Schedules PSA	NO	NO	YES	YES	NO	NO	NO	NO	NO	NO	NO	NO	NO	NO	NO	No Date Delimitation
Daily Work Schedule PSA Mapping	NO	NO	NO	NO	NO	YES	NO	NO	NO	NO	NO	NO	NO	NO	NO	
Work Break Schedules	NO	NO	NO	NO	NO	YES	NO	NO	NO	NO	NO	NO	NO	NO	NO	
Daily Work Schedules	NO	NO	NO	NO	NO	YES	NO	NO	NO	NO	NO	NO	NO	NO	NO	
Period Work Schedules	NO	NO	NO	NO	NO	YES	NO	NO	NO	NO	NO	NO	NO	NO	NO	
Public Holiday Calendars	NO	NO	YES	YES	YES	NO	YES	NO	NO	NO	NO	NO	NO	NO	NO	No Date Delimitation
Work Schedules	NO	NO	NO	NO	NO	YES	NO	NO	NO	NO	NO	NO	NO	NO	NO	
Attendance Absence Groupings for subsystem	NO	NO	NO	NO	NO	NO	NO	NO		NO	NO	NO	NO	NO	NO	Freely Determined

Figure 2.4 Time Management Groupings Screen Group 1 of 10

Category	EG	ESG	PA	PSA	Employee Subgroup Group for Work Schedules	PSA for Daily Work Schedules	Holiday Calendars	PSA Groupings for Substitutions	PSA Grouping for Attendances & Absences	Employee Subgroup Grouping for Time Quotas	PSA Grouping for Time Quotas	PSA Grouping for Availability	PSA Grouping for Time Recording	PSA Grouping for Leave Types	Groupings for Subsystems	Notes
Attendances and Absence Reasons for Subsystems	NO	NO	NO	NO YES	YES	NO	NO	NO	NO	NO	NO	NO	NO	NO	YES	
Personnel Subarea Groupings for Substitutions	NO	NO	YES	YES	NO	NO	NO	NO	NO	NO	NO	NO	NO	NO	NO	No Date Delimitation Functionality
Definition of substitutions Types	NO	NO	NO	NO	NO	NO	NO	YES	NO	NO	NO	NO	NO	NO	NO	
Group Personnel Subareas for Absences and Attendances	NO	NO	YES	YES	NO	NO	NO	NO	NO	NO	NO	NO	NO	NO	NO	No Date Delimitation Functionality
Define Absence Types	NO	NO	NO	NO	NO	YES	NO	NO	YES	NO	NO	NO	NO	NO	NO	
Absence-Determine Entry Screens and Time Constraint Classes	NO	NO	NO	NO	NO	NO	NO	NO	YES	NO	NO	NO	NO	NO	NO	
Absence-Define Counting Classes for Period Work Schedule	NO	NO	NO	NO	NO	NO	NO	NO	NO	NO	NO	NO	NO	NO	NO	
Employee	YES	YES	NO	NO	NO	NO	NO	NO	NO	NO	NO	NO	NO	NO	NO	

Figure 2.5 Time Management Groupings Screen Group 2 of 10

Category	EG	ESG	PA	PSA	Employee Subgroup Group for Work Schedules	PSA for Daily Work Schedules	Holiday Calendars	PSA Groupings for Substitutions	PSA Grouping for Attendances & Absences	Employee Subgroup Grouping for Time Quotas	PSA Grouping for Time Quotas	PSA Grouping for Availability	PSA Grouping for Time Recording	PSA Grouping for Leave Types	Groupings for Subsystems	Notes
Deduction Rules for Attendances Quotas	NO	NO	NO	NO	NO	NO	NO	NO	NO	YES	YES	NO	NO	NO	NO	
Assign Counting Rules to Absences	NO	NO	NO	NO	NO	NO	NO	NO	YES	NO	NO	NO	NO	NO	NO	
Determine Daily Work Schedule Variants for absence	NO	NO	NO	NO	NO	YES	NO	NO	YES	NO	NO	NO	NO	NO	NO	Based on same groupings as daily work
Determine Indicators for Personal Calendar	NO	NO	NO	NO	NO	NO	NO	NO	YES	NO	NO	NO	NO	NO	NO	
Determine Calendar Indicators for absences and attendances	NO	NO	NO	NO	NO	NO	NO	NO	YES	NO	NO	NO	NO	NO	NO	
Link Absences to Additional Absence Data	NO	NO	NO	NO	NO	NO	NO	NO	YES	NO	NO	NO	NO	NO	NO	
Maternity Types of Birth	NO	NO	NO	NO	NO	NO	NO	NO	YES	NO	NO	NO	NO	NO	NO	
Maternity Protection Periods	NO	NO	NO	NO	NO	NO	NO	NO	YES	NO	NO	NO	NO	NO	NO	
Maternity Default	NO	NO	NO	NO	NO	NO	NO	NO	YES	NO	NO	NO	NO	NO	NO	

Figure 2.6 Time Management Groupings Screen Group 3 of 10

Category	EG	ESG	PA	PSA	Employee Subgroup Group for Work Schedules	PSA for Daily Work Schedules	Holiday Calendars	PSA Groupings for Substitutions	PSA Grouping for Attendances & Absences	Employee Subgroup Grouping for Time Quotas	PSA Grouping for Time Quotas	PSA Grouping for Availability	PSA Grouping for Time Recording	PSA Grouping for Leave Types	Groupings for Subsystems	Notes
Military Definition of Periods	NO	NO	NO	NO	NO	NO	NO	NO	YES	NO	NO	NO	NO	NO	NO	
Definition of Attendances	NO	NO	NO	NO	NO	NO	NO	NO	YES	NO	NO	NO	NO	NO	NO	Same as absences
Attendance – Determine Entry Screens and Time Constraint Classes	NO	NO	NO	NO	NO	NO	NO	NO	YES	NO	NO	NO	NO	NO	NO	
Attendance – Define Counting Classes for Period Work Schedule	NO	NO	NO	NO	NO	YES	NO	NO	NO	NO	NO	NO	NO	NO	NO	
Attendance Assign Counting Rules to Attendance Types	NO	NO	NO	NO	NO	NO	NO	NO	YES	NO	NO	NO	NO	NO	NO	
Attendance – Set Groupings for Attendance Counting	NO	NO	NO	NO	NO	NO	NO	NO	YES	NO	NO	NO	NO	NO	NO	
Group Personnel Subareas for Availability	NO	NO	YES	YES	NO	NO	NO	NO	NO	NO	NO	YES	NO	NO	NO	No Date Delimitation Functionality
Define	NO	NO	NO	NO	NO	NO	NO	YES	NO	NO	NO	NO	NO	NO	NO	

Figure 2.7 Time Management Groupings Screen Group 4 of 10

Category	EG	ESG	PA	PSA	Employee Subgroup Group for Work Schedules	PSA for Daily Work Schedules	Holiday Calendars	PSA Groupings for Substitutions	PSA Grouping for Attendances & Absences	Employee Subgroup Grouping for Time Quotas	PSA Grouping for Time Quotas	PSA Grouping for Availability	PSA Grouping for Time Recording	PSA Grouping for Leave Types	Groupings for Subsystems	Notes
Determine Work Schedule Rules for Availability	NO	NO	NO	NO	YES	YES	YES	NO	NO	NO	NO	NO	NO	NO	NO	
Employee Subgroup Grouping for Time Quota Types	YES	YES	NO	NO	NO	NO	NO	NO	NO	NO	NO	NO	NO	NO	NO	
Personnel Subarea Grouping for Time Quota Types	NO	NO	YES	YES	NO	NO	NO	NO	NO	NO	NO	NO	NO	NO	NO	No Date Delimitation Functionality
Define Absence Quota Types	NO	NO	NO	NO	NO	NO	NO	NO	NO	YES	YES	NO	NO	NO	NO	
Define Attendance Quota Types	NO	NO	NO	NO	NO	NO	NO	NO	NO	YES	YES	NO	NO	NO	NO	
Calculate Absence Quotas	NO	NO	NO	NO	NO	NO	NO	NO	NO	YES	YES	NO	NO	NO	NO	
Define Personnel Subarea Grouping for Time Recording	NO	NO	YES	YES	NO	NO	NO	NO	NO	NO	NO	NO	NO	NO	NO	No Date Delimitation Functionality
Quota Base Entitlements	NO	NO	NO	NO	NO	NO	NO	NO	NO	YES	YES	NO	NO	NO	NO	
Quota Validity and Deduction	NO	NO	NO	NO	NO	NO	NO	NO	NO	YES	YES	NO	NO	NO	NO	

Figure 2.8 Time Management Groupings Screen Group 5 of 10

Category	EG	ESG	PA	PSA	Employee Subgroup Group for Work Schedules	PSA for Daily Work Schedules	Holiday Calendars	PSA Groupings for Substitutions	PSA Grouping for Attendances & Absences	Employee Subgroup Grouping for Time Quotas	PSA Grouping for Time Quotas	PSA Grouping for Availability	PSA Grouping for Time Recording	PSA Grouping for Leave Types	Groupings for Subsystems	Notes
Define Generation Rules for Quota Type Selection	NO	NO	NO	NO	NO	NO	NO	NO	NO	YES	YES	NO	YES	NO	NO	
Define Validity Intervalfor Time Quota Accruals	NO	NO	NO	NO	NO	NO	NO	NO	NO	YES	YES	NO	NO	NO	NO	
Quota Assign Deduction Rules to Counting Rules	NO	NO	NO	NO	NO	NO	NO	NO	NO	YES	YES	NO	NO	NO	NO	
Valuate Absences Using Quota Deduction in Payroll	NO	NO	NO	NO	NO	NO	NO	NO	NO	YES	YES	NO	NO	NO	NO	
Define Time Quota Compensation (IT 416)	NO	NO	NO	NO	NO	NO	NO	NO	NO	YES	YES	NO	NO	NO	NO	
Wage Type Permissibility for Infotype 416	YES	YES	YES	YES	NO	NO	NO	NO	NO	NO	NO	NO	NO	NO	NO	
Assign Wage Types to Quota to be Compensated	NO	NO	NO	NO	NO	NO	NO	NO	NO	YES	YES	NO	NO	NO	NO	
Personnel Subarea Grouping for Leave	NO	NO	YES	YES	NO	NO	NO	NO	NO	NO	NO	NO	NO	NO	NO	No Date Delimitation Functionality

Figure 2.9 Time Management Groupings Screen Group 6 of 10

Category	EG	ESG	PA	PSA	Employee Subgroup Group for Work Schedules	PSA for Daily Work Schedules	Holiday Calendars	PSA Groupings for Substitutions	PSA Grouping for Attendances & Absences	Employee Subgroup Grouping for Time Quotas	PSA Grouping for Time Quotas	PSA Grouping for Availability	PSA Grouping for Time Recording	PSA Grouping for Leave Types	Groupings for Subsystems	Notes
Personnel Time Events – Maintain Absence / Attendance Reasons	NO	NO	NO	NO	YES	NO	NO	NO	YES	NO	NO	NO	NO	NO	NO	
Personnel TimeEvents – Grouping for Access Control	NO	NO	NO	NO	NO	NO	NO	NO	NO	NO	NO	NO	YES	NO	NO	
PDC – Settings for Pair Formation	NO	NO	NO	NO	NO	NO	NO	NO	NO	NO	NO	NO	YES	NO	NO	
TE – Define Settings for Pair Formation	NO	NO	NO	NO	NO	NO	NO	NO	NO	NO	NO	NO	YES	NO	NO	
TE – Employee Subgroup Grouping for PCRand CAP	YES	YES	YES	NO	NO	NO	NO	NO	NO	NO	NO	NO	NO	NO	NO	
TE – Define Time Types	NO	NO	NO	NO	NO	NO	NO	NO	NO	NO	NO	NO	YES	NO	NO	
TE (Clock Times) – Calculation Rule MODT	-	-	-	-	-	-	-	-	-	-	-	-	-	-	NO	PCR that can be customized
TE (Clock Times) – Dynamically Set Work Schedule	NO	NO	NO	NO	NO	YES	NO	NO	NO	NO	NO	NO	NO	NO	NO	

Figure 2.10 Time Management Groupings Screen Group 7 of 10

Category	EG	ESG	PA	PSA	Employee Subgroup Group for Work Schedules	PSA for Daily Work Schedules	Holiday Calendars	PSA Groupings for Substitutions	PSA Grouping for Attendances & Absences	Employee Subgroup Grouping for Time Quotas	PSA Grouping for Time Quotas	PSA Grouping for Availability	PSA Grouping for Time Recording	PSA Grouping for Leave Types	Groupings for Subsystems	Notes
TE (Clock Times) Set Time Type Determination T555Z	NO	NO	NO	NO	NO	NO	NO	NO	NO	NO	NO	NO	YES	NO	NO	Also used time type determination group from
TE (clock Times) Indicate Absences to be shortened	NO	NO	NO	NO	NO	NO	NO	NO	YES	NO	NO	NO	NO	NO	NO	
TE (Clock Times) Absence Input Checks	NO	NO	NO	NO	NO	NO	NO	NO	YES	NO	NO	NO	NO	NO	NO	
TE (Clock Times) Set Log Time for Overtime Quotas	NO	NO	NO	NO	NO	YES	NO	NO	NO	YES	YES	NO	NO	NO	NO	
TE (Clock Times) Define Valuation Class for Period Work Schedules	NO	NO	NO	NO	NO	NO	NO	NO	NO	NO	NO	NO	NO	NO	NO	
TE (Clock Times) Define Limits for Time Balances	NO	NO	NO	NO	NO	NO	NO	NO	NO	NO	NO	NO	YES	NO	NO	
TE (Clock Times) Time Evaluation Messages	NO	NO	NO	NO	NO	NO	NO	NO	NO	NO	NO	NO	YES	NO	NO	
TE (Clock Times) Define	NO	NO	NO	NO	NO	NO	NO	NO	NO	NO	NO	NO	YES	NO	NO	

Figure 2.11 Time Management Groupings Screen Group 8 of 10

43

Category	EG	ESG	PA	PSA	Employee Subgroup Group for Work Schedules	PSA for Daily Work Schedules	Holiday Calendars	PSA Groupings for Substitutions	PSA Grouping for Attendances & Absences	Employee Subgroup Grouping for Time Quotas	PSA Grouping for Time Quotas	PSA Grouping for Availability	PSA Grouping for Time Recording	PSA Grouping for Leave Types	Groupings for Subsystems	Notes
TE (Clock Times) Define Rules for Transfer to Absence Quotas	NO	NO	NO	NO	NO	NO	NO	NO	NO	NO	NO	NO	YES	NO	NO	
TE (Clock Times) Time Wage Type Selection Rule	-	-	-	-	-	-	-	-	-	-	-	-	-	-	NO	Based on MODIF W = and MODIF
TE (Without Clock Times) Determine Time Class for Attendances	NO	NO	NO	NO	NO	NO	NO	NO	YES	NO	NO	NO	NO	NO	NO	
TE (Without Clock Times) Determine Processing Type/Time Type Class for Absence and Attendance V_554S_F	NO	NO	NO	NO	NO	NO	NO	NO	YES	NO	NO	NO	NO	NO	NO	
TE (Without Clock Times) Assign Processing Type/Time Type	NO	NO	NO	NO	NO	NO	NO	NO	NO	NO	NO	NO	YES	NO	NO	Time Type Determination Group MODIF and
CE-Message	NO	NO	NO	NO	NO	NO	NO	NO	NO	NO	NO	NO	YES	NO	NO	

Figure 2.12   Figure 2.12 Time Management Groupings Screen Group 9 of 10

Category	EG	ESG	PA	PSA	Employee Subgroup Group for Work Schedules	PSA for Daily Work Schedules	Holiday Calendars	PSA Groupings for Substitutions	PSA Grouping for Attendances & Absences	Employee Subgroup Grouping for Time Quotas	PSA Grouping for Time Quotas	PSA Grouping for Availability	PSA Grouping for Time Recording	PSA Grouping for Leave Types	Groupings for Subsystems	Notes
TMW–Assign Processing Messages to Message Types	NO	NO	NO	NO	NO	NO	NO	NO	NO	NO	NO	NO	YES	NO	NO	
TMQ–Define Time Data IDs	NO	NO	NO	NO	NO	NO	NO	YES	YES	NO	NO	YES	NO	NO	NO	
Availability–Specify Information On Availability	NO	NO	NO	NO	NO	NO	NO	NO	YES	NO	NO	NO	NO	NO	NO	
Shift Planning – Substitution Types Called In Planning	NO	NO	NO	NO	NO	NO	NO	NO	NO	NO	NO	YES	NO	NO	NO	
Incentive Wages – ESG Grouping for Incentive Wage Participation	YES	YES	NO	NO	NO	NO	NO	NO	NO	NO	NO	NO	NO	NO	NO	

Figure 2.13 Figure 2.13 Time Management Groupings Screen Group 10 of 10

2.3   Time Management Sample Blueprinting Questions

The blueprinting portion of the project is not limited to just defining the key structural areas that are shared between all ERP HCM components. You will also need to review all of the functionality that Time Management offers and determine whether or not it should be implemented. You should also be working with members from other teams, such as project systems and logistics, to determine if their business requirement dictates the availability of particular time-related data.

This is a massive data-gathering exercise and care should be taken so that you have adequate time to cover each topic. Before you even blueprint, you will need to gather your thoughts, form questions, and be prepared to discuss the various functionality within the system, the integration points to other SAP components or bolt-on systems, and the overall data flow through the system.

The following are some data points that you should be obtaining and forming your questions around. This is a general guideline and is not meant to be an all-inclusive list as HR policies and pay practices vary. You should also request all union contracts if they are applicable as they contain a lot of information you'll need to digest to begin to envision the overall design of the system. Sometimes, these union contracts will provide you with great insight into how the Enterprise Structure and Personnel Structure should be established. The following is a list of questions broken down by high-level topics.

▸ **Work Schedules** — Request a list of all work schedules that employees are currently working. Are there any particular shifts, such as first shift, second shift, or third shift? What are the hours of the shifts, the start times, end times, etc? Are you willing to maintain an accurate work schedule or keep them as generic as possible? You can review the configuration in Chapter 5 to determine all of the data points that may be necessary.

▸ **Attendances and Absences** — Request a list of all of the particular codes that are in use today. You should also obtain any special rules that pertain to each code, such as who can use them, when they should be used, etc. Are there any shift differentials? If so, what are they, how much and under what conditions should they be paid?

▸ **Holiday calendars** — Request a list of holiday calendars and for whom the particular calendars apply.

▸ **Master data** — Request the types of information that the current system is storing and perhaps what the vision for data storage is for the future. Based on this, you can then research which infotypes SAP offers that you can use. Chapter 4 provides a lot of details surrounding the infotypes and what they can store.

▸ **Time entry** — How is time entered into the system? Is this purely an SAP time-keeping solution or will you have third-party vendor software capture the time and pass it to the SAP system for processing. Are you going to capture clock times or just capture the number of hours? Will there be approvals of the time?

▸ **Time calculations** — What kind of time calculations are required? Examples include overtime, shift differentials, specific calculations to your organization, etc.

▸ **Substitutions** — Will you utilize the Substitutions Infotype for short-term variations to employees work schedules?

▸ **Quotas** — Do you track quotas such as vacation, holiday, or other types of absences? If so, what are they and how much quota is allotted? Who is eligible and what are all of the rules surrounding the processing.

▸ **Shift planning** — Do you have the need for managers or time keepers to establish particular shifts and manage the workforce from those shifts? If so, then perhaps shift planning should be explored.

There are many more questions and much more detail per the preceding questions that should be determined and documented. The more efficient and better you are at collecting and consolidating the data, the better chance you have at designing the system with minimal revisions.

2.4   Summary

In this chapter, you have learned about some of the key areas to consider when blueprinting. Luckily, you are most likely not starting from scratch as a legacy system is probably up and running with many of the requirements already in use in your production environment. Inviting the right people to your meetings will make all the difference in the world when gathering requirements. This chapter has provided you with the key areas to consider when designing all of the structures. In the following chapter, you will learn about integrating time-related information with other SAP software components.

Because Time Management can involve other areas of business outside of Human Resources (HR), it's important to have a software tool that can work with the business processes in a variety of areas. In this chapter, we'll discuss the integration points between the SAP ERP HCM Time Management functionality and other SAP components.

3 Overview of Integrating Time Management with Other Components

During your blueprinting sessions, you most likely had meetings with other teams to decide how data was going to flow through the system. You decided which attendances and absences would be used, what they would be called, and the types of data that should be associated with each attendance and absence. Perhaps, during one of your sessions, a request was made that the system must allow for particular attendance types to track specific pieces of information related to the other components, such as a cost center or an order number. How is SAP software equipped to handle such a requirement?

The Time Management Implementation Guide (IMG) has a section called Integrating Time Management with Other SAP Applications. This section of customization enables the Time Management infotype data the ability to enter other component-related data that can be tracked. After it passes through payroll, all time-related data is sent to the Finance and Controlling components. Usually, the time entered flows through an employee's normal cost centers and other finance and controlling component structures.

But what would happen if an employee works in a different department for the day? Should the cost associated with those hours be sent to their normal work location, or should the new location incur the cost for the one day the employee worked there. You might want to book those hours against a different cost center. In this example, the system would need to allow you the flexibility to change the cost-related information for just the eight hours of attendance entered.

You also have the ability to dictate that the cost of the eight attendance hours entered should be allocated to a different cost center than the rest of the employee's normal earnings. The basic premise is to provide you the ability to alter types of time-related data in those situations that fall outside of the norm. The system is delivered with most of the settings you will ever need. They are rarely used on an everyday basis and you really should not have to make any changes to the standard configuration to support integration with other SAP software components.

The Time Management functionality can be integrated with two basic categories of components:

- ▶ **External Components** — SAP considers these to be components outside of the SAP system, such as a time-keeping solution provided by another vendor.

- ▶ **Internal Components** — SAP considers these the integration points between the various components provided by SAP.

Let's move on to discuss both in more detail.

3.1 External Components

In general, external components include the following items:

- ▶ A third-party time collection system transferring clock-time-related data to Infotype 2011 Time Events.

- ▶ A third-party time collection subsystem transferring time-related data to the Cross-Application Time Sheet (CATS).

Even though they aren't technically part of this section or configuration, time entry does arrive from external systems and resides in the same tables as CATS. Once it has arrived, it can be considered internal for the purposes of transferring data to other SAP components.

Now let's look at internal components. We'll discuss the integration points from CATS, however, the main configuration considered within this section of the IMG relates to allowing particular absences and attendances to hold other components data that can be sent through payroll.

3.2   Internal Components

The internal components that we refer to, and which are truly the basis for this chapter, generally include the following processing procedures.

▸ CATS to the HCM component. You can transfer time data directly to the HR components.

▸ CATS to the Finance and Controlling component. You can transfer time data to the Finance and Controlling components.

▸ CATS to the Plant Maintenance/Customer Relationship Management (CRM) component. You can transfer time data to the Plant Maintenance and CRM component.

▸ CATS to the Project System component. You can transfer time data to the Project System component.

▸ Transferring Time Confirmations from the Logistics component including Plant Maintenance. Time-related data can be pulled via confirmations from logistics to the Attendance infotype.

▸ Updating various data elements for infotype records that are directly maintained on the infotypes. These are basic updates, such as a temporary cost center change for particular time codes.

The first four bullet points relate to transferring time data from CATS directly to the other components. The fifth bullet point refers to the logistics components pushing time-related data to the HR component. The final bullet point is in reference to the majority of the configurations within this section and that allow the entry of other components' data directly on the applicable time-related infotypes. The items in Figure 3.1 are the delivered integration points between CATS and the various components. The time sheet automatically pulls in each component's data so that they are available for dropdown selection when associated with an attendance or absence record.

Figure 3.1 shows an overview of the various integration points between SAP Time components and other SAP components.

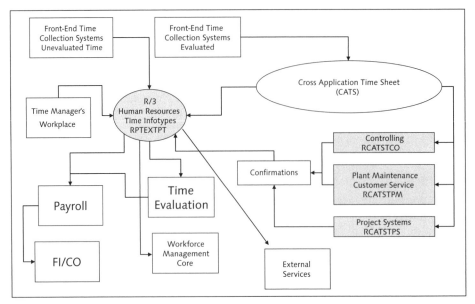

Figure 3.1 Integration to Other SAP Applications

Once you know which components you want to integrate with, you need to ensure the system is set up to accommodate your requirements. This involves a number of steps, which we review in the next section. The configuration for integrating to other SAP applications can be found in the IMG under menu path TIME MANAGE-MENT • INTEGRATING TIME MANAGEMENT WITH OTHER SAP APPLICATIONS.

Now we'll learn how the various internal components can be set up in the IMG.

3.3 Configuration with Internal Components

Let's explore the various configuration settings required to set up the system so that data can flow from one component to another. We'll start by discussing logistics confirmation data.

3.3.1 Retrieving Logistics Confirmation Data

Within the Plant Data Collection (PDC) component of logistics, you can schedule confirmations to be transferred to the Time Management component as atten-dances. This data normally comes from the SAP Plant Maintenance component,

Customer Service component, or the Project Systems component. In order to use this functionality, you need to establish the integration configuration within the plant data collection section of the IMG. If you were to select that particular node under plant data collection, the IMG would take you to program RPWI1100.

SAP delivers a program that is the main integration point between logistics confirmations and the creation of HR infotype records. Program RPWI1100 reads the interface file and generates the session to create the Time Management infotypes.

Figure 3.2 shows program RPWI1100 and the various fields that you can update. After you select which confirmations you would like to process, you can then define whether the confirmations should post as time tickets or attendances. You can then enter which attendance or absence type the confirmation should create. When the program is run, the infotype records will be created automatically.

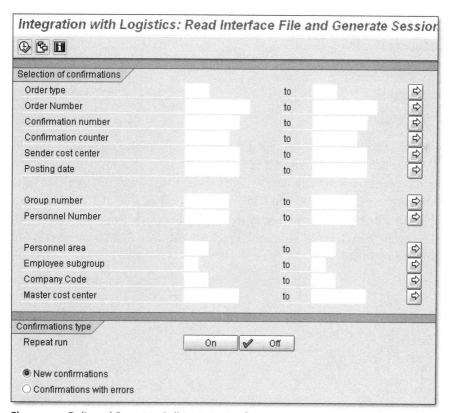

Figure 3.2 Delivered Report to Pull Logistics Confirmation to HR

The next section of configuration discusses setting up the system so that various components can determine which employees are available.

3.3.2 Specify Information on Availability Functionality

Within the Logistics component, there is a subcomponent called Project Systems. This is where you can define particular projects, assign employees, cost-related information, and other tracking information for that particular project.

In order for the Project System's component to determine employee availability, you need to establish which attendance and/or absence codes that are linked to an employee will actually help the project system determine their availability. For each attendance and absence type, the Availability field allows you to choose one of three options that will drive the availability functionality. Figure 3.3 shows the screen and field for availability. This functionality not only integrates with project systems, but also with functions within Time Management, such as shift planning, training, and event management. The following setting options are available:

▶ Blank — Not Available

▶ 1 — Available

▶ 9 — Irrelevant

These codes are utilized by a delivered Business Application Programming Interface (BAPI) called BAPI_TIMEAVAILSCHEDULE_BUILD. This BAPI serves as the integration point between the components so that they can communicate. The programming within the BAPI pulls the codes 1 for available and blank for not available. This BAPI utilizes the codes to determine which employees are available. The code "9 Irrelevant," will not be picked up by the BAPI because it is not programmed to do so.

Figure 3.3 shows the integration points for absences and attendances.

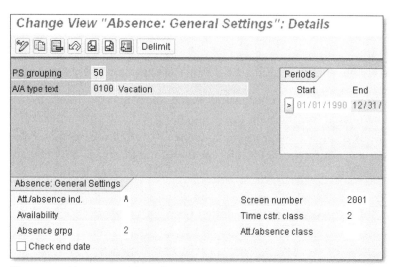

Figure 3.3 Absence- and Attendance-type Integration Points

3.4 Infotype Integration

Accounting- and logistics-related information can be linked to particular infotypes so that, during time entry, a user can assign particular values that would pass to accounting or logistics. An example of this might be a cost center override for particular hours worked on a particular day. In order to allow the user the ability to enter this data, you need to ensure that the particular infotypes have been set up to allow for this integration. Infotypes are covered in detail in Chapter 4. This particular customization for integration is merely a checkbox that allows additional costing information to be associated with the infotype record. The following infotypes are available for customization:

▸ Infotype 0014 Recurring Payments and Deductions — Utilized for payroll processing

▸ Infotype 0015 Additional Payments — Utilized for payroll processing

▸ Infotype 2001 Absences —Utilized for Time Management processing

▸ Infoytpe 2002 Attendances — Utilized for Time Management processing

▸ Infotype 2003 Substitutions — Utilized for Time Management processing

- ▸ Infotype 2004 Availability — Utilized for Time Management processing
- ▸ Infotype 2005 Overtime - Utilized for Time Management processing
- ▸ Infotype 2010 Employee Remuneration Information — Utilized for payroll processing
- ▸ Infotype 2011 Time Events — Utilized for Time Management processing

Depending on your overall time solution and which infotypes you choose to utilize to store time-related information, this configuration allows some flexibility because the various infotypes that can be configured cover all time-related infotypes and a few, such as Infotype 0014, Infotype 0015, and Infotype 2010, that are used for payroll. Figure 3.4 shows the integration checkbox configuration.

Change View "Infotype with Acct./Logictics Data": Overview

Infotype	Infotype text	Accounting/logistics data
0014	Recurring Payments/Deductions	✔
0015	Additional Payments	✔
2001	Absences	✔
2002	Attendances	✔
2003	Substitutions	✔
2004	Availability	✔
2005	Overtime	✔
2010	Employee Remuneration Info	✔
2011	Time Events	✔

Figure 3.4 Infotype Integration Points

As you can see in Figure 3.4, all of the infotypes are delivered with the integration turned on. If you decide you don't want to allow integration for a particular infotype, you can deselect the checkbox.

The next section discusses setting the system up to enable cost assignment specifications.

3.4.1   Cost Assignment Specifications

The cost assignment specification allows you to determine which of the infotypes you will allow additional costing information to be associated with. The checkboxes shown in Figure 3.5 represent the various functionalities of the infotypes for accounting and logistics specifications. By deselecting the checkboxes, the functionalities become grayed out on the infotype screen. Figure 3.5 shows Infotype 2002 Attendances. You should notice the Cost assignment button. If you were to deselect the checkbox in Figure 3.5 under Cost assignment, then this button would remain on the screen, however, a user would not be able to select it.

Figure 3.5 shows the cost assignment specification configuration.

Infotype	Infotype text	Pers.cal.	Import peri...	Import peri...	ScrNo	Remuneration spec.	Cost assignment	Act. allocation	Ext. services
2001	Absences	1	01	01	4000	☑	☑	☐	☐
2002	Attendances	1	01	01	4050	☑	☑	☑	☑
2003	Substitutions		01	01	4100	☑	☑	☐	☐
2004	Availability		01	01	4150	☑	☑	☐	☐
2005	Overtime		01	01	4200	☑	☑	☐	☐
2006	Absence Quotas		01	01	4250	☐	☐	☐	☐
2007	Attendance Quotas		01	01	4300	☐	☐	☐	☐
2010	Employee Remunerati...		01	01	4450	☐	☑	☑	☐
2011	Time Events				4500	☑	☑	☐	☐
2012	Time Transfer Specific...				4550	☐	☐	☐	☐
2013	Quota Corrections				4600	☐	☐	☐	☐
2052	Weekly Entry w/Activity ...				7150	☐	☐	☐	☐

Figure 3.5 Cost Assignment Specifications

As you can see in Figure 3.5, there are multiple columns of checkboxes. You can specify the following functionality per infotype:

▶ Remuneration Specifications

▶ Cost Assignments

▶ Activity Allocations

▶ External Services

As with cost assignment, you can also deactivate particular buttons on the screen by infotype. This provides you some flexibility if you are trying to restrict what infotype can be entered on which infotype.

After you have set up the cost assignments for the various infotypes, the next item of configuration is to determine which objects are permitted. By objects, we mean the particular fields that are available for input, which are illustrated in Figure 3.6.

Within the function module RP_TIME_COBL_002, you can establish which fields are eligible for entry for the cost assignment specifications. This functionality works in two parts.

▶ **Part 1** — Establish which fields you want to display for each particular infotype. You can find a complete list by looking at the structure COBL (via Transaction code SE11) by utilizing the data-type radio button. Figure 3.6 shows the function module RP_TIME_COBL_002. Within that function module you will see a list of fields. Those fields translate into what the user would see if they were maintaining cost-related information on the infotype. Figure 3.6 also shows the actual fields that would display on the infotype. By using this configuration, you can add or remove the fields from the screen the user would see. You really shouldn't have to change this configuration, however, if you need to add or remove fields, this is how it would be done.

▶ **Part 2** — After you define which fields you would like the user to maintain, you can now assign those fields so they populate on the screen. To do this, you utilize a feature. You can identify the variable key if you have various versions of screen fields that you would like to display. Feature DOKNT (via Transaction code PE03) is a feature that calls the previous parts configuration. The variable key is called in the feature based on the decisions that have been set up within the feature. The feature for the United States is set to blank. Notice in Figure 3.6 that the fields listed in the variable name have a blank listed in the variable key to the left.

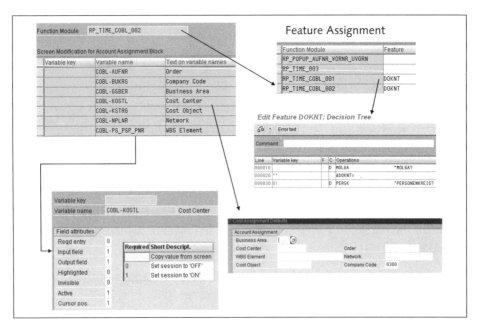

Figure 3.6 Screen Configuration Set Up for Cost Assignment

This setup is how you can map particular fields to display on the infotype screens. Let's apply this to a practical example.

Example

You have two different companies within your organization. For company code 0001, you want to only show the cost center and company code fields. For company code 0002, you want to use the standard SAP screen. The first step would be to define the fields. Just as in Figure 3.6, you would set up the company code and cost center fields, however, under the variable key of the table, you would associate a particular code. We will use 1234. So, in the table for the function modules, you have the variable key set to blank with the standard fields set up that company code 0002 will use, and you also have variable key 1234 with both company code and cost center assigned.

You then proceed to the feature DOKNT and make a decision off of company code. If the company code in the feature is 0001, then you would set up the feature for that line item to read &DOKNT=1234. Company code 0002, which uses the standard SAP screen, would show &DOKNT=. This way each company code would have a different screen when maintaining cost assignment information. Figure 3.6 shows the various configuration screens.

In the next section, we will discuss the configuration for activity allocation specifications.

3.4.2   Activity Allocation Specifications

The activity allocation specifications follow the same configuration as the cost assignment specifications and utilize the same tables and feature. Figure 3.7 shows the configuration table where you link infotypes to account assignments.

Infotype	Infotype text	Pers.cal.	Import peri...	Import peri...	ScrNo	Remuneration spec.	Cost assignment	Act. allocation	Ext. services
2001	Absences	1	01	01	4000	✔	✔	☐	☐
2002	Attendances	1	01	01	4050	✔	✔	✔	✔
2003	Substitutions		01	01	4100	✔	✔	☐	☐
2004	Availability		01	01	4150	✔	✔	☐	☐
2005	Overtime		01	01	4200	✔	✔	☐	☐
2006	Absence Quotas		01	01	4250	☐	☐	☐	☐
2007	Attendance Quotas		01	01	4300	☐	☐	☐	☐
2010	Employee Remunerati..		01	01	4450	☐	✔	✔	☐
2011	Time Events				4500	✔	✔	☐	☐
2012	Time Transfer Specific..				4550	☐	☐	☐	☐
2013	Quota Corrections				4600	☐	☐	☐	☐
2052	Weekly Entry w/Activity ..				7150	☐	☐	☐	☐

Figure 3.7 Activity Allocation Infotype Integration Checkbox

The next section, similar to that of cost assignment, discusses how to set up the fields that you would like to make eligible for entry. Figure 3.8 shows the configuration setup.

The fields utilize the same configurations that were available for cost assignment, but also include fields that reside on structure PSREF. You can view the structure via Transaction code SE11. You should select the data type option and select the structure PSREF. There you will see a list of available fields.

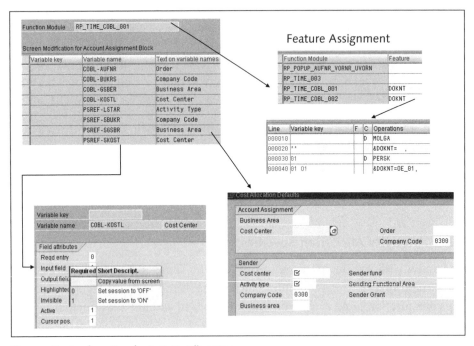

Figure 3.8   Configuration for Activity Allocation

Program RPTPDOC0 can be used to transfer additional data for activity allocation to accounting and those entries tied to Wage types that are processed through payroll and then posted to accounting. Figure 3.9 shows the report selection screen.

Transfer Additional Data for Activity Allocation to Accounting

Status information

| User name | bschaer |

Status	New	Incorrect	
∞	☑ 0	☑ 0	Posting documents
∞	☐ 0	☑ 0	Additional time data

Selection conditions for additional time data

Personnel number		to	
Valid from date		to	
Infotype		to	

Status

○ New
○ With errors
◉ New and with errors

Restrictions for incorrect records

Last retrieved by			
Last retrieved on		to	
Last retrieved at	00:00:00	to	00:00:00

Other data

| Posting date | 09/22/2008 |

☑ Transfer personnel number
☐ Detailed log

Figure 3.9 Report RPTPDOC0

The following section discusses the configuration of external services. This external service should not be confused with bolt-on software to the SAP system, such as a third-party time-keeping system.

3.5   Recording External Services

External services functionality utilizes the Materials Management (MM) component to check the time data entered and account for the time against what is expected per the setup in the MM component. The Time infotypes store the MM external services–related information and are processed through Time Evaluation. SAP delivers Time Evaluation schema TM02 for such processing. Time Management schemas TM00 and TM04 are discussed in detail in Chapters 8 and 9. Schema TM02 is a different variation of these two schemas with the main difference being that schema TM02 includes the function MMSRV, which provides the time data back to the external services component. This way, the evaluated time in Time Evaluation can be compared against the values the MM component stored.

Let's use an example to illustrate the point. Say you decide to use an external employee, such as a subcontractor, to conduct a security analysis of your office location. In order to begin the work, you have signed the contracts and entered a purchasing document in the MM component. As part of that purchase document, you filled in particular items that generate a purchase order. When your subcontractor fills in their time in the time sheet, they fill in the purchase order number with each hour worked. When Time Evaluation finishes processing, the function MMSRV will export the total hours worked on a Wage type that can be validated within the MM component and used as a basis of payment to the subcontractor.

Let's have a look at Figure 3.10, which shows where this purchasing document is attached to the time entered. In this figure you see the external services integration point to HR infotypes. In this example, we will utilize Infotype 2002 — Attendances. As you can see, the External Services button is shown on the infotype screen. This is very similar to activity allocations and cost assignments functionality previously discussed. Continuing our example, the time-related data is entered into the system. The dropdown menus for the purchasing information are obtained from the MM component. The record is saved and ready for Time Evaluation.

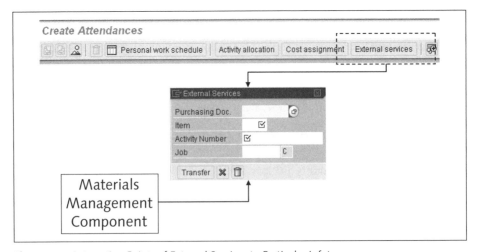

Figure 3.10   Integration Points of External Services to Particular Infotypes

Now that you have seen the various integration points, let's have a look at how you might further change the look and feel of a particular screen. The next section discusses user interfaces, which are the screens an employee would see when entering or maintaining data.

3.5.1 User Interfaces Configuration

The user interfaces section allows you to customize the "List Entry" selections of the time infotypes. Like most infotypes, you can customize which fields are required, optional, output, or hidden. Using the previous example, by updating the external services information for Infotype 2002, let's say you want the job number field to be a required field. The job is the last field on the user interface. By utilizing the functionality to alter these screens, you can make the fields required. Figure 3.11 shows how you can set up a screen field to be required, display-only field, hidden, etc.

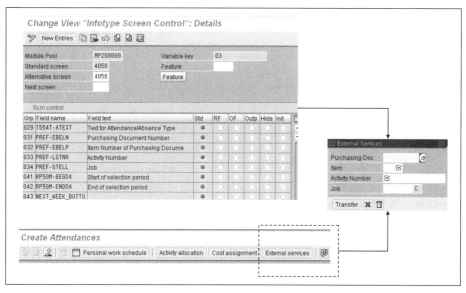

Figure 3.11 External Services User Interface Screens

You can see the various fields in Figure 3.11. In our example, if you elected to change the job number field to required, you would just change the radio button next to the job number field from STD to RF.

Now let's move on to discuss the use of customer enhancements.

3.5.2 Customer Enhancements

Enhancements allow you to insert custom coding into the system to update particular fields or validate what has been entered. By doing so, you can speed up the time it takes to enter data and also ensure the correct data is entered.

The enhancements available for integration to other components include the following:

▶ PTIM2001 — Time recording — Default values for activity allocation

▶ PTIM2002 — Time recording — Default values for cost assignment

▶ PTIM2003 — Time recording — Default values for external services

▶ PTIM2004 — Time recording — Check activity allocation

▶ PTIM2005 — Weekly screen for time recording — Default attendance and absence types

▶ PTIM2006 — Weekly screen for time recording — Complete check

Now that we have covered customer enhancements, it's time to see a very simple table that is set up to help enable integration with external applications.

3.5.3 External Application for Integration with Personnel Time Management

This basic customization allows you to define the specific external applications that will integrate with Time Management. You need to establish a name for each external application. Figure 3.12 shows an example of the delivered external application codes. If you have a couple of different third-party time collection systems, then create a name for each system so they can be identified.

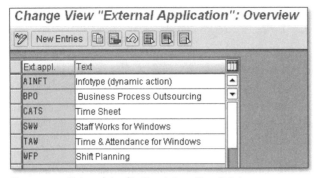

Figure 3.12 External Application Integration Points

The final section of configuration discusses setting the system up for what is called the Workforce Management Core.

3.5.4 Workforce Management Core Integration

Workforce Management Core is an application used in the retail industry for managing employee time data. In order to interface with the application, the Workforce Management Core integration configuration allows you to map time-related infotypes and subtypes to time specification types created in Workforce Management. You can also link the period work schedules into the infotype field and the daily work schedule into the subtype field so that working and break times can also be transferred to the Workforce Management component. Figure 3.13 shows the configuration table.

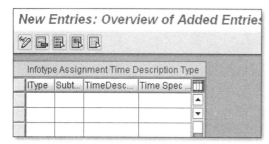

Figure 3.13   Workforce Management Integration Point

This concludes the configuration of the IMG for integrating Time Management with other SAP software components.

3.6 Summary

In this chapter, we covered the Time Management integration points with other SAP software components through the configuration steps of the IMG. You learned how you can customize the various infotype screens to allow users to enter the additional data related to the infotype record. This data is obtained from other SAP software components. The next chapter is an overview of all of the various infotypes related to the Time Management component.

In this chapter, you'll learn about the infotypes in SAP ERP HCM Time Management used to track employee-related information that is used as your employee master data. Each section will explain the infotypes in detail by defining their fields and functionality.

4   Time Management Master Data

Within the SAP ERP HCM Time Management functionality, there are a variety of infotypes used to create your employee master data. You are not required to implement every infotype; however, based on your goals for the system, some infotypes are required.

Throughout this chapter we will review each of the time-related infotypes, explain what they are used for, and detail why you may want to use each piece of master data to track your employee information. A table format is used throughout the chapter that provides the field name, a description, and, where applicable, the purpose and some insight on how to use the particular field.

We will be reviewing the following infotypes:

- Infotype 0005 Leave Entitlement
- Infotype 0007 Planned Working Time
- Infotype 0008 Basic Pay
- Infotype 0050 Time Recording Information
- Infotype 0080 Maternity Protection
- Infotype 0081 Military Service
- Infotype 0082 Additional Absence Data
- Infotype 0130 Test Procedures
- Infotype 0315 Time Sheet Defaults
- Infotype 0416 Time Quota Compensation
- Infotype 0672 FMLA Event
- Infotype 2001 Absences

- Infotype 2002 Attendances
- Infotype 2003 Substitutions
- Infotype 2004 Availability
- Infotype 2005 Overtime
- Infotype 2006 Absence Quotas
- Infotype 2007 Attendance Quotas
- Infotype 2010 Employee Remuneration
- Infotype 2011 Employee Time Events
- Infotype 2012 Time Transfer Specifications
- Infotype 2013 Quota Corrections
- Infotype 2050 Annual Calendar
- Infotype 2051 Monthly Calendar
- Infotype 2052 Weekly Calendar

4.1.1 Infotype 0005 Leave Entitlement

It's important to know about Infotype 0005 because you will see it on the Infotype dropdown menu, but based on current updates, you should not use it any longer. Infotype 0005 was originally created to store leave entitlements such as sick days, vacation days, and relocation days. However, Infotypes 2006 and 2007 are now the preferred method for tracking time awarded to employees.

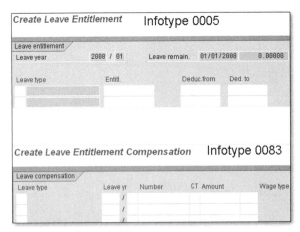

Figure 4.1 Infotype 0005

4.1.2 Infotype 0007 Planned Working Time

Infotype 0007 is a required infotype for Time Management and Payroll because it contains information that enables employees to enter attendances and absences. It also provides Time Evaluation with the data required for calculating each day's time. This is a required infotype if you plan on using any portion of Time Management or Payroll (Figure 4.2). You can utilize this infotype to drive pay practices, such as shift differentials for employees working the night shift. In this case, you can set up the system to look for particular work schedule rules associated with an employee and generate shift differentials for only that employee.

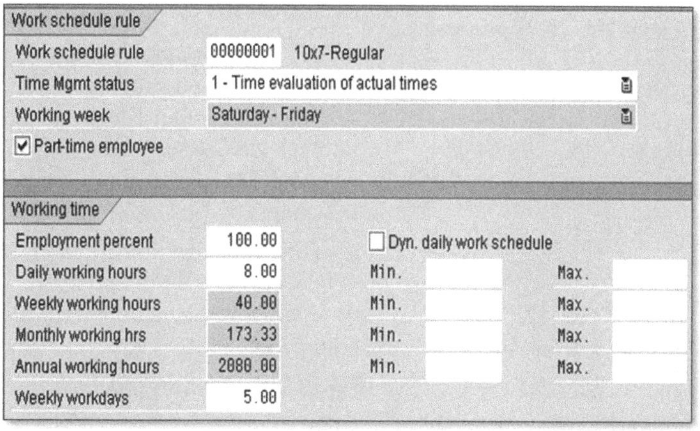

Figure 4.2 Infotype 0007 Planned Working Time

Table 4.2 explains the various fields of Infotype 0007.

Field	Description	Purpose/Impact
Work schedule rule	This field is the foundation of Time Management. This rule has levels of configuration behind it that drives how the system will react to various situations.	Configured behind the rule are daily work schedules, break schedules, period work schedules, and other information. Careful consideration should be given to the design of work schedules and how they will be used to drive time bucket calculations, payment calculations for payroll, and integration to other features, such as month-end accruals.

Table 4.2 Infotype 0007 Fields

Field	Description	Purpose/Impact
Time Mgmt status	This field is the decision key on how the Time Evaluation program (RPTIME00), used in Transaction code PT60, will react to the employee.	1 – Process actual times entered into the system. This is the option used in most scenarios for hourly or salary Nonexempt employees who enter time via a time-keeping system.
		2 – Process PDC (Plant Data Collection) times entered into the system.
	This field can either be populated manually or defaulted from feature TMSTA. All features can be accessed via Transaction code PE03.	7 – Process time without integration to payroll.
		8 – Processing is intended for nonemployees whereby lump-sum times are entered into Infotype 2002 Attendances to be processed as required in Time Evaluation.
		9 – Process planed time for employees. This is the option used for most salaried exempt employees
Working week	This field enables the Time Evaluation schema to accurately determine the week on an individual basis for overtime calculations.	Set up using table T559A and defaulted using feature WWEEK. The working week is freely definable. The table also has a start date and start time.
Part-time employee	This field enables further functionality whereby decisions can be made off this field in Time Evaluation through custom rules.	The activation of this checkbox displays the dynamic work schedule functionality.
	This field can also be used to designate part-time employees if the grouping within the Enterprise Structure is not granular enough to properly report.	See the dynamic daily work schedule functionality.

Table 4.2 Infotype 0007 Fields (Cont.)

Field	Description	Purpose/Impact
Employment percent	This field is populated to 100% based on the work schedule configuration assigned to the work schedule rule. If alterations are made to the percentage, then the daily work hours, weekly work hours, monthly work hours, and annual work hour's fields are automatically adjusted.	Reducing the percentage impacts the amount of absence hours that can be entered into Infotype 2001. The system adjusts the hours down to the target time. If the percentage is adjusted, then all infotype records for Infotypes 2001 and 2002 for the given date range are displayed upon saving so that they can be reviewed.
Daily working hours	This field is also enabled to be manually changed, however, with any changes in this field, similar to the employment percentage changes, the other fields change in conjunction to the value entered.	The four fields (daily work hours, weekly work hours, monthly work hours, and annual working hours) can be altered to allow entry on Infotype 0007. Only two fields can be set up at any one time for entry. The feature WRKHR drives the entry possibilities on Infotype 0007.
Weekly working hours	This field displays the weekly working hours defaulted from the work schedule rule. If they system is set up to allow direct entry, the other fields will change in conjunction to the value entered.	
Monthly working hours	This field displays the monthly working hours defaulted from the work schedule rule. If the system is set up to allow direct entry, the other fields will change in conjunction to the value entered.	

Table 4.2   Infotype 0007 Fields (Cont.)

Field	Description	Purpose/Impact
Annual working hours	This field displays the annual working hours defaulted from the work schedule rule. If the system is set up to allow direct entry, the other fields will change in conjunction to the value entered.	
Weekly workdays	The work days are defaulted from the work schedule and can be overwritten without impacting the four fields referenced earlier.	
Additional Time Indicator	This field is a user-defined field that can be used in Time Evaluation per specific user requirements.	This field is most likely hidden and can be activated to display on Infotype 0007.

Table 4.2 Infotype 0007 Fields (Cont.)

One of the main fields of Infotype 0007 is the work schedule rule. Chapter 5, "Work Schedules," explains the work schedule rule in detail and provides you with guidance on how to set each of the pieces up in the system.

4.1.3   Infotype 0008 — Basic Pay

Infotype 0008 has a variety of fields that are populated from the Payroll configuration. There are two fields, however, that are linked to Infotype 0007 that are addressed here. The reason the two fields are linked is due to the fact that a reduction in work schedule hours can sometimes affect an employee's compensation. The system can be linked so that if you reduce an employee's hours in half, the fields on Infotype 0008 will move to 50% and thus reduce the compensation in half. Figure 4.3 displays the Infotype screen.

Table 4.3 explains the various fields of Infotype 0008 so you can understand the options available, and Figure 4.4 displays the Infotype screen.

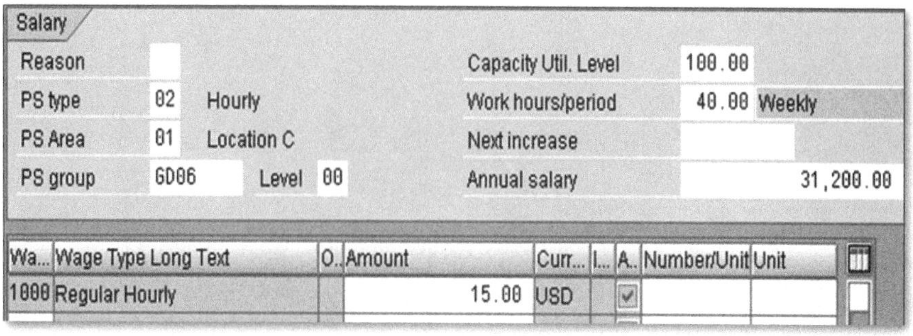

Figure 4.3 Infotype 0008 Basic Pay

Field	Description	Purpose/Impact
Capacity Util. Level	This is the percentage of the normal, standard working time an employee works.	Infotype 0007 Employment percent field drives the value of this field.
Work hours/ period	This is the amount of hours the employee is scheduled to work in the payroll period.	This field is defaulted based on the capacity utilization level percentage of work hours.

Table 4.3 Infotype 0008 Fields

4.1.4 Infotype 0050 Time Recording Information

Infotype 0050 is normally used for providing data to a time-keeping system via a mini-master data download. The mini master download is a basic extraction of the required master data to a different software system so that the other system can process the employee correctly. The fields can be set up and mapped to other systems so that the combination of fields can drive time collection rules configured in various systems. By using a mini-master, you will only need to maintain master data in one system and export that data out to all of the other systems. In addition, the fields are used within Time Evaluation and can be leveraged to make decisions on various groups to accommodate business requirements. For example, the particular fields are populated so that the data entered on this infotype maps directly to particular data fields of a bolt-on time collection system via a custom interface.

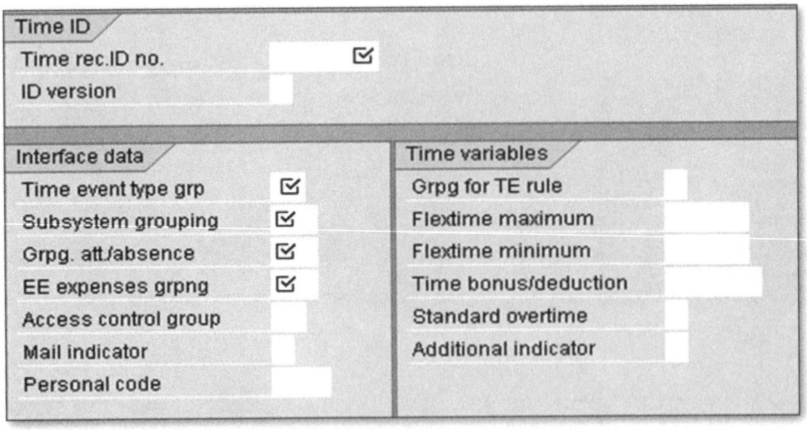

Figure 4.4 Infotype 0050 Time Recording

You can see the various fields available for Infotype 0050 in Table 4.4.

Field	Description	Purpose/Impact
Time Rec.ID number	Time Recording ID number.	This is the number associated with the time collected in a subsystem or bolt-on time-keeping system.
ID version	Version of ID number	This is a version control on the ID card for employees. Should an employee lose a card, they can keep the same time recording ID number, but then be assigned a new ID version.
Time event type group	Work time event type group	This field allows for a grouping to be associated with the employee on particular types of time activities that can be entered during time collection.
Subsystem grouping	Grouping for subsystems	Controls how groups of data can be sent to various subsystems via a download.
Grpg. Att/ absence	Attendance and absence grouping	Groups various attendances and absences that particular employees or groups of employees will be able to utilize at the subsystem terminal.
EE expenses grouping	Grouping for employee expenses	Groups various expense-related entries together for employees to utilize at the subsystem terminal.

Table 4.4 Infotype 0050 Fields

Field	Description	Purpose/Impact
Access control group		Controls time-restricted access authorizations. Used in conjunction with the subsystem setup to control when and how employees can enter time.
Mail indicator		Enables the subsystem to display text for employees during the entry of time at a subsystem. This field works in conjunction with the subsystem setup where the actual messages are maintained.
		This field also allows you to generate messages in Time Evaluation to be viewed during error handling.
Personal code		This field is a code that the employee may need to enter to fully access the time-keeping system. If the subsystem supports this functionality, this field can act like a password.
Grpg for TE rule	Grouping for Time Evaluation Rule	Freely definable field that allows flexibility for custom calculations depending on how you categorize the codes used in this field. Based on the values, you can create your own Time Evaluation rule to process employees differently.
Flextime maximum		Used in Time Evaluation for custom rules on flextime balances.
Flextime minimum		Used in Time Evaluation for custom rules on flextime balances.
Time bonus/ deduction		Used in Time Evaluation to build user-defined balances or calculations.
Standard overtime		Used to assign a blanket approval for individual overtime hours. This would override the need for an Infotype 2007 quota for the overtime.
		This field can also be used for any custom rules required.
Additional indicator		Used as a freely definable user indicator for custom business processing rules.

Table 4.4 Infotype 0050 Fields (Cont.)

4.1.5   Infotype 0080 Maternity Protection

Infotype 0080 is used to track an employee's expected and actual start of their maternity leave period. The absence entered is stored on Infotype 2001 Absences. The data on this infotype is used for reporting purposes and is not processed directly in Time Management. The absence, however, will be pulled into Time Evaluation for processing (see Figure 4.5).

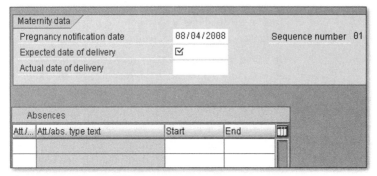

Figure 4.5   Infotype 0080 Maternity Protection

Table 4.5 explains the various fields of Infotype 0080.

Field	Description
Pregnancy Notification date	Date on which the company was notified.
Expected date of delivery	
Actual date of delivery	
Attendance/Absence type	
Start/End date	

Table 4.5   Infotype 0080 Fields

4.1.6   Infotype 0081 Military Service

Infotype 0081 is used to store additional data for an absence. The information entered on this infotype is stored on Infotype 2001 Absences. The absences will be pulled directly into Time Evaluation for processing. This infotype isn't used that often unless you have a need to track specific information relative to the individuals, association with the military (such a rank), etc. (see Figure 4.6).

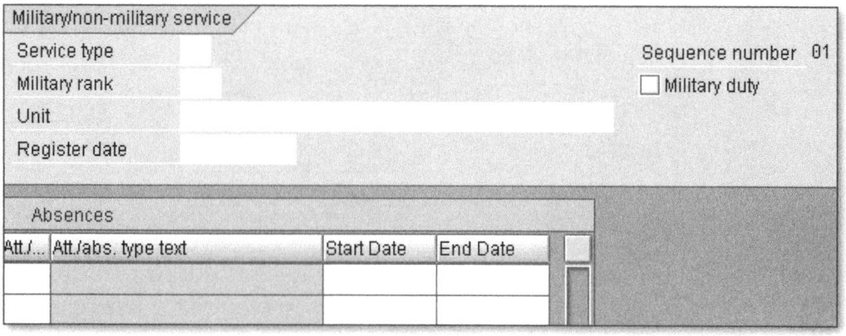

Figure 4.6 Infotype 0081 Military Service

Table 4.6 explains the various fields of Infotype 0081.

Field	Description
Service type	Type of service being tracked.
Military rank	Tracks the rank of the employee.
Unit	Tracks the particular unit the employee is assigned.
Register date	Date of military registration.
Attendance/Absence Type	The attendance or absence used to track military service.
Start/End Date	The date range of the particular event.
Military duty	Used to specify whether or not military service is optional.

Table 4.6 Infotype 0081 Fields

4.1.7 Infotype 0082 Additional Absence Data

Infotype 0082 is used to store exactly what it says, additional absence data (Figure 4.7). In particular, you can link to specific events and create worker's compensation–related information. Just like all other infotypes, this functionality allows you to track more detailed information than the normal Infotype 2001 Absences screen allows. You can also report off of the information. Let's say, for example, that you wanted to track an absence called Work Accident and the information on the screen, such as when the accident occurred. You would set up the absence type and link it to the additional data so that the relevant information can be entered.

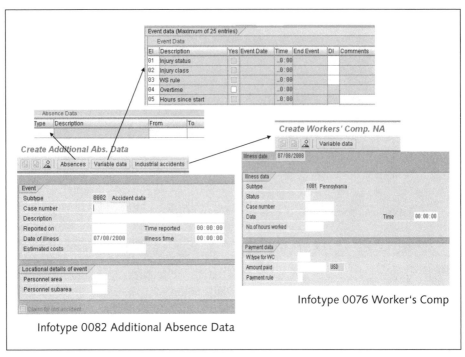

Figure 4.7 Infotype 0082 Additional Absence Data and Infotype 0076 Workers' Compensation

Table 4.7 explains the various fields of Infotype 0082 and Infotype 0076.

Field	Description	Purpose/Impact
Subtype	Description of the types of absence data captured.	
Case number	Tracks the particular occurrence by a unique code assigned.	
Description	Freely definable description of the situation.	
Reported on	Utilized to record the specific date the situation was reported.	
Date of illness	Utilized to record the specific date on which the situation occurred.	

Table 4.7 Infotype 0082 Additional Absence Data and Infotype 0076 Worker's Compensation Fields

Field	Description	Purpose/Impact
Estimated costs	Used to track what the dollar amount of the situation may cost.	
Time reported	Used to record the actual time the situation was reported.	
Illness Time	Used to record the actual time the specific situation occurred.	
Personnel area	General location of the event.	
Personnel subarea	Further breakdown of where the event occurred.	
Claim for Industrial accidents	Industrial accident claim indicator.	Flag used

Table 4.7 Infotype 0082 Additional Absence Data and Infotype 0076 Worker's Compensation Fields (Cont.)

4.1.8 Infotype 0130 Test Procedures

Infotype 0130 allows an administrator or employee to enter time, an administrator, or manager to check the time, and have the time be released for processing by a time administrator with a test procedure.

Using this functionality, you can set control points where it takes two individuals to get time entered and approved for processing.

The individual entering the time has update access to the infotypes, but does not have write access to Infotype 0130 (Figure 4.8). The individual approving the records has write access and approves the time by running a test procedure through a particular date. After the test procedure is conducted, the individual entering the time may not be able to alter the original record. Any changes would need to be done by someone with write authorization to both the infotypes and the test procedures.

The report for Time Leveling RPTAPPU0 can be utilized for this process.

Figure 4.8 Infotype 0130 Test Procedures for Time Evaluation

Table 4.8 explains the various fields of Infotype 0130.

Field	Description	Purpose/Impact
Test for	Specifies the particular test that is going to run.	You can configure the system to link particular infotypes to a particular code.
Released by	Specifies the date up to which the test was run and for all records that are now available for further processing.	
Tested by	Defaults based on tester.	
Tested using	Indicates the program used to test.	
Tested on	Date the test last occurred.	
Tested at	Time of the last test.	

Table 4.8 Infotype 0130 Fields

4.1.9 Infotype 0315 Time Sheet Defaults

Infotype 0315 is used for defaulting information into the timesheet for external and internal employees. If you are using the External Service component (MM-SRV) and transferring time, then this infotype is required. Figure 4.9 displays the infotype. An example of why you might want to explore using this infotype would be if you hire subcontractors to help on a particular internal project for the company. These individuals have been set up in your system with minimal master data. They will also enter their time they are working on the project in the Cross-Application Time Sheet (CATS). By utilizing this infotype, you can set a default for where you would like their costing information sent for the hours worked and vendor-related information to validate the billing invoice against.

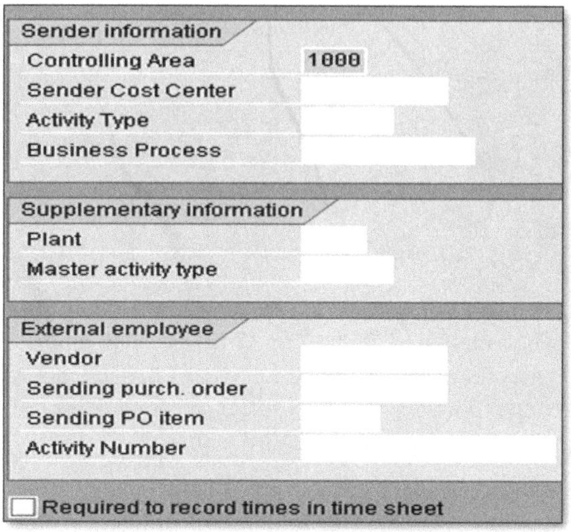

Figure 4.9 Infotype 0315 Time Sheet Defaults

Table 4.9 lists the various fields of Infotype 0315.

Field	Description	Purpose/Impact
Controlling Area	Identifies the highest organizational level in the Controlling component.	
Sender Cost Center	Identifies the sender cost center to book amounts against.	
Activity Type	Identifies the type of activity to book amounts against.	
Business Process	Identifies a process defined in activity-based costing to book amounts against.	
Plant	Identifies a Logistics organizational component to book amounts against.	

Table 4.9 Infotype 0315 Timesheet Default Screen Fields

Field	Description	Purpose/Impact
Master activity type	Identifies the highest level activity type that can be internally allocated further.	
Vendor	Identifies the vendor number to book amounts against.	Required if using external employees
Sending purch. order	Identifies the Logistics component order ID number.	
Sending PO item	Identifies a further breakdown of the purchase order.	
Activity Number	Identifies the number of the activity from the service master record.	
Required to record times in time sheet	Identifies the employee as required to enter a timesheet according to the Time Sheet Leveling report.	The Time Sheet Leveling report can be found via Transaction code CATC or program RCATSCMP.

Table 4.9 Infotype 0315 Timesheet Default Screen Fields (Cont.)

When an employee terminates and hasn't used up all of their vacation time, you normally need to pay them what is remaining. To do this, you use Infotype 0416.

4.1.10 Infotype 0416 Time Quota Compensation

Infotype 0416's function is to payout remaining quota due to the employee that has not been decreased by absences entered into the system. Typically, this is used during the termination process and payment for an employee. The quota is taken directly from Infotype 2006 Absence Quotas. The amount to be compensated is then passed to payroll for processing.

The infotype allows for processing specific absence types configured behind each compensation rule, or the system can be set up so that you can enter whichever quota type you like and the amount of payment. Figure 4.10 displays the infotype.

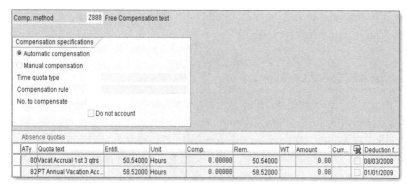

Figure 4.10 Infotype 0416 Time Quota Compensation

Table 4.10 explains the various fields of Infotype 0416.

Field	Description	Purpose/Impact
Compensation method	A description of the type of compensation to be paid out.	Configuration for the method will enable data to default during the selection.
Automatic compensation	Pays out the whole quota amount.	You select the type of quota to payout if one is not linked to the compensation method.
Manual compensation	Allows the user to process specific amounts of the particular quota.	You select the number of hours, the Wage type, or a dollar figure to compensate.
Time quota type	The particular quota type from Infotypes 2006 and 2007 that should be paid out.	
Compensation rule	Rule that specifies the order in which the quota should be taken.	
No. to compensate	Managed in days or hours, this is the value that will be compensated.	
Do not account	Specifies that the quota should not be processed in payroll.	

Table 4.10 Infotype 0416 Time Quota Compensation Fields

When certain absences happen, you may need to be able to track them to comply with the FMLA laws using Infotype 0672.

4.1.11 Infotype 0672 FMLA Event

Infotype 0672 is actually a structure to store the related data for FMLA occurrences resulting from the FMLA Workbench. The workbench can be accessed via Transaction code PTFMLA. The data on the screen in Figure 4.11 has been used to give you an idea of the type of data that is available for custom reports as the SAP system does not currently provide a report for the workbench. FMLA allows you to track particular absences against an FMLA reason such as adoption, sick family members, maternity leave, etc. The tracking mechanisms allow you to review how much time has been taken off against the three-month allowance granted by law. By tracking these occurrences of absence, an employer would have a good sense of how close an employee is to their maximum allowance of time off and can then terminate the employee once the maximum time is taken and they have not returned back to work. The SAP system does not offer a standard report to view the data that is tracked; however, this infotype is listed so that you know which data is available so you can develop a custom report.

Table: PA0672
Displayed Fields: 47 of 47 Fixed Columns: 3 List Width 1023

	Client	Personnel no.	Subtype	Object ID	Lock indicator	End Date	Start Date	IT record no.	Changed on
☐	220	00003167	001			01/11/2006	01/10/2006	000	03/23/2006
☐	220	00003167	001			01/11/2006	01/10/2006	001	03/23/2006
☐	220	00003167	001			03/31/2006	03/01/2006	000	05/23/2006

Historical rec.	Text exists	Ref. exists	Conf.fields ex.	Screen control	Change Reason	Reserved Field/Unused Field
	X					

Grouping Value	FMLA Rule	FMLA Reason	Request No.	Status	Continuity ID	Planned Hours	Certificate Provided	Requested on
	001	BAFC	000000002001	A	C	0.00		03/23/2006
	001	SICKF	000000001902	A	C	0.00		03/23/2006
	001	SICKF	000000001904	P	C	0.00	X	03/23/2006

Rolling	Deduction from	Deduction to	Converter	Eligibility	Creditable Hrs	Service	Checked on	CreditableHrs(old)
12	00/00/0000	00/00/0000	3.3300	2	40.0000	001	00/00/0000	40.0000
12	00/00/0000	00/00/0000	3.3300	2	40.0000	001	00/00/0000	40.0000
12	00/00/0000	00/00/0000	26.0000	2	312.0000	002	00/00/0000	312.0000

LengthofService	Checked on	Event No.	Log. system	Seniority	Working Hours	FMLA Entitlemnt	Remainder
001	00/00/0000	000000000000004002	SRACLNT220	012	1,250.00	12.00	0.4260
001	00/00/0000	000000000000003802	SRACLNT220	012	1,250.00	12.00	0.4260
002	00/00/0000	000000000000003806	SRACLNT220	012	1,250.00	12.00	0.4260

Figure 4.11 Infotype 0672 FMLA Event

4.1.12   Infotype 2001 Absences

Infotype 2001 is one of the main infotypes and it's used to process absences entered into the SAP system. The absence can come from a variety of sources.

▶ Direct entry on the infotype itself

▶ CATS Entry

▶ Third-party time subsystem that interfaces with the CATS database

▶ Time Manager's Workbench

Absences are described by absence types. These can be configured to either be paid or unpaid events. The absence can also be configured to reduce a quota that is linked on Infotype 2006 Absence Quotas. Examples might include vacation time, holiday time, and FMLA time as noted in the previous section. This infotype is a required infotype if you want to process absences entered by employees. Figure 4.12 displays the infotype 2001, and Figure 4.13 is a continuation of Infotype 2001.

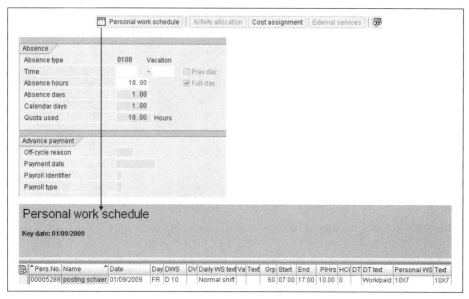

Figure 4.12   Infotype 2001 Absences

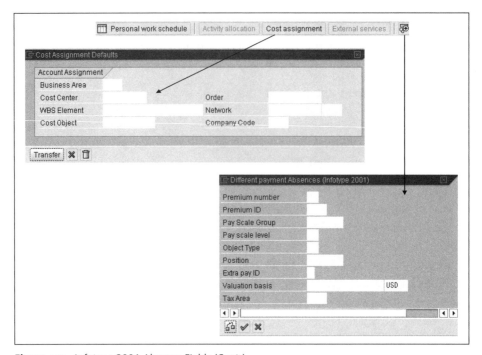

Figure 4.13 Infotype 2001 Absence Fields (Cont.)

Field	Description	Purpose/Impact
Absence type	A descriptive code of the type of absence that will be entered.	Examples would include vacation, leave without pay, etc.
Time	The start and end times of the absence.	Records have a cap of 24 hours.
Absence hours	The total amount of hours of the absence.	This can either be typed in or driven from the State and End Times entered.
Absence days	The number of days accounted for.	If you enter a date range, this field will calculate the number of days between the two dates; however, the full planned time will be used.
		This field will also display a 1 for a single date entry where the hours equal the total planned time from the work schedule.
		This field will show the percentage of a work day if the hours are less than the hours based on the work schedule.

Table 4.12 Infotype 2001 Fields

Field	Description	Purpose/Impact
Calendar days	Total calendar days calculated.	If you enter a date range, this field will calculate the number of days between the two dates; however, the full planned time will be used.
		This field will also display a 1 for a single date entry where the hours equal the total planned time from the work schedule.
		This field will display zero hours if the absence hours are less than the planned working time from the daily work schedule.
Quota used	The amount of hours that will be deducted from the quota that the absence is linked to.	
Prev. day	Indicates that the absence will be associated with the previous day.	This is useful for when employees work shifts that cross over into the next day. It can help award overtime to the appropriate week.
Full-day	Indicates that a full day has been accounted for based on a comparison against the daily work schedule's planned hours.	

Table 4.12 Infotype 2001 Fields (Cont.)

Table 4.13 explains the various fields of Infotype 2001. These fields are part of the infotype and allow you to control, by absence type, which information should be stored on each. For example, you normally have a cost center assigned on Infotype 0001 Organizational Assignment. This is where an employee works and where his costs should be assigned. If you are temporarily working on a different assignment and the cost or any of the other following fields differ from what is the norm, then you have the opportunity to place a different value in any one of these fields. In our example, by entering a different cost center on this particular absence type, then only these hours are booked to a different cost center.

Field	Description	Purpose/Impact
Business Area	Financial Accounting organizational unit.	
Cost Center	Controlling organizational unit.	
WBS Element	Production Planning Work Breakdown Structure.	
Cost Object	Identification number of the cost object in Controlling.	
Order	Logistics order number.	
Network	Project Systems structure identifying a task or an entire project.	
Company Code	Financial Accounting organizational unit.	
Premium number	Number used to identify the premium that should be paid.	Table V_T510P
Premium ID	Identification to pass the value of the premium to payroll for processing.	
Pay Scale Group	Selects the value of the Pay Scale Group in conjunction with the Pay Scale Level and uses that rate for payment.	
Pay scale level	Further description of the Pay Scale Group.	
Object Type	Represents a specific kind of Personnel Development object, such as a position.	
Position	Defaults the payment attributes of a position.	

Table 4.13 Infotype 2001 Fields

Field	Description	Purpose/Impact
Extra pay ID	Indicator that specifies how the valuation basis field should be used.	Blank — the valuation basis is taken as entered (+) — the valuation basis is increased by the value (–) — the valuation basis is decreased by the value
Valuation basis	The dollar amount that will be the new rate to be associated with the hours.	
Tax Area	The work tax area for tax purposes.	

Table 4.13 Infotype 2001 Fields (Cont.)

Similar to absences, attendances are required if you are paying employees in the payroll system that require the tracking of specific type of attendance. So let's look at Attendances.

4.1.13 Infotype 2002 Attendances

Infotype 2002 is used to process all attendance-related time information entered into the system. The attendance can come from a variety of sources.

▶ Direct entry on the infotype itself

▶ CATS Direct Entry

▶ Third-party time subsystem that interfaces to the CATS database

▶ Time Manager's Workbench

Attendances are described by attendance types. These can be configured to either paid or unpaid events. An example of using an attendance includes regular time for your hourly employees. The attendance can also be configured to reduce a quota that is linked on Infotype 2007 Attendance Quotas (Figure 4.14).

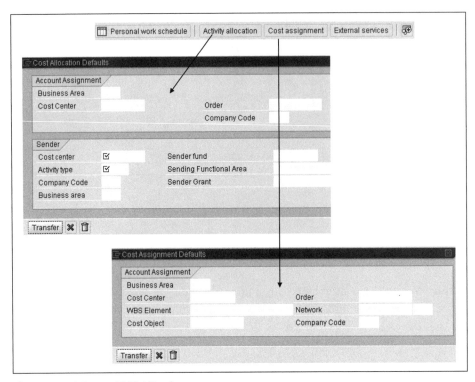

Figure 4.14 Infotype 2002 Attendances

Table 4.14 explains the various fields of Infotype 2002.

Field	Description	Purpose/Impact
Attendance type	The description of the attendance being entered.	
Time	The start and end times of the attendance stored in format HH:MM.	
Attendance hours	The number of hours directly entered or derived from the start and end times of the attendance.	

Table 4.14 Infotype 2002 Attendances Screen Fields

Field	Description	Purpose/Impact
Attendance days	Indicates a percentage of the day worked compared to the planned working time from the daily work schedule.	
Previous day	Indicates that the attendance should be allocated to the previous day for Time Evaluation calculations.	Useful in determining overtime when an employee works the night shift that carries over into the next day. If the next day happened to be the beginning of a new work week, the hours should be credited to the previous week's hours bucket to determine if overtime compensation is warranted.
Full-day	Indicates the attendance is a full day compared to the planned working time from the daily work schedule.	
Calendar days	Indicates the number of days between the begin date and end date of the record.	
Payroll hours	The number of payroll hours determined for the day.	This amount does not necessarily have to equal the amount entered based on customizing settings. Can be overwritten by Business Add-Ins (BAdIs) in the Implementation Guide (IMG) under Time Data Recording and Administration.
Payroll days	Indicates a percentage of the day worked compared to the planned working time from the daily work schedule.	This amount does not necessarily have to equal the amount entered based on customizing settings. Can be overwritten by BAdIs in the IMG under Time Data Recording and Administration.

Table 4.14 Infotype 2002 Attendances Screen Fields (Cont.)

Field	Description	Purpose/Impact
Overtime comp. type	Used to determine if compensation and or the credit toward time off should be calculated in Time Evaluation.	
Eval type att/ abs	Can be customized for user requirements so that special calculations can occur in Time Evaluation.	

Table 4.14 Infotype 2002 Attendances Screen Fields (Cont.)

Figure 4.15 is a continuation of Infotype 2002. This is very similar to the functionality we discussed for absences in that you can overwrite a particular value for a particular attendance.

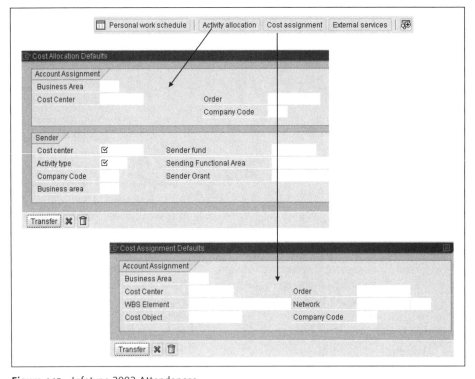

Figure 4.15 Infotype 2002 Attendances

Table 4.15 explains the various fields of Infotype 2002.

Field	Description	Purpose/Impact
Business Area	Financial Accounting Component organizational unit	
Cost Center	Controlling Component organizational unit	
WBS Element	Number associated with a particular task	
Cost Object	Financial Accounting Component organizational unit	
Order	Logistics order number	
Network	Used to identify the activity type by a cost center	
Company Code	Financial Accounting organizational unit	

Table 4.15 Infotype 2002 Attendance Screen Fields

Figure 4.16 is a continuation of Infotype 2002. These fields allow you to tie back to the Materials Management (MM) component–related information and provide additional pay type–related to the record. For example, in Figure 4.16 you can see the Valuation Basis field. If an employee normally receives $8 an hour pay and you decide to pay him $10 an hour for a particular period of time, such as four hours, then you can assign 10 in the valuation basis field. When payroll is processed, the $8 per hour will be overwritten with $10 for this particular attendance only.

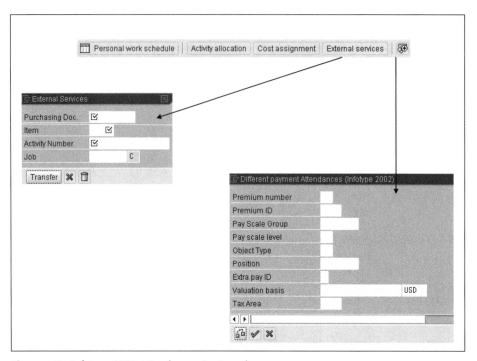

Figure 4.16 Infotype 2002 Attendances Continued

Table 4.16 explains the various fields of Infotype 2002.

Field	Description	Purpose/Impact
Purchasing Doc.	Document number from External Services.	
Item	The particular item number from within the purchasing document.	
Activity Number	The number of the activity from the service master record for each service.	
Job	A particular job identification number.	
Premium number	Used to grant extra compensation premiums to employees for particular conditions.	Driven from table V_T510P

Table 4.16 Infotype 2002 Attendance Screen Fields

Field	Description	Purpose/Impact
Premium ID	Indicator that determines the value of the awarded premium.	
Pay Scale Group	A grouping of pay scale–related rates that can be associated with increases or decreases in hourly rates.	
Pay scale level	The variation of the pay scale group that holds the actual rate to be assigned.	
Object Type	Used to select different types of specific objects defined in the system.	Examples (position - S, work center - A)
Position	Used to select the attributes of a particular position.	
Extra pay ID	Controls how the valuation basis will be used.	Blank — No extra pay: Valuation basis used as is. (–) — Valuation basis used as amount deducted. (+) — Valuation basis used as amount added.
Valuation basis	Used to hold an amount that will override Infotype 0008's rate.	
Tax Area	Used as a work tax area override to Infotype 0208 Work Tax Area.	

Table 4.16   Infotype 2002 Attendance Screen Fields (Cont.)

So, what happens when you have a temporary change in a work schedule? You have to use substitutions – Infotype 2003.

4.1.14   Infotype 2003 Substitutions

Infotype 2003 is used to enter overrides to an employee's existing work schedule on Infotype 0007 Planned Working Time. These are typically short-term changes to a schedule. If you plan to make the change permanent, then it is recommended to go ahead and change the work schedule rule on Infotype 0007. There are a variety of ways a substitution can be entered and the durations can be anywhere from a period within a day to spanning as many calendar days as necessary (Figure 4.17). Substitutions can be created in the following manner.

▶ Directly on the infotype itself

▶ Via a third-party time-keeping system

▶ Via a shift substitution in Shift Planning

▶ Entry via Time Manager's Workplace

Note that you cannot enter a substitution through CATS.

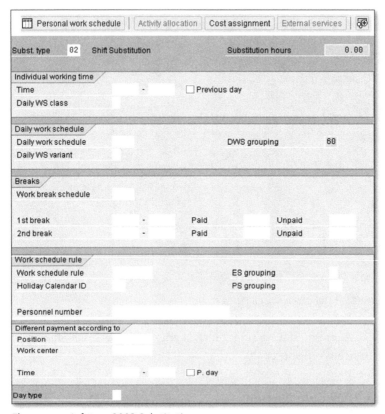

Figure 4.17 Infotype 2003 Substitutions

When you create a substitution, there are a variety of fields that can be entered so the system knows that there is an alteration to the normal working schedule.

Table 4.17 explains the various fields of Infotype 2003.

Field	Description	Purpose/Impact
Substitution type	Substitution describing why there is an override to an employee's schedule.	
Time	Start and End Time of the substitution.	
Previous day	Used to assign time entered to the previous days time buckets.	
Daily WS class	Overrides the particular daily work schedule class assigned to the normal daily work schedule.	Can be used to override the way attendance and absences are compensated, counted, and which Wage types are generated.
Daily work schedule	Overrides the entire day with the functionality of that particular daily work schedule.	Includes information such as: ▶ Planned Time ▶ Flextime ▶ Core time ▶ Breaks ▶ Tolerances ▶ Overtime ▶ Daily Work Schedule Class ▶ Infotype 2005 Overtime Reactions
Daily WS variant	Works in conjunction with the daily work schedule, however, it allows a particular version of the schedule if one exists.	
Work break schedule	Defaults based on Personnel Area/Subarea grouping and cannot be changed.	
1st break	Overrides the particular break schedule for the time period specified.	
2nd break	Allows customer-specific overrides to break schedule.	
Work schedule rule	Overrides the entire work schedule rule from Infotype 0007.	

Table 4.17 Infotype 2003 Substitutions Screen Fields

Field	Description	Purpose/Impact
Holiday Calendar ID	Overrides the holiday calendar.	
Personnel number	Used to default fields based on what the personnel number selected has on their master data.	Defaults the work schedule rule, holiday calendar, ES grouping, and PS grouping.
ES grouping	Employee subgroup grouping for work schedules.	
PS grouping	Personnel Subarea grouping for work schedule.	
Position	Used to pay employees differently based on the position.	
Work center	Used to pay employees differently based on the work center.	
Time	Used to compensate the employee differently for a set period of daily time.	
P. day	Used to specify the substitution that should be allocated to the previous day.	This previous day indicator is similar to the previous day check box used for individual working time however this particular check box is for different payments.
Day type	Specifies if the day is a working day or not.	

Table 4.17 Infotype 2003 Substitutions Screen Fields (Cont.)

Once you make a substitution, you may need to find a substitute for another worker, or add an extra person to a shift. To know who is available, you'll use Infotype 2004 Availability.

4.1.15 Infotype 2004 Availability

Infotype 2004 is used to determine when an employee may or may not be available for a shift. The availability is based on time periods outside of the planned working time in the work schedule rule associated with the employee on Infotype 0007 Planned Working Time (see Figure 4.18).

You can enter availability based on three criteria:

▸ Fixed Times — Used to enter times outside the normal, planned work schedule times

▸ According to Daily Work Schedule — Used to enter daily work schedules that are configured to allow for availability processing

▸ According to Work Schedule Rule — Used to enter availability for longer durations or for those that follow the working pattern associated with the work schedule rule

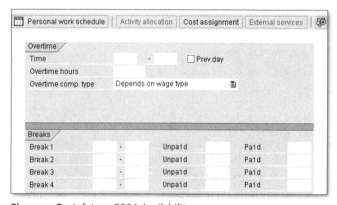

Figure 4.18 Infotype 2004 Availability

Table 4.18 explains the various fields of Infotype 2004.

Field	Description	Purpose/Impact
Availability type	Defines the type of availability being tracked.	Typical examples include on-call or a percentage availability.
Time	Specifies the time the employee is tracked as available.	
Prev. day	Indicates the availability is tracked toward the previous day.	
Daily work schedule	Indicates the availability based on the configuration of the daily work schedule.	

Table 4.18 Infotype 2004 Availability Fields

Field	Description	Purpose/Impact
DWS grouping	Defaults from the grouping of the Personnel Area/Subarea combination.	
Daily WS variant	The variation of the daily work schedule.	
ES grouping	Employee subgroup grouping for work schedules.	
Holiday Calendar ID	Holiday calendar ID for work schedules.	
PS grouping	Personnel Subarea grouping for work schedules.	
Work schedule rule	Based on the combination of the preceding three fields, the list of work schedule rules will be presented.	

Table 4.18 Infotype 2004 Availability Fields (Cont.)

4.1.16   Infotype 2005 Overtime

Infotype 2005 is used to enter overtime to be paid to an employee. This functionality is usually not required if Time Evaluation is processed because overtime rules in Time Evaluation automatically determine the appropriate amount of overtime based on Federal and State regulations. You may want to use this infotype to determine if the employee is actually permitted to have overtime calculations processed and for which times of the day or the total amount of overtime that would be permitted (Figure 4.19).

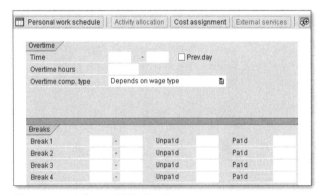

Figure 4.19   Infotype 2005 Overtime

Table 4.19 explains the various fields of Infotype 2005.

Field	Description
Time	The time period by which an employee can be paid overtime.
Prev. day	Indicates that the record should be allocated to the previous day.
Overtime hours	The number of over-time hours to be processed.
Overtime comp. type	Indicates whether or not the time should be compensated or not.
Break	Additional data points to establish periods of break between the start and end times.

Table 4.19 Infotype 2005 Overtime Screen Fields

Now let's look at how you use the quota infotypes to track an employee's allotted time against what has been used.

4.1.17 Infotype 2006 Absence Quotas

Infotype 2006 is used to hold the allotted time for each type of quota that is tracked. This infotype can be updated by the following methods.

▸ Time Evaluation accrual

▸ Front loaded via Time Evaluation program

▸ Direct entry on the infotype

The amounts remaining at the end of the year or during a termination from employment can be paid out via Infotype 0416 Time Quota Compensation. Upon entry into the system, absences that are linked to the quota type validate that a sufficient quota number remains to take the absence. Once accepted, the quota is reduced by the amount of hours from the absence. The quota can be set up for hours or days (see Figure 4.20). Using, as an example, an allotment of 15 vacation days for an employee, the Infotype 2006 would show 120 hours of vacation available. Any time an employee takes a vacation day, you would see the hours tracked and the infotype would show the remaining amount available.

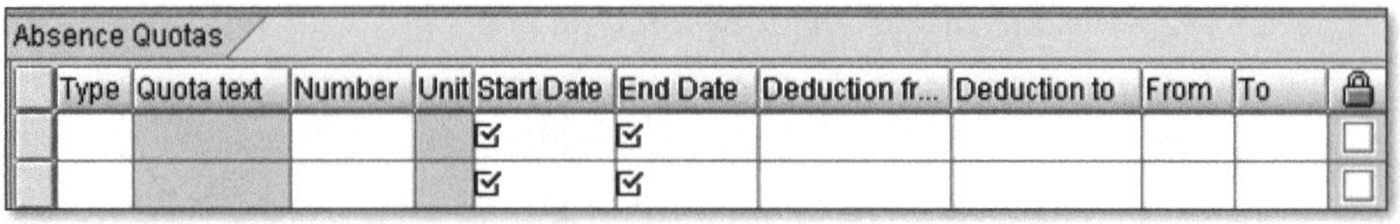

Figure 4.20 Infotype 2006 Absence Quotas

Table 4.20 explains the various fields of Infotype 2006.

Field	Description
Type	The description of the absence.
Number	The number of hours that the employee is entitled to.
Start Date	The date on which the quota can be taken.
End Date	The date on which the quota is valid to.
Deduction from	Defines the period the employee can take the quota.
Deduction to	Defines the period the employee can take the quota.
From	The begin time that the quota can be taken.
To	The end time that the quota can be taken.
Locked	Indicates that the record is locked and will not be processed.

Table 4.20 Infotype 2006 Absence Quota Screen Fields

4.1.18 Infotype 2007 Attendance Quotas

Infotype 2007 is used to track various categories of attendance, such as training. The attendance quotas also allow you to specify a time frame by which the attendance can be validated against. This would allow you to specify that particular types of entries are only valid for a particular date range and time period. Quotas can be entered in hours or days.

This infotype can be updated by the following methods:

- Time Evaluation accrual
- Front loaded via a Time Evaluation program
- Direct Entry on the infotype

The amounts remaining at the end of the year or during a termination from employment can be paid out via Infotype 0416 Time Quota Compensation. At the point of entry into the system, attendances linked to the quota type validate that a sufficient quota number remains to take the attendance. Once accepted, the quota is reduced by the amount of hours from the attendance. The quota can be set up for hours or days (see Figure 4.21).

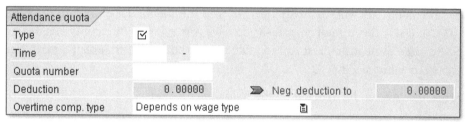

Figure 4.21 Infotype 2007 Attendance Quotas

Table 4.21 explains the various fields of Infotype 2007.

Field	Description
Type	The type of attendance quota.
Time	The time frames in which the attendance must be entered to qualify.
Quota number	The amount of quota available.
Deduction	The amount of deduction taken.
Overtime comp. type	Indicates whether or not the quota should be compensated or not.
Negative deduction to	The limit by which the quota can go negative.

Table 4.21 Infotype 2007 Attendance Quota Screen Fields

Now that you've tracked the employee's working time and absences, you'll need to determine how much they should be paid for that period. For this step, you'll use Infotype 2010 Employee Remuneration.

4.1.19 Infotype 2010 Employee Remuneration

Infotype 2010 is used to process payments for payroll (Figure 4.22). This infotype is not available for processing in Time Evaluation. Using, as an example, a third-party time-keeping system, you don't necessarily have to use SAP's Time Evaluation program to process time-related information. You can have your interface from the external time-keeping system process all of the calculations and then pass the information to the SAP system where it can be stored on this infotype. This would allow you to bypass processing SAP's Time Evaluation steps. Instead of the other time-keeping system passing 5 different records of 8 hour regular times and 4 different records of overtime at 2 hours each, you could simply pass 1 record with 40 hours of regular time and 1 record with 8 hours of overtime. Should you process your data this way? It really depends on all of your business requirements. You may actually need to pass the individual entries to Infotype 2002 and skip this infotype because you have particular requirements that dictate SAP's Time Evaluation must run to build certain buckets of time that a particular interface would need.

This infotype can be updated by the following methods:

▶ CATS

▶ Direct entry

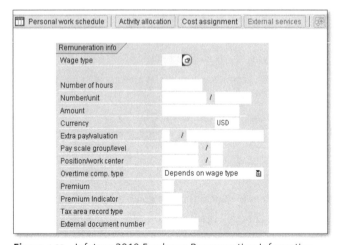

Figure 4.22 Infotype 2010 Employee Remuneration Information

Table 4.22 explains the various fields of Infotype 2010.

Field	Description	Purpose/Impact
Wage type	The code entered by which a payment will be made in payroll.	
Number of hours	The number of hours that will be compensated in payroll.	
Number/unit	The number of hours combined with a unit qualifier.	
Amount	The dollar amount that should be paid.	
Currency	The currency the amount will be compensated in.	
Extra pay/ valuation	Controls how the valuation basis will be used.	Blank — No extra pay: Valuation basis used as is: (–) — Valuation basis used as amount deducted. (+) — Valuation basis used as amount added.
Pay scale group/level	The pay scale group and level by which the rate will be taken from.	
Position/ work center	The position or work center by which defaults values will be taken.	
Overtime comp. type	The type of processing that should occur.	This can included compensation or time off.
Premium	The number assigned with a premium that will provide an additional payment during payroll processing.	
Premium Indicator	Used to determine the actual value of the premium.	
Tax area record type	Work tax area override.	
External document number	Used to specify a number uniquely identifying the payment to a particular source.	

Table 4.22 Infotype 2010 Employee Remuneration Information Screen Fields

Attendance and absences Infotypes 2002 and 2001 are used for processing evaluated time that has a start and end time. But for employees who have to clock in, you'll need to use Infotype 2011 Employee Time Events.

4.1.20 Infotype 2011 Employee Time Events

Infotype 2011 is used to store the actual clock-in and clock-out entries received from a third-party time collection system (Figure 4.23). The time entries can also be entered and corrected via the Time Manager's Workplace, which we'll discuss in Chapter 11. You'll want to utilize this infotype if you have swipe-card systems at certain facilities that allow an employee to clock in and out during the day. The swipe-card systems capture the data and time stamp it as clock in or clock out throughout the day. This infotype would store each swipe and then Time Evaluation will review each of the entries and form the daily hours worked.

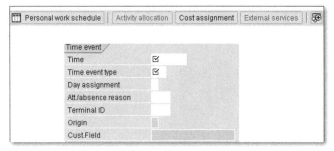

Figure 4.23 Infotype 2011 Time Events

Table 4.23 explains the various fields of Infotype 2011.

Field	Description	Purpose/Impact
Time	The clock time for the record.	The data is stored in HH:MM:SS format.
Time event type	The type of time that is being entered.	These are the time events configured in table T705P for the particular grouping of employees.

Table 4.23 Infotype 2011 Employee Time Events

Field	Description	Purpose/Impact
Day assignment	Determines if the time is associated with the current day or the previous day.	(=) — current day (<) — previous day (+) — manual override current day (-) — manual override previous day
Att./absence reason	The reason for the time entry, which will create a Wage type during Time Evaluation.	Configuration is in table V_T705A.
Terminal ID	Displays the identification code of the point of entry subsystem terminal.	
Origin	Displays whether or not the entry was made in the SAP system directly or from a subsystem.	The following codes are available: Blank — Subsystem entry M — Entered or changed by time administrator G — No current use E — Employee Self-Service (ESS) entry S — Subsystem entry, process in ESS
Cust. field	Customer field that is freely definable.	An enhancement can be used to populate the fields.

Table 4.23 Infotype 2011 Employee Time Events (Cont.)

Sometimes in the system, there will be situations where all of the business rules you've setup are not flexible enough for certain situations. To alter values that drive some of the calculations, you'll use Infotype 2012 Transfer Specifications.

4.1.21 Infotype 2012 Time Transfer Specifications

Infotype 2012 allows the user three options to change various time balances. The transfers are conducted in the Time Evaluation schema using FUNCTION P2012.

- ► Time Type — Table V_T555J
  - ► Update Time type balances
  - ► Transfer amounts from one Time type to another Time type
- ► Wage Type — Table V_T555K
  - ► Transfer amounts from a Time type to a Wage type
  - ► Transfer amounts to a Wage type
- ► Quota Type — Table V_T555L
  - ► The quota must exist in order for a change to be available

By using this functionality, you can change certain values during the processing. For example, let's say you are running Time Evaluation and you have certain rules in the system that will only process if a Time type value is equal to 1. The employee's history in the system has not allowed for that setting of a Time type to be set to 1 so the employee will not process through those specific calculation rules. By utilizing Infotype 2012, you can enter a Time type with the value of 1 and the rules will now engage. This example of functionality offers you a lot of options when you are trying to design a system with very strict pay practice calculations, however, the business needs flexibility to adjust the rules in particular cases. You can design your system with all of the rules, but also allow for flexibility by using the three options listed earlier. Figure 4.24 shows Infotype 2012.

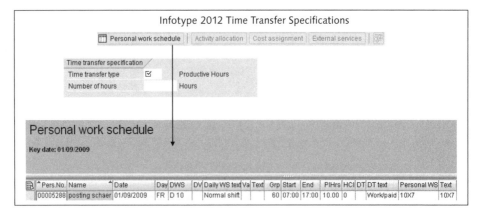

Figure 4.24 Infotype 2012 Time Transfers

Table 4.24 explains the various fields of Infotype 2012.

Field	Description	Purpose/Impact
Time transfer type	The type of time transfer the user needs to process.	The configuration of the time transfer type will dictate whether or not time will be taken from a specific Time type or if the amount entered under the number of hour's field will be the final number used.
Number of hours	The amount of hours to be transferred.	If you have an amount from a Time type, you can also use the number of hour's field to adjust the hours where necessary.

Table 4.24 Infotype 2012 Time Transfer Screen Fields

Just as with Infotype 2012 in which you can make certain adjustments, you may also need to make adjustments to the quota calculations if you generate them through Time Evaluation. To make these adjustments, you'll use Infotype 2013 Quota Corrections.

4.1.22 Infotype 2013 Quota Corrections

Infotype 2013 is used to adjust quotas that were generated via Time Evaluation using only the radio button Increase (Figure 4.25).

You have three options when changing a quota correction:

1. Increase the generated entitlement.
2. Reduce the generated entitlement
3. Replace the generated entitlement
    ▶ You use select Transfer collected entitlement immediately below
    ▶ Only enter one entry per day otherwise the first entry will be overwritten

You also have three options on when to transfer the quota correction:

1. Do not change transfer time
    ▶ The system will transfer the update when Time Evaluation generates the actual quota
    ▶ The quota changes will not be available until the accrual rules generate the next allotment of hours

2. Transfer collected entitlement immediately

▶ The system will transfer the amount on the next Time Evaluation run in conjunction with any new entitlements

3. Only transfer quota correction immediately

▶ The system will transfer the amount on the next Time Evaluation run

This infotype comes in handy if, for example, you have set up the system to grant an employee 80 hours of vacation each year, but because they are a savvy employee with hard-to-find technical skills, such as SAP time or payroll, they negotiated an extra 40 hours of vacation. The normal Time Evaluation process would grant the employee 80 hours. You are still 40 hours short. Instead of configuring the system for all of these different situations, you can enter 40 hours on Infotype 2013 and it will be processed during the next Time Evaluation run. The employee's vacation quota would then be changed to 120 hours.

These changes will only take place during the next Time Evaluation run.

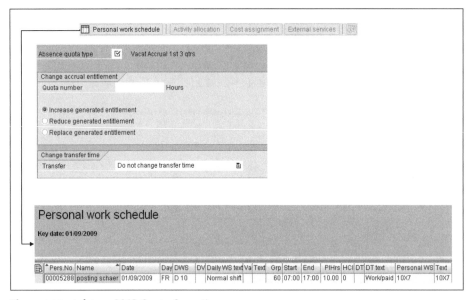

Figure 4.25 Infotype 2013 Quota Corrections

Table 4.25 explains the various fields of Infotype 2013.

Field	Description
Absence quota type	Describes the actual quota that will be updated.
Quota number	The amount of the change to the quota type.
Increase generated entitlement	Increases the quota by the quota number.
Reduce generated entitlement	Reduces the quota by the quota number.
Replace generated entitlement	Creates or replaces the quota by the quota number.
Transfer	Specifies the method by which to transfer the change.

Table 4.25 Infotype 2013 Quota Corrections Screen Fields

Sometimes it is useful to see an employee's absence and attendance across a greater span of time than 1 day. Infotype 2050 Annual Calendar provides this information.

4.1.23   Infotype 2050 Annual Calendar

Infotype 2050 allows you to quickly view and create full-day attendances and absences for a single employee at a time. You select the category code that is linked to the attendance or absence. Upon saving, the record is automatically generated on the absence Infotype 2001 or attendance infotype 2002 based on your code selection (Figure 4.26).

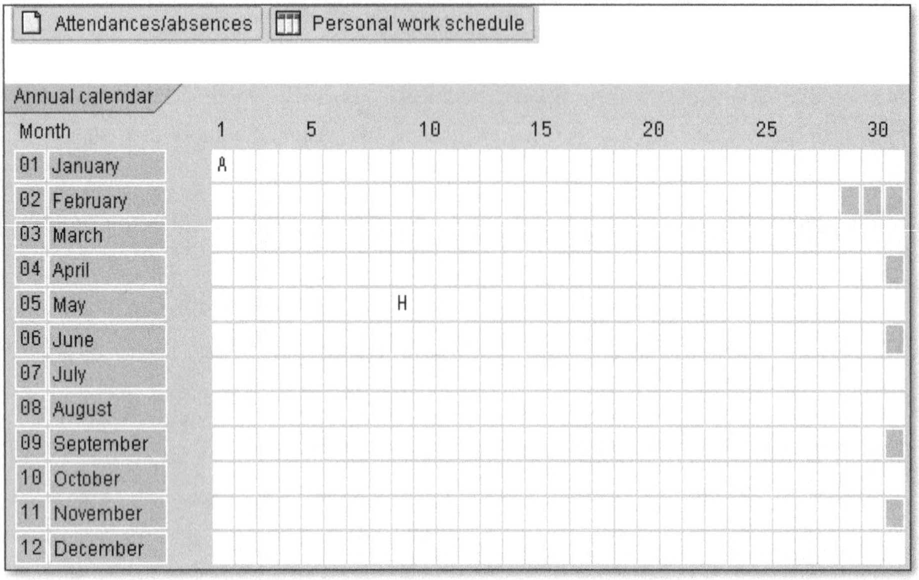

Figure 4.26 Infotype 2050 Annual Calendar

In Figure 4.26, the 'H' represents a regular holiday and the 'A' represents an attendance.

Similar to the annual calendar, it's sometimes useful to see what daily work schedule an employee will be utilizing over a monthly period of time using Infotype 2051 Monthly Calendar.

4.1.24 Infotype 2051 Monthly Calendar

Infotype 2051 allows you to adjust the employee's monthly calendar. Specifically, you can change the daily work schedule, the daily work schedule variant, and, like Infotype 2050, you can create attendances or absences infotypes directly by entering a particular code (Figure 4.27).

Now let's consider what happens if you have a group of attendances for an employee and as a time administrator, you receive an email to change each attendance so that a different cost center is used. Instead of going 1 by 1 through Infotype 2002, you can use utilize Infotype 2052 to quickly view and change the data to the new cost center.

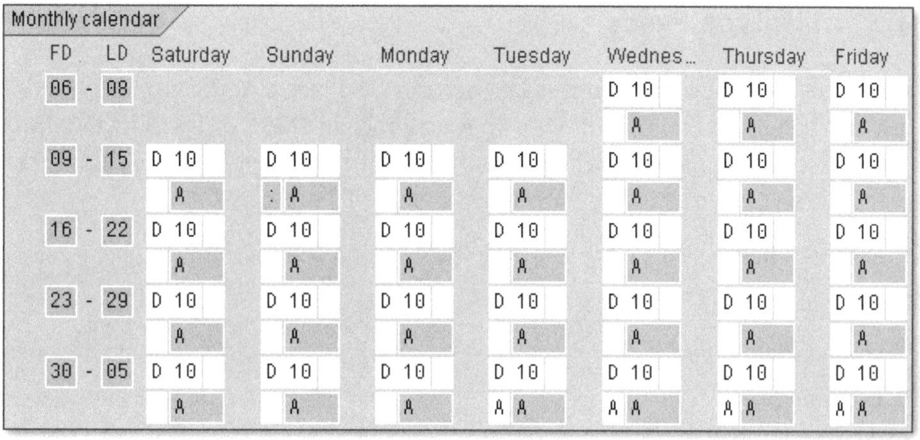

Figure 4.27 Infotype 2051 Monthly Calendar

4.1.25 Infotype 2052 Weekly Calendar

Infotype 2052 allows you to enter attendances or absences for an employee using a weekly view. In addition, records that already exist on Infotype 2001 and Infotype 2002 will automatically be pulled into the screen. You then have the opportunity to adjust the records accordingly and add a variety of activity allocations to the time entries similar to the functionality that is delivered on both Infotype 2001 and Infotype 2002 — should you have entered them directly there (see Figure 4.28).

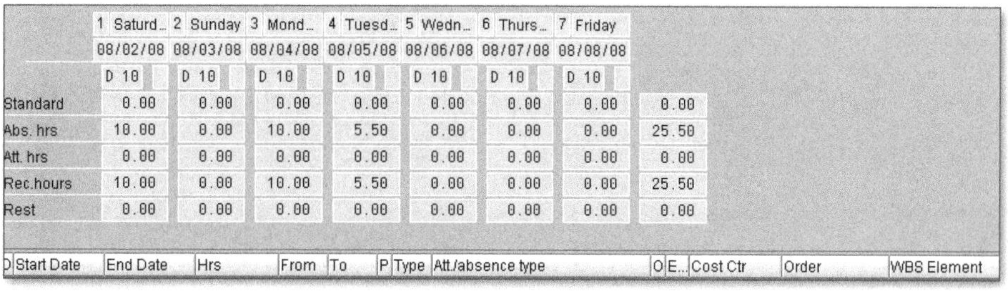

Figure 4.28 Infotype 2052 Weekly Entry Activity Allocations

This concludes the individual infotype discussion. The next section describes how you may want to customize particular fields on an infotype screen.

4.2 Infotype Fields

All of the infotypes listed in this chapter can be altered. You can make the following changes in table T588M via Transaction code SM31 or by following IMG path PERSONNEL MANAGEMENT • PERSONNEL ADMINISTRATION • CUSTOMIZING USER INTERFACES • CHANGE SCREEN MODIFICATIONS (see Figure 4.29).

► Required field

► Optional field

► Output Field only

► Hide the field

► Hide and initialize, which stores any date that is automatically populated in the hidden field when new records are created or copied.

Figure 4.29 displays the table entry for Infotype 0007 Planned Working Time.

Change View "Infotype Screen Control": Details

New Entries

Module Pool	MP000700	Variable key	10
Standard screen	2000	Feature	
Alternative screen	2000	Feature	
Next screen			

Scrn control

Grp	Field name	Field text	Std	RF	OF	Outp	Hide	Init
001	P0007-SCHKZ	Work Schedule Rule	◉	○	○	○	○	○
002	P0007-ZTERF	Employee Time Management Status	◉	○	○	○	○	○
003	P0007-EMPCT	Employment percentage	◉	○	○	○	○	○
004	P0007-TEILK	Indicator Part-Time Employee	◉	○	○	○	○	○
004	P0007-TEILK	Indicator Part-Time Employee						
005	P0007-ARBST	Daily Working Hours	◉	○	○	○	○	○
006	P0007-MINTA	Minimum number of work hours per	◉	○	○	○	○	○
007	P0007-MAXTA	Maximum number of work hours per	◉	○	○	○	○	○
008	P0007-WOSTD	Hours per week	◉	○	○	○	○	○
009	P0007-MINWO	Minimum weekly working hours	◉	○	○	○	○	○
010	P0007-MAXWO	Maximum number of work hours per	◉	○	○	○	○	○

Figure 4.29 Setup for Infotype 0007 Planned Working Time

The key to the infotype in Figure 4.29 is based on a Module Pool and the standard screen. In you are not familiar with this concept or unsure exactly which module pool or screen you should select, you can easily find out by conducting the following steps:

▶ Open an infotype record via Transaction code PA30

▶ Once inside the record, follow menu path SYSTEM •STATUS.

You will see a screen that provides a lot of useful information. In particular, Figure 4.30 illustrates the section of data that will help you determine the module pool and screen number.

SAP data	
Repository data	
Transaction	PA30
Program (screen)	MP000700
Screen number	2000
Program (GUI)	MP000700
GUI status	MOD

Figure 4.30 System Status Technical Information

4.3 Summary

This chapter was designed to give you an exposure to the various infotypes for the ERP HCM Time Management Master Data. The infotypes were focused toward most United States–related implementations, but other infotypes for your particular country maybe available. You can find a complete list of all infotypes in table V_T582A. You are not required to implement all of them, but based on your project's requirements you will most likely use a few of them. Most often the following infotypes are used:

▶ Infotype 0007 Planned Working Time

▶ Infotype 0008 Basic Pay

▶ Infotype 0050 Time Recording Information (only if using third-party time systems, or if special processing in Time Evaluation is needed and there isn't another way to store the data you need to make decisions in custom personnel calculation rules)

- ▶ Infotype 0416 Time Quota Compensation
- ▶ Infotype 2001 Absences
- ▶ Infotype 2002 Attendances
- ▶ Infotype 2006 Absence Quotas
- ▶ Infotype 2010 Employee Remuneration
- ▶ Infotype 2012 Time Transfer Specifications

The other infotypes may or may not be used based on your requirements.

In the following chapters, we'll discuss the configuration that supports the Time Management infotypes discussed here. In particular, Chapter 5 will teach you about the Work Schedule rules that reside in Infotype 0007. This configuration forms the foundation of how you can build personnel calculation rules in Time Evaluation to make decisions and generate Wage types to compensate your employees.

In this chapter, you'll learn about key areas to consider during the configuration of Work Schedules that reside in Infotype 0007 Planned Working Time. At the conclusion of this chapter, you should understand the concepts and setup process of Work Schedule rules.

5   Work Schedules

Work Schedules are the foundation of Infotype 0007 Planned Working Time. They represent various pieces of information that make up an individual's defined working time no matter how specific or generic you decide the overall schedules need to be. The Work Schedule configuration supports SAP ERP HCM Time Management in the following ways:

▶ Facilitating time entry inside and outside SAP's time capturing components

▶ Processing specific calculations in Time Evaluation

▶ Displaying availability for shift planning

▶ Running Payroll Processing

▶ Integrating with the Logistics component

Key Management Decision Points — Work Schedule Decisions

The following items are key decision points for the implementation of Work Schedules.

▶ The scope by which SAP's ERP HCM Time Management functionality will calculate various categories of time, such as breaks, overtime, and holidays, depends on how detailed the configuration is to support such processing. For instance, if your business requirements are such that Time Management is going to merely process the time that was entered manually into a time collection system, taking into account the individual entering the time factors and the various business rules and laws, and if there are not any systematic business requirements to determine when an employee should work or when they would be available for work, then the Work Schedule rule functionality should be kept as generic as possible. This will minimize the time needed to capture the various system requirements and configure and test them. Using as generic a Work Schedule as possible will also reduce the overall ongoing maintenance costs of having detailed Work Schedules in the system to maintain and support.

▶ If your business would like to systematically determine all calculations based on time entry, and possibly take into account substitutions to Work Schedules and shift planning, then this part of the configuration will be extremely detailed. You should be sure to budget and provide the appropriate amount of time to the team to prototype and build a proof of concept so end users can review how the system would work in a production environment.

▶ Part of determining the complexity of the Work Schedule is to determine the willingness of your business to maintain appropriate master data related to Work Schedules or Substitutions. Obviously, there will be some people who would prefer to manage the day-to-day aspects of their business instead of moving employee master data around to accommodate pay practices. So, you will need to determine the overall commitment level to ensure that the appropriate level-system setup is conducted.

▶ The first step will be to determine if SAP ERP HCM Payroll's Month-End Accrual functionality will be required when posting payroll results to accounting. For example, the Month-End Accrual functionality can be based on three criteria when calculating the factoring rates for the accrual:

  ▶ Calendar Days

  ▶ Payroll Days

  ▶ Payroll Hours

If you elect to set up the system with generic Work Schedules such that an employee is scheduled 7 days a week 24 hours a day, then the Month-End Accrual functionality will need to be reviewed further to determine if a custom payroll function should be created for a new calculation. Otherwise, the accruals would use 31 days for that particular month instead of 20 in the calculations.

5.1 Overview

Work Schedules create the foundation for determining when an employee is supposed to be working and how that employee should be compensated for their time. Work Schedule rules are made up of various pieces that, when properly strung together, create the desired schedule per employee (see Figure 5.1)

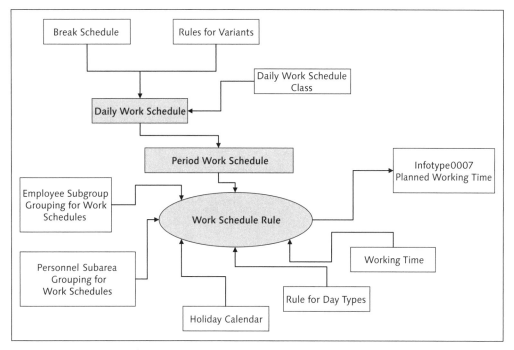

Figure 5.1 Components of the Work Schedule Rule for Infotype 0007

Figure 5.1 illustrates the various components that make up the Work Schedule rule that will be associated with an employee on Infotype 0007. The shaded items are the main building blocks of the Work Schedule rule. The Work Schedules require each component, which will be described in more detail in the next section.

5.1.1 Work Schedule Components

The SAP ERP HCM Time Management functionality can be set up to automatically generate specific holidays that an organization specifies as a day off whether it be paid or unpaid.

Holiday Classes

Public holiday classes are the building blocks for the actual holiday. Once established, the holiday classes are linked to a holiday calendar, which in turn are linked to a Work Schedule rule.

The public holiday classes are used by the system to determine daily work schedule variant rules, absence counting, and selection of time Wage types, as shown in Figure 5.2.

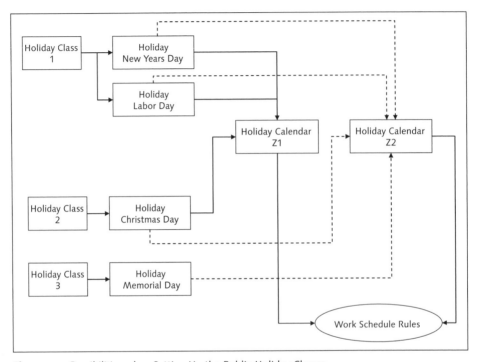

Figure 5.2 Possibilities when Setting Up the Public Holiday Classes

Notice that there are three holiday classes illustrated. Holiday Class 1 is associated with two holidays, Holiday Class 2 is associated with one holiday, and Holiday Class 3 is associated with one holiday. You are probably asking yourself why you wouldn't just associate the same holiday class of one with all four types of holidays. The simple answer is you would, unless your business requirements were such that you were going to implement the Time Evaluation functionality covered later in this book. And as a part of that functionality, you had captured specific requirements around the various holidays during the blueprinting stage of the project.

Examples

▶ New Years Day should be a paid holiday

▶ Labor Day should be a paid holiday

▶ Christmas Day should be a paid holiday; however, if any regular working time is entered into the system on that day, the employee should be paid for the holiday, receive payment for the regular time entered, and the employee should also receive $100 extra for working that day.

To accommodate this requirement, you will need some type of identifier during the Time Evaluation processing to flag the day as Christmas day. The holiday class is available for such decisions in Time Evaluation. A custom time rule, which will be covered further and in more detail in the Time Evaluation sections of this book, would make a decision based on this holiday class to determine if it was a 2. If it wasn't, then the custom calculation rule would merely ensure the holiday was paid. In this example, the holiday in question is Christmas Day and the employee also worked on that day so the custom rule would need to go further to determine if the time entered qualified for the $100 bonus and if so, create a new time bucket to hold a qualifier for the $100 bonus and also pay out the hours entered on the attendance. All three pieces of time (Christmas Day, regular time, and $100 bonus) would be passed to payroll for compensation.

Now that you are familiar with what holiday classes are, let's have a look at your options for setting up a holiday calendar. The configuration for holidays can be found in the IMG under menu path TIME MANAGEMENT • WORK SCHEDULES • DEFINE PUBLIC HOLIDAY CLASSES.

There are five basic ways to set up a holiday:

1. With a Fixed Date
2. With a Fixed Day From Date
3. Distance from Easter
4. Easter Sunday
5. Floating Public Holiday

The following sections will go into more detail regarding the five ways to set up a public holiday.

5.1.2   With a Fixed Date

Figure 5.3 shows the various fields at your disposal under the Fixed Date option. This option is used when the holiday falls on the same calendar month and day each year.

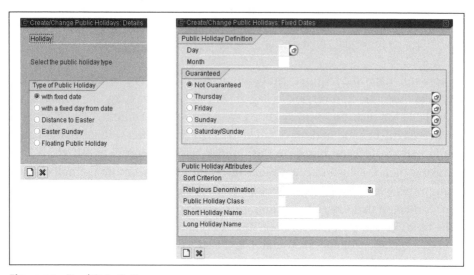

Figure 5.3   Fixed Date Options

You will notice in Figure 5.3 a section called Guaranteed. This section allows you to further define when the holiday will be observed. For example, Saturday/Sunday is most commonly used and allows the holiday to be observed on Friday if it falls on a Saturday, or on Monday if it falls on Sunday.

Additional settings are available under the Public Holiday Attributes section including:

- **Sort Criterion** — A three-character key that allows you to sort the holidays in a particular fashion when searching for holidays to link to a holiday calendar.

- **Religious Denomination** — A delivered list of religion categories to further describe the holiday.

- **Public Holiday Class** — Used to identify if the holiday is a holiday or not. Blank represents the date is not a public holiday. One and two represent delivered holiday classes. Three through nine represent available customer holiday classes.

▶ **Short Holiday Name** — Abbreviated description of the holiday.

▶ **Long Holiday Name** — Extended description of the holiday that will display in the holiday calendar.

Let's have a look at the second option — With a Fixed Day From Date.

5.1.3   With a Fixed Day From Date

Figure 5.4 illustrates the various fields at your disposal under the With a Fixed Day From Date option.

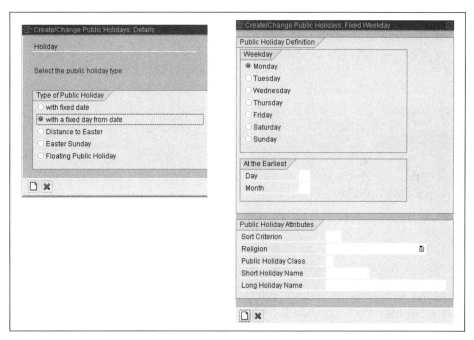

Figure 5.4   Setup Using With a Fixed Day From a Date

This holiday definition allows you to set up the holiday on a particular weekday. The key to the holiday generation date is the At the Earliest section whereby the day and month should be populated.

For example, the public holiday is set up for Tuesday. The At the Earliest section is set up for 7/2 or July 2, July 2, 2008 falls on a Wednesday. The system will then associate the holiday to be observed on July 8, the following Tuesday.

Let's now have a look at the third option — Distance From Easter.

5.1.4   Distance From Easter

This holiday definition allows you to set up the holiday by defining the number of days prior to Easter, or the number of days after Easter. When defining this section, you can only select one of the options. Figure 2.5 illustrates the set up using Distance to Easter.

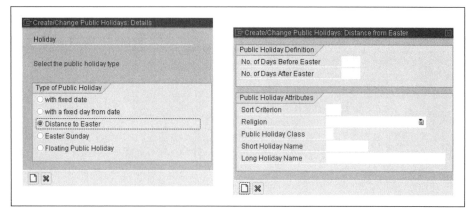

Figure 5.5   Setup Using Distance to Easter

For example, Easter in 2008 is defined as Sunday, March 23. If you had entered 2 in the field No. of Days Before Easter, then Friday, March 21, would be the date in the system that the holiday calendar would generate the public holiday.

Using the same configuration, in 2009, Easter is defined as Sunday, April 12. The holiday would then be generated on Friday, April 10.

Now let's have a look at the fourth option — Easter Sunday.

5.1.5   Easter Sunday

This holiday definition allows you to set up the holiday by using only Easter Sunday. There are no other selections for the date available. The SAP system knows which date to use (see Figure 5.6).

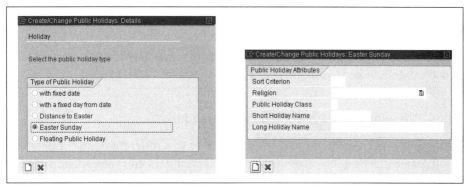

Figure 5.6 Setup Using Easter Sunday

Let's take a look at the fifth and final option — Floating Public Holiday.

5.1.6 Floating Public Holiday

This holiday definition allows you to set up the holiday by defining particular days of the month for each year the holiday is applicable. The holiday can be defined for multiple times throughout the year (see Figure 5.7).

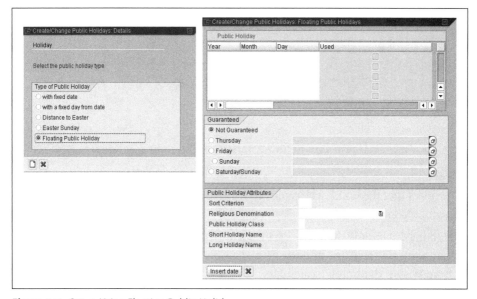

Figure 5.7 Setup Using Floating Public Holidays

As with the public holiday setup using a fixed date, you can further define the observed date using the Guaranteed section.

Now that you have a grasp on the various ways to create a holiday, let's have a look at the holidays linked to a holiday calendar.

5.1.7 Viewing Holidays Linked to a Calendar

Figure 5.8 shows a solid line and a dotted line to two different holiday calendars. Holiday calendars can leverage the same public holidays and can pick and choose which public holidays are applicable.

Change Public Holiday Calendar: Details			

◀ Calendar ▶ Calendar 🗒 🗒

Calendar ID   US USA

Valid   From   1995
      To   2010

Assigned Public Holidays

Selected	Public Holiday	Valid From	Valid To
☐	Christmas Day (guaranteed)	1900	2098
☐	Memorial Day	1900	2098
☐	Independence Day	1900	2098
☐	Labor Day	1900	2098
☐	Thanksgiving Day	1900	2098

Figure 5.8 Linkage of Public Holidays to a Holiday Calendar

Here are some final notes on defining and changing public holidays:

▸ Changing a public holiday type after it is associated with a holiday calendar requires that the holiday be removed from the holiday calendar prior to changes being made.

▸ Holiday calendars should be transported manually as these changes are not automatically sent in the transport. To do this, select CALENDAR • TRANSPORT from within the holiday calendars.

Now that we know how to set up holidays, let's review what the primary keys are for the Work Schedule configuration.

Personnel Subarea Groupings

For Work Schedules, the Personnel Area/Subarea combination is used to associate a grouping. This grouping does not have date delimiting functionality. Using the example from the blueprinting section, we can see that different Personnel Area/Subarea combinations can utilize the same grouping of Work Schedules (see Figure 5.9).

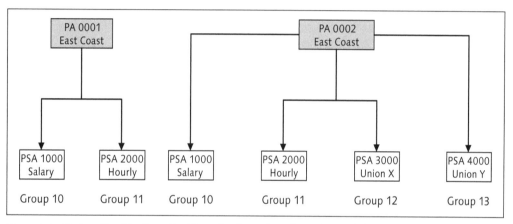

Figure 5.9 Various Combinations Can Share the Same Grouping or Have Their Own Grouping

In addition to the grouping for Work Schedules, there is also a grouping for daily Work Schedules. The daily Work Schedules, which will be explained later in the chapter, is the lowest level configuration of a Work Schedule rule. During the design phase of your system setup you will need to determine whether or not the Personnel Area/Subarea combinations share enough common characteristics to utilize the same configuration of daily Work Schedules, or if there is a valid reason to configure daily Work Schedules for each grouping of Personnel Area/Subarea combinations (see Figure 5.10).

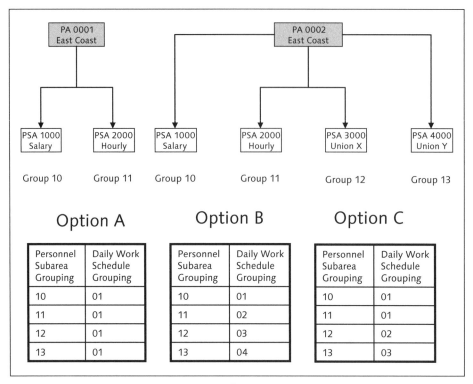

Figure 5.10 Various Options on the Groupings for Daily Work Schedules

▶ **Option A** — Each of the Personnel Area/Subarea combinations share the exact same daily work schedule grouping.

▶ **Option B** — Each of the Personnel Area/Subarea combinations has their own daily work schedule grouping.

▶ **Option C** — This is a variation of option A and B where Personnel Area/Subarea grouping 10 and 11 share the same daily Work Schedule while Personnel Area/ Subarea 12 and 13 have their own daily Work Schedule grouping.

Work Schedule configurations can be found in the IMG under the menu path TIME MANAGEMENT • WORK SCHEDULES.

Now that we have reviewed how various groupings can leverage the same configuration, let's take a look at how to set up a daily Work Schedule.

Daily Work Schedules

The daily Work Schedules are comprised of:

▸ Work Break Schedules

▸ Rules for Variations of daily Work Schedules

▸ Other various settings on the setting itself

Work Break Schedules

After break schedules have been configured and Work Schedules have been generated, any changes to a break schedule require you to re-evaluate the daily Work Schedules associated with those break schedules (see Figure 5.11).

	Grpg	Break	No	End	P	Unpaid	Paid	After	RefTim	Type 1	Type 2
	01	AFTN	01	21:00	✔	1.00					
	01	ERLY	01	08:00	☐		0.25				
	01	ERLY	02	10:30	☐		0.50				
	01	ERLY	03	12:45	☐		0.25				
	01	EXEC	01	12:30	☐	0.50					
	01	GLZ	01	10:00	☐	0.25					
	01	GLZ	02	13:30	☐	0.75					
	01	GLZ	03	22:10	☐	0.17				0	

Figure 5.11 Makeup of Work Break Schedule

Table 5.1 describes the fields of the break schedule.

Field	Description	Notes
Grpg	Personnel Subarea grouping for daily Work Schedules	
Break	Four-character alphanumeric code identifying the break schedule	
No	Sequence number of the break	
Start	Start time of the break	
End	End time of the break	

Table 5.1 Work Break Schedule Fields

Field	Description	Notes
P	Previous day indicator.	
Unpaid	The duration of the break that will be unpaid.	
Paid	The duration of the break that will be paid.	The unpaid and paid entries cannot exceed the amount of time between the start and end times entered in the START and END fields.
After	This field holds the number of hours an employee must work before taking a break.	
RefTim	This is the reference time for dynamic breaks taken at unspecified times.	Option 1 = blank "start of planned working time." Option 2 = N "start of normal working time."
Type 1	Used to determine which break types can be imported by Time Evaluation processing.	Option 1 = "blank" normal break. Option 2 = "O" overtime break.
Type 2	Freely definable field used during importing breaks and processing in Time Evaluation.	

Table 5.1 Work Break Schedule Fields (Cont.)

The next section of configuration involves defining particular variations of the daily Work Schedule.

Rules for Variations of Daily Work Schedules

In this section, we will look at the rules to determine where the variants for the monthly Work Schedule generation are set up. Upon generating the work schedule, the entries shown in Figure 5.12 will be plugged into the various days of the period schedule. The following fields in Figure 5.12 are available during the setup and are further described in Table 5.2.

Rules to determe variant for monthly WS rule generation					
Rule	No	Holiday cla...	HolClNextDay	Day	Variant
Z2	01	.X........	XXXXXXXXXX	XXXXXXX	
Z2	02	X.X.......	XXXXXXXXXX	XXXXXXX	A

Figure 5.12 Rules for Daily Work Schedule Variants

Field	Description	Notes
Rule	Daily Work Schedule selection rule.	This rule will be assigned directly to a daily work schedule.
No	Sequential number.	Different versions of the same rule.
Holiday class	Checks the current day to determine if a holiday is going to occur.	There are 10 entries or positions that can be made. Position 1 = no holiday Positions 2-9 = the holiday class configured on the particular holidays in the holiday calendar.
Holiday Class Next Day	Used to check the subsequent day to determine whether or not a holiday is going to occur.	There are 10 entries or positions that can be made. Position 1 = no holiday Positions 2-9 = the holiday class configured on the particular holidays in the holiday calendar.
Day	The seven days in the week.	Monday equals position 1 Tuesday equals position 2 Wednesday equals position 3 Thursday equals position 4 Friday equals position 5 Saturday equals position 6 Sunday equals position 7
Variant	The variation of the daily Work Schedule to be used	

Table 5.2 Fields for Rules of Daily Work Schedule Variants

In the example in Figure 5.13, the Work Schedule should generate daily Work Schedule variant A for all non-holidays and those holidays in which the holiday class is a 2. Figure 5.13 illustrates the example by highlighting the particular day that has been assigned the daily Work Schedule variant of A. All other days in the month use the baseline variant of blank. By setting up the system this way, you could have associated four hours for variant A instead of the eight hours normally worked.

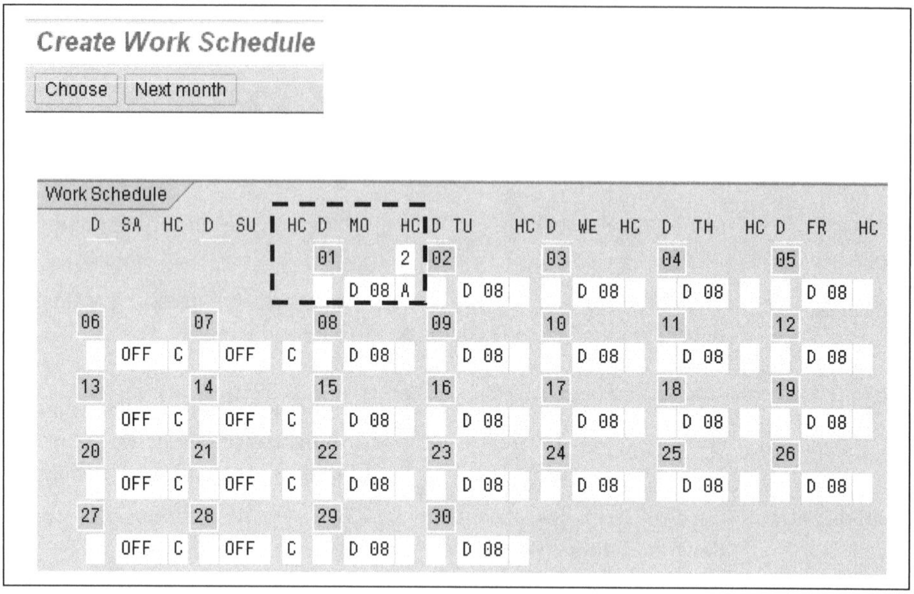

Figure 5.13 Daily Work Schedule Variant of A Associated with the Holiday Class of 2 for the Particular Holiday

Daily Work Schedule Definition

Daily Work Schedules are set up in the system to allocate planned working time on a particular day to an employee. Daily Work Schedules are strung together by each day of a week to create a period schedule. These period schedules are then associated with a Work Schedule rule that is ultimately associated with an employee's Infotype 0007 Planned Working Time record.

In addition to providing the planned working time, the daily Work Schedule, if implemented properly, can also provide the foundation for seeking which employees may or may not be available for work on a particular day.

Employees whose daily work schedule shows that the employee has zero planned hours will not be able to enter an absence through the Cross-Application Time Sheet (CATS) on these days without losing the hours on the CATS screen. To avoid such processing, either dynamic daily Work Schedules based on absences or substitutions for the day in question should be set up on Infotype 2003 (see Figure 5.14).

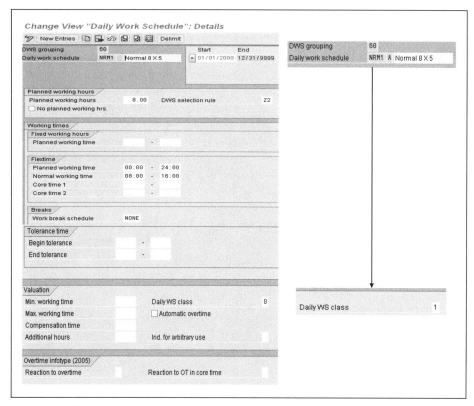

Figure 5.14 Daily Work Schedule Configuration Table

Table 5.4 explains each of the fields that are available for customization.

Field	Description	Notes
DWS grouping	Grouping of daily Work Schedule based on Personnel Area/Subarea combination.	Daily Work Schedule groupings can be set up so that any combination of Personnel Area/Subarea combinations that utilize the same daily Work Schedules, period Work Schedules, and break schedules can utilize the same grouping.

Table 5.4 Displays a Sample Daily Work Schedule

Field	Description	Notes
Daily work schedule	Description of the particular schedule being set up.	▸ Four alphanumeric fields. ▸ Examples include first, second, third shift. ▸ Naming convention key to minimize Time Evaluation maintenance if certain custom personnel calculation rules will utilize the daily Work Schedule description.
Daily work schedule variant	Used to define versions of the same daily Work Schedule rule. Sample business requirement: Set the daily work schedule to be four hours when a holiday is on a Friday. Daily Work Schedule would be Z999 Variant Blank for Monday through Friday except when a Friday occurs where the holiday class is 1. In this case, the Friday daily Work Schedule would be set to Z999 Variant A.	▸ Used in monthly Work Schedule rule generation to provide a different daily Work Schedule based on holiday classes and a particular day of the week. ▸ Used in dynamically assigning daily Work Schedule based on absence entered.
Planned working hours	The amount of hours the employee should be working.	▸ An employee cannot enter more absence hours than planned hours on a particular day, unless a substitution is entered on Infotype 2003 to override the daily work schedule. ▸ The part-time checkbox on Infotype 0007 will further reduce the planned hours of an employee's daily Work Schedule by the amount entered in the daily working hours field or the percentage field.

Table 5.4 Displays a Sample Daily Work Schedule (Cont.)

Field	Description	Notes
DWS selection rule	Used to associate a particular version of a daily Work Schedule when generating the monthly Work Schedule rule.	Based on the setup of the daily Work Schedule selection rule, the generation of the actual Work Schedule rule will insert various daily Work Schedules on particular days where conditions for those daily Work Schedules are satisfied.
No planned working hrs.	Selection of this checkbox sets the daily Work Schedule hours to zero.	▶ Day will be categorized as a day off. ▶ No absences will be entered unless a substitution is entered, dynamic assignment of daily Work Schedules based on absences is set up, or if the Work Schedule is changed.
Planned working time (fixed)	Used to specify when the employee's work should start and finish.	
Planned working time (flextime)	Used to specify when the employee's work should start and finish.	▶ Used as the period of time the employee can record clock times. ▶ The system will take any planned working time above the normal working time as overtime.
Normal working time (flextime)	Used to determine clock in/out entries that are missing in Time Evaluation.	Can be used to calculate missing hours.
Core time 1 (flextime)	Used to define periods of time during the daily Work Schedule when the employee should be at work.	
Core time 2 (flextime)	Used to define periods of time during the daily Work Schedule when the employee should be at work.	

Table 5.4 Displays a Sample Daily Work Schedule (Cont.)

Field	Description	Notes
Work break schedule	Used to identify periods of time when the employee should be on a paid or unpaid break.	Configured as a separate piece of the Work Schedule and then selected during the daily Work Schedule setup.
Begin tolerance	Used to round clock entries up or down based on the period of time they are entered into the system.	Can be used as a preventative measure in Time Evaluation for creating messages or additional time entries that would result in overtime.
End tolerance	Used to round clock entries up or down based on the period of time they are entered into the system.	
Min. working time	Minimum amount of time that should be entered.	Only used in Time Evaluation processing. Can be called using operation HRS=SMIN.
Max. working time	Maximum amount of time that should be entered.	Only used in Time Evaluation processing. Can be called using operation HRS=SMAX.
Compensation time	Used to compensate time within Time Evaluation.	Only used in Time Evaluation processing. Can be called using operation HRS=SADV.
Additional hours	Used to hold hours over and above the planned hours.	Only used in Time Evaluation processing. Can be called using operation HRS=SADD.
Daily WS class	Used as an additional way of evaluating a daily Work Schedule.	Used to define daily Work Schedules. Can drive different time wage–type selection rules, and counting of absences and attendances. Used in Time Evaluation using operation VARSTDPRCL.

Table 5.4 Displays a Sample Daily Work Schedule (Cont.)

Field	Description	Notes
Automatic overtime	Used to flag the daily work schedule so that a custom personnel calculation rule can be created to satisfy a particular business requirement.	Only used in Time Evaluation processing. Used in Time Evaluation using operation VARSTOVPOS.
Ind. for arbitrary use	Used to flag the daily work schedule so that a custom personnel calculation rule can be created to satisfy a particular business requirement.	
Reaction to overtime (Infotype 2005)	Used to determine how the system should react when overtime is directly entered into the system.	Used only in flextime daily Work Schedules. Specifies reaction to overtime via no message, a warning, or an error.
Reaction to OT in core time	Used in conjunction with Infotype 2005.	Used only in flextime daily Work Schedules. Specifies reaction to overtime via no message, a warning, or an error. Used only for overtime entered during the core time of a daily Work Schedule.

Table 5.4 Displays a Sample Daily Work Schedule (Cont.)

Now that we have reviewed how to create a daily Work Schedule, it's time to discuss the next building block of a Work Schedule rule. This object is called a period Work Schedule.

Period Work Schedules

Period Work Schedules are based on the Personnel Area/Subarea combination. The period Work Schedule is based on daily Work Schedules for a particular period and continues to repeat the pattern. The period Work Schedules are usually set up on a seven-day cycle and can either repeat each week or, based on a particular sequence, can change to a different set of daily Work Schedules the following week. This rotating schedule would then repeat upon completion of the initial cycle through the sequence of period Work Schedules. See Figure 5.15 for an example of a different period Work Schedules.

Grpg	PWS	Period WS text	W...	01	02	03	04	05	06	07
01	3-WK	3week Rotating Shift	001	DAY	DAY	DAY	DAY	DAY	FREI	FREI
01	3-WK	3week Rotating Shift	002	AFTN	AFTN	AFTN	AFTN	AFTN	FREI	FREI
01	3-WK	3week Rotating Shift	003	NGHT	NGHT	NGHT	NGHT	NGHT	FREI	FREI
01	EXEC		001	EXEC	EXEC	EXEC	EXEC	EXEC	FREI	FREI
01	GLZ	Flextime	001	GLZ	GLZ	GLZ	GLZ	GLZ	FREI	FREI

Figure 5.15   Example of Different Period Work Schedules

Another element that is utilized within a Work Schedule rule is a day type.

Day Types

Day types are used in the system to define which particular calendar days are actually working days paid and which particular calendar days are days that would be paid, however, an attendance at work is not required for payment. An example of this would be a holiday. A holiday would receive a day type of "1" while the rest of the normal work week would have a "0." Any day type other than "0" is considered a day off.

Day types can influence the following:

▶ the relevance of the type of payment

▶ absence counting

The following day types are delivered and should never be changed:

▶ Blank—Employee is supposed to work and be paid

▶ 1 — Employee is off from work and is to be paid

▶ 2 — Employee is off from work and is not to be paid

▶ 3 — Employee is off from work, however, the system can be configured to pay or not based on the business requirements

In addition to day types, there are Selection rules. These are associated with daily Work Schedules and enable the system when generating a Work Schedule to determine which day type should be associated with work days, public holidays, and weekends.

Work Schedule Rules and Work Schedules

This is the final section of the IMG where you create the Work Schedule rules. The IMG menu path is TIME MANAGEMENT • WORK SCHEDULES • WORK SCHEDULE RULES AND WORK SCHEDULES. The first section of configuration is to define Employee Subgroup groupings for the Work Schedule.

Employee Subgroup Groupings

SAP software delivers many options for employee subgroup groupings for Work Schedules. Normally, hourly employees use Subgroup grouping 1 and salaried employees use Subgroup grouping 2. New entries can be created to satisfy business requirements. The groupings will be associated with the Employee Group/Subgroup combination. By using this, you can establish a specific list of Work Schedules for each group. That way, you can control the various Work Schedule rules that are available for selection on the dropdown menus of Infotype 0007.

Table 5.5 lists the single field that is available.

Field	Description	Notes
ES GRPG	Employee Subgroup grouping for Work Schedule	0 — Applicants
		1 — Hourly wage earners
		2 — Salaried employees
		3 — Executive
		4 — Executive PH
		6 — Holder
		7 — Non-holder

Table 5.5 Employee Subgroup Groupings for Work Schedules

Using the Table 5.5 configuration, the Employee Group/Subgroups combination is associated with the new Employee Subgroup grouping for Work Schedules. In this example, all salaried Employee Subgroups will share the same Work Schedules. If the business requirement was such that the part-time population required a new set of Work Schedules only visible to that group, then different Employee Subgroup groupings should be used. The groupings allow the system to only display the Work Schedules that belong to that population of employees. Table 5.6 shows some sample groupings and how they could be defined for the particular Employee Groups and Subgroups.

Employee Group	Description	Employee Subgroup	Description	Employee Subgroup Grouping
1	Full-Time	01	Salary	2
1	Full-Time	02	Hourly	1
1	Full-Time	03	Officer	2
2	Part-Time	01	Salary	2
2	Part-time	02	Hourly	1
2	Part-Time	04	Seasonal	1
3	Retiree	05	With Benefits	3
3	Retire	06	Without Benefits	3

Table 5.6 Sample Employee Subgroup Groupings

Table 5.7 shows an example of how to link the holiday calendars to Personnel Area/Subarea combinations.

Personnel Area	Description	Personnel Subarea	Description	Holiday Calendar
0001	East Coast	1000	Salary	Z1
0001	East Coast	2000	Hourly	Z1
0002	East Coast	1000	Salary	Z1
0002	East Coast	2000	Hourly	Z2
0002	East Coast	3000	Union X	Z3
0002	East Coast	4000	Union Y	Z4

Table 5.7 Sample Holiday Calendar Assignments

In the example in Table 5.7, all of the salaried Personnel Subareas across the organization share the same holiday calendar. The hourly population of Personnel Area 0001 also shares the Z1 calendar. The hourly population under Personnel Area

0002 has its own holiday calendar of Z2 and each union Personnel Subarea also has its own calendar.

Figure 5.16 Shows a diagram based on the data in table 5.7.

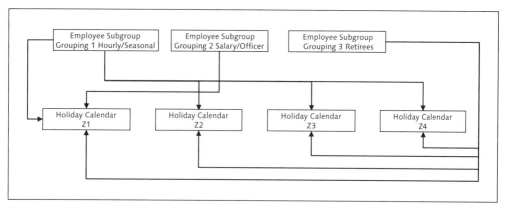

Figure 5.16   Sample Holiday Calendar Assignments

Finally, we have reached the point where we actually get to create the Work Schedule. All of the configuration thus far for Work Schedules will be pulled into the Work Schedule rule based on the settings you make. The following section explains the configuration.

Work Schedule Rules

The primary keys of the Work Schedule rule table is the combination of:

► Employee Subgroup grouping

► Holiday calendar

► Personnel Subarea grouping

For all combinations where an employee resides, a valid Work Schedule needs to be created for the combination of these three keys. Figure 5.17 shows the various fields for a Work Schedule rule.

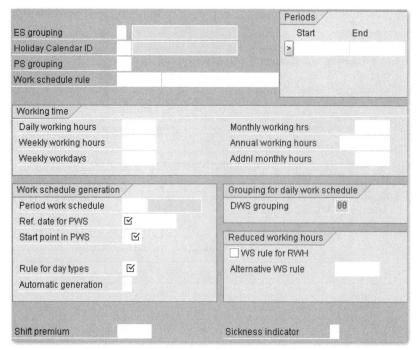

Figure 5.17 Various Fields Available for a Work Schedule Rule

Table 5.8 explains the various fields associated with Figure 5.17.

Field	Description	Notes
Employee Subgroup grouping	Grouping associated with Employee Group/Subgroup combinations.	
Holiday Calendar ID	Grouping associated with Personnel Area/Subarea combinations.	
Personnel Subarea grouping	The third element of the key to the table in which the Work Schedule rules will be applicable.	
Work schedule Rule	The final definition of the Work Schedule whereby the period Work Schedule is linked.	▸ Eight character field ▸ Can be queried in Time Evaluation using operation OUTWPSHIFT

Table 5.8 Work Schedule Rule Fields

Field	Description	Notes
Daily working hours	The hours per day that will be displayed on Infotype 0007 Planned Working Time.	The target hours on the time sheet are driven from the daily Work Schedule, not the daily working hours of this field. Can be queried in Time Evaluation using operations TABLE 508A and HRS=TDAHRS.
Weekly working hours	The weekly working hours that will be displayed in Infotype 0007.	Can be queried in Time Evaluation using operations TABLE 508A and HRS=TWEHRS.
Weekly workdays	The weekly working days that will be displayed in Infotype 0007.	Can be queried in Time Evaluation using operations TABLE 508A and HRS=TWKWDY.
Monthly working hrs	The monthly working hours that will be displayed in Infotype 0007.	Can be queried in Time Evaluation using operations TABLE 508A and HRS=TMOHRS.
Annual work hours	The annual working hours that will be displayed in Infotype 0007.	Can be queried in Time Evaluation using operations TABLE 508A and HRS=TYEHRS.
Addnl working hours	Used in the processing of reduced working hours.	Can be queried in Time Evaluation using operations TABLE 508A and HRS=TM2STD.
Period work schedule	Used to generate the monthly Work Schedule.	
Ref. date For PWS	Date on which the period Work Schedule will be generated.	
Start point in PWS	Works in conjunction with the reference date for the period Work Schedule generation.	
Rule for day types	Used to determine which days are going to be working days, weekend days, or public holidays upon the generation of the Work Schedule.	

Table 5.8 Work Schedule Rule Fields (Cont.)

Field	Description	Notes
Automatic generation	Used by the system on how to react if the monthly Work Schedule has not been generated when the personal Work Schedule is entered.	Options include: ▸ Blank — Regenerate internally, issue message ▸ A — Regenerate internally, no message ▸ M — Do not regenerate, issue error message
DWS grouping	Grouping for daily Work Schedules.	Defaulted from the Personnel Subarea grouping of the primary key.
WS rule for RWH	Used to flag the Work Schedule rule for reduced working hours.	Used in conjunction with Infotype 0049 Reduced Hours/Bad Weather.
Alternative WS Rule	Work Schedule rule assigned to employees operating under the reduced working hours processing.	
Shift premium	Used to enter a percentage that an employee can receive additional compensation for specific working conditions.	Used in Time Evaluation and payroll.
Sickness indicator		Used in Austria.

Table 5.8 Work Schedule Rule Fields (Cont.)

We have now completed the configuration on how to set up Work Schedules. The following schedule explains a topic called the Dynamic Daily Work Schedule (DWS), which allows you to assign a daily Work Schedule based on certain parameters in the system.

Dynamic Daily Work Schedules

The DWS selection rule is comprised of particular parameters under the grouping for attendance and absences. The X under grouping 2 is linked to the particular absence configuration under the absence grouping field. Under this scenario, the absence will create four hours of absence when the normal daily work schedule of OFF did not have any planned hours (see Figure 5.18).

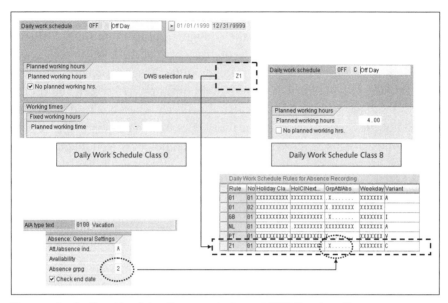

Figure 5.18 Configuration Setup Necessary to Support DWS Based on Absences

Figure 5.19 shows the actual processing of the time-related data in the CATS.

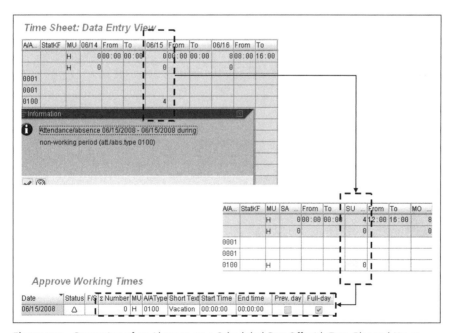

Figure 5.19 Processing of an Absence on a Scheduled Day Off with Zero Planned Hours

In the examples shown in Figures 5.18 and 5.19, an absence of eight hours is entered on a planned day off. Because the configuration is set up so that when a vacation absence is entered on a day off, the variant C of the DWS selection will place four hours of vacation into the Infotype 2001 Absences record. You will notice that the record will show zero hours on both the CATS screen and on the time-approval screen. You should notice that the full-day checkbox is selected. The system will not allow you to override the four hours. You can configure the system to have multiple variants of the Work Schedule rule, however, you might need to force the business process to enter the absence twice if you want the flexibility of deducting half day and full day as it equates to an eight-hour schedule.

Now that we have explained how to process DWS, the next topic is how to generate a Work Schedule. To use any new or to change schedules, they must be generated so that they are available for use.

Generation of Work Schedules

Creating, changing, or deleting Work Schedules can be accomplished manually. When making minor changes or generating a few Work Schedule rules, this method can be used. If, however, you are creating a large set of Work Schedule rules, as in Figure 5.20, it can be done through batch input (see Figure 5.21).

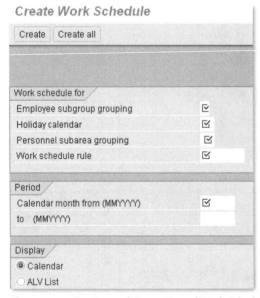

Figure 5.20 Creating and Generation of Work Schedules Manually

You can create Work Schedule rules a month at a time, viewing and changing data where necessary, or you can create all of them at once. This offers you the ability to see each month's worth of Work Schedule–related data prior to moving on to the subsequent month.

Figure 5.21 shows the batch scheduling of Work Schedule generation. Batch scheduling allows you to generate the Work Schedule in the background. The main difference between Figure 5.21 and Figure 5.20 is that you will not be able to see or change any of the data on the screen compared to Figure 5.20, where you can generate the schedule and view each month before proceeding to the next month.

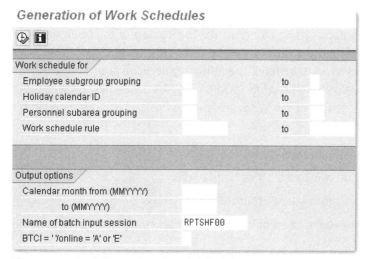

Figure 5.21 Batch Generation of Work Schedules

The batch generation of Work Schedules allows you to select multiple entries of the various groupings, holiday calendars, Personnel Subarea groupings, and Work Schedule rules. This is the preferred method of generation when working with significant numbers of Work Schedules.

You have the following options when using the batch input method for generating Work Schedule rules:

▸ Blank — A batch input session is created and then must be manually started

▸ A — The session is started immediately with all screens displayed

▶ E — The session is processed immediately, however, screens encountering errors are displayed

▶ N — The session is processed immediately without any screens being displayed

We have now concluded the sections of the IMG where you configure Work Schedules. The following section provides some insight and guidance on how certain pieces of the Work Schedule should be configured.

5.1.8   Design Implications

If Time Evaluation is in scope for the implementation, there are personnel calculation rules that can be customized. The customization has some preset pieces of information that decisions can be based off of. The section of the book on Time Evaluation will provide more details on personnel calculation rules and Time Evaluation processing. For Work Schedules, the following decision points are available under the standard delivered operation VARST for Work Schedules. Each of these decision points are based off of the Work Schedule associated with an individual's Infotype 0007.

▶ **varstDAYTP** – decision is based off of the day type

▶ **varstHOLCL –** decision is based off of holiday class

▶ **varstNHYHC** – decision is based off of the holiday class

▶ **varstFREE** – decision is based off of the daily work schedule settings for planned hours

▶ **varstDAYPG** – decision is based off of the daily work schedule

▶ **varstVARIA** – decision is based off of the variant of the daily work schedule

▶ **varstDPRCL** – decision is based off of the daily work schedule class

▶ **varstBREAK** – decision is based off of the work break schedule

▶ **varstTIMMD** – decision is based off of the period work schedule

▶ **varstTIMCL** – decision is based off of the valuation class of the period work schedule

▶ **varstSUBST** – decision is based off of the substitution type entered on Infotype 2003 substitutions. This infotype overrides the existing work schedule settings for that particular date range.

- **varstPRSNT** – decision to determine if the employee is supposed to be at work

- **varstPRSWD** – decision to determine based off of infotype 2002 if the employee was present for the entire day

- **varstABSCE** – decision to determine if the employee is absent

- **varstABSWD** – decision to determine if employee is absent for the entire day

In Addition to the operation VARST, there are a few other operations when working with Work Schedule–related information:

- **HRS1S** – Daily Work Schedule, with a variety of options

- **HRS1I** – Planned Working Time

- **HRS1T** – Configuration Table T508A. Used in conjunction with operation TABLE

- **OUTWPSHIFT** – Work Schedule Rule

Based on these decision points, the overall design of the Work Schedule should be such that creating new personnel calculation rules or altering some of the delivered rules will not create an ongoing maintenance nightmare.

Let's look at the following example to see how it works. A corporation is implementing Time Evaluation and will utilize Work Schedules to calculate a majority of the payment rules associated with the business. During the blueprinting phase, it was determine that there were three shifts (Day, Afternoon, and Evening).

The team has the requirement to generate shift differentials automatically based on regular hours worked on certain Work Schedules.

The team has the following options:

- Set up the Work Schedule rules and place each rule into the customized personnel calculation rule to generate X hours of shift differential if the employee is on a Work Schedule rule designated as a shift differential Work Schedule.

- Under this design, what would happen if the requirements were such that the Work Schedule rule was not built based on a period work schedule where the employee was always on a particular shift? Instead, the employee worked a rotating schedule whereby the first week was a day shift, the second week was the afternoon shift, and the third week of the rotation placed them onto the third shift?

▶ If the personnel calculation rule that creates the shift differential is based off of the Work Schedule rule, the employee would be paid incorrectly.

▶ In order to pay the employee correctly, the business would either have to change Infotype 0007 for each change in schedule or create a substitution infotype for the change in Work Schedule. Both of these options are usually unacceptable due to the massive amounts of master data changes that would be required.

▶ The second option, and a better approach to the requirement, would be to write the rule based on a piece of the overall work schedule called the daily Work Schedule. Figure 5.22 shows an example of the naming conventions of the daily Work Schedules and how that could impact a personnel calculation rule that makes decisions based on those codes.

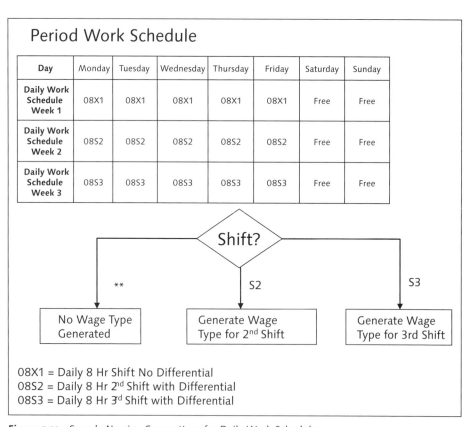

Figure 5.22 Sample Naming Conventions for Daily Work Schedules

If the company only has a few Work Schedules, then making the decision based on the Work Schedule rule might be acceptable. As referenced in Appendix D, we saw a listing all possible combinations of a work-week schedule, so there could be many different Work Schedule rules. When this is the case, it would prove more beneficial to make the decision on shift differentials based on the daily Work Schedule. The design should be laid out to maximize as few daily Work Schedules as possible.

On the day time is entered, if the employee has the daily Work Schedule of 08S3, then the third-shift Wage type would be generated. If the employee instead has a daily Work Schedule of 08S2, then the second-shift Wage type would be generated. If neither of these conditions is met, then there will not be a shift differential Wage type generated.

This example also denotes a decision based on the last two characters of the daily Work Schedule. By using Time Evaluation operations VALEN and VAOFF a query can be conducted based on the last two characters. We illustrated the last two characters in case the business requirements change and the business needs second and third shift daily Work Schedules, which would not require shift premiums.

5.1.9 Things to Consider

The overall design should take into account all time functionality. For instance, during the design phase of the Work Schedules, there are various decisions that can be made within the Time Evaluation schema.

Ensure that the naming conventions and configuration assigned with each aspect of the Work Schedules is granular enough to accommodate all of the business requirements and is maintainable during production support of the system.

5.2 Summary

In this chapter, you learned about the concepts surrounding what a Work Schedule rule is comprised of. You have learned about each piece of the equation, how they interact with each other, and some of the possibilities of how the various settings should be configured to accommodate your business requirements. The concepts take time to digest and it is advisable to spend time in the system setting up basic examples and testing them through the system.

The next chapter will explain the functionality surrounding Time Data Recording.

In this chapter, you will learn about the Time Data Recording and Administration functionality within SAP ERP HCM Time Management and find out how to configure it.

6 Time Data Recording and Administration

Time Data Recording is a section of functionality that allows you to enter time, such as absences and attendances. This is where you configure specific codes to track time. For example, attendances such as regular time, off-site training, and absences, including vacation or jury duty would be set up in this section.

The Implementation Guide (IMG) for Time Data Recording and Administration can be located in the IMG under the menu path TIME MANAGEMENT • TIME DATA RECORDING AND ADMINISTRATION, and is broken down into the following sections:

▶ Substitutions

▶ Absences

▶ Attendances

▶ Overtime

▶ Availability

▶ Management of Time Accounts using quotas

▶ System reactions to overlapping time infotypes (time constraints)

▶ Business Add-Ins (BAdIs)

Each of these sections are covered to demonstrate the system setup, including the configuration tables that support each area and tables listing the various fields that are contained within. We will also explore when you may need to use each particular infotype.

Figure 6.1 provides an overview of what we will be covering.

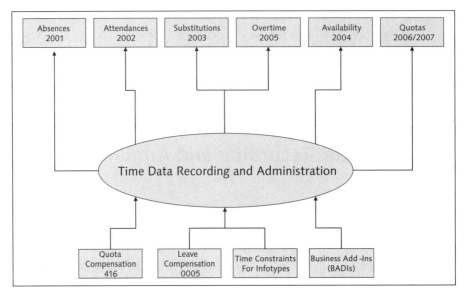

Figure 6.1 Time Data Recording and Administration Overview

> **Note**
>
> Infotype 2011 — Time Events — is an infotype that holds time-related data similar to what will be covered in this chapter; however, it will not be covered here because it heavily supports the Personnel Time Events functionality and, therefore, has been placed in Chapter 7, "Personnel Time Events."

Let's begin with Substitutions and then move on to Absences and Attendances.

6.1   Substitutions

Substitutions are variances to an individual employee's normal Work Schedule driven from the Work Schedule rule on Infotype 0007 Planned Working Time. For example, let's say an employee normally works the first shift and, due to production demands, the supervisor requests that the employee work the second shift instead. The second shift receives a shift bonus that is set up in the system to generate based on an employee's work schedule. Instead of changing Infotype 0007, you can use Infotype 2003 to put a temporary change that would make the employee eligible for the shift differential compensation. Infotype 2003 has a lot of flexibility and is the preferred method over Infotype 0007, because you can also put a time frame on the employee's eligibility, whereas Infotype 0007 is for an entire day.

Keep in mind, however, that for the supervisor to use the substitutions infotype for an employee, that employee must reside in a Personnel Area and Personnel Subarea combination that has a grouping that has been configured with a substitution subtype. Without the substitution type configured for the Personnel Area/Subarea combination, you will not be able to save the infotype record. The subtype is a required field for the substitution Infotype 2003.

The Personnel Subarea groupings are driven from the combination of Personnel Area/Subareas. These groupings allow the same substitution types to be eligible for a particular grouping. By utilizing these groupings, you can set up the system so that different substitution types can be used by different groups of employees. Figure 6.2 shows the configuration table and part of the actual infotype where the dropdown list of Substitution Types appears, and Table 6.1 lists the fields available for substitution configuration. The substitutions configuration can be located in the IMG under the menu path TIME MANAGEMENT • TIME DATA RECORDING AND ADMINISTRATION • SUBSTITUTIONS.

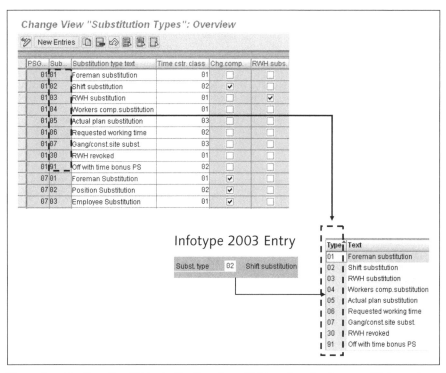

Figure 6.2 Configuration Tables to the Dropdown List Based on the Personnel Subarea Grouping for Substitutions

Field	Description	Purpose/Impact
PSG	Grouping of Personnel Areas/Subareas for substitution types and availability types.	Controls which subtypes appear on the dropdown menu.
Substitution type	A description or reason for the occurrence of the substitution.	
Substitution type text	Further description of the substitution type.	
Time cstr. class	Settings for the system to determine how to react to various entries on other time data infotypes for a given day where there is overlap.	It is a way to establish collisions when multiple records exist on either the same infotype or other time entry–related infotypes.
Chg.comp	This is an indicator for shift change compensation.	If the employee is working a different shift than normal and there is a disparity between the two rates of pay, then the payroll system can be set up to determine how to fairly compensate the employee without penalizing them.
RWH subs.	This is an indicator for the reduced working hours substitution.	Used only in Germany – country code 01. The system will not take into account during the absence hours, counting rules nor the personal Work Schedule set up. In addition, if the substitution is flagged, the system will only process the record if a corresponding record on Infotype 0049 — Reduced Hours/Bad Weather — has a valid record.

Table 6.1 Substitution Configuration Fields

The following Feature VTART allows you to select which substitution type will default upon entering Infotype 2003. The feature is shown in Figure 6.3

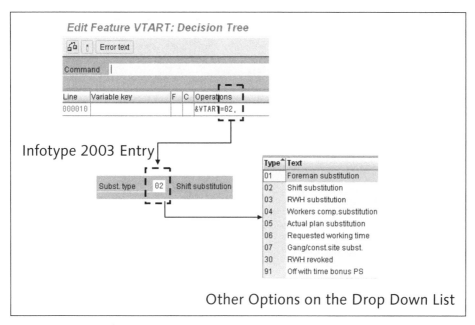

Figure 6.3 Linkages from the Feature That Can Be Set Up to Default Certain Substitution Types to the Actual Record Creation

Figure 6.4 shows you an example of a structure that is linked to Feature VTART. The fields that you see are standard delivered fields for the structure. The fields are available so that you can make decisions based on them. You are not required to use any or all of them but they are at your disposal. For example, if your company has two company codes, which is the first field in Figure 6.4. Your business requirement is that company code 0001 should only have one substitution type called shift change. Company code 0002 should also be able to see substitution 01 but they also have a second substitution type (02) for emergency shift change. You would like to default substitution type 01 for company code 0001 and further default substitution type 02 for company code 0002. By using the Company Code field, you can decide which substitution type is defaulted for which company code.

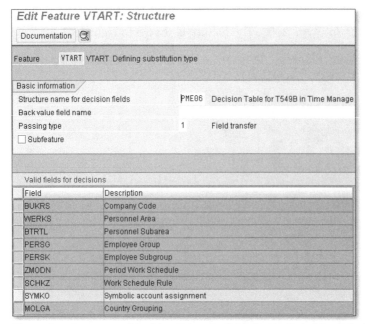

Figure 6.4 Structure and Decision Points Available for the Defaulting Substitution Types

There are basically four ways to create an Infotype 2003:

▶ Direct entry on Infotype 2003

▶ Utilizing Time Managers Workplace to process the substitution

▶ Shift Planning

▶ A third-party time collection system that in the interface to the SAP system, populates table PTEX2003GEN and PTEX2003SPEC. Upon transfer to the infotypes via Transaction code CAT6, the infotype record will be created.

It should be noted that the SAP system cannot create a substitution via direct time entry through the portal or the Cross-Application Time Sheet (CATS). Any substitutions entered on Infotype 2003 will cascade back to the Time Sheet to allow entry of more specific time where prior to the Infotype 2003 record it was not possible.

Example

Let's say you have a salaried employee who works Monday through Friday and, according to their work schedule, they are off on Saturday and Sunday. During the course of operation, you decide to have the employee begin working five consecutive days starting on Wednesday; however, you have elected to not set up any other Work Schedule rules that would accommodate this requirement. The employee is now working Wednesday through Sunday, and Monday and Tuesday are technically off days. The employee calls in sick on a Saturday and attempts to enter eight hours of absence. The CATS screen will not allow the hours and blanks them out on the screen. In order to fix this, you would either have to change them to a valid Work Schedule if one exists, create a new schedule if one does not exist, or change your business requirements so that generic work schedules are used, such as seven-day-by-eight-hour work schedules. Using a generic work schedule would work as long as you are tracking actual schedules in the system.

Let's move on to the next section of the IMG, which covers Absences.

6.2   Absences

Absence and Attendance types share the same Personnel Area/Subarea groupings. As you saw in Chapter 2, "Time Management Blueprint Considerations," there is a lot of functionality derived by assigning groupings to the combination of Personnel Areas/Subareas. Absences and Attendances have not been broken into distinct areas so they share the same grouping. This means that if you define an absence called Vacation and another part of the business uses the term PTO for personnel time off, you need to decide if both should show up on the Absences dropdown list for employee's to select from, or if you really need to limit who can see which absence. If you need to limit access to the particular codes, then you will need to assign different groupings.

Once you decide on how many groupings you will need, it is then time to create the particular absences. The next section will show you how to do that. The absence configuration can be found in the IMG under the menu path TIME MANAGEMENT • TIME DATA RECORDING AND ADMINISTRATION • ABSENCES.

6.2.1   Definition of Absence Types

When you went through your blueprinting phase of the project, you acquired a list of reasons people may be absence from work. The reasons become absence types and need to be set up in the system. These are reasons such as holiday, vacation, unpaid absence, military leave, etc. The definition of absence types can be located in the implementation guide under the menu path TIME MANAGEMENT • TIME DATA RECORDING AND ADMINISTRATION • ABSENCES. Figure 6.5 displays the configuration screen for setting up absences. Table 6.2 will explain the functionality of each of the fields.

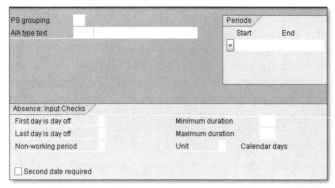

Figure 6.5 Configuration Table for Absence Inputs

Field	Description	Purpose/Impact
PS grouping	Grouping of Personnel Areas and Subareas for absence and attendance types.	
A/A type text	Absence or attendance type and description.	Four-digit alphanumeric field that will be displayed on the infotypes.
First day is day off	Relates to how the system should react should an entry be made on the first day that is a scheduled day off according to the Work Schedule.	Four possibilities: ▶ E — Reject Entry, issue error message ▶ W — Accept Entry, issue warning ▶ I — Accept Entry, inform user ▶ Blank — Accept Entry, no message is issued
Last day is day off	Relates to how the system should react should an entry be made on the last day that is a scheduled day off according to the Work Schedule.	Four possibilities: ▶ E — Reject Entry, issue error message ▶ W — Accept Entry, issue warning ▶ I — Accept Entry, inform user ▶ Blank — Accept Entry, no message is issued

Table 6.2 Fields Available for Absences

Field	Description	Purpose/Impact
Non-working period	Relates to how the system should react should an entry be made for an entire period that is a scheduled day off according to the Work Schedule.	Four possibilities: ▶ E — Reject Entry, issue error message ▶ W — Accept Entry, issue warning ▶ I — Accept Entry, inform user ▶ Blank — Accept Entry, no message is issued
Minimum duration	This is the minimum duration allowed for the entry. Blank represents any entries less than 1 work day. This field works in conjunction with the Unit field.	
Maximum duration	This is the minimum duration allowed for the entry. Blank represents any entries less than 1 work day. This field works in conjunction with the Unit field.	
Unit		Four possibilities: ▶ Blank — Calendar Days ▶ K — Calendar Days ▶ A — Attendance and absence Days ▶ R — Payroll Days
Second date required	This checkbox forces the time infotype data entry screen to enter an end date. If the checkbox is not selected, then the end date will default from the start date.	

Table 6.2 Fields Available for Absences (Cont.)

Figures 6.6 and 6.7 illustrate what the various settings will show the user when they are entering absences into the system. As an example, we will use the field First Day is Day Off.

Based on the settings for the First Day is Day Off field, the following messages in Figure 6.6 are displayed when a time is entered.

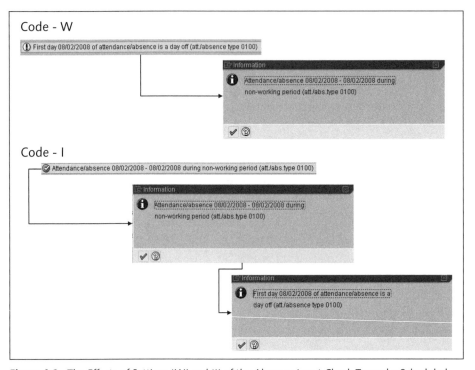

Figure 6.6 The Effects of Settings 'W' and 'I' of the Absence Input Check Toward a Scheduled Day Off

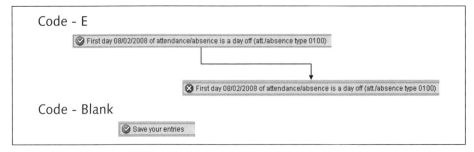

Figure 6.7 The Effects of Settings 'E' and 'BLANK' of the Absence Input Check Toward a Scheduled Day Off

This covers the first field in the lower left-hand corner of Figure 6.5. Another field for customizing is the Second Date required checkbox. The following section describes this functionality.

6.2.2 Second Date Required Illustration

When an absence is entered on Infotype 2006 Absence Quotas you need to enter the date it is applicable for. You can set up the system so that a user only has to enter the first day and the end date will default to the first date. If you check the Second Date Required checkbox, then the user will be forced to enter the end date, which in most cases is the same as the start date. Based on the settings, the following messages in Figure 6.8 are displayed when time is entered.

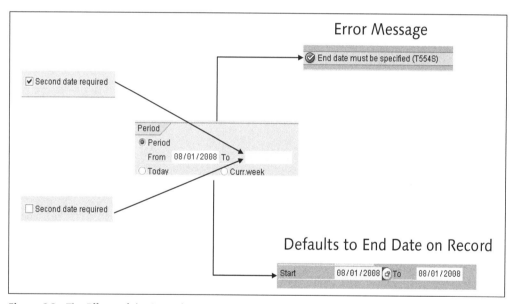

Figure 6.8 The Effects of the Second Date Required Field on the Infotype Screen

We've seen two examples of how the configuration affects what the user sees when interacting with the screens. Let's look at a third and final example for absences. Figure 6.8 shows a few fields that deal with the minimum and maximum amounts that can be entered. You can use this functionality to control how much time is entered on a particular day for a particular absence type.

6.2.3 Minimum and Maximum Duration Examples

Based on the settings, the following messages are displayed in Figure 6.9 when time is entered that falls outside of the range defined as Calendar days, Attendance and Absence days, and Payroll days.

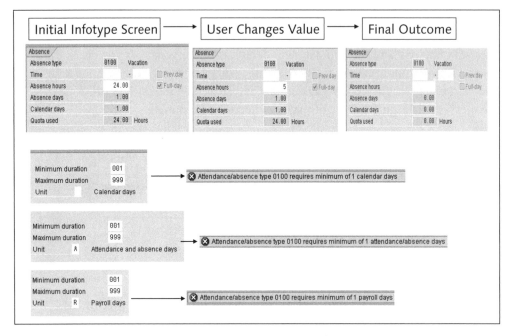

Figure 6.9 The Messages Delivered Based on Minimum and Maximum Duration Settings

Now that you've set up an absence, it's time to make additional settings that will not only allow the absence into the SAP system, but also that the absence can be made available to other functionalities, such as Availability and Time Evaluation. (Time Evaluation is discussed in Chapters 8 and 9.)

The general absence settings allow you to set up various pieces of information that will be called by other areas of Time Management. Figure 6.10 shows the configuration screen. Table 6.3 explains the impacts of the fields on processing and making the data available for other areas, such as Time Evaluation or tracking employee availability.

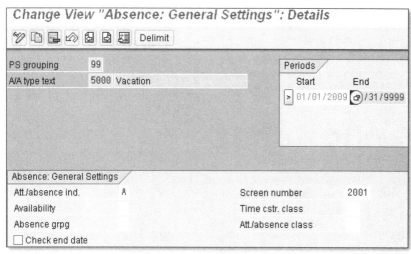

Figure 6.10 The Configuration Table for General Setting

Field	Description	Purpose/Impact
PS grouping	Grouping of Personnel Areas and Subareas for absence and attendance types.	
A/A type text	Absence or attendance type and description.	Four-digit alpha numeric field that will be displayed on the infotypes.
Att./absence ind.	Drives which screen number can be used. Determines processing type for Time Evaluation for attendances and absences.	A — Used for absences P — Used for attendances Utilized during time wage–type selection. Utilized in Time Evaluation processing types tables T555Y and T555Z.
Availability	Used to identify an employee's availability if particular attendances or absences have been entered.	Three possibilities: ▶ Blank — Not Available ▶ 1 — Available ▶ 9 — Irrelevant

Table 6.3 Absence Settings Configuration Fields

Field	Description	Purpose/Impact
Absence grpg	Used to identify which attendances or absences will drive the Work Schedule to use a variant Work Schedule.	Groupings from table V_550X_B — Determination of daily Work Schedule variants. Groupings Blank and 1 through 9 are available.
Check end date	This checkbox forces the time infotype data entry screen to enter an end date. If this checkbox is not selected, then the end date will default from the start date.	
Screen number	Specifies which screen number will be utilized for particular records when entering the infotype. The fields will be different based on the screens selected. The screens can be viewed via table T588M for the particular module pool (MP200000) you are after.	Seven Possibilities for absences: ▸ Infotype 2000 —Absences General ▸ Infotype 2001 —Quota Deductions ▸ Infotype 2002 — Work Incapacity (Germany) ▸ Infotype 2003 — Maternity Protection ▸ Infotype 2004 — Military Service ▸ Infotype 2005 — Work Incapacity (Netherlands) ▸ Infotype 2008 — Work Incapacity General Two possibilities for attendances: ▸ Infotype 2050 — Quota Deduction ▸ Infotype 2051 — No Quota Deduction

Table 6.3 Absence Settings Configuration Fields (Cont.)

Field	Description	Purpose/Impact
Time cstr. class	Used to detect collisions between infotype records. The system can validate against other infotypes for overlapping time records and deal with them accordingly.	▸ V_554Y_B Infotype Reaction ▸ V_T554Y Global View
Att./absence class		

Table 6.3 Absence Settings Configuration Fields (Cont.)

Now that we have created Absences and assigned various settings that impact the processing of the absence, it's time to discuss Time Constraints. The following section discusses what Time Constraints are and how they can affect you.

6.3 Time Constraint Classes

Time Constraints are basic settings within the system used to control how various time entries should react to other entries on an infotype. The Time Constraint class is linked to the absence type in the general settings section of the configuration. This way, you can control the time entry by absence type. What do we mean by control? Well, let's say you don't want any employees to enter an absence if a full-day attendance is already in the system. After all, we don't want them getting paid for working a full day of regular time and vacation time on the same day. By using Time Constraints, you can tell the system how infotype records will react to other infotype records that are already in the system. Using our earlier example, you could prevent vacation time from ever being entered into the system. Using Time Constraints, you can control how time entries react to other time entries of the same infotype or other infotypes, such as attendances.

Figure 6.11 shows an example of a Time Constraint class configuration.

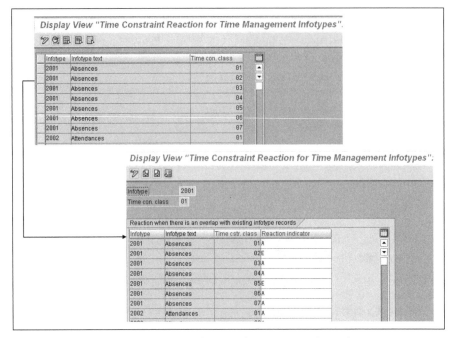

Figure 6.11 Delivered Time Constraint Classes and Reactions to Those Classes

The table is broken down by the Time Constraint class. Within each class you can see all of the infotypes and the reactions configured for each under the specific Time Constraint class.

The reactions are as follows:

▶ A — The old record is delimited

▶ E — New record creation is not possible

▶ W — A warning is issued for a new record

▶ N — A new record is created without the message being issued

Using this flexibility, you can assign two different absence or other infotype records to behave differently based on the reaction indicator. For instance, your vacation absence code could be configured to code E, which would not allow an entry if a full-day attendance is already entered and vice versa. This would prevent an employee from potentially receiving overtime if too many hours were entered for that particular day. Meanwhile, an absence that is not related to compensation could be entered without any negative ramifications to compensation.

Figure 6.12 shows the Time Constraint class using the global view table V_T554Y.

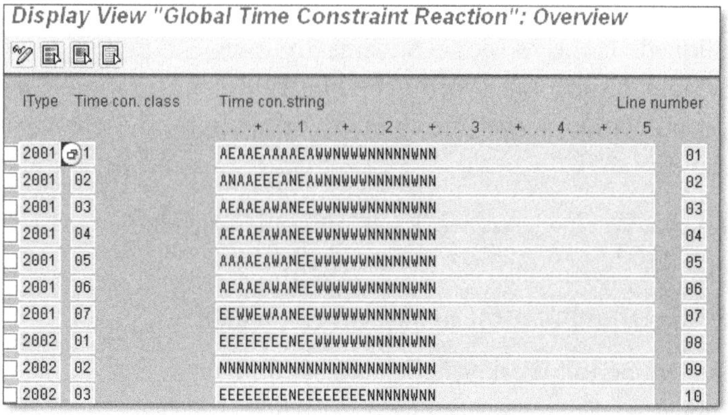

Figure 6.12 Global View of the Time Constraint Class

Now that we've defined how absences should react to other absences and attendances, it's time to define how we should count an absence. The following section describes an overview of the absence counting section.

6.3.1 Absence Counting

This section of the IMG pertains to how absences will be accounted during entry. The sections include the following areas:

- Counting classes for the period Work Schedule
- Rule for absence counting
- Assignment of counting rules to absence types
- Determine daily Work Schedule variants for absences
- Defining indicators for the personal calendar

Groupings for counting rules include the following:

- Employee Subgroup grouping for time quotas is based on Employee Group/ Subgroup combinations
- Personnel Subarea grouping for time quotas is based on Personnel Area/ Subarea combinations

In the next section, we'll discuss counting classes for period Work Schedules.

6.3.2 Counting Classes for the Period Work Schedule

The Counting class is linked via the Personnel Subarea grouping and period Work Schedule that was created during the Work Schedule rule configuration. The Counting class sets the foundation to evaluate absences based on the period Work Schedule.

For instance, at a high-level, you have two work schedule rules each linked to their own period work schedule.

▶ Work Schedule 8X5 has period Work Schedule 8x5 configured.

▶ Work schedule 10X4 has period Work Schedule 10x4 configured.

In this example, you could set up the first schedule to Counting class 1 and the second schedule to Counting class 2. When establishing the Counting class rules, you can say that any Counting class of 1 will deduct 8 hours of quota versus a Counting class of 2, which would deduct 10 hours of quota. Figure 6.13 shows the Counting class configuration table.

	Grpg	Period WS	Description	Start Date	End Date	Cntg class

Figure 6.13 Configuration Table for Period Work Schedule Counting Class

Once you set up the Counting classes for period Work Schedules, you need to define what those classes mean. Let's look at the actual rules.

6.3.3 Rules for Absence Counting

Absence counting rules have the following groupings to determine who should be assigned to which sets of rules.

▶ Employee Subgroup grouping for time quotas

▶ Personnel Subarea grouping for time quotas

Within the configurations, you need to decide if there should be any rounding of the values that are determined.

6.3.4 Absence Counting Rounding Rules

Rounding rules can be configured and attached to the counting rules. These allow you some flexibility in determining how particular absences can be rounded up or down. It is not necessary to establish every range if your ranges follow a set pattern. You can use the Roll checkbox to accommodate this requirement. For example, you may want all absences rounded to eight hours no matter how many hours were actually entered. By creating a rounding rule and ultimately assigning that rounding rule to an absence via a counting rule, this requirement can be achieved. Figure 6.14 shows a Rounding rule. Within the rounding rule you can define the lower and upper limits by which a rule is selected. Once selected, the target value is the new value that will be used. Let's say the rounding rule was for any amount between 7.50 and 8.05 with a target value of 8. If the employee has 7.51 hours entered, the system will round the hours up to 8.

RoRul	Name	No.	Lower limit	Incl.	Upper limit	Incl.	Target value	Roll.
				☐		☐		☐
				☐		☐		☐

Figure 6.14   Example of Absence Rounding Table

Now that we've talked about counting rules, let's see how they are configured.

6.3.5 Counting Rule

Figures 6.15 and 6.16 show a counting rule configuration. There are a lot of pieces of configuration that can offer you flexibility when establishing counting rules, and the decisions you made on your Work Schedule rule setup can impact the counting rule configuration.

The groupings of the counting rule include:

▸ Employee Subgroup grouping for time quota types

▸ Personnel Subarea grouping for time quota types

▸ The actual counting rule that you create

ESG Time quota types	
PS Grpg Tm Quota Typ	
Counting rule	
Sequential no.	

Applicability of rule

Conditions for current day

Weekday

☐ Monday ☐ Wednesday ☐ Friday ☐ Sunday
☐ Tuesday ☐ Thursday ☐ Saturday

Holiday class	Day type
☐ Not a public holiday	☐ Work acc. to work schedule
☐ Holiday class 1 - public hol.	☐ Day type 1: Day off
☐ Holiday class 2 - public hol.	☐ Day type 2: Day off
☐ Holiday class 3 - public hol.	☐ Day type 3: Day off
☐ Holiday class 4 - public hol.	☐ Day type 4: Day off
☐ Holiday class 5 - public hol.	☐ Day type 5: Day off
☐ Holiday class 6 - public hol.	☐ Day type 6: Day off
☐ Holiday class 7 - public hol.	☐ Day type 7: Day off
☐ Holiday class 8 - public hol.	☐ Day type 8: Day off
☐ Holiday class 9 - public hol.	☐ Day type 9: Day off

Conditions for work schedule

Counting class for period work schedule	Daily work schedule class
☐ Counting class 0	☐ Daily work schedule class 0
☐ Counting class 1	☐ Daily work schedule class 1
☐ Counting class 2	☐ Daily work schedule class 2
☐ Counting class 3	☐ Daily work schedule class 3
☐ Counting class 4	☐ Daily work schedule class 4
☐ Counting class 5	☐ Daily work schedule class 5
☐ Counting class 6	☐ Daily work schedule class 6
☐ Counting class 7	☐ Daily work schedule class 7
☐ Counting class 8	☐ Daily work schedule class 8
☐ Counting class 9	☐ Daily work schedule class 9

Condition for planned hours

☐ Planned hours = 0 ☐ Planned hours > 0

Condition for absence/attendance

☐ < 1 day ☐ Full-day

Figure 6.15 Counting Rule

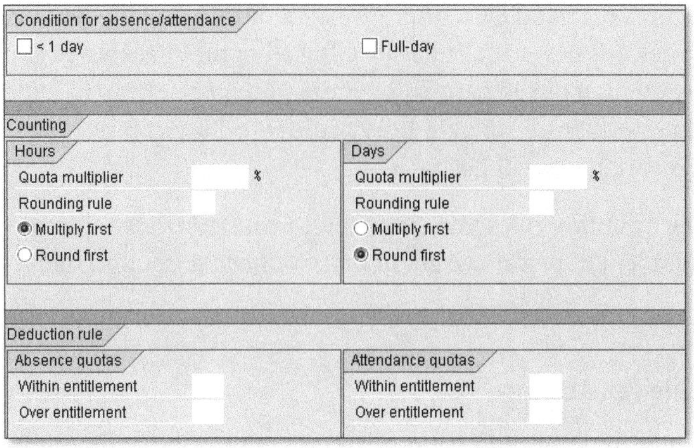

Figure 6.16 Counting Rule Continued

The counting rule is made of the following sections. If the checkbox is selected, the rule looks at the particular day in question to determine if all conditions have been satisfied.

▶ Day of the week — Self-explanatory.

▶ Holiday class — Based on the holiday calendar that is linked to the Work Schedule rule.

▶ Day type — Based on the daily Work Schedule configuration that is linked to the Work Schedule rule.

▶ Counting class for period Work Schedule — Based on the period work schedule that is linked to the work schedule rule.

▶ Daily Work Schedule Class — Based on the daily Work Schedule configuration that is linked to the Work Schedule rule.

▶ Conditions for planned hours — Checks the planned hours from the daily Work Schedule.

▶ Conditions for absences and attendances — Checks how many hours have been entered on the infotype.

▶ Quotas hours and days calculations — Calculates what percentage of hours or days will be deducted from the quotas and if any rounding rules should be applied.

▶ Deduction rules — Deduction rules link a particular absence or attendance quota to a particular counting rule via a deduction rule.

As you can see from Figures 6.15 and 6.16, there are a lot of things going on with the setup of counting rules. It's best to start by selecting all of the checkboxes and then removing the ones you don't need based on your requirements. Keep in mind that your Work Schedules design can play a heavy role into how complex your counting rules and their variations will become.

After you complete your counting rules you still need to configure how absences are linked to a counting rule. But before we get to that, we need to set up a deduction rule.

6.3.6 Deduction Rule for Absence

Deduction rules are created and linked to counting rules. You can specify multiple quota types to one deduction rule and the priority of which quota type should be taken in which order. By setting up a deduction rule, you can control how your quotas, such as vacation, are reduced by particular absences. Figure 6.17 shows the fields of a deduction rule.

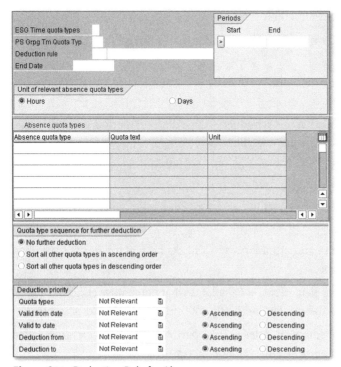

Figure 6.17   Deduction Rule for Absences

Now it's time to link an absence to a counting rule.

6.3.7 Assigning Counting Rules to Absence Types

This section discusses the link between absence types and the counting rule. You have the option of specifying if a quota deduction should be taken. Once linked, an absence will validate that there is a sufficient amount of quota remaining in order to satisfy the total amount of hours entered. For example, let's say you have a new employee who starts a new job and is granted six hours of vacation right away. The employee decides to take their first Friday off, which is eight hours. Because the employee only has six hours allowed, you will not be able to enter the full eight hours. Technically, the employee should probably be working two hours and then taking the rest of the day off, but that's another issue. For the purposes of this example, you need to link the vacation absence to Counting rule 010 via a Quota deduction as shown in Figure 6.18.

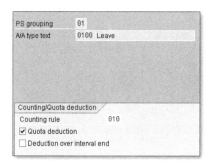

Figure 6.18   Counting Rule Assignment to Absence Type

This completes the basic absences configuration setup. But there is one more thing we need to discuss — daily Work Schedule variants.

6.3.8 Determine Daily Work Schedule Variants for Absences

Daily Work Schedule variants can be established for particular absence codes. There are four basic steps for this configuration:

1. Create the variants for the particular daily Work Schedule

2. Assign the absence grouping code in the absence general settings

3. Define the rules for checking the daily Work Schedule

4. Assign the daily Work Schedule selection rule to the particular daily Work Schedule

Based on this configuration, you can specify which daily Work Schedule variant, if any, should overwrite the existing daily Work Schedule for processing. If you use this functionality, the hours entered will always equal the planned hours. You won't be able to overwrite these amounts for that particular variant. Figure 6.19 shows the various configuration settings in order to set up this functionality.

Example

For example, let's say that during the summer your company makes every fourth Friday a four-hour workday. To prevent employees from entering a full-day absence for that particular Friday and receiving extra pay, you can set up a new absence type called Fourth Friday. You could then link this absence type through the configuration by utilizing daily Work Schedule variants. By doing this, if an employee enters time not equal to four, the daily Work Schedule dynamically changes and places the planned four hours, which you configured to be the default hours for the day.

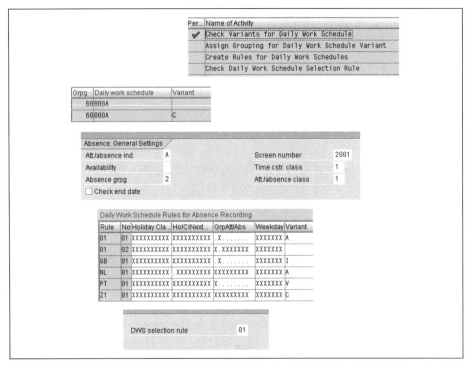

Figure 6.19 Dynamic Daily Work Schedule Variant Setup

There is one more step within the Absence configuration. You need to decide if you're planning on using any personnel calendars, such as Infotype 2050 — Annual Calendar. If so, then the following section explains the functionality.

6.3.9 Defining Indicators for the Personnel Calendar

This configuration allows you to create codes that are linked to particular absence types. The codes will be a shorthand abbreviation that are displayed on the personnel calendars and are in the dropdown selection. By utilizing these special codes, you can select a value and, based on the configuration that links the value to an absence type, the Infotype 2001 Absences records will automatically be created for you. Figure 6.20 shows the configuration table.

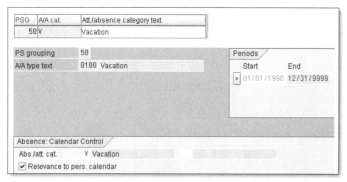

Figure 6.20 Personal Calendar Assignment

There is also additional functionality under the absences IMG, so let's take a look.

6.3.10 Special Absence Data

Special absence data is where SAP ERP HCM Time Management uses specific infotypes to allow further storage of information related to absences. The software allows you to store data in the following areas:

▶ General additional absence data (Infotype 0076, Worker's Compensation, and Infotype 0082, Additional Absence Data)

▶ Maternity protection (Infotype 0080 — Maternity Protection)

▶ Military and Nonmilitary service (Infotype 0081 — Military Service)

> **Note**
>
> We covered these infotypes in Chapter 4, "Time Management Master Data."

- In this section, you specify how the data can be entered and what particular absences can be linked to each infotype.

- This concludes our coverage of Absence configuration. Now we'll move on to the Attendance configuration.

6.4 Attendances and Actual Working Times

As we mentioned, Absence and Attendance types share the same Personnel Area/Subarea groupings. In addition, the configuration setup between the two is very similar. The configuration for Attendances can be found in the IMG under the menu path TIME MANAGEMENT • TIME DATA RECORDING AND ADMINISTRATION • ATTENDANCES.

Figure 6.21 shows the general settings for Attendances.

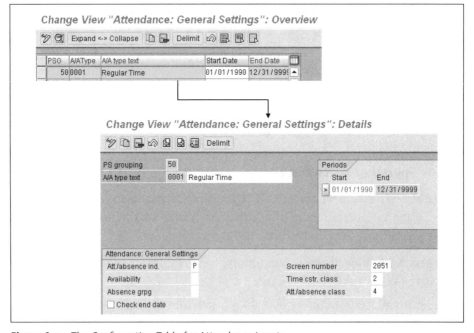

Figure 6.21 The Configuration Table for Attendance Inputs

Table 6.4 lists the fields for Attendances.

Field	Description	Purpose/Impact
PSG	Grouping of Personnel Areas and Subareas for absence and attendance types.	
A/A type text	Absence or attendance type and description.	Four-digit alphanumeric field that is displayed on the infotypes.
Att./absence ind.	Drives which screen number can be used. Determines processing type for Time Evaluation for attendances and absences.	A — Used for absences P — Used for attendances Utilized during time wage–type selection. Utilized in Time Evaluation processing type tables T555Y and T555Z.
Availability	Used to identify an employee's availability if particular attendances or absences have been entered.	Three possibilities: ▶ Blank — Not Available ▶ 1 — Available ▶ 9 — Irrelevant
Absence grpg	Used to identify which attendances or absences will drive the Work Schedule to use a variant Work Schedule.	Groupings from table V_550X_B — Determination of daily Work Schedule variants. Groupings Blank and 1 through 9 are available.
Check end date	This checkbox forces the time infotype data entry screen to enter an end date. If the checkbox is not selected, then the end date will default from the start date.	

Table 6.4 Attendance General Settings

Field	Description	Purpose/Impact
Screen number	Specifies which screen number will be utilized for the record when entering the infotype. The fields will be different based on the screens selected. The screens can be viewed via table T588M for the module pool (MP200000) you are after.	Seven possibilities for absences: ▶ Infotype 2000 — Absences General ▶ Infotype 2001—Quota Deductions ▶ Infotype 2002 — Work Incapacity (Germany) ▶ Infotype 2003 — Maternity Protection ▶ Infotype 2004 — Military Service ▶ Infotype 2005 — Work Incapacity (Netherlands) ▶ Infotype 2008 — Work Incapacity General Two possibilities for attendances; ▶ Infotype 2050 -Quota Deduction ▶ Infotype 2051 — No Quota Deduction
Time cstr. class	Used to detect collisions between infotype records. The system can validate against other infotypes for overlapping time records and deal with them accordingly.	▶ V_554Y_B Infotype Reaction ▶ V_T554Y Global View
Att./absence class	Used to help drive Time type creation under specific conditions.	

Table 6.4 Attendance General Settings

Now let's look at determining how the particular Attendances should be counted using Counting classes.

6.4.1 Counting Class

The Counting class is linked via the Personnel Subarea grouping and period Work Schedule created during the Work Schedule rule configuration. This Counting class sets the foundation to evaluate absences based on a period Work Schedule. Figure 6.22 shows the Counting classes linked to a period Work Schedule and how the various counting rule checkboxes apply.

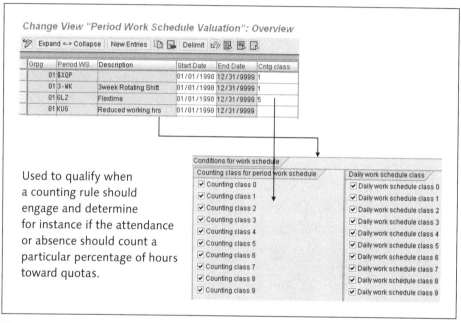

Figure 6.22 How a Counting Class Is Linked to a Counting Rule

Based on Figure 6.22, you could set up a counting rule to activate if an employee has a counting class of 5 linked to their Work Schedule. Under the counting rule in the Conditions for work schedule section, you would uncheck all of the checkboxes except for Counting class 5.

Another Attendance configuration option involves overtime compensation types.

6.4.2 Overtime Compensation Types

Overtime compensation types allow you to define Attendance configuration so that custom processing in Time Evaluation can compensate this Attendance accordingly. It is merely a code assignment that can be made in Time Evaluation to make processing decisions based on a particular overtime compensation type. Figure 6.23 shows how the configuration is displayed on an infotype screen, such as Attendances. You will likely never use this field, but it's there just in case. One example of a situation when you might use it would be to utilize one Attendance code, such as Regular Time, but then allow an administrator to use various values in the overtime compensation type field. Based on the values entered, Time Evaluation could be set up to generate different Wage types.

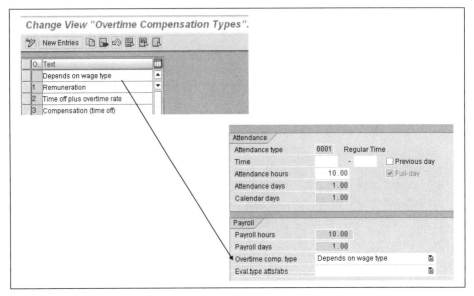

Figure 6.23 Overtime Compensation Link to the Attendance

In addition to the overtime compensation types that show up in Infotype 2002, you can also set up the evaluation type field for Infotype 2002. The following section explains the evaluation type for attendances.

6.4.3 Evaluation Type for Attendances

Evaluation types for attendances can be configured so that Time Evaluation or Payroll can compensate the attendance according to your business requirements. In Time Evaluation, a decision can be made on operation VARPREVLTP. Figure 6.24

shows the link between the field in Infotype 2002 and the configuration table. Similar to the overtime compensation type, you could also leverage this field to make decisions in Time Evaluation so that various employees could use the same attendance type; however, based on the value of the evaluation type, a custom personal calculation rule would process differently by making decisions off of the value.

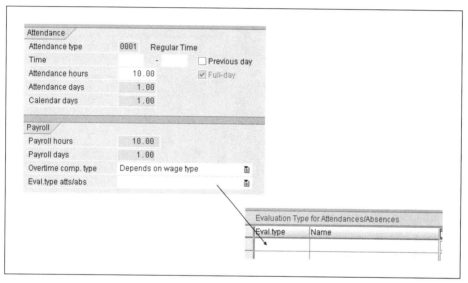

Figure 6.24 Evaluation Type Attributes Linkage

Let's move on to the overtime compensation type.

6.5   Overtime

The overtime compensation type discussed earlier is applicable to multiple infotypes. Figure 6.25 illustrates the various infotypes and how the configuration is linked to them. Decisions can be made in Time Evaluation using operation VARPRVERSL. If you decide to utilize this functionality, be aware that the field values you enter in the configuration will be shown on a couple of different infotypes. The overtime configuration can be found in the IMG under the menu path TIME MANAGEMENT • TIME DATA RECORDING AND ADMINISTRATION • OVERTIME.

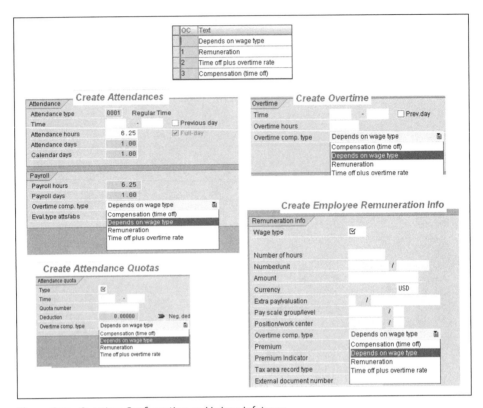

Figure 6.25 Overtime Configuration on Various Infotypes

Now let's see how to set up the system to allow managers to see who may or may not be available for a particular shift.

6.6   Availability

This grouping is based on the same Personnel Subarea groupings for the Substitutions functionality. Under this section of configuration, you specify the types of availability, how time constraints should work for the availability type, and how an employee is deemed available if they are assigned the availability type. This configuration is also utilized by the Shift Planning component. The availability type can be found in the IMG under the menu path: TIME MANAGEMENT • TIME DATA RECORDING AND ADMINISTRATION • AVAILABILITY.

PSG...	AvailType	Availability type text	Avail.type	TCC	Avail	Cal	Shift	Shift
01	01	On-call duty	R	01		◉	○	○
01	02	Availability <=10%	1	02		◉	○	○
01	03	Availability <=25%	2	02		◉	○	○
01	04	Availability <=40%	3	02		◉	○	○
01	05	Availability <=49%	4	02		◉	○	○
10	01	On-call duty	R	01		◉	○	○

Daily Work Schedule

Grpg	Daily work schedule	Variant	Daily WS text	Start Date	End Date	Availability
01	GLZ		Flextime	01/01/1990	12/31/9999	☑
01	GLZ	A	Flextime	01/01/1990	12/31/9999	☐
01	GLZ	B	Flextime	01/01/1990	12/31/9999	☐
01	N-11		Night shift	01/01/1990	12/31/9999	☐

"Work Schedule Rule: Availability".

ES g...	ES grpg for ...	Holiday...	Text	PSG	WS rule	Start ...	End Date	Availability
								☐
								☐

Figure 6.26 Availability Configuration Tables

You'll want to use this functionality if you have the need for SAP to help you determine who may or may not be available for particular shifts or in the case of an emergency. Many managers keep paper copies or other forms to track employee's schedules, by using the Availability functionality, you are leveraging your investment in the SAP system and using real-time data to help in your decision-making process.

After you have completed the set up of determining which Work Schedule will determine which employees may be available for work in the system, the next section consists of managing quotas, such as vacation. The following section explains the quota configuration.

6.7 Managing Time Accounts Using Attendance and Absence Quotas

Absence quotas are driven based on two groupings:

- Employee Subgroup grouping based on Employee Group/Subgroup combinations
- Personnel Subarea grouping based on Personnel Area/ Subarea combinations

The time quota configuration can be found in the IMG under the menu path TIME MANAGEMENT • TIME DATA RECORDING AND ADMINISTRATION • MANAGING TIME ACCOUNTS USING ATTENDANCE AND ABSENCE QUOTAS.

Figure 6.27 shows the quota type configuration table.

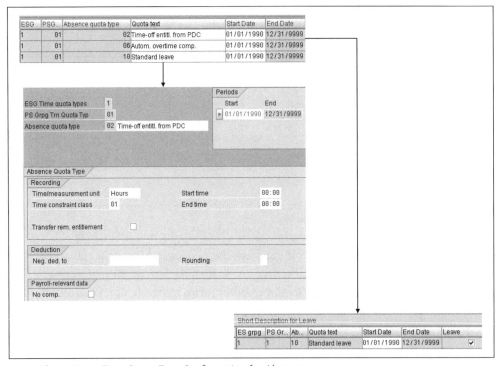

Figure 6.27   Time Quota Type Configuration for Absences

6.7.1   Time Quota Types

The absence quota types are held in Infotype 2006 and attendance quotas in Infotype 2007 and they contain the days or hours buckets allocated to employees. Figure 6.28 shows the configuration table for attendance quotas.

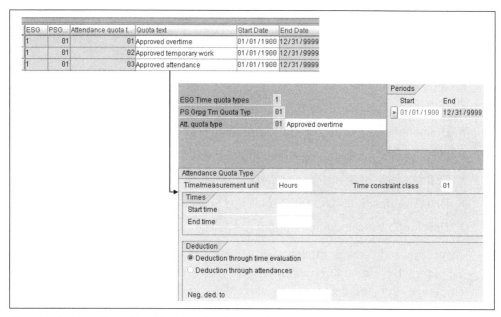

Figure 6.28 Time Quota Type Configuration for Attendances

After you have created all of your attendance and absence quotas, you now need to determine exactly how much an employee is entitled to receive per year. The following section on calculating absence entitlements will explain the configuration.

6.7.2   Calculating Absence Entitlements

There are two ways to generate quotas:

▶ No generation — The report RPTQTA00 is processed using the configuration rules to create the quotas.

▶ Time Evaluation — The Time Evaluation schema generates quotas based on the configuration supporting the type of quota. You can set up quotas to increase or replace quotas.

Each quota can be set up for either hours or days calculations.

The following sections of configuration will outline the configuration opportunities available when setting up quotas.

- Specify Rule Groups for Quota Type Selection
- Set Base Entitlements
- Determine the Validity and Deduction Periods
- Define Rules for Reducing Quota Entitlements
- Define Rules for Rounding Quota Entitlements
- Define Rules for Transferring Quota Entitlements
- Define Generation Rules for Quota Type Selection
- Develop Enhancement for Quota Type Selection

As we proceed through this section, we will use two employees as an example. Employee 1 is a new hire within company code 0001. Employee 2 has been an employee with the company for over 15 years and resides in company code 0002.

6.7.3   Rule Groups for Quota Type Selection

There are two ways for you to establish the quota type grouping that will be used during the selection rules for quota types:

- **Personnel Calculation Rule MODT** — This option offers the most flexibility when determining the quota type group using Time Evaluation processing. The operation MODIF Q= is used to establish the grouping.

- **Feature QUOMO** — Used when report RPTQTA00 is used to generate the quotas in Time Evaluation.

By using one of the two options for generating quotas, we can determine which groupings should be associated with employee 1 versus employee 2. By doing so, we have the ability to have different types of quotas for each employee. Figure 6.29 shows the two options.

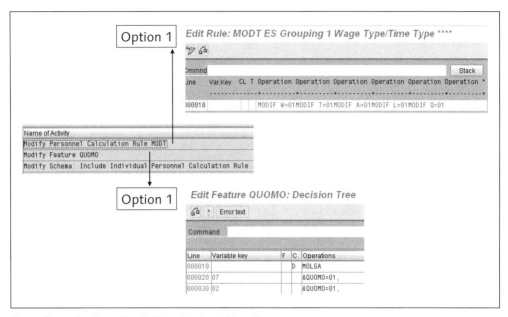

Figure 6.29 Configuration Options for Quota Type Groups

After you decide which method you would prefer for both employees 1 and 2, you then need to determine how much quota should be granted. The base entitlements section describes this functionality.

6.7.4 Base Entitlements

The base entitlement is the foundation for providing the amount of quota that will be granted for the established requirements.

The groupings for the table include the following:

▶ Employee Subgroup grouping for time quotas

▶ Personnel Subarea grouping for time quotas

▶ Personnel Subarea grouping for time recording

▶ Absence quota type (driven from personnel calculation rule MODT or Feature QUOMO)

The rule can be used to establish entitlements based on seniority or age requirements with the sequential number being variations of the amount of quota to be granted. This way, you can have different rules for different populations of employees with multiple levels of quota.

The entitlement can be as follows:

- ▶ **Constant** — This is a specific amount that is granted.

- ▶ **12-day balance** — This option allows you a lot of flexibility. You can set up custom personnel calculation rules and Time types that hold specific values. All of these calculations allow you to link the final Time type to the entitlement for those amounts to be awarded.

- ▶ **Period balance** — Similar to 12-day balance, except the amount is taken from the period table instead of the daily table.

The final section allows you to define the period in which the quota rules will take effect. There are six different options:

- ▶ **Calendar year** — One calendar year from January 1 through December 31.

- ▶ **Accrual period** — Time period the entitlement is based on.

- ▶ **Time Evaluation period** — Based on the period parameters of table V_T539Q Period Parameters.

- ▶ **Payroll period** — Payroll period associated with the end of the accrual period.

- ▶ **Other period** — Payroll period defined in payroll period parameters.

- ▶ **Relative to date type** — You can select a date type that is stored on Infotype 0041 — Date Specifications. You can further define a length of time relative to the date type selected.

Continuing with our example, Company code 0001 offers two weeks of vacation time to all employees regardless of years of service. Company code 0002 offers 2 weeks of vacation for 0 to 10 years of service and 4 weeks of vacation for those from 11 years on. By setting up the base entitlement, you specify how much is granted based on years of service. Figure 6.30 shows the configuration table for base entitlement.

After you define all of the various levels of vacation based on years of service, it is then time to define when those entitlements will be available. The following section on validity and deduction periods is where you define the periods that enable an employee to record vacation time absences.

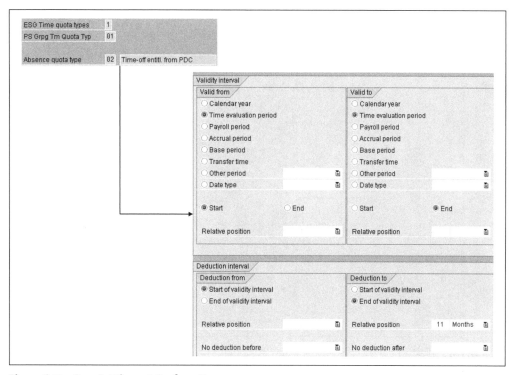

Figure 6.30 Base Entitlement Configuration

6.7.5 Validity and Deduction Periods

The configuration of this step establishes the date requirements that will populate the quota infotypes and the date range by which an absence can reduce the quota. The periods under the validity period have similar characteristics, as shown in Figure 6.31.

In our example, employee 1 and employee 2 could also take vacation in different periods. Under this section, you can specify that employee 1 must use their vacation in the calendar year, however, employee 2 can also take up to the first quarter of the following year to use their quota. By adjusting the various radio buttons for End Date, you could specify a relative position of 15 months for the end date.

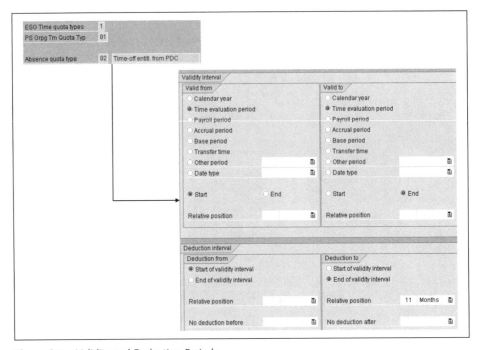

Figure 6.31 Validity and Deduction Periods

After you define the periods, then it is time to create any necessary reductions for the amount of quota that will be generated. The following section will show the configuration for reducing quota entitlements.

6.7.6 Define Rules for Reducing Quota Entitlements

This section allows you to establish reduction rules to determine how, if at all, part-time employees will have their entitlement reduced. When analyzing this option, you need to determine how the organization plans to maintain the Infotype 0007 part-time employee checkbox, and if quotas should be reduced according to any of the options under this section. The reduction indicator for the particular absence dictates to the system that the day should be considered inactive for calculation purposes.

Continuing with our example, employee 1 becomes a part-time employee during the middle of the month. They were awarded 6.67 hours for the month, but they shouldn't be entitled to the full amount because they have become part-time. By utilizing this configuration, you can tell the system how to reduce the quota entitlement so that employee 1 gets a portion of the monthly amount of quota. Figure 6.32 shows the quota reduction configuration.

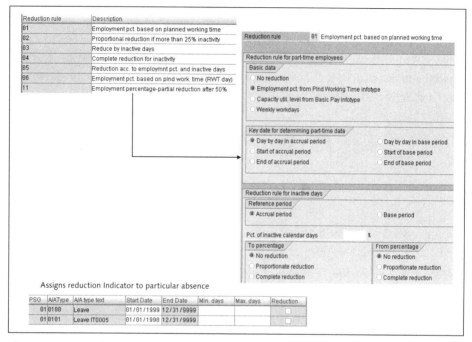

Figure 6.32 Rules for Reducing Quotas

Once you define any reduction rules, you may also have requirements to round the particular amounts generated.

6.7.7 Define Rules for Rounding Quota Entitlements

Similar to absence rounding rules, this section of the configuration allows you to round, per your requirements, the particular quota value that will be generated. When setting up the lower and upper limits, you can specify if the equal-to value should be considered. By checking the Roll Interval checkbox, you don't necessarily need to set up every possible lower and upper limit if they fall into a set pattern of time difference between each level. Figure 6.33 shows the rounding rule configuration table. You can specify the Lower and Upper limits for when the rule should engage based on the value of the quota being generated.

RoRul	Name	No.	Lower limit	Incl.	Upper limit	Incl.	Target value	Roll.
01	Round up or down...	001	0.50000	☑	1.50000	☐	1.00000	☑
02	Round percentage...	001		☐	0.25000	☐		☐

Figure 6.33 Rules for Rounding Quota Entitlements

The next step of the configuration involves defining when the quota will be transferred to Infotype 2006 or Infotype 2007. This is called Define Rules for Transferring Quota Entitlements. These rules are specifically designed for New Zealand and Australia and, as such, will not be covered in this chapter. Figure 6.34 shows the standard delivered table entries.

Quota Generation: Rule for Transfer Times	
Transfer	Rule for transfer times
001	Long Service Leave 10 / 15 years
002	NZ LSL 10/15/20 Years

Figure 6.34 Rules for Transfer Time

The next section of configuration regards when the quota will actually be created on Infotype 2006 Absence Quotas or Infotype 2007 Attendance Quotas. The rules contain all of the configuration required to process and create quotas for employees.

6.7.8 Define Generation Rules for Quota Type Selection

Generation rules are where most of the setup for quotas is maintained. This configuration uses all of the previous configuration steps of this section, and allows you the ability to link everything together. Upon entering the rule, there will be six tabs where quota-related data is maintained:

▶ Applicability

▶ Accrual Period

▶ Base Entitlement

▶ Accrual Entitlement

▶ Transfer Time

▶ Total Entitlement

Figures 6.35 through 6.39 show the various tabs of the selection rule.

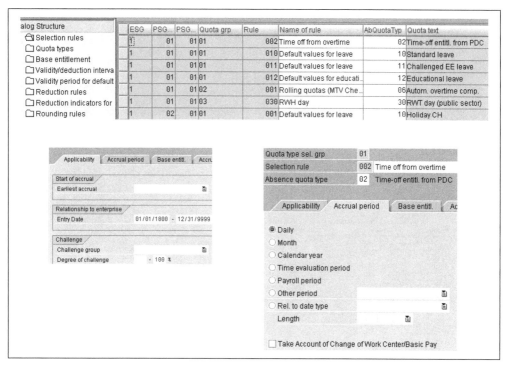

Figure 6.35 Applicability and Accrual Period Tabs

Using our example of the two employees, the initial grouping for quota types that was established is now used. Here is where you define the generation rules for each quota type that is linked to each company code in our example.

The two key tabs shown in Figure 6.35 are:

▶ Applicability — This tab allows you to define when the earliest accrual can occur, the employees relationship hire date, and a challenge group that is pulled from Infotype 0004 — Challenge — which allows you to make further processing restrictions based on challenge group.

▶ Accrual period — This tab allows you to select one option for the accrual period.

Back to our example, this is where you would link the two ranges for employee 2, whose benefits department has two ranges for quota entitlement based on years of service. For employee 1, you would only see one base entitlement.

Base entitlement is shown in Figure 6.36.

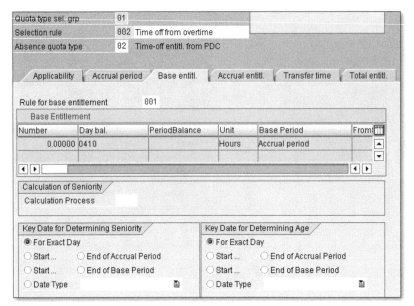

Figure 6.36 Base Entitlement Tab

▶ Base Entitlement — This tab allows you to link a base entitlement rule and a calculation for the employee's seniority. Seniority and age allow you to further define the rules for determining the dates.

Figure 6.37 shows three tabs:

▶ Accrual Entitlement — This tab allows you to specify prorations on the calculation, the use of Time types for multiplication purposes, reduction rules, rounding rules, and maximum entitlements.

▶ Transfer Time — This tab allows you to define when Infotype 2006 or 2007 is created.

▶ Total Entitlement — This tab allows you to define the rounding rule and the maximum amount of quota that should be granted.

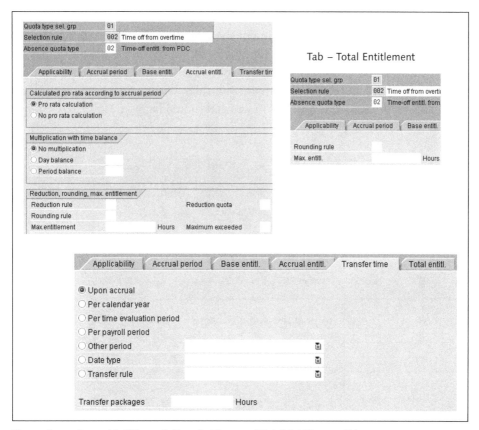

Figure 6.37 Accrual Entitlement, Transfer Time, and Total Entitlement Tabs

After you have completed the configuration for your quotas, there is a section called Deduction Rule for Quotas.

6.7.9 Deduction Rules for Quotas

The deduction rule allows you to define which quotas are deducted and in which particular order based on the assignment of deduction priorities. These deduction rules are associated with a counting rule. This configuration might look familiar as it is configured in the absence deduction rule section of the IMG and leveraged in the quota configuration.

To conclude our example, employee 2 of Company code 0002 is allowed to carry over any unused portion of vacation entitlement into the following year. Employee

2 can already take up to the first quarter of the following year to use their vaca-tion quota; however, at the beginning of the 2nd quarter, the remaining amount is moved to a different quota type. Employee 2 now has two different quotas on Infotype 2006. When the employee enters a vacation day, which quota should be deducted first? By setting up a deduction rule, you can specify which quotas should be deducted and the priority in which it should happen. Figure 6.38 shows a deductions rule.

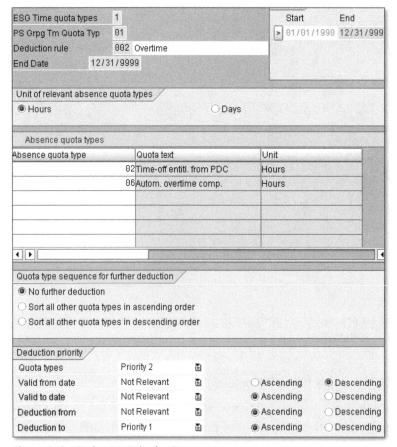

Figure 6.38 Deduction Rules for Quotas

That concludes the setup of quotas. What happens, however, if employee 2 termi-nates their employment and has a remaining vacation quota balance? Let's look at Time Quota Compensation and find out.

6.7.10 Time Quota Compensation

Time Quota Compensation is the methodology by which you would pay out any quotas remaining to an employee, either at the end of each year, if accumulation of quotas is not allowed, or more commonly during termination of employment. This infotype is processed during payroll.

The setup consists of two basic parts:

▶ Part 1 is the definition of the compensation method. This will be the drop-down figure on Infotype 0416 — Time Quota Compensation. You can specify a deduction rule or a quota type that can be linked directly to the compensation method.

▶ Part 2 is a further description of who is authorized to see the compensation methods based on Employee Subgroup groupings and Personnel Subarea groupings. Under this section you can further define the payout by specifying which quota types apply, the number to compensate, an amount to compensate, a particular year, a percentage factor to utilize, and which Wage type should hold the calculation amount in payroll.

Figure 6.39 shows the configuration of a time quota compensation type and how to link a Wage type so that payroll will compensate the amount during processing.

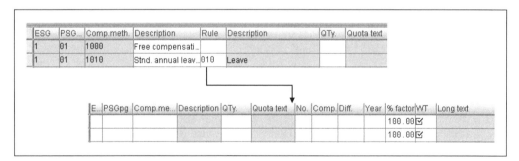

Figure 6.39 Time Quota Compensation Tables

As you can see, there is a lot of configuration to conduct when setting up the quotas. In the next section, we'll review a possible workaround to updating all of the various tables.

6.7.11 Develop Enhancements for Quota Type Selection

You can use the SAP enhancement HRPTIM03 for quota type selection. There may be times that the standard tables do not provide enough flexibility to set up your requirements or you may determine it is easier for you to leverage custom coding instead. The following enhancement provides you some flexibility in setting up your system to generate quotas.

You can use the enhancement to refine the criteria available for creating absence quotas in the following areas:

- Applicability of the selection rule EXIT_SAPLHRV_001
- Defaults for processing accrual entitlements determined by Time Evaluation EXIT_SAPLHRV_002
- Rules for reducing quota entitlements EXIT_SAPLHRV_003
- Defaults for determining base entitlements EXIT_SAPLHRV_004
- Default for transfer: Change results of quota generation EXIT_SAPLHRV_005
- Processing individual regulations for determining the employee's start and end dates EXIT_SAPLHRV_006

Depending on your requirements, it may be easier and more efficient to set up all of your requirements using these user exits instead of the table configurations.

Now there are just two other items to cover in the IMG pertaining to Time Management status. Let's look at them in the following sections.

6.7.12 Time Management Employee Status

Within the system, SAP delivers the following Time Management statuses that can be used on Infotype 0007. These statuses also dictate if and how Time Evaluation will process for these employees. The following statuses are available in the standard system. Each of these will help enable Time Evaluation processing so that the appropriate employees are selected at the beginning of running the program for Time Evaluation.

- 0 — No Time Evaluation
- 1 — Time Evaluation of actual times
- 2 — Plant Data Collection (PDC) Time Evaluations

- 7 — Time Evaluation without Payroll integration
- 8 — External services
- 9 — Time Evaluation of planned times

6.7.13 Permitting Attendances and Absences to Be Recorded Without Clock Times

This functionality is driven by Feature HRSIF, which can be referenced via Transaction code PE03. This is a very easy step to configure and is a basic setting that allows various time-related infotypes, such as absence and attendance, to hold start and end times, or just hold the total hours. This feature allows you to define whether or not hours entered on the time infotypes required start and end times, or if you can just enter a lump-sum amount of hours.

The feature has two basic values that can be entered:

1. Employees can enter time on the infotypes by entering a number instead of start and end times.
2. Employee's clock times are generated based off of the Work Schedule when the times entered are less than the planned working time.

This concludes our discussion of the configuration of Time Data Recording and Administration.

6.8 Summary

In this chapter, you learned about the various sections of configuration under Time Data Recording and Administration. You learned what the various areas are comprised of, such as absences and attendances, and how they can be set up to facilitate specific functionality. In the next chapter, we will discuss Personnel Time Events, which facilitate the processing of clock-in and clock-out processing.

In this chapter, you'll learn about key areas to consider during the configuration of Personnel Time Events that are used to communicate and process time-related information to external Time Management subsystems. After reading the chapter, you should be knowledgeable of the concepts and understand how to set up interfacing to a third-party time collection system or the SAP Logistics component.

7 Personnel Time Events

Personnel Time Events are the actual time postings captured in a third- party time collection system and then passed to the SAP system for further processing. Examples of such Time Events are clock-in and clock-out times used during a standard workday.

SAP ERP HCM uses the HR Plant Data Collection (HR PDC) to interface with a third-party time collection system and the PDC function to interface with SAP Logistics.

There are two communication methodologies for interfacing with a third-party time collection system when capturing Personnel Time Events:

- PDC Employee Times and Expenditures
  - Valid as of release 4.5A
  - Preferred method
- Communication Channel 1 (CC1)
  - Valid as of release 3.0, considered obsolete by some

If you are implementing a third-party time collection system that will evaluate the time prior to entering the SAP system, then the Personnel Time Events functionality is not required unless you intend to use the SAP Portal and utilize the clock-in and clock-out functionality.

Key Management Decision Points — Personnel Time Events

The following items are key decision points for the implementation of Personnel Time Events:

▸ The stakeholders of the implementation should try to have the third-party time collection system vendor available during the blueprinting phase of the project.

▸ Most third-party time collections systems have a generic interface that may or may not need to be customized based on your implementation requirements. You will want to validate which methodology they use and leverage their prior implementations when interfacing to the SAP system.

▸ Personnel Time Events require the use of Time Evaluation with Clock Times to evaluate the Time Events sent from third-party time collection systems.

▸ The team responsible for implementing this functionality requires basis support to establish the communication parameters between the systems. They will also need Advanced Business Application Programming (ABAP) support to build any interfaces that are required to upload the data into the SAP system via Intermediate Documents (IDOCs). They will establish communication between the consultants or team members responsible for setting up the third-party time collection systems, and with your functional team to configure the various elements, and determine the batch scheduling processing for all of the various components.

▸ Deciding which communication parameters to use: HR PDC, CC1, or both in parallel.

The configuration for Personnel Time Events is broken into three basic areas in the Implementation Guide (IMG):

1. General Settings

2. Personnel Time Events

3. Employee Expenditures: External, Cafeteria, and Service Station

The configuration section of the IMG for Personnel Time Events can be found under the men path TIME MANAGEMENT • PERSONNEL TIME EVENTS.

7.1 General Settings

Within the general settings section of the configuration, you can enable communication with other time recording systems. So let's look at the general settings you need to set up to use Time Events.

7.1.1 Specify Communication Parameters

The first step in your general settings is to specify the communication parameters. During this part of the setup, you specify the communication parameters between the SAP system and the third-party time collection system. Without this setup, the SAP system will not know how to communicate with the third-party time collection systems and you will not be able to import the various time records, such as absences and attendances. The interfaces are asynchronous and utilize the SAP system's Business Application Programming Interface (BAPI). SAP delivers three options during this setup that you can specify:

1. Specification "Blank" — HR PDC available as of release 4.5a

2. Specification 1 — CC1, available as of release 3.0A and may not receive support after release 6.0, but will not be removed

3. Specification 2 — HR PDC and CC1 that run in parallel

Next you need to configure the number range for the Time Events.

7.1.2 Create Number Range for Time Events and Account Assignment Data

The number range object for Time Events and plant data is PD_SEQ_NR. It is used for all Time Events and integration points with other components' tables that are required when interfacing with Human Resources (HR). The other components include:

▶ Controlling

▶ Material Management (MM)

▶ Plant Maintenance (PM)

▶ Project Systems (PS)

The number range interval is delivered by SAP and is set to '01.' It's recommended that you not change this interval. The next section of configuration under the general settings is to group the Personnel Time Events that will be used. The following section explains how to set up such groupings.

7.1.3   Grouping Personnel Time Events

The grouping of Personnel Time Events controls which Time Events an employee is able to see and use. The groupings configured under this step become part of the master data selection on Infotype 0050 — Time Recording Information. Based on the master data of the employee and the configuration behind the settings, you can control the eligibility of different types of Time Events for different groups of employees.

So the question is, what are Time Events and how are they actually used in the system? Let's look at an example.

> **Example**
>
> When an employee reports for a shift at the distribution center, there is a clock-in terminal on the wall. The employee has been given a swipe card that he swipes through on the terminal. This particular terminal does not give the employee an opportunity to specify any more details other than he clocked in. At this point, we know that he clocked in, but how? The Personnel Time Events are codes that are created when the swiping in and out through the day are recorded. The information is stored on these codes and passed to the SAP system. You can group Personnel Time Events so that groups of particular codes may be available for different groups of people.

So in this example, how does the employee get assigned to particular Time Events? One of the fields in Infotype 0050 is called the Time Event type grouping. This is the grouping that dictates an employee will receive a specific set of Personnel Time Events. The functionality would let you define that 1 employee may be able to see 5 Personnel Time Events while another employee might have access to 10 Personnel Time Events to track various clock-in and clock-out times.

SAP delivers all of the available Time Events, however, you can decide which of the various groupings you would like to use. Figure 7.1 shows you the Time Events delivered in the system. The Time Events starting with a 'P' should be utilized.

Now that you have seen the Personnel Time Events delivered in Figure 7.1, how can you control other information that can be used at the employee level? The following section explains how you can utilize the SAP system for this requirement.

01	Clock-in	P01	Clock-in/-out
02	Clock-out	P02	Start or end of break
03	Clock-in/-out	P03	Start or end of off-site work
04	Start of off-site work	P04	Start or end of off-site work at home
05	End of off-site work	P05	Interim entry
06	Start or end of off-site work	P10	Clock-in
07	Start of off-site work at home	P11	Change
08	End of off-site work at home	P15	Start of break
09	Start or end of off-site work at home	P20	Clock-out
A10	Start teardown PP	P25	End of break
A20	Partial teardown PP	P30	Start of off-site work
A30	Interrupt teardown PP	P35	Start of off-site work at home
A40	Finish teardown PP	P40	End of off-site work
B10	Start processing PP	P45	End of off-site work at home
B20	Partial processing PP	P50	External wage type
B30	Interrupt processing PP	P60	Information entry
B40	Finish processing PP	R10	Begin setup PP
I20	Time ticket PM partial confirmation	R20	Partial setup PP
I40	Time ticket PM final confirmation	R30	Interrupt setup PP
K10	Currently not in use	R40	Finish setup PP
K20	Currently not in use	S10	Start of malfunction (not yet released)
K30	Currently not in use	S40	End of malfunction (not yet released)
L20	Time ticket PP partial confirmation	T20	Time ticket PS partial confirmation
L40	Time ticket PP final confirmation	T40	Time ticket PS final confirmation
N10	PM work start	V20	Partial variable activity PP
N20	PM work part-finish	V40	Finish variable activity PP
N30	PM work interruption	W10	PS work start
N40	PM work finish	W20	PS work part-finish
		W30	PS work interruption
		W40	PS work finish

Figure 7.1 Various Time Events Delivered in the System

7.1.4   Set Groupings for Connections to the Subsystem

Set groupings are utilized for grouping particular objects for distribution to various subsystems. What are objects? Objects are a generic term referring to any fields or pieces of master data on an employee's record. The groupings configured under this step become part of the master data selection in Infotype 0050. We covered Infotype 0050 in Chapter 4, "Master Data." Within Infotype 0050, there are various fields that can help you determine what kinds of data a particular employee should be able to see in a subsystem. In particular, the Subsystem Grouping field is where this configuration is utilized on an employee's master data record. The groupings help you determine which employee master data in your custom interfaces will be sent to the subsystems. For example, you might have a couple different versions of time collection systems throughout the country. Some of these systems might require more employee master data than others. By setting up these groupings, when your custom interface is processed, you can make decisions on which master data should be pulled out of the SAP system and sent to the subsystem.

The final configuration under the general settings section is called enhancement for link to time recording systems. We will cover this next.

User Exit	Description	Category
EXIT_SAPLRPTC_001	Downloading HR mini master	Personnel Time Events **
EXIT_SAPLRPTC_002	Downloading personnel time balances	Personnel Time Events **
EXIT_SAPLRPTC_005	Downloading attendances and absence reasons	Personnel Time Events
EXIT_SAPLRPTC_006	Downloading cost centers	Personnel Time Events
EXIT_SAPLRPTC_008	Downloading internal orders	Personnel Time Events
EXIT_SAPLRPTC_009	Downloading objects	Personnel Time Events
EXIT_SAPLRPTC_010	Downloading time event groups	Personnel Time Events
EXIT_SAPLRPTC_011	Downloading projects	Personnel Time Events
EXIT_SAPLRPTC_003	Uploading time events	Personnel Time Events **
EXIT_SAPLRPTC_001	Downloading HR mini master	Employee Expenditures **
EXIT_SAPLRPTC_002	Downloading permitted employee expenditures	Employee Expenditures
EXIT_SAPLRPTC_010	Downloading time event groups	Employee Expenditures
EXIT_SAPLRPTC_004	Uploading employee expenditures	Employee Expenditures **

Figure 7.2   Various User Exits Available within Enhancement HRPTIM05

7.1.5   Enhancement for Link to Time Recording Systems (HR-PDC)

The enhancement HRPTIM05 contains numerous user exits that allow customization for various upload and download programs. Enhancements are provided throughout all SAP components and are available just in case the standard delivered tables are not robust enough for you to configure all of your requirements. The enhancements allow you to develop custom code to satisfy your business requirements. Figure 7.2 shows the exits available. Those user exits flagged with an ** allow for customer fields within the exit. In addition, the source code for the user exits can be displayed via Transaction code SE37. As you can see from Figure 7.2, the first exit is used for downloading the HR mini-master. This basically means, which employee master data needs to be taken out of the SAP system and sent to the external time-keeping systems? Continuing with our example, we can use the groupings to send master data to one time-keeping system, and different master data to another time-keeping system based on the employee. The user exit is where you would make decisions based on the groupings to determine which master data to send.

We have now finished the section for Personnel Time Events general settings. Let's continue our discussion with the second section of the configuration — Personnel Time Events.

7.2   Personnel Time Events Configuration

As we mentioned at the beginning of the chapter, Personnel Time Events are the time postings made by employees throughout the course of the day. Time Events might include clock-in and clock-out, breaks etc. This section of configuration allows you to define master data that will be maintained in Infotype 0050 and translate the particular clock entries to Wage types during Time Evaluation processing. Let's have a look at the first section of configuration.

7.2.1   Setting Up Attendance/Absence Groupings for the Subsystem

This section of configuration is for grouping reason codes. What are reason codes? Let's say you have a time-keeping system in which your employees swipe in, and he can also provide more detail regarding that particular swipe. A monitor screen recognizes his swipe entry, displays the information, and he then can define why he's swiping his card. One reason might be to just start work. Another reason might be he is leaving for an appointment. But if you're using Personnel Time Events and the code only says P01 for clock-in, how is the SAP system going to know that the employee left for an appointment and how is Time Evaluation going to generate a Wage type for the unpaid absence because of this appointment? Well, the system uses Reason Codes. Reason codes area a further description that an employee can associate with their swipe entries so that you can determine the reason for such an entry.

As we noted in the previous sections, you might have a variety of different time collection systems across the country. This configuration setting allows you to establish a grouping that will become part of the master data selection on Infotype 0050 Time Recording Information. So let's see how this works. In the next section we'll create reason codes and associate them with attendance or absence types.

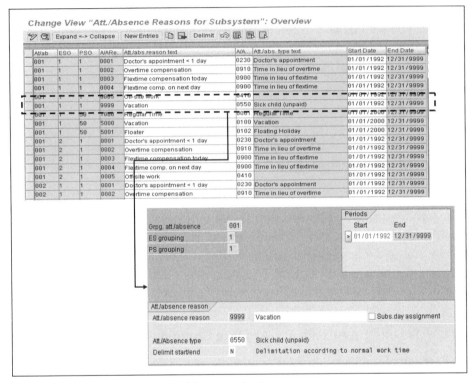

Figure 7.3 Various Data Points Available During the Setup

7.2.2 Maintain Attendance/Absence Reasons

This configuration is for setting up the system to allow the user at the third-party time entry subsystem terminal to associate particular reasons for the type of time entry being entered. We just explained what reason codes could be used for (see Figure 7.3), so let's see what it looks like. If the employee is assigned reason code 9999 with their swipe entry, then that reason code can be translated into absence type 0550 during the Time Evaluation process. In addition, during Time Evaluation processing, you can set up the system so that Time Events that have a reason code corresponding to an attendance or absence, automatically create an Infotype 2001 Absences or Infotype 2002 Attendances during Time Evaluation processing. An administrator can then use the Time Management Pool Error Handling to review the locked records and unlock those, which in turn approves them for processing. This would be beneficial if you need some sort of an approval of particular reason codes before the employee was eligible to be compensated for those hours.

Now let's take a closer look at some of the fields in Figure 7.3.

The key for the table is based on the combinations of the following fields:

▶ Att./absence

▶ ES grouping

▶ PS grouping

During the setup, the following fields are available:

▶ **Att./absence reason** — A reason for why the Time Event is entered into the system.

▶ **Subs. day assignment** — This indicator flags the Time Event to record a full-day attendance or absence on the subsequent day.

▶ **Att./Absence type** — Used to generate the attendance or absence type in Time Evaluation. This level of detail allows the user to maintain what kind of payments should or should not be made.

▶ **Delimit start/end** — Used to determine the missing Time Pair when one does not exist or when less than one working day is entered.

To determine how to delimit the time, there are four options available:

  ▶ **Blank** — Delimitation of the Time Pair is controlled in Time Evaluation

  ▶ **C** — Delimitation is based on the core working times from the daily Work Schedule for that day

  ▶ **N** — Delimitation is based on the normal working times from the daily Work Schedule for that day

  ▶ **P** — Delimitation is based on the planned working times from the daily Work Schedule for that day

The next section of configuration under Personnel Time Events is to determine which data should be displayed at time-keeping subsystem terminals.

7.2.3 Determine Data to be Displayed at the Terminal

Within the IMG, the determination of data displayed at the terminals is broken into two parts. The first part is to check the time balance configuration, which we refer to as Time types. The second part is to determine the particular employee master data that they will see when entering their clock times. The data is sent in the HR mini-master outbound file to the subsystems. Let's have a look at the two parts in more detail.

▶ **Time types** — Used to store time-related buckets that can be pushed out to the third-party time collection system terminals. There is a configuration setting that must be selected if you want employees to view particular balances of time. The "Store for the Time Accounts" option in table V_T555A must be selected. Why would you use this? You might find this beneficial to provide employees with a total number of hours they have worked for the week. You could also provide any overtime-related information that was generated in Time Evaluation so that the employees are aware that their time is accurately accounted for.

The second part is to determine which master data should be sent to the subsystems.

▶ **Master Record Information** — The following are a few examples of the data you could send:

  ▷ Date — The most recent payroll run date.

  ▷ Quota Information from Infotype 2006 and Infotype 2007— Entitlement, remaining quota, total remaining. In addition, the quota type, and those managed in days and hours are available.

  ▷ Leave remaining from Infotype 0005 — Leave Entitlement.

  ▷ Incentive Wages Data — Individual and group incentives.

The next section of configuration under Personnel Time Events is called Groupings for Access Control.

7.2.4   Set Groupings for Access Control

Throughout this chapter we keep reverting back to Infotype 0050. This infotype is the key ingredient to successfully setting up employees in subsystems for a variety of functionalities, such as clocking in and out of the system. This grouping for access control is no different than the other settings we have covered for Infotype 0050. This grouping establishes when an employee can access certain locations. These time-restricted groupings are based on Personnel Subarea groupings for Time Recording. The groupings configured under this step become part of the master data selection in Infotype 0050. This setting is just a grouping. The third-party time-keeping system must support this functionality for it to work.

For example, you might want to control when employees have authorization to a restricted area. Obviously the SAP system doesn't control when they can or cannot enter this area, but you can establish the grouping on the employee master data record. The grouping is translated by whatever software you are using to control access to the restricted area to determine if an employee is permitted.

This concludes the configuration review for the second section — Personnel Time Events. The third section of configuration is called Employee Expenditures, which we discuss in the next section.

7.3   Employee Expenditures: External Cafeteria and Service Plans

The configuration of the employee expenditures: external cafeteria and service plans is smaller than the previous two sections. What are employee expenditures? Does your company have a cafeteria? Wouldn't it be nice if you could just take your ID badge and have the cost of your meal taken as a payroll deduction? This is an example of what expenditures processing is all about. The following section allows you to determine groupings that are used during this process.

7.3.1   Determine Grouping for Employee Expenditures at the Subsystem

This grouping establishes which groupings of personnel can charge various items via a badge or swipe card. The postings are transferred to SAP Time Events via Time Event P50. If you refer back to Figure 7.1, you can see that Time Event P50 is an identifier for an external Wage type. The groupings configured under this step become part of the master data selection in Infotype 0050. The employee expenses grouping field is where this configuration is shown on the employee master data.

The following section allows you to define the level of detail that can be utilized when using employee expenditures.

7.3.2 Maintenance of Wage Types

Wage types are the methodology by which expenditures are deducted from an employee's payroll. This configuration links the grouping for expenditures to a Wage type that will ultimately end up on Infotype 0015 Additional Payments and Deductions, or Infotype 2010 Employee Remuneration Information. It is in this step that you could, for example, define all of the various levels or descriptions of employee expenses, such as meals, company store purchases, etc.

This concludes our review of the entire configuration for Personnel Time Events. We discussed interfacing to various subsystems so that they can collect employee time information. The next section shows you the various reports that can be run to select data from the SAP system to send to various subsystems.

7.4 Interface Processing via Subsystem Connections

This section goes into more detail regarding the processing of information to and from the third-party time-keeping subsystems. You may decide to use all or just a few of the specific reports that are shown based on your requirements and the actual amount of data that your subsystems require. The report names basically explain the functionality they provide. For example, report RPTCC105 is called Download Time Event Groupings. This means it takes your configuration, downloads it from the SAP system and makes it available to be uploaded or interfaced into various subsystems. Figure 7.4 shows the data flow from the SAP system to the subsystems and then back to the SAP system.

Now let's have a look at Figure 7.5, which shows the specific reports that are covered in the rest of this chapter. As you can see from Figure 7.5, we listed the various programs that flow out of the SAP system to the subsystems. Please note that the dotted box represents the SAP processing.

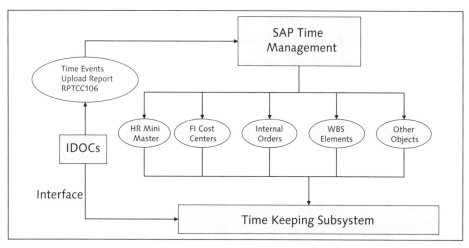

Figure 7.4 Generic View of the Data Flow to the Third-party Time Collection Subsystem

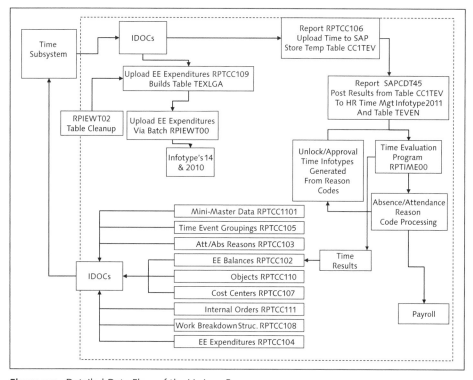

Figure 7.5 Detailed Data Flow of the Various Programs

Now let's review the various processing from the subsystem connections via Transaction code PT80.

7.5 Transaction Code PT80 Time Events

The first area we will cover is the subsystem connection that is displayed form Transaction code PT80. As you can from Figure 7.6, information is provided regarding the connection between the SAP system and the subsystems.

Communication log	Time events	Employee expend.	Logistics integr.

Log of Communication Between Subsystem and SAP System

🕐 Times of transfer

Logical system	Description	Date	Time
			00:00:00
			00:00:00
			00:00:00

Figure 7.6 Overview of Transaction Code PT80

As seen in Figure 7.6, there are four tabs that are available for the various processing programs:

▶ **Communication Log** – Displays the communication data between the SAP system and the subsystem

▶ **Time Events** – Allows the user to manually process Time Events in related data to and from the third-party time collection system

▶ **Employee Expenditures** – Allows the user to manually process employee expenditures to and from the third-party time collection system

▶ **Logistics Integration** – Allows the user to manually process information sent from SAP's Logistics component

Let's take a look at the second tab – Time Events. Figure 7.7 shows the tab for Time Events. We referenced the particular programs next to each button. As we discussed in the first half of this chapter, certain data can be sent to the subsystem. Each of these reports lists the kind of data that can be sent.

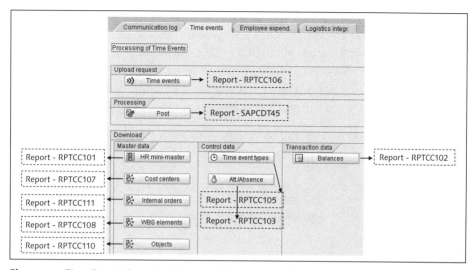

Figure 7.7 Time Events Overview Screen and the Various Delivered Programs That Are Attached to Each Command Button

Report RPTCC106 communicates a request for uploading Time Events from the third-party time collection system. The Time Events that have been entered into the time-keeping system are then uploaded into table CC1TEV (see Figure 7.8).

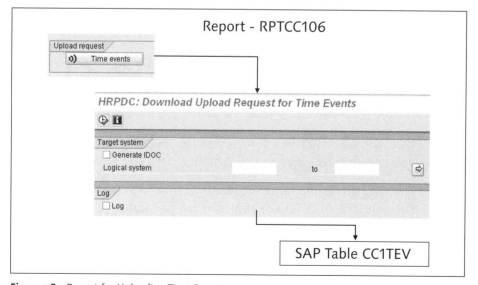

Figure 7.8 Report for Uploading Time Events

This report pulls in the data from table CC1TEV and stores the information on Infotype 2011 Time Events. After the successful posting of such Time Events they are then removed from the table CC1TEV. Occasionally, certain Time Events will fail to post to Infotype 2011. They remain in table CC1TEV for future posting runs to occur. The most likely reason of such a failure is due to the master data record being locked for master data maintenance at the point of posting.

The next report, SAPCDT45 in Figure 7.9, is used to process the various Time Events that were uploaded into the system.

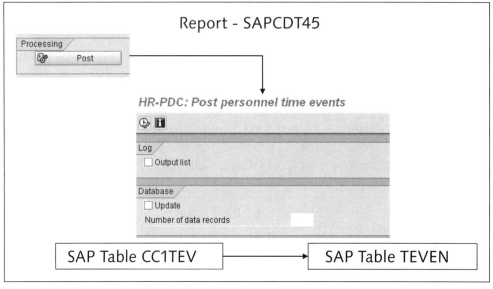

Figure 7.9 Report for Posting the Time Events from the Events Temporary Table CC1TEV

Report RPTCC101, shown in Figure 7.10, is used for downloading the mini-master file. The mini-master download uses the IDOC basic type HRCC1DNPERSO01.

There are 24 fields that are populated in the IDOC to send to the third-party time collection system. The fields and descriptions can be located in the system via Transaction code WE60. The IDOC gathers its information from Infotype 0001, Organizational Assignment; Infotype 0002, Personal Data; and Infotype 0050, Time Recording Information.

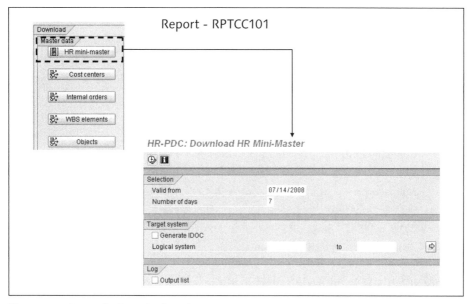

Figure 7.10 Report for Downloading the HR Mini-master

There are numerous fields in the mini-master that are available for you to download. Table 7.1 provides a quick reference of the available fields.

#	Field	Source	#	Field	Source
1	Logical system	Manual Insert	2	Time Recording ID Number	Infotype 0050
3	Start Date		4	End Date	
5	ID Version	Infotype 50	6	Personnel Number	
7	Formatted Name of Employee		8	Employee Name	
9	Language Key		10	ISO Language	
11	Personnel Subarea Grouping for Abs/Att Types		12	Country Grouping	
13	Grouping for Connection to Subsystem	Infotype 0050	14	Employee subgroup grouping for work schedule	

Table 7.1 Fields Available in the IDOC

#	Field	Source	#	Field	Source
15	Access Control Group	Infotype 0050	16	Personal Code	Infotype 0050
17	Mail Indicator	Infotype 0050	18	Grouping for Att/Abs Reasons	Infotype 0050
19	Grouping for Employee Expenses	Infotype 0050	20	Work Time Event Type Group	Infotype 0050
21	Company Code	Infotype 0001	22	Cost Center	Infotype 0001
23	Multi-Purpose Field time Results Confirmation		24	Customer Specific Field	

Table 7.1 Fields Available in the IDOC (Cont.)

Report RPTCC107 is utilized to download the cost centers from the SAP system. This report allows you to download the cost centers from the SAP system and send them to the third party time collection system so that employee's can enter time against various cost centers for work they are doing. Figure 7.11 shows the report selection screen.

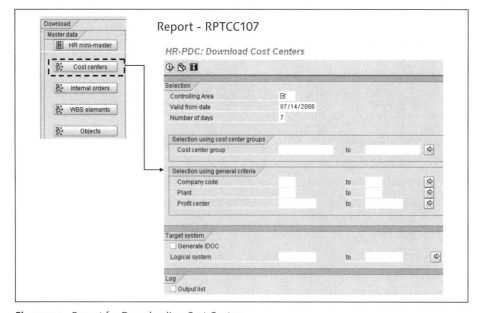

Figure 7.11 Report for Downloading Cost Centers

The next report deals with the ability to download internal orders.

Report RPTCC111 allows you to download internal orders from the SAP system and send them to the third-party time collection systems. You would use the report if the SAP Projects System's component required that employees allocate their time to internal order. Figure 7.12 shows the report.

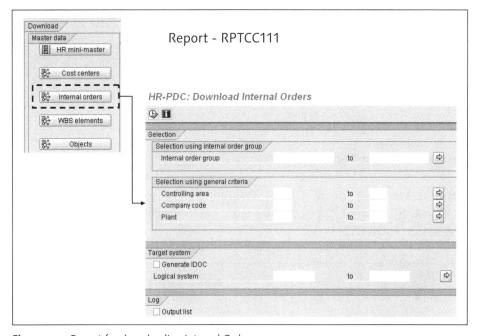

Figure 7.12 Report for downloading Internal Orders

The next report we will cover is report RPTCC108, which is used to download Work Breakdown Structure (WBS) elements. These breakdown structures allow you to assign your time so that they can be tracked against the structure defined in the Logistics component. Figure 7.13 shows the report.

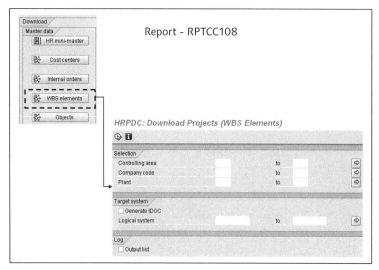

Figure 7.13 Report for Downloading WBS Elements

The next report is report RPTCC110. This report allows you to download particular objects from the SAP system and send them to the third-party time collection system (see Figure 7.14).

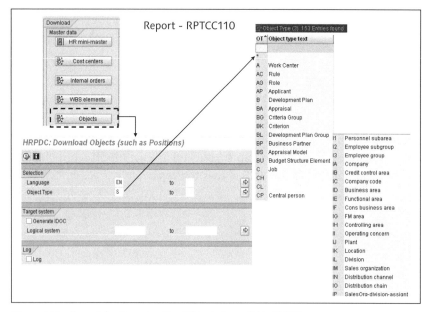

Figure 7.14 Report for Downloading Objects from Table T528B

Report RPTCC105 determines which time event type groupings are displayed on the third-party time collection system terminals. These groupings were defined in the first three sections of the IMG configuration. Figure 7.15 shows the report.

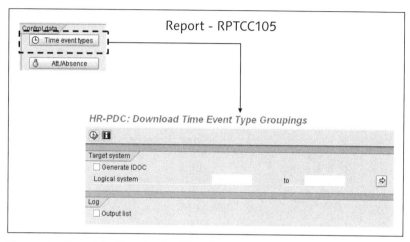

Figure 7.15   Report for Downloading Time Event Type Groupings

Earlier in this chapter we reviewed how reason codes can drive what kind of clock entry the employee is entering into the time system. Once you create your configuration, or make changes to existing configuration, you can use report RPTCC103 to download the reason codes. Figure 7.16 shows the report.

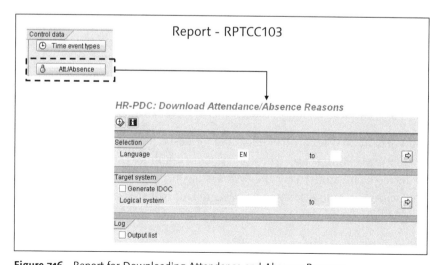

Figure 7.16   Report for Downloading Attendance and Absence Reasons

The final report under the Time Events tab is to download employee balances, such as the overtime hours we discussed earlier in the chapter (see Figure 7.17). Report RPTCC102 is used to send an employee's Time Evaluation results to the third-party subsystems.

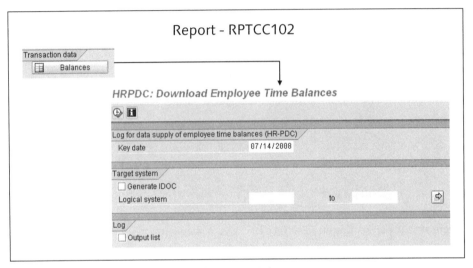

Figure 7.17 Report for Downloading Employee Time Balances

This concludes the listing of reports that are delivered under the Time Events tab. The third tab of Transaction PT80 is for employee expenditures.

7.6   Transaction Code PT80 Employee Expenditures

The Employee Expenditures tab has various reports that can be called directly from Transaction code PT80. Figure 7.18 shows an overview of the Employee Expenditure tab and lists each of the report names that are available.

Let's begin with the first report for uploading requests. Report RPTCC109 is used to request that the external time-keeping system submit any employee expenditures that have been captured by the SAP system for processing. This program uploads the various employee expenditures and stores the data on table TEXLGA (see Figure 7.19).

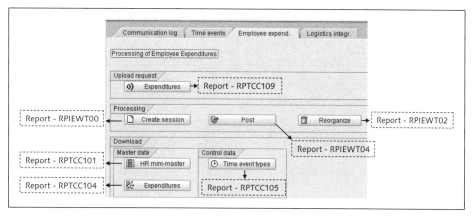

Figure 7.18 The Employee Expenditures Overview Screen and the Programs That Are Attached to Each Command Button

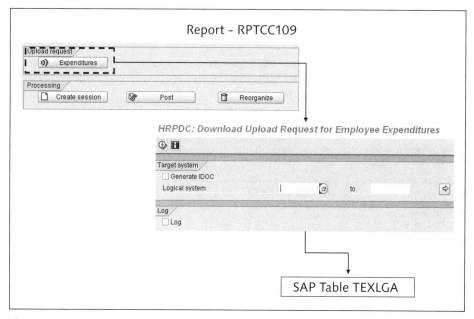

Figure 7.19 Report to Upload Expenditures

After the employee expenditures have been uploaded to the SAP system, the next step is to begin processing the data so that it can be stored on the employee's master data record. Report RPIEWT00 is used to create the input sessions that are used to create the records for the employees. Figure 7.20 shows the report.

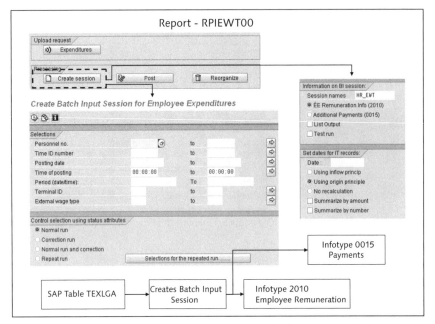

Figure 7.20 The Report to Create Batch Input Sessions for the Creation of Infotype 0015, Additional Payments, and Infotype 2010, Employee Remuneration

Once you have created the input data via the report in Figure 7.21, it is time to use report RPIEWT04 to process the data from the previous step. This processing is the step where the records are created on the employee's master data record.

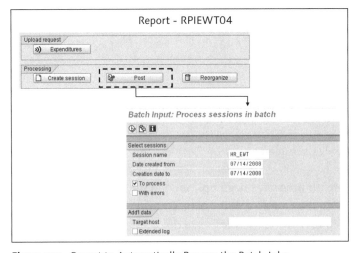

Figure 7.21 Report to Automatically Process the Batch Jobs

Every now and then, it is good to conduct some system maintenance to clear out old data. Our next report is provided to help in that endeavor. Report RPIEWT02 is used to delete any employee expenditures from the temporary tables that have already been processed and loaded onto the employee's record (Figure 7.22).

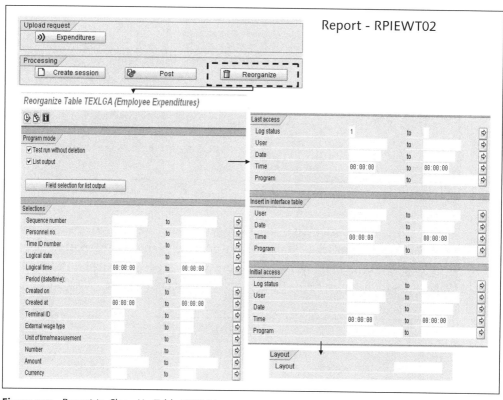

Figure 7.22 Report to Clean Up Table TEXLGA

The next report is the same report that you saw under the Time Events tab. This report, RPTCC101, is used to download the various master data fields that your subsystem might require (Figure 7.23).

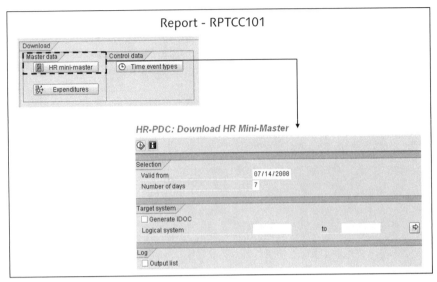

Figure 7.23 Report to Download the HR Mini-Master File

Similar to sending master data, you also need to send the subsystems the various employee expenditures that employees are allowed to enter. The report RPTCC104 is used to send the employee expenditure Wage types and eligibility for those Wage types to the subsystem. This report can be seen in Figure 7.24.

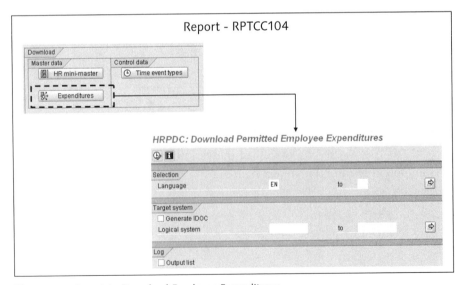

Figure 7.24 Report to Download Employee Expenditures

There is one final report that you can run under the Employee Expenditures tab. Report RPTCC105, which can also be viewed under the Time Events tab, sends the subsystems the various groups for Time Events that you have created (Figure 7.25).

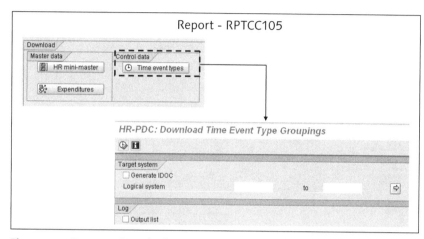

Figure 7.25 Report to Download Time Event Type Grouping

7.7 Transaction Code PT80 Logistics Integration

The fourth and final tab for Transaction code PT80 is for integration between SAP Time Management and the SAP Logistics component. These reports follow the same basic premise as before in that you can download and upload data between the components. Figure 7.26 shows the Logistics Integration tab and the various reports that are delivered by the SAP system.

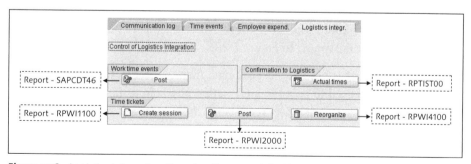

Figure 7.26 Logistics Integration Overview Screen and the Various Reports

Let's begin with the first report for uploading Time Events from Logistics. Report SAPCDT45 is used to request that the Logistics Component submit Time Events to Time Management. The report used to initiate the posting of Time Events is stored in table EVHR by the Logistics component into the Time Management component or Infotype 2011 (Figure 7.27).

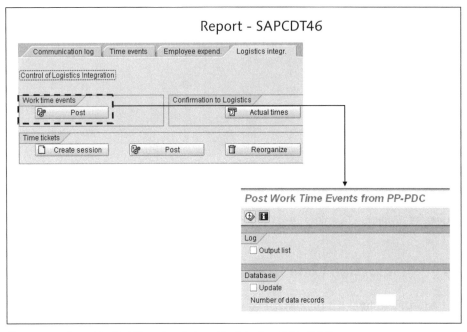

Figure 7.27 Report to Post Time Events from the Interface Table EVHR

After we have made the request for data from the Logistics component, we then need to process the information so that it can be stored in Time Management. Report RPWI1100 creates a batch input session that, when executed, will retrieve the logistics confirmations and store then as either Time Tickets or attendances. Let's have a look at the report in Figure 7.28.

The following report is used to post the data that was generated in Figure 7.28. Report RPWI200 is used to post the information obtained from the Logistics component and create the master data records for the employees. Figure 7.29 shows the report.

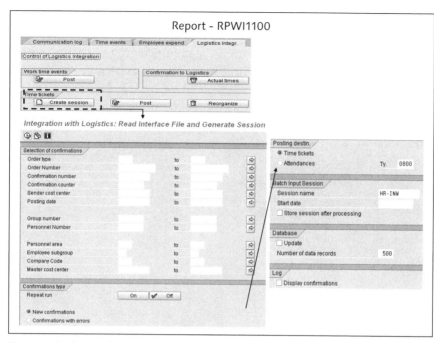

Figure 7.28 Report That Generates the Batch Input Session Using the Interface Table between HR and Logistics

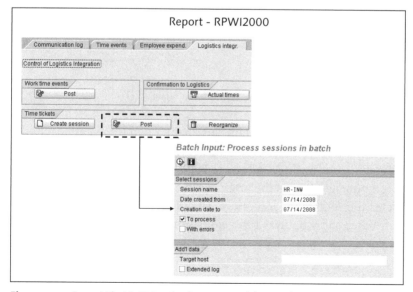

Figure 7.29 Report That Initiates the Processing of the Batch Input Sessions

Similar to the Employee Expenditures tab, the SAP system also offers a maintenance tool to clean up and delete old data that has been transferred between the two SAP components. Report RPWI4100 is the maintenance utility that reorganizes the table between Logistics and Time Management as seen in Figure 7.30.

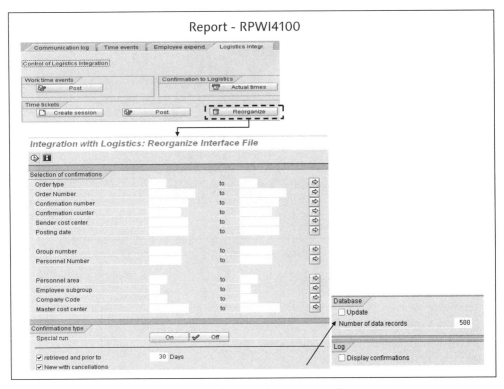

Figure 7.30 Report That Reorganizes the HR and Logistics Interface

There have been a lot of reports shown in this chapter and we are almost done. The final report is RPTIST00 (Figure 7.31). This report is used to send actual work times determined in Time Evaluation back to Logistics for comparison purposes. The logistics component contains the original Time Events; however, Time Evaluation calculates the time more accurately. The difference between what Time Evaluation calculates and what was received is sent back to Logistics.

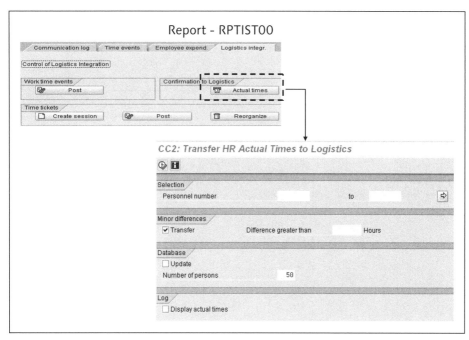

Figure 7.31 Report Comparing Values of Time from Logistics and HR and Transfers

This concludes our review of the various reports within Transaction code PT80.

7.8 Summary

In this chapter, you learned about the concepts surrounding the setup and process-ing of Personnel Time Events to and from a third-party time collection subsystem. There is additional information surrounding the processing of Personnel Time Events provided in Chapter 8, "Time Evaluation with Clock Times." A key point to remember is to be very thorough when testing new time entries, changes to time entries, and deletions of time entries that enter into the SAP system from outside time-keeping systems.

In the next chapter we will explain the functionality surrounding Time Evaluation with Clock Times.

In this chapter, you will learn about key areas to consider when configuring Time Evaluation with Clock Times functionality.

8   Time Evaluation with Clock Times

Time Evaluation is a program in SAP ERP HCM that allows the system to process time-related data on employee master data infotypes. The processing usually takes place daily, and the program evaluates the data and generates and updates data in the system. Both Time Evaluation with Clock Times and Time Evaluation without Clock Times, which we'll cover in the next chapter, share the same operational program, but there are differences in their processing. We will not analyze every personnel calculation rule in this chapter, but you should be knowledgeable of the core concepts and how to set up and process Time Evaluation with Clock Times by the time we're through.

Throughout this chapter, we will focus on the following examples:

▶ Generating absence and attendance Wage types

▶ Calculating and generating overtime Wage types

▶ Quotas that can be updated

▶ Custom calculations

So let's begin looking at time evaluation. In general, Time Evaluation is done for those companies that wish to calculate specific time so that payroll can compensate employees for hours worked. Within Time Evaluation, you can set the system up to generate overtime based on all of the regular time that has been entered into the system.

Time Evaluation is usually scheduled for every day; however, if any data is entered into the system that is earlier than the last date on which Time Evaluation has run, then the system can force a retroactive processing to pick up any historical changes that might impact any calculations of time. Infotype 0003 Payroll Status is used for both Payroll and Time Evaluation to determine if various programs need to use an earlier date other than the current date for processing. Historical record changes automatically set the date in Infotype 0003. Time Evaluation looks for these dates to determine the first date of processing for a particular employee. Time Evaluation, like Payroll, utilizes this infotype to determine how far back to go for each employee, however, the infotype has designated fields so that Time Evaluation will know how far back to process — and so will Payroll. Each program could retro for different reasons.

For example, let's say an employee was paid 38 hours for regular time this week. After receiving his paycheck, he determines he forgot to enter, or the manager forgot to approve, one of the day's time entries. The employee is short four hours. Today's date is June 15 and somebody went back to June 11 and either enter or approve the time. What will be the date value of Infotype 0003 so that Time Evaluation knows when to start processing? June 11 is set. When Time Evaluation begins for this employee, June 11 is the first date that is processed. As Time Evaluation catches up, the employee now receives two hours of overtime for the payroll check that he just received. During the next payroll, the employee will receive the additional amount.

Throughout this chapter, we will reference time tables that are used to store Time Evaluation results. For example, the ZL table holds Wage types that are generated in Time Evaluation and are passed to Payroll to compensate employees for their hours worked. Appendix E lists all of the various tables and the fields within the tables.

Key Management Decision Points — Time Evaluation with Clock Times

The following items are key decision points for the implementation of Time Evaluation with Clock Times:

▶ Determine if the use of third-party time collection systems will send unevaluated time or if the portal's clock-in and clock-out functionality will capture Time Events. If either of these cases is true, then you need to implement Time Evaluation with Clock Times. Sufficient time should be placed in the overall project plan to allow for the complexity and testing of this clock time functionality to ensure that not only are the calculations correct, but that you've also had ample time to conduct negative testing to ensure all employees are processed correctly.

▶ The scope by which SAP ERP HCM Time Management has been laid out dictates how complex your Time Evaluation customization will become. Normally, union regulations determine most of the custom calculations, however, it should be emphasized that even minor, non-union business rules take time to set up.

▸ Time Evaluation only processes for active employees. This means that the STAT2 (Employment status) value for Infotype 0000 Actions must be a '3' (Active) in order for Time Evaluation to process. You will need to keep this in mind when determining your Time Management and Payroll requirements to ensure that you are not creating gaps in functionality by placing employees in an inactive status, but yet needed to process Time Evaluation.

8.1 Schema Terminology

Before we move ahead, it might be helpful to quickly review some key terms you've been exposed to and introduce you to some new ones you'll come across in this chapter.

▸ **RPTIME00** — The actual program that is used to process Time Evaluation. The program is where the schema is called. You can run different versions of the schema with the same program.

▸ **Schemas** — Delivered and customized processing procedures used to calculate, evaluate, and store time-related data. SAP delivers numerous functions that process set pieces of ABAP code, called delivered rules, and customer-specific functionality.

▸ **Subschemas** — Delivered and customized processing procedures similar to schemas. Subschemas allow the main schema to call sets of code and logic that are grouped together for like functionality.

▸ **Functions** — Delivered functionality used to process very specific elements of functionality.

▸ **Personnel calculation rules** — Delivered and customizable pieces of code logic called by a function.

▸ **Variable keys** — An element of a personnel calculation rule where by the answer to a decision is found. This is the left side of a personnel calculation rule that enables the rule to find a particular section of logic to process.

▸ **Operations** — Delivered logic that is embedded into a personnel calculation rule to accommodate specific processing. A personnel calculation rule can have numerous operations in one rule. Each operation is processed prior to the next operation. Operations have various settings that can be specified to drive the outcome of the processing.

You'll come across these terms frequently, so keep them in mind. Now let's get started with Time and Payroll Constants and other useful programs that will provide you with the tools to help in your design, processing, and support of the system.

8.2 Listing of Time and Payroll Constants

The following is a list of constants tables that house both delivered and custom constant values. These tables are available when creating custom rules to hold various amounts for calculations in your schemas. SAP delivers these constants tables to aid in their program processing and they are available for your use as well. One example would be to set up a Constant XXXXX with a value of eight hours. You could then take your Time Evaluation rules for daily overtime and compare the amount worked against eight hours. Instead of hard coding eight hours in the rules, you have a table entry in the constant table that can be changed should the law regarding eight hours change to nine hours.

▶ V_T510H — Payroll Constants for Time Unit

▶ V_T510J — Constant Valuations

▶ V_T510K — Constant Valuation of Wage types

▶ V_T510P — Premium Table

▶ V_T511K — Payroll Parameters

▶ V_T511P — Payroll Parameters

In addition to the various Constants tables that you might find handy, we have included other useful programs that aren't directly linked to transaction codes. These may be useful as you learn to use the system.

8.3 Useful Programs

There are a number of programs that can be useful when you are working with schemas and rules. For example, if you are creating your own personnel calculation rule and plan to use a specific operation, you can run this program to see how that particular operation may be used in existing calculation rules. This can give you some ideas about how to use them in addition to what you'll find in the help text. The programs in the following list allow you to display rules or update parameters of rules, such as who is the owner.

▶ RPCPE02N — Displays personnel calculation rules in editor mode.

▶ RPDASC00 — Displays the whole schema and allows you to download to a text file.

▶ RPUCTC00 — Lists all of the personnel calculation rules.

▶ RPUCTF00 — Allows you to change the attributes of a rule or schema. This is helpful in case changes to a rule are needed and the user locked the rule so that only updates by their user ID are possible.

▶ RPUCTJ00 — Displays personnel calculation rules that are not utilized in a schema.

▶ RPUCTX00 — Copies rules from the client 000.

▶ RPUCYD00 — Displays a directory of all of the personnel calculation rules.

Now let's move on to the configuration in the Implementation Guide (IMG) that supports Time Evaluation with Clock Times. The following section begins the configuration of the schema.

8.4   Configuration and Schema Overview

We'll start with an in-depth look at the various sections of Time Evaluation Schema TM00 — Time Evaluation with Clock Times. You will use these frequently, so it's important to have a good understanding of them.

8.4.1   General Settings

The general settings section provides configuration tools, including the following sections. When you are setting up Time Evaluation, you need to set up each of these sections based on your requirements. These sections can be found in the IMG under the menu path TIME MANAGEMENT • TIME EVALUATION WITHOUT CLOCK TIMES.

Let's begin with the first step of configuration — settings for pair formation.

Define Settings for Pair Formation

Time Pairs are the foundation for clock time entries from time entry terminals where employees clock in and clock out throughout a work day. We spoke of Infotype 2011 Time Events and the various codes that determine the type of time entered in Chapter 7. Those codes process statuses and are used to develop Time Pairs during Time Evaluation with Clock Times processing. Figure 8.1 shows some of the processing statuses.

PS...	Status	Processing status text	Start Date	End Date	Reaction
01	A00	Repeated posting of time events	01/01/1900	12/31/9999	
01	A01	First record of day	01/01/1900	12/31/9999	
01	A03	Employee has day off - start/end of day is ...	01/01/1900	12/31/9999	
01	A04	Employee has day off - start/end of day is ...	01/01/1900	12/31/9999	
01	A05	Time events which follow in quick succes...	01/01/1900	12/31/9999	
01	A06	Value limit for time events which follow in ...	01/01/1900	12/31/9999	
01	A07	Assigning a Time Event to the Current or ...	01/01/1900	12/31/9999	
01	A10	Clock-in or clock-out	01/01/1900	12/31/9999	

Figure 8.1 Plant Data Collection Processing Statuses

Most third-party bolt-on time-keeping systems also advertise that they use these codes as well so that integration between the systems is easier to maintain. You should validate this with your external time system.

The next section of configuration under the general settings is to establish when Time Evaluation processes.

Schedule Time Evaluation

Time Evaluation is usually run every night. Like all programs within the SAP system, you can define variants for the program to use when processing. Examples of data that might be within the variant include payroll area and time statement form. You schedule the job to run overnight for each variant that needs to be processed.

The following section of the general settings is to establish what the earliest date Time Evaluation will run.

Set Modifier for Earliest Recalculation Date and Set Earliest Recalculation Date for Pair Formation and Time Evaluation

The earliest date that Time Evaluation is run is controlled by a table entry and Feature TIMMO, which reads that particular table entry. The next two sections of the IMG work together to form the earliest date in which Time Evaluation can process. For example, let's say you have used the SAP system for the last year, but only for maintaining master data with both Time Management and Payroll outsourced. Your company then decides to bring Time Management and Payroll into the SAP system instead of using third-party vendors. When you are ready to go live with Time Management and Payroll, you would only want the system to retro back to the first day that you are live with the new functionality. To accomplish this, you can set the date and link it to a code. In Figure 8.2, you set the date of the new functionality and link it to code 01. You would then utilize Feature TIMMO and link your employees to the 01 code so that they use the earliest date for running Time Evaluation. This would prevent the system from processing any time that may have been entered prior to the Time Management and Payroll go-live date.

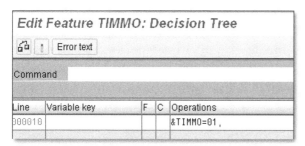

Figure 8.2 Earliest Recalculation Date

The following configuration step is used to establish the period for Time Evaluation.

Determine Time Evaluation Period

The system is set up for monthly processing and it is recommended not to change this.

The next section of the IMG is for configuring Time Evaluation settings.

8.4.2 Time Evaluation Settings

You can use Time Evaluation settings to set up four basic areas that Time Evaluation utilizes during processing. The Time Evaluation settings section of configuration is comprised of the following:

► Personnel Subarea grouping for Time Recording

► Group Employee Subgroups for the personnel calculation rule

► Set Employee groupings for the Time Evaluation rule

► Define Time types

Let's look at each of these in more detail.

Personnel Subarea Grouping for Time Recording

Chapter 2, "Time Management Blueprint Considerations," provided a listing of Time Management functionality and the various components of the HCM structures that are the primary keys to determining the configuration tables. The Time Recording information is a grouping of Personnel Areas and Personnel Subareas. By setting this grouping, the Personnel Areas/ Subarea combination utilizes the same Time types, time transfer specification from Infotype 2012, access control groups, and message types. By using these groupings, you can parse out various groups of employees that may need to utilize these different items, such as Time types. For example, let's say you have one Personnel Area called East coast, with two Personnel Subareas. Should you break them out into two different groupings? If you have a really valid business reason then this might be a good option.

But, let's say that Personnel Subarea 0001 uses all of the Time types defined within the grouping. Personnel Subarea 0002 only uses 50% of those Time types. Should you create two grouping so that Personnel Subarea 0002 only has those Time types that it normally uses? The answer really depends on how much configuration you would like to do in the system. If you want to create different groupings for Time types, you should also consider the ramifications of that decision on other areas of configuration that also use these particular groupings. For example, if you were to break out the time recording groupings into grouping 50 for Personnel Subarea 0001 and grouping 60 for Personnel Subarea 0002, you would then need to create all of the Time types within each grouping 50 and 60. You would also need to replicate configuration into both groupings for time transfer specifications, access control groups, and message types. This would cause an unnecessary amount of configuration and ongoing maintenance. Besides, as you will learn later in this chapter, employees don't have direct access to Time types because they are an element utilized within Time Evaluation processing.

Let's move on to setting up employee subgroups for personnel calculation rules.

Group Employee Subgroups for the Personnel Calculation Rule

Personnel calculation rules are items used within Time Evaluation to process calculations for various groups of employees. Typically, your hourly group may have a different set of rules than your salaried group. But do you really want to make a decision about each and every rule to determine what kind of employee you are processing? Probably not. So, by utilizing Employee Subgroup groupings for personnel calculation rules, you can establish, based on an Employee Group/Subgroup combination, a particular code that is used as a head of the personnel calculation rule to determine which part of the rule should be processed. Hourly employees typically have a 1 and your salaried population typically gets a 3. The personnel calculation rules have one set of processing instructions for grouping 1 and potentially a different set of rules for grouping 3.

The next section of configuration is called Employee Groupings for the Time Evaluation Rule

Set Employee Groupings for the Time Evaluation Rule

This section of configuration allows you to further define particular groups of employees. Because your business rule may not fit neatly into the Employee Group/Subgroup combinations, you have this opportunity to define codes and write custom personnel calculation rules to process a particular calculation for the employees. The codes defined here are associated with an employee on Infotype 0050 Time Recording Information which was covered in Chapter 4, "Master Data."

Overview of Time Types

Time types are the buckets that Time Evaluation uses to store all time-related information. Time types can be used to drive payments to employees, provide decision points in the schema processing, or merely hold information for processing at a later time.

Figure 8.3 provides a list of some of the delivered Time types. You can also create your own; however, it is not a good idea to delete any of the standard Time types, because they may be called within the delivered personnel calculation rules causing you major issues with errors during Time Evaluation processing. A complete listing of Time types can be found via table V_T555A and can be accessed via Transaction code SM31.

Time Type	Description	Time Type	Description	Time Type	Description
0000	Utility time type 1	0200	Core time	0811	Leave deduction in hours
0001	Utility time type 2	0210	Core time Attendance	0812	Leave prev.month in hrs
0002	Planned time	0220	Core time Absence	0891	Time-off entitlement
0003	Skeleton time	0230	Core time Off-site	0892	Time-off ent.: Prev.month
0005	Flextime balance	0235	Core time violation	0893	Tm/lieu:month before last
0006	Flextime excess/deficit	0300	Unapproved overtime	0895	Transfer to 0893
0007	Flextime offset	0301	Overtime	0900	Daily overtime after x hr
0008	Flextime (prev. period)	0310	Overtime Attendance	0901	Weekly overtime
0010	Attendance	0320	Overtime Absence	0902	Weekly overtime
0020	Absence	0330	Overtime Off-site	0903	Utility tm.type: OT/week
0030	Off-site work	0406	Time-off quota 04	0904	Util.time EE/next week
0040	Overtime worked	0407	Overtime offset	0905	Sequence attendance days
0041	Overtime to compensate	0408	TimeOff/overtime prev.mo.	0906	Begin time working week
0042	Overtime to remunerate	0410	Time off from overtime	0907	Weekly overtime part-time
0043	Overtime basic/time off	0411	Overtime exceeding quota	0908	Overtime limit, part-time
0044	Guaranteed overtime hours	0420	Approved auxiliary work	0910	Guar.pair - start time
0045	OT isolated from DWS	0421	Aux.work exceeding quota	0911	Util.time type guar.- EE
0046	Overtime compensation day	0500	Break	0912	Begin planned block
0050	Productive hours	0510	Break Attendance	0913	End planned block
0051	Cumul.productive hours	0520	Break Absence	0914	Length max. GMA-pair/day
0080	Annual attendance days	0530	Break Off-site	0920	OT/Wk: Daily planned time
0090	Auto. leave accrual (=)	0540	Break paid	0921	OT/Wk: Prelim. overtime
0091	Auto. leave accrual (+)	0600	Absence on public holiday	0922	OT/Wk: Addit.planned time
0092	Quota gen. - actual time	0601	Holiday on a Sunday	0923	OT/Wk: Revised overtime
0093	Quota gen. - actual/plnd	0700	Transfer FLEX to overtime	0924	OT/Wk:Weekly planned time
0094	Transfer remaining quota	0701	Transfer overtime to FLEX	0925	OT/Wk: Weekly overtime
0095	Leave from previous year	0702	Revision off-site work	0926	OT/Wk: Add.wkly.plan.time
0097	Annual leave entitlement	0710	Repost flextime	0927	OT/Wk: Overtime
0098	Annual leave taken	0711	Repost overtime	0928	OT/Wk: Transfer spec.(wk)
0099	Remaining annual leave	0740	Overtime remuneration	0929	OT/Wk: Daily overtime
0100	Fill time	0800	Compensation time	0930	Util.time type att.flag
0110	Fill time Attendance	0801	Reduc.of compensation tm.	0931	Util.time type cost dist.
0120	Fill time Absence	0802	Comp.time - prev.month	0932	Cost distribution open
0130	Fill time Off-site	0810	Leave surplus in hours	0933	Cost distribution OK

Figure 8.3 Delivered Time Type Examples

Time types are not just four characters and some text. Each Time type has various settings that control how they are stored in the system. Figure 8.4 shows the configuration details of a Time type. You decide how the data is stored, whether it be daily or via a cumulative table. You can also set up Time types to determine how they are processed from previous periods and if the Time type will be stored so that the Time Management pool, which is discussed in Chapter 10, "Evaluation and Time Management Pool," can report on the particular Time types.

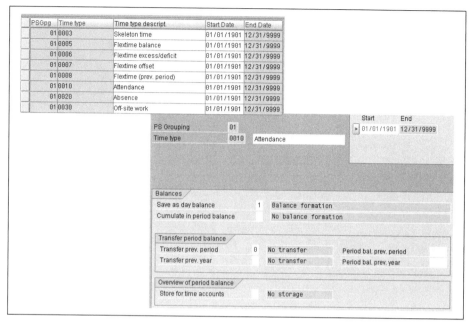

Figure 8.4 Definition of Time Types

We are now finished with the basic settings used in Time Evaluation processing. Now it's time to jump right into what a schema is comprised of and what the various sections of the schema do. The following section is the beginning of the schema setup. For Time Evaluation with Clock Times, we will use Schema TM00, which can be accessed via Transaction code PE01.

8.5   Time Evaluation Schemas

The Time Evaluation schemas are made up of subschemas, functions, personnel calculation rules, and operations. Each of these is processed according to either ABAP code delivered for the particular component, or to the customization that you put into the system. There is a logical sequence of processing within the schema that explains the order of the functions and where they reside within the schema. For example, you can't calculate overtime if you don't know how many regular hours an employee has worked. Therefore, we must follow a logical sequence of processing within the schema to ensure that we calculate everything correctly.

Figure 8.5 illustrates Schema TM00 — Processing Sections.

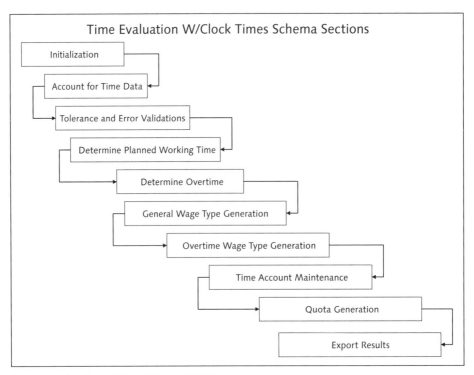

Figure 8.5 Sections of Time Schema TM00

All Time Evaluation schemas are broken down into various sections. The example about calculating overtime based on knowing regular hours worked represents delivered Schema TM00 — Time Evaluation with Clock Times. All schemas tend to share some basic characteristics and the methodology behind how the data processing is sequenced is basically the same, as you'll see when we discuss Schema TM04 — Time Evaluation without Clock Times in Chapter 9. What you find after reading both chapters and reviewing both schemas is that there are a lot of common elements to both. For example, both Schema TM00 and Schema TM04 need to gather time master data to determine attendances. Schema TM00 gathers its data from Infotype 2011 and Schema TM04 gathers data from Infotype 2002 Attendances. They are different infotypes, but the methodology of the infotype master data section is basically the same. There are some differences and those differences mainly stem from specific functionality that might be the main reason for the schema or subschema. For example, a schema or subschema may include various functions and calculation rules to generate messages for situations where an employee is missing a clock-out entry on a particular day. If you are running

Schema TM04, you shouldn't be processing clock times because the records entering the system from Infotype 2002 already have a defined number of hours.

Schema TM00 is broken down into the following processing sections:

- Initialization
- Accounting for time data
- Tolerances and error validations
- Determination of planned work time
- Determination of overtime
- General Wage type generation
- Overtime Wage type generation
- Time account maintenance
- Quota generation
- Exploration of the Time Evaluation results

Let's look at each of these parts of the Time Evaluation schema in detail, beginning with the initialization of the schema.

8.5.1   Initialization

This is the first step of the schema. There are basic validation points that are processed to determine what should be picked up in the schema.

One main ingredient of the equation is driven off of the Time Management status that resides in Infotype 0007 Planned Working Time. The following is a list of the delivered Statuses and a description of what each means.

- 0 — Indicates that Time Evaluation will not process.
- 1 — Indicates that Time Evaluation will processes for actual times entered. This is sometimes referred to as positive time entry whereby an employee only gets paid for time entered and processed in the system.
- 2 — Indicates that Time Evaluation will process for Plant Data Collection (PDC) time

- ▶ 7 — Indicates that Time Evaluation will process without integration to Payroll. This is utilized when outsourcing the payroll processing, however, it requires the SAP system to calculate the time-related hours for payment.

- ▶ 8 — Indicates that external services will be processed.

- ▶ 9 — Indicates that Time Evaluation will be processed for planned times. This is referred to as exception-based time recording. The employees would enter absences or attendance overrides to their basic work schedule. Time Evaluation would use the planned time in their Work Schedule to build the hours related to payment.

At the beginning of every schema, you will see the CHECK function. Of the various parameters available for this function, you can set up the initialization to select employees with the specific status covered earlier. SAP help explains all of the various parameters you can make for a given function or operation. You can view help by placing your cursor on the function or operation and selecting the F1 key, or utilizing Transaction code PE04 to view the documentation associated with each function or operation.

After you select which employees will process in a particular schema, it's time to establish some groupings that will be utilized throughout the schema.

8.5.2 Groupings for Time Management

If there's one thing that the Time Management functionality isn't lacking, it's groupings. It seems that there are groupings for just about everything, and it can be one of the hardest things to keep straight as you are setting up the system. While we are on the topic, let's discuss some other groupings.

SAP ERP HCM offers a personnel calculation rule that enables you to set groupings at the beginning of the schema. These groupings can be changed during subsequent processing based on specific requirements. The rule that sets the initial groupings is MODT and can be referenced via Transaction code PE02. You will notice that the groupings describe tables that hold data to support various processing. The groupings within the rule set the primary key for each of the tables listed. The following types of groupings can be established:

- ▶ W = Table T510S Wage Type Selection Rule
- ▶ T = Table T555Z Time Type Determination Group

- A = Table T554C Absence Valuation Employee Grouping
- D = Table T510S Day Grouping for Wage Type Selection Rule
- S = Table T552W Dynamic Work Schedule Assignment
- Q = Table T559L Quota Type Selections
- L = Table T559P Time Balance Rule Group for Value Limits

Figure 8.6 provides an example of the personnel calculation rule MODT. In this example, you will notice a number 1 located at the top. Recall when we discussed that hourly employees typically process with a grouping 1 and salaried employees processes with group 3, you can see that this particular example is for an hourly employee.

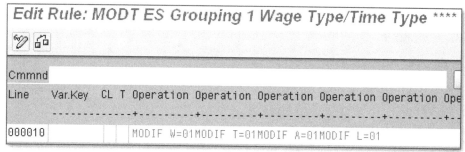

Figure 8.6 Example of the Personnel Calculation Rule That Determines the Groupings

Note

Please keep in mind that you are not required to use all of the hourly or salaried groupings; it really just depends on your particular situation.

You can also copy the rule, customize the rule according to your business requirements, and insert the new rule into the subschema to be processed. If you need to make changes to a standard rule, it is a Best Practice to make a copy and change your version. This way your changes will not be overwritten should SAP decide to make a change to the standard personnel calculation rule. Once you place your rule into the schema, you should comment out or delete the original entry in the subschema so that it will not be processed. You can use the * to comment out the rule, leaving it in the schema for reference purposes.

The next section of processing is to pull in Work Schedules and working time entered into the system.

8.5.3 Account for Time Data

This section of the schema processes the time-related information from the Time Management infotypes. In addition to the infotypes, Work Schedules play a large role in processing. Reduced working hours processing and general validation of the time entered are also processed. For example, if an employee enters his time at the warehouse by swiping his ID badge at a terminal, how is Time Evaluation going to get that clock-in entry? Prior to reaching Time Evaluation, his clock-in entry is stored on Infotype 2011. This particular section now pulls in that record, and all others for that particular day, and begins to process them to determine how may total hours were actually worked. Figure 8.7 shows this portion of the schema. Within this figure you'll see a description next to each function to give you an idea of the kind of processing occurring.

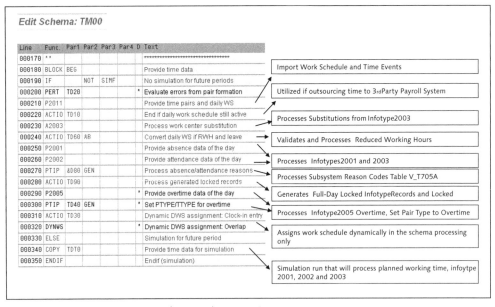

Figure 8.7 Schema Section for Providing Time Data

After you pull in all of the applicable master data for processing, it's now time to determine if everything looks okay, and then generate any messages, if necessary, to notify a time administrator of any issues.

8.5.4 Tolerances and Error Validations

This section of processing allows you to define what the tolerances are for particular calculations and when messages should be generated that will be stored in the messages table FEHLER of the B2 time cluster. For example, based on Work Schedule configurations, you may have set up a Work Schedule rule so that any Time Pair with a begin time within 15 minutes of the actual start time will be changed to the start time of the Work Schedule. This might be beneficial when large numbers of employees are trying to clock-in, because if there are not enough time clocks long lines can form. If the employee is in line, they shouldn't be punished for clocking in late because they had to wait in line. You can set up the SAP system to set the start times to whatever you need, and it can generate any type of messages you want. Figure 8.8 shows the section of the schema and describes each function.

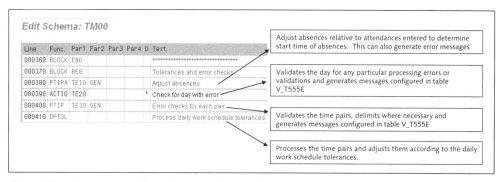

Figure 8.8 Schema Section for Tolerance and Error Checks

After you generate messages, the Determined Planned Time section of the schema is used to determine any elements of the Work Schedule rule that will help in the processing of employee data.

8.5.5 Determine Planned Time

This section of the schema takes into account your Work Schedule and those planned times that reside in the configuration behind the Work Schedule rule associated with the employee on a particular day of processing. As part of this processing, any Time Pairs that are in the system are translated into Time types and assigned various codes specific to absences or attendances. For example, a Time

Pair after processing through this section is changed to Time type 0010 — regular hours. Because it was an attendance, the Time type is flagged as an attendance. Figure 8.9 shows this section of the schema.

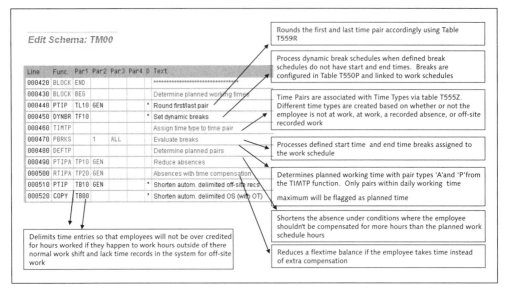

Figure 8.9 Schema Section for Determining Planned Time

8.5.6 Determination of Overtime

Figure 8.10 shows the various functions that can calculate overtime. This overtime is not related to calculating overtime based on any hours greater than 40 in a given work week. Instead, various settings on the employee's master data may dictate that overtime should be granted. For example, Infotype 0050 has a field called standard overtime. If this field was populated, you could have written a custom rule to generate a Time type with X amount of overtime hours based on your business rules.

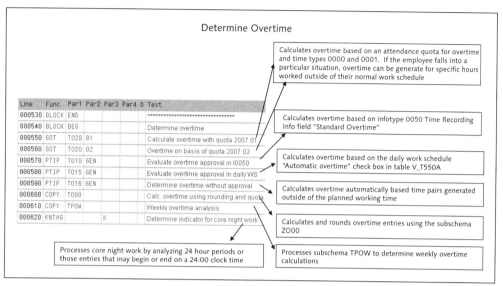

Determine Overtime

Calculates overtime based on an attendance quota for overtime and time types 0000 and 0001. If the employee falls into a particular situation, overtime can be generate for specific hours worked outside of their normal work schedule

Calculates overtime based on infotype 0050 Time Recording Info field "Standard Overtime"

Calculates overtime based on the daily work schedule "Automatic overtime" check box in table V_T550A

Calculates overtime automatically based time pairs generated outside of the planned working time

Calculates and rounds overtime entries using the subschema ZO00

Processes core night work by analyzing 24 hour periods or those entries that may begin or end on a 24:00 clock time

Processes subschema TPOW to determine weekly overtime calculations

Line	Func.	Par1	Par2	Par3	Par4	D	Text
000530	BLOCK	END					************************************
000540	BLOCK	BEG					Determine overtime
000550	GOT	T020	01				Calculate overtime with quota 2007 01
000560	GOT	T020	02				Overtime on basis of quota 2007 02
000570	PTIP	T010	GEN				Evaluate overtime approval in I0050
000580	PTIP	T015	GEN				Evaluate overtime approval in daily WS
000590	PTIP	T016	GEN				Determine overtime without approval
000600	COPY	T000					Calc. overtime using rounding and quota
000610	COPY	TPOW					Weekly overtime analysis
000620	KNTAG			K			Determine indicator for core night work

Figure 8.10 Attendance Quota Overtime Processing

At this point if the schema processing, the result of all of the various sections was to generate Time types. Now we need to translate those Time types into Wage types so that Payroll can use the Wage types to compensate the employees. Let's look at how to generate Wage types.

8.5.7 General Wage Type Generation

This section of the schema is for generating the actual Wage types passed to Payroll by storing them on the ZL table of the B2 time cluster. The B2 cluster is the storage location where all of the Time Evaluation results reside. The generation of Wage types takes into account table V_T510S — Time Wage type selection rule — whereby rules are established on when particular Wage types can be generated. For example, Time type 0010, which stands for regular time, may have been generated at some point in the schema processing. We need a mechanism to translate Time type 0010 to a Wage type. (An example is provided later in the chapter.) This section of the schema sets the groupings for employees so that they can access the appropriate time Wage type selection rules (see Figure 8.11).

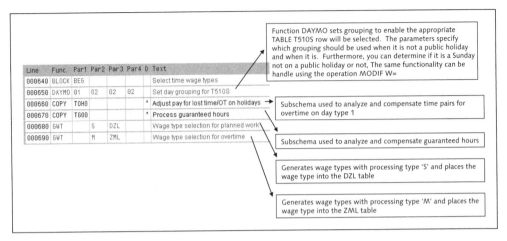

Figure 8.11 Schema Section for General Wage Type Generation

After you generate regular Wage types, the next section of the schema calculates any overtime based on hours worked.

8.5.8 Overtime Wage Type Generation

This section of the schema is for generating overtime Wage types based on delivered rules. More often than not, you will need to change the overtime calculations for the particular states that have 8-, 10-, and 12-hour shift laws surrounding compensation (see Figure 8.12).

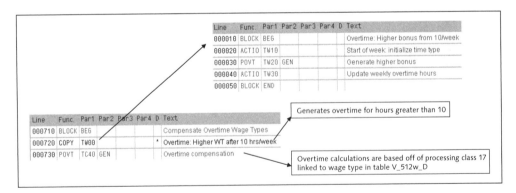

Figure 8.12 Schema Section for Overtime Wage Type Generation

8.5.9　Time Account Maintenance

This section of the schema process the day balances of the Time types. You can set rules for when to form the day balances and at what limit they should be created. You can also adjust any day balances or Wage types by using Infotype 2012 Time Transfer Types to enter the manual adjustments that are processed in the schema. In addition, this is also the section where Function QUOTA is processed. This function is for generating quotas and should only be called once in the schema (see Figure 8.13)

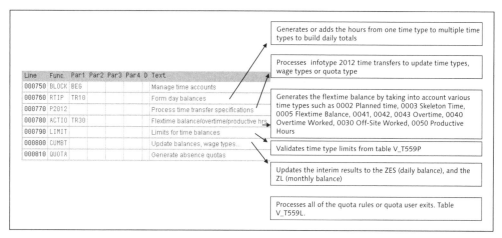

Figure 8.13　Schema Section for Time Account Maintenance and Quotas

After all of the Wage types have been created and Time type balances updated, the schema is almost done. The final section of the schema processing is to export the results to the B2 cluster.

8.5.10　Exporting the Time Evaluation Results

The final section of the schema takes all of the stored temporary data and writes the final results to the B2 time cluster for the particular day. When the data is written to the B2 cluster, the information is available for Time Management reporting (see Figure 8.14).

Line	Func.	Par1	Par2	Par3	Par4	D	Text
000830	EDAY						End of day processing
000840	* *						If last day of period
000850	BEND						Final processing
000860	IF			EOM			If last day of period
000870	P2007	TS20	GEN			*	Transfer excess flextime to overtime
000880	LIMIT						Adjust flextime balance
000890	ENDIF						Endif (last day of period)
000900	EXPRT						Export evaluation results
000910	EEND						End of processing block

Figure 8.14 Exporting the Time Revaluation Results

This concludes the overview of the various sections of the schema. Now we'll look at the various tables used during the processing.

8.6 Time Evaluation Table Details

Now that you have a general understanding of the various sections of a schema, let's have a look at some of the key tables that help enable the processing. This section is broken into three basic parts:

- Configuration Tables
- B2 Cluster Tables
- Internal Processing Tables

Let's begin by looking at the key configuration tables that support the schema processing.

8.6.1 Configuration Tables

There are various configuration tables used throughout the schema, but it's not possible to cover them all here, so we will only cover the key tables in this section. However, you will find a list of all of the tables in Appendix E, so be sure to reference that appendix as well. Let's begin with the Time type Determination table.

Time Type Determination

This table is called from Time Evaluation function TIMTP during the determination of planned time processing. The main goal of this table is to generate the appropriate Time type and associate it with the hours that are being processed. The Time type will be evaluated later to determine if a Wage type should be created. Table 8.1 includes the fields and descriptions of table V_T555Z.

Field	Description
PSG	Personnel Subarea grouping for time recording.
Group	Time type determination group. The employee is associated with this group ID via operation MODIF T = XX, where XX equals the group ID. This is set during the personnel calculation rule MODT.
ID	This identification code is associated with the daily Work Schedule and is generated automatically so that the appropriate line of table V_T555Z can be engaged. Examples include: 01 Overtime, 02 Fill Time, 03 Core Time, 04 Core Time Break, 05 Fill Time Break, 06 Paid Break, 07 Unpaid Infotype 2005 Break, 08 Paid Infotype 2005 Break, and 09 Overtime Break.
PType0	Used to determine the Time type when the employee is not at work.
TType0	The actual Time type associated with the record.
PType1	Used to determine the Time type when the employee is at work.
TType1	The actual Time type associated with the record.
PType3	Used to determine the Time type when the employee works off-site.
TType3	The actual Time type associated with the record.

Table 8.1 Fields and Descriptions from Table V_T555Z

Time types are generated via Time Evaluation with the help of table V_T555Z. Figure 8.15 shows the configuration table, and you can see the groupings on the left side of the table that we covered earlier in this chapter. The table is basically broken down into four sections distinguished by particular columns:

▸ PType0 — Pair type for not at work

▸ PTYP1 — Pair type for at work

▸ Ptype2 — Pair type for recorded absence

▸ Ptype3 — Pair type for off-site work

Each pair type has a corresponding Time type. This way, for a particular grouping of employees, you can assign Time types for when they aren't working, when they are working, when they are absent, or if they are working off-site.

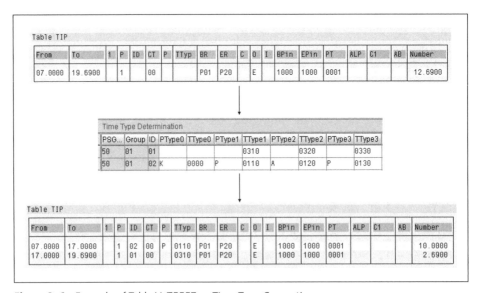

Change View "Time Type Determination": Overview

PSG...	Group	ID	PType0	TType0	PType1	TType1	PType2	TType2	PType3	TType3	Start Date	End Date
01	01	01				0310		0320		0330	01/01/1900	12/31/9999
01	01	02	K	0000	P	0110	A	0120	P	0130	01/01/1900	12/31/9999
01	01	03	K	0235	P	0210	A	0220	P	0230	01/01/1900	12/31/9999
01	01	04	K	0000	K	0510		0520	K	0530	01/01/1900	12/31/9999
01	01	05	K	0000	K	0510		0520	K	0530	01/01/1900	12/31/9999
01	01	06	K	0000	A	0540	A	0540	A	0540	01/01/1900	12/31/9999
01	01	07	K	0000	K	0510		0520	K	0530	01/01/1900	12/31/9999
01	01	08			M	0540	M	0540	M	0540	01/01/1900	12/31/9999
01	01	09	K	0000	K	0510		0520	K	0530	01/01/1900	12/31/9999
01	02	01	-		M	0310	A	0320	M	0330	01/01/1900	12/31/9999
01	02	02			S	0110	S	0120	S	0130	01/01/1900	12/31/9999
01	02	03			S	0210	S	0220	S	0230	01/01/1900	12/31/9999
01	02	04			K	0510		0520	K	0530	01/01/1900	12/31/9999

Figure 8.15 Time Type Determination Table V_T555Z

Figure 8.16 illustrates how the table is used during the processing.

Table TIP

From	To	1	P	ID	CT	P	TTyp	BR	ER	C	O	I	BPin	EPin	PT	ALP	C1	AB	Number
07.0000	19.6900	1			00			P01	P20		E		1000	1000	0001				12.6900

Time Type Determination

PSG...	Group	ID	PType0	TType0	PType1	TType1	PType2	TType2	PType3	TType3
50	01	01				0310		0320		0330
50	01	02	K	0000	P	0110	A	0120	P	0130

Table TIP

From	To	1	P	ID	CT	P	TTyp	BR	ER	C	O	I	BPin	EPin	PT	ALP	C1	AB	Number
07.0000	17.0000	1		02	00	P	0110	P01	P20		E		1000	1000	0001				10.0000
17.0000	19.6900	1		01	00		0310	P01	P20		E		1000	1000	0001				2.6900

Figure 8.16 Example of Table V_T555Z — Time Type Generation

You'll notice in Figure 8.16 that the employee's daily Work Schedule rule dictates that they should work 10 hours. In this example, in the Table TIP section, you'll see the From and To times. These are the clock-in and clock-out times that arrive via Infotype 2011 Time Events for 12.69 hours. The system looks at the Work Schedule to determine that the employee is scheduled and that there should be 10 hours on that day.

Because they are scheduled, the column PType1 is engaged and the record is split into two records. Ten hours of the record fall into identification code 02, which is Fill Time. In addition, the table associates the processing type of P with the record designating that as planned time and Time type 0110 is now associated with the record to be processed later in the schema. The remainder of the time, or 2.69 hours, is determined to be overtime based on the 10 hours from the daily Work Schedule. The record is associated with identification number 01 for overtime and is not associated with a processing type because there isn't one defined. The Time type 0310 is now associated with the record and can be processed according to the business processing rules later in the schema.

These Time types can be set up under the time Wage type selection rule table V_T510S to generate a Wage type, if necessary, or a custom personnel calculation rule could be written to generate the Wage type. So, let's look at the time Wage type selection rule next.

Time Wage Type Selection Rule

The time Wage type selection rule table is where the Time types that were generated earlier in the schema are now evaluated based on set criteria to determine if a Wage type should be generated. Table 8.2 provides the fields and descriptions of table V_T510S.

Field	Description
Time WT sel.rule grp	Defined in personnel calculation rule MODT, operation MODIF W = XX where XX is the grouping.
Day grouping	The DAYMO function, or personnel calculation rule MODT operation MODIF D = XX, where XX is the grouping sets, the grouping key for the table.

Table 8.2 Fields and Descriptions of Table V_T510S

Field	Description
Valid processing types	Codes associated with Time types throughout the schema processing. These codes allow you to further define when a Wage type should be generated.
Conditions Day	This is a series of criteria you can set to determine when a Wage type should be generated. You have the following options: ▸ Weekday ▸ Public holiday on the previous day ▸ Public holiday on the current day ▸ Public holiday on the subsequent day ▸ Valuation class ▸ Daily Work Schedule class ▸ Day type
Conditions Time	Similar to the daily conditions, you can also make certain conditions for the time of the day. You can specify the following: ▸ Start and end times ▸ Minimum and maximum time for a processing type ▸ Relevant processing types where you can look at all of the assigned processing types to determine the minimum and maximum amounts ▸ Interval checkbox that engages only if the minimum and maximum are between the two values
Control	The following options are available: ▸ Insert a fixed amount of hours ▸ Exit the rule if the condition is satisfied ▸ Stop time Wage type selection processing when a condition is met

Table 8.2 Fields and Descriptions of Table V_T510S (Cont.)

The time Wage type selection rule is used to determine when particular Wage types should be generated. In order for a Wage type to be generated, all of the conditions of the rule must be true. Figure 8.17 shows a sample Wage type selection rule.

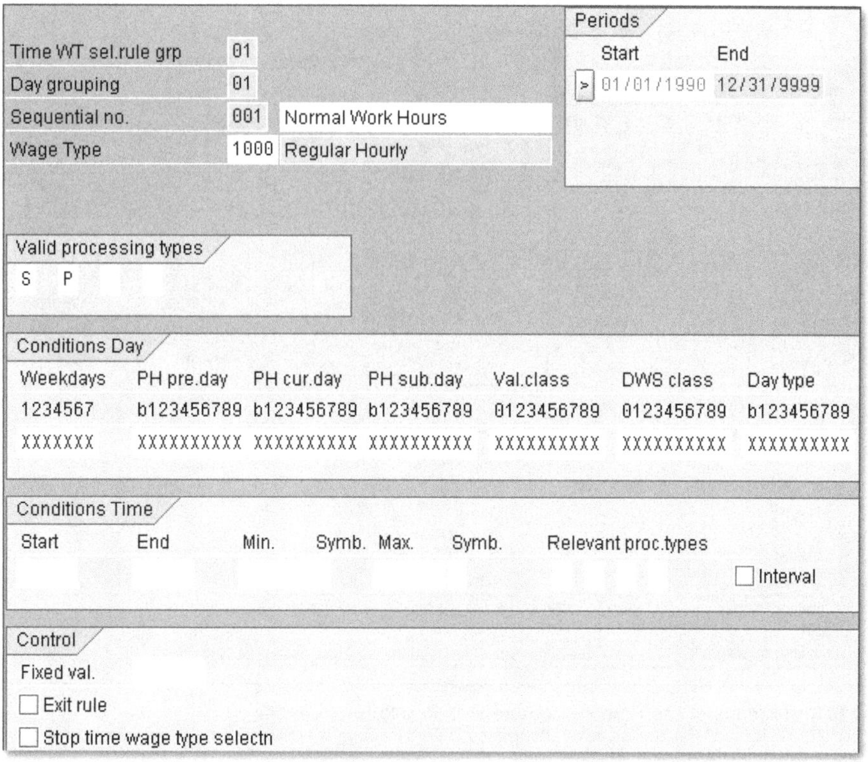

Figure 8.17 Time Wage Type Selection Rule

Now that you've seen the configuration of a rule, let's see what the rule looks like when processing in the schema. Figure 8.18 shows the time Wage type selection rule in action. You'll notice three entries on the first table — TIP. This is the input table. In this example, we'll follow the TIP entry for regular time designated by Time type 0110. You will also notice that Time type 0110 has a code of "S" in the column right next to the Time type. This designates it as planned time. The overtime Time type has an "M." Now look at the processing section in Figure 8.18. You'll see toward the top the words "Processing type" followed by SP. This is the first condition that must be met. Because our Time type 0110 has an "S," the condition is met and the next condition is processed. As you can see, there are numerous conditions that must be met in order for our Wage type to be generated. In our example, we were successful in turning an Infotype 2011 time entry into a Time type, and then into a Wage type that is now ready for Payroll.

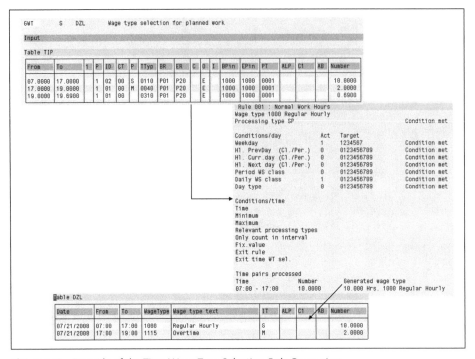

Figure 8.18 Example of the Time Wage Type Selection Rule Processing

In this example, we looked at processing type S, but there are also a number of other processing types that you should know about.

Processing Types

Processing types are codes assigned to Time Pairs within Time Evaluation. They are used for processing, evaluating, and generating Time types and Wage types throughout the Time Evaluation schema. They can either be inserted into a Time type using a table or by a personnel calculation rule using operation FILLPV for Time types (see Figure 8.19).

Let's switch gears and look at a way we can process all absences and attendances without calling each specific code for a particular absence or attendance in a custom rule. We can use table V_554S_E and associate the class field to a particular absence or attendance. By doing so, we can write a rule that takes any absences with a code of 02 and processes them differently than any absence with a class of 03. Table 8.3 provides the table fields names.

	Processing Type	Processing type text
	1	Availability < 10 %
	2	Availability < 25 %
	3	Availability < 40 %
	4	Availability < 49 %
	A	Absence
	C	On-call shift
	G	Guaranteed hours
	H	Assumed overtime
	J	Break for "as if" time
	K	Break
	M	Overtime
	N	Overtime (paid + comp)
	O	Overtime (comp only)
	P	Attendance
	R	On-call duty
	S	Planned work
	X	Public holiday

Figure 8.19 Table V_T510V Processing Types

Absence Evaluation V_554S_E

Field	Description
PSG	Personnel Subarea grouping for absences and attendances.
A/AType	Absence and attendance type.
Class	The Absence Evaluation class allows you to group similar absences for subsequent processing within Time Evaluation. A decision can be made using operation VARABCAT. Within the standard system the following codes have been utilized: ▶ 01 — If compensated absence is less than one working day, reduce the time once planned hours is reached ▶ 02 — If non-compensated absence is less than one working day, do not reduce the working time if planned time is reached ▶ 03 — Utilized for determining leave status

Table 8.3 Fields and Descriptions of Table V_554S_E

Field	Description
P/T (Processing Type/Time Type Class)	Used to group absences and attendances together for like processing. A decision can be made in Time Evaluation using operation OUTTPCLTIM for your custom rules. In addition, table T555Y can generate particular Time types based on the P/T assignment.

Table 8.3 Fields and Descriptions of Table V_554S_E

Figure 8.20 shows table V_554S_E.

Change View "Absence: Time Evaluation": Overview

Expand <-> Collapse   Delimit

	PSG	A/AType	A/A type text	Start Date	End Date	Class	P/T
	01	0100	Leave	01/01/1999	12/31/9999	03	
	01	0101	Leave IT0005	01/01/1990	12/31/9999	03	
	01	0110	Leave 1/2 day	01/01/1999	12/31/9999	03	
	01	0190	Educational leave	01/01/1990	12/31/9999	03	
	01	0200	Illness with certificate	01/01/1990	12/31/9999	02	
	01	0210	Illness w/o certificate	01/01/1990	12/31/9999	02	

Figure 8.20 Table V_554S_E Absence Evaluation

Sometimes, during the processing, we have to make exceptions for particular employees. These exceptions require us to alter particular time values during the schema processing. This is accomplished using time transfers.

Time Transfers

The time transfer specifications allow you to utilize Infotype 2012 Time Transfer Specifications to update three different buckets in Time Evaluation. By doing so, you can update the three types of buckets with an override amount that can be factored into the equation. For example, let's say your benefits department granted a bonus for hours worked and only those above 2,200 hours receive the year-end bonus. Your system is working just fine until a new hire negotiates a 1,000 hour credit toward their year-end total. How are you going to update the system for 1000 hours if the employee just started working? By using time transfers and writing a few custom rules, you can set up the system so that the Infotype 2012 entry of 1,000 hours will be added to the Time type bucket used to determine the year-end bonus eligibility. Figure 8.21 shows the various configuration options.

- Time types
- Wage types
- Quota types

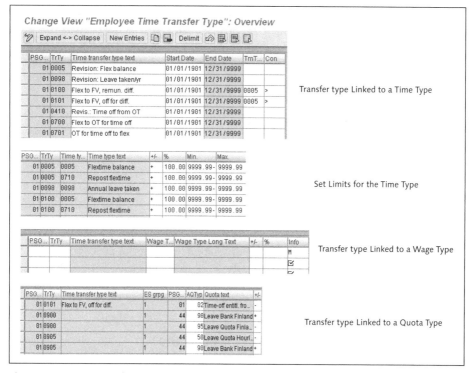

Figure 8.21 Time Transfer Configuration Tables

The next section allows you to define limits for Time types.

Limits Table

Table V_T559P allows you to specify limits for time balances based on a variety of conditions, generate messages under specific conditions, and move time data from Time types to other Time types and Wage types (see Figure 8.22).

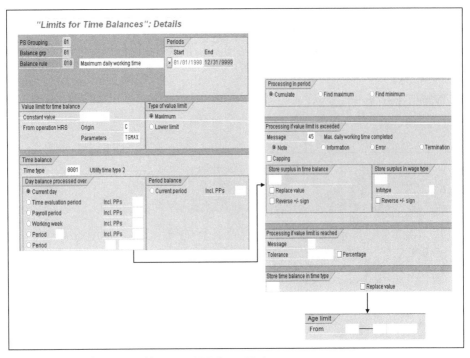

Figure 8.22 Configuration Table V_T559P Balance Limits

We covered a few of the tables used by the schema during the processing, so now let's take a look at some of the operations that can be used within personnel calculation rules. A complete list can also be found in Appendix G.

8.7 Sample Time Evaluation Operations

Operations are used within personnel calculation rules and were defined at the beginning of this chapter. Now let's discuss the sample Time Evaluation operations that enable you to make particular decisions when processing, fill particular field's values, change particular field values, and call particular data during the processing. One of the most difficult lessons to learn is what's possible using standard SAP ERP HCM functionality. In this section we will provide you with a baseline for the available data and how you might be able to utilize the standard functionality for your business requirements. After reviewing some of these options, you can compare them against the various Time Pair, Time type, and Wage type data that flows through the system to determine what may or may not be possible to change during processing. For example, you may want to change a Time type from processing type "S," as in our previous examples, to processing type "M" so that overtime will be paid instead of regular time.

We will cover the following options and list all of the available field options:

▸ FILLP — Change Time Pair Information

▸ FILLW – Fill Wage Type Data

▸ TFLAG – Change Status Data a Day

▸ VARAB – Provide Information on Absences

▸ VARPR – Provide Data on Current Attendance

▸ VARST – Provide General Fields

▸ HRS – Edit Number of Hours Field

▸ OUTTP – Provide Time Pair Information

Let's start with the first operation called FILLP. This operation allows you to change the Time Pair information listed in Table 8.4.

Operation	Description	Operation	Description
FILLP1.	Status STAT1	FILLPM....	End terminal
FILLPA	Master CCenter in C1	FILLPN	Number of hours
FILLPB.	Start time	FILLPO	End att./abs. reason
FILLPC	Clearing type	FILLPP	Pair type
FILLPE	End time	FILLPT	Time identifier
FILLPF	Start of record type	FILLPV	Processing type
FILLPG	End of record type	FILLPW	TIP-VAR01
FILLPH	Origin indicator	FILLPX	TIP-VAR02
FILLPI	Start att./abs. reason	FILLPY	Init. all fields
FILLPK	Internal key — INTKY	FILLPZ	Initialize arrow
FILLPL	Start terminal		

Table 8.4 Operation FILLP Change Time Pair Information

Similar to changing Time Pairs, the next section is an operation on how to change Wage type–related information. Operation FILLW in Table 8.5 allows you to make manual changes to Wage types during the schema processing.

Operation	Description	Operation	Description
FILLWA	Fill Wage type abs.	FILLWI.	Fill Wage type IFTYP
FILLWB...	Fill C1 split	FILLWL...	Fill ALP split
FILLWC.	Fill WT comp. key	FILLWT...	Fill Wage type time

Table 8.5 Operation FILLW — Fill Wage Type Data

The next operation is called TFLAG.

Operation TFLAG in Table 8.6 allows you to change the status data for a particular day. For example, you could change the status of the day being processed from an attendance day to an absence day. By doing so, you can control the way in which the day is being processed.

Operation	Description	Operation	Description
TFLAGA	Flag = absence	TFLAGP	Flag = attendance
TFLAGB	Read overtime breaks	TFLAGB1	Read break type 1
TFLAGK	Flag = core night work	TFLAGB2	Read break type 2

Table 8.6 Operation TFLAG — Change Status Data a Day

The next operation is very useful in providing information on the absences that have been entered into the system and processed in Time Evaluation. By using operation VARAB, you can make decisions on the fields listed in Table 8.7. Based on these decisions, you can write rules to process your business requirements. For example, if you were tracking how many full-day absences where encountered during a work week, you could use the VARABDAY operation to determine if it was a full-day absence. If so, you could create a counter and for every day that a full-day absence occurred, the counter would increase by one.

Operation	Description	Operation	Description
VARABABSTP	Abs. type cal. entry	VARABPSS	Abs. type from PSOLL
VARABCAT	Abs. type in VarKey	VARABTIM	Grpg for PType/TType
VARABDAY	Full-day absence?	VARABTYP	Abs. category in variable key
VARABOCABS	Offcycle payroll ID	VARABVCL	Abs. class in variable key

Table 8.7 Operation VARAB — Provide Information on Absences

The SAP system also has a similar operation that is used for attendances called VARPR. Table 8.8 shows the various fields that can be used to make decisions in your rules.

Operation	Description	Operation	Description
VARPRABSTP	Att. type cal. entry	VARPRTIM	Assign cls. in v. key
VARPRCAT	Time Eval. class	VARPRTYP	Att. category in variable key
VARPRDAY	Full-day attendance?	VARPRVCL	Att. class in variable key
VARPREVLTP	Evaluation type	VARPRVERSL	Overtime calculation

Table 8.8 Operation VARPR — Provide Data on Current Attendance

The next operation is called VARST. This operation is very useful in providing data by which you can make particular decisions from within your rules. Table 8.9 lists the various options available to you.

Operation	Description	Operation	Description
VARSTABSCE	Employee absent	VARSTMOD W	Day Grouping for Wage type selection table T510S
VARSTABSWD	EE absent for day	VARSTNDYAC	Subsequent day active?
VARSTBREAK	Break schedule	VARSTNDYHC	Public Holiday class subs. day
VARSTCURMO	Current period	VARSTNDYNE	Sub. day Negative time ev.
VARSTCURYR	Current year	VARSTNDYPO	Sub. day Pos. time ev.
VARSTDAYPG	Daily Work Schedule	VARSTNOTIM	Data without times
VARSTDAYTY	Day type	VARSTOVPOS	Auto. overtime
VARSTDPRCL	Daily WS class	VARSTP2000	Place Time Pair in TIP
VARSTFDY01	First day PERMO=01	VARSTP2001	Absence in TIP
VARSTFDYPP	First day of pay period	VARSTP2002	Attendance in TIP
VARSTFDYWW	First day of work week	VARSTP2004	On-call in TIP

Table 8.9 Operation VARST — Provide General Fields

Operation	Description	Operation	Description
VARSTFIRST	First pair	VARSTP2005	Overtime in TIP
VARSTFREE	Planned hrs. DWS = 0?	VARSTP2011	Time events exist
VARSTHOLCL	Public holiday class	VARSTPRSNT	Employee at work
VARSTLAST	Last pair	VARSTPRSWD	EE at work whole day
VARSTLDAYP	Last of period	VARSTRDY01	Relative day of pay period
VARSTLDWDY	Last weekday LDAYW	VARSTRDYPP	Relative day of pay period
VARSTLDY01	Last day PERMO=01	VARSTRDYWW	Relative day working week
VARSTLDYPP	Last day of pay period	VARSTREDAY	Relative day of period
VARSTLDYWW	Last day working week	VARSTSIM	Simulation
VARSTLRD	Leave — deduction?	VARSTSUBST	Substitution type
VARSTLRD01	Leave 01—deduction?	VARSTTIMCL	Val. class PWS
VARSTLWDY1	Weekday 1 LDAYW	VARSTTIMMD	Period WS
VARSTLWDY2	Weekday 2 LDAYW	VARSTTIMQU	Att. quota type
VARSTLWDY3	Weekday 3 LDAYW	VARSTTPLN	Target planning
VARSTLWDY4	Weekday 4 LDAYW	VARSTTQU01	Att. quota 01 avail.
VARSTLWDY5	Weekday 5 LDAYW	VARSTVARIA	Daily WS variant
VARSTLWDY6	Weekday 6 LDAYW	VARSTWDY 1	Weekday 1

Table 8.9 Operation VARST — Provide General Fields (Cont.)

Operation	Description	Operation	Description
VARSTLWDY7	Weekday 7 LDAYW	VARSTWDY 2	Weekday 2
VARSTMOD A	MODIF T554C	VARSTWDY 3	Weekday 3
VARSTMOD D	DAYMO T510S	VARSTWDY 4	Weekday 4
VARSTMOD L	GRBAL T559P	VARSTWDY 5	Weekday 5
VARSTMOD Q	QUOMO T559L	VARSTWDY 6	Weekday 6
VARSTMOD S	DYTPE T552W	VARSTWDY 7	Weekday 7
VARSTMOD T	MODIF T555Z	VARSTWEDAY	Relative weekday

Table 8.9 Operation VARST — Provide General Fields (Cont.)

The next operation may be one of the most used operations. This operation is called HRS and allows for a lot of different calculations in the system. For example, any time you make a decision based on the hours of a Time type, you use function HRS=D0010. This would set the hours equal to the daily balance of Time type 0010. You could then compare that value to eight. Using the operation hours again, hrs?8 is how the next use of the operation would work. You then answer the question in the rule for when the hours equal, are less than, or greater to build whatever calculation you need based on your requirements. Table 8.10 lists the various ways you can use operation HRS.

Operation	Description	Operation	Description
O	Time type zzzz is put in the No. of hours field from table SALDO (previous month balance table)	I	The following is provided from Infotype 0007 — Planned Working Time : operation HRS1I
M	Time type zzzz is put in the No. of hours field from table SALDO (monthly balance table)	N	The following is provided from Infotype 0008 — Basic Pay: operation HRS1N
D	Time type zzzz from the previous day is put in the No. of hours field from table ZES	V	The following is provided from Infotype 0050 — Time Recording: operation HRS1V

Table 8.10 Operation HRS — Edit Number of Hours Field

Operation	Description	Operation	Description
LzzzzA	Time type zzzz from the last day before the current day on which the employee worked and whose time recording status is not equal to zero is put in the No. of hours field from table ZES	Q	The following is provided from Infotype 2007, Attendance Quota, and Infotype 2006, Absence Quota : operation HRS1Q
W	Time type zzzz cumulated for the current week and in the No. of hours field; current day is not taken into account in this accumulation	F	The following is provided Infotype 2006: operation HRS1F
X	Time type zzzz is cumulated from the previous days of the current payroll period; the current day is not taken into account in this accumulation	G	The following is provided from Infotype 2007:operation HRS1G
P	The following is provided from the current pair: operation HRS1P	T	The following field is provided from the customizing table: operation HRS1T
A	The following is provided from the current absence pair: operation HRS1A	C	The constant zzzzz is provided from the payroll constants table (T511K). Special processing. See operation HRS1C
E	The following is provided from table DZL: operation HRS1E	%	The following are provided from the Wage type valuation table (T512W): operation HRS1%
Z	The following is provided from table ZML: operation HRS1Z	B	The following system fields are provided: operation HRS1B

Table 8.10 Operation HRS — Edit Number of Hours Field (Cont.)

Operation	Description	Operation	Description
Kxxxx	The variable balance for identifier xxxx is read from table VS. Beforehand, you must structure the variable key as for operation ADDVS	Y	Time interval between two date entries is calculated: operation HRS1Y
S	The following is provided from the daily work operation HRS1S	R	The result of the last HRS operation is put in the No. of Hours Field. **Exception**: If the last operator equals "?," then the difference between the No. of hours field minus operand 2 of the last HRS operation is put in the No. hours field.
U	Same as HRS=S, however, without taking substitutions into account	Kxxxx	The variable balance for identifier xxxx is read from table VS. Beforehand, you must structure the variable key as for operation ADDVS
H	The following is provided from Infotype (0005) — Leave Entitlement: operation HRS1H		

Table 8.10 Operation HRS — Edit Number of Hours Field (Cont.)

The next operation is called OUTTP and is used to provide specific Time Pair information so that you can make decisions within the rule. Table 8.11 lists the various fields of operation OUTTP that you can make decisions from.

Operation	Description	Operation	Description
OUTTPABTYP	Absence type	OUTTPEUSER	Pair end Infofield
OUTTPALSET	ALP pointer set	OUTTPEXBTM	Start time exists?
OUTTPBGCOD	Beg. posting AbReason	OUTTPEXETM	End time exists?
OUTTPBRTYP	Beg. post. record type	OUTTPEXTIM	Times exist?
OUTTPBTERM	Beg. posting terminal	OUTTPINTKY	Internal key

Table 8.11 Operation OUTTP — Provide Time Pair Information

Operation	Description	Operation	Description
OUTTPBUSER	Infofield pair start	OUTTPORIGS	Origin status
OUTTPC1000	Present 2002/2011?	OUTTPPRTYP	Attendance type
OUTTPC1SET	C1 pointer set	OUTTPPTYPE	Pair type
OUTTPCLTIM	Cl. PType/Time type	OUTTPSTAT1	STAT1
OUTTPCLTYP	Comp. key in v. key	OUTTPTIMDS	Time ID
OUTTPCOGOS	Att. from pair form.	OUTTPTITYP	Time type
OUTTPEGCOD	End posting AbReason	OUTTPVAR01	Var. field in VarArg
OUTTPERTYP	End post. record type	OUTTPVAR02	Var. field in VarArg
OUTTPETERM	End posting terminal	OUTTPVTYPE	Processing Type

Table 8.11 Operation OUTTP — Provide Time Pair Information (Cont.)

This concludes our coverage of the most frequently used operations. As a final note, Time Evaluation with Clock Times utilizes Schema TM00. In this schema, one of the main differences compared to Schema TM04, Time Evaluation without Clock Times, is the utilization of Infotype 2011, Time Events. In addition, there are custom rules for building Time types based on the Time Pairs entered. The overtime rules are also a bit different than those delivered in Schema TM04. To truly understand Schema TM00, you should walk through it and become familiar with the details of the processing. Once you have completed that task, conduct the same exercise with Schema TM04, which is covered in Chapter 9.

8.8   Summary

In this chapter, you learned about the concepts surrounding Time Evaluation Schema TM00. You learned about each section of the schema and what is happening during the functions when they are processing. Time Evaluation is probably the hardest element of the SAP ERP HCM Time Management functionality to master. The concepts take time to digest, so you should spend time in the system setting up and testing basic examples, using the delivered rules and schemas. In the next chapter we will look at the Time Evaluation without Clock Times functionality.

In this chapter, you will learn about key areas to consider during the configuration of the Time Evaluation without Clock Times functionality. This chapter, and the previous chapter on Time Evaluation with Clock Times, share the same program; however, there are various differences in their processing. At the conclusion of this chapter, you should be knowledgeable of the concepts and steps to set up and perform processes with Time Evaluation without Clock Times.

9 Time Evaluation Without Clock Times

The general and Time Evaluation settings sections were covered in Chapter 8, "Time Evaluation with Clock Times," so they will be not be covered here. This chapter explains the elements of the Time Evaluation schema that processes time-related data. In addition, we will further explain some of the personnel calculation rules by providing a description of what the rule is actually doing. By understanding the material in this chapter, you should have baseline knowledge of how to customize the system for your requirements. Throughout the chapter, we will describe the personnel calculation rules and what is happening within each of them as they process. Each of the rules can serve as a model by which you can base your own rules.

You will use Time Evaluation Without Clock Times for situations when your payroll system requires time-related information to pay employees correctly.

Example

If you have an employee who takes a vacation day without having enough vacation quota, you may need to reduce their salary by one day's pay. To do this, you can have the employee enter an unpaid absence, which will be processed by Time Evaluation to generate a no-pay Wage type. This Wage type is then passed to payroll, which reduces the employee's salary for the payroll period.

9.1 Time Valuation without Clock Times Schema Overview

The key decision points for management when implementing Time Evaluation Without Clock Times are the same as those for Time Evaluation With Clock Times, so we won't repeat them in this chapter. If you would like to review them, please refer back to chapter 8.

The Time Evaluation schema processes time-related records entered into the time infotypes from various sources. Then it converts the records into the appropriate Wage types that are used by payroll and then posted to the SAP ERP Financial component. You will want to implement Time Evaluation if you intend to run payroll within the SAP system, or if you plan to export the time-related data records to a third-party payroll system. Regardless of the final system setup, you need to review every section of the Implementation Guide (IMG) for the functionality to determine the system impact and if it's a required piece of configuration to support the processing of your business requirements. Figure 9.1 illustrates the various elements involved in the process during Time Evaluations, including how data enters the system, and the terminology of the buckets that hold the data as it flows through the SAP system. Figure 9.1 also outlines the data processing flow of time entered into the system to when it is posted to the general ledger accounts.

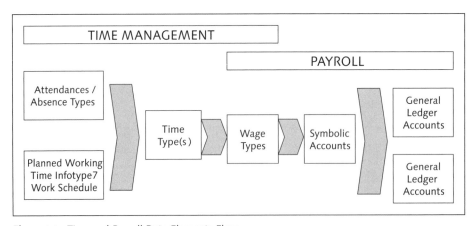

Figure 9.1 Time and Payroll Data Elements Flow

It is very helpful to understand how the data flows through the system. So let's look at the date elements involved during Time Evaluation and when they are created.

▶ **Absence and attendance type** — As we discussed in Chapter 6, these are created when time is entered into the SAP system. It then resides in various infotypes, such as Infotype 2001, Absences; or 2002, Attendances. Absence and attendances types can also be generated within Time Evaluation based on Infotype 2011 Time Events.

▶ **Planned working time** — The configuration that supports the Work Schedule rules that reside on Infoytpe 0007 Planned Working Time is leveraged in Time Evaluation to create time-related records during Time Evaluation processing. This is normally reserved for negative recording employees that only enter exceptions to their normal Work Schedule. Time Evaluation takes the Work Schedule, determines the times, and generates a Time type.

▶ **Time types** — These are created during Time Evaluation processing using a variety of methods, such as:

  ▸ Based on the configuration of absence and attendance types. The configuration can link a processing type/Time type class to a particular Time type configured in table T555Y.

  ▸ Based on the planned time from the Work Schedule configuration. The Time Pairs created also utilize table T555Y to create the applicable Time types.

  ▸ Created by a custom personnel calculation rule.

  ▸ Attendances and absence types are linked to processing type/Time types via tables V_554S_E for absences and V_554S_F for attendances.

▶ **Wage types** — Are created by either a custom personnel calculation rule or by utilizing table T510S — Wage type generation.

▶ **Symbolic account** — Maps Wage types to general ledger accounts for posting to accounting.

▶ **General ledger accounts** – Actual accounts where the Wage type numbers and amounts are posted.

9.2 Configuration Initial Steps

This section of the customization allows you to further define which employees will be processed by this particular schema. Depending on how you choose to set up your system, you can have various groups of employees share the same schema, or you can even create a different schema for the various groups. You can access

the customizing table via the IMG menu path TIME MANAGEMENT • TIME EVALUA-
TION • TIME EVALUATION WITHOUT CLOCK TIMES • INITIAL STEPS.

9.2.1   Check Function

The check function allows you to specify how and for whom Time Evaluation
will process. The CHECK function, and its various delivered parameters, tells the
schema important information during the initialization. The following CHECK
functions are delivered:

▶ **PON** — Positive or negative time recording parameters are determined based
on the Time Management status field from Infotype 0007. Time Evaluation
selects all employees that don't have a 0 for this value.

▶ **TRC** — Employees with Time Management status of 1 are selected.

▶ **PDC** — Employees with Time Management status of 2 are selected.

▶ **TS7** — Employees with Time Management status of 7 are selected.

▶ **SRV** — Employees with Time Management status of 8 are selected.

▶ **NEG** — Employees with Time Management status of 9 are selected

▶ **INFT** — The system checks if Infotypes 2001, Absences, 2002 Attendances,
2004 Availability, 2005 Overtime and 2012 Time Transfer specifications are
processed within the schema.

▶ **NOTR** — The system will not read Infotype 0050 Time Recording
Information.

▶ **BP** — Infotype 0008 Basic Pay is read and stored in the Work Pay Basic Pay
(WPBP) table.

▶ **CHAL** — Infotype 0004 Challenge is read and made available during the quota
processing, if you have based your quota configuration to leverage the challenge infotype.

▶ **FUT** — Allows the system to evaluate future days when processing.

▶ **RPR** — Sets the retroactive indicator for periods where data has changed for
previously processed payroll runs.

▶ **NOB1** — Tells the system not to import the B1 cluster information during
processing.

This setup is very useful because you can check an employee's master data to determine if they should be processed through this schema. You can use this to establish initial settings that determine the groups of employees to process.

9.2.2 Define Groupings

SAP offers a personnel calculation rule that allows you to set particular groupings at the beginning of the schema. These groupings can be changed during subsequent processing based on specific requirements. The rule that sets the initial groupings is TMON and it can be referenced via Transaction code PE02. The following types of groupings can also be established:

▶ W = Table T510S Wage Type Selection Rule

▶ T = Table T555Z Time Type Determination Group

▶ A = Table T554C Absence Valuation Employee Grouping

▶ D = Table T510S Day Grouping for Wage type Selection Rule

▶ S = Table T552W Dynamic Work Schedule Assignment

▶ Q = Table T559L Quota Type Selections

▶ L = Table T559P Time Balance Rule Group for Value Limits

Figure 9.2 shows an example of the personnel calculation rule used to set the various groupings for these particular groupings just listed. You can utilize this type of approach to process a group of employees in a similar manner by leveraging table entries to help derive particular calculations.

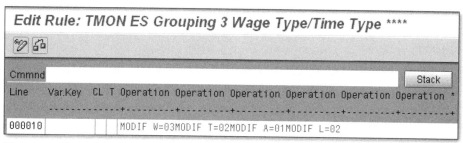

Figure 9.2 Personnel Calculation Rule TMON

> **Note**
>
> You are not required to use all of the groupings. It really just depends on your situation. You can also copy the rule, customize the rule according to your business requirements, and insert it into the subschema to be processed. You will want to comment out or delete the original entry in the subschema that you copied from.

In the next section, we will review how time data is brought into the schema for processing.

9.3 Providing Time Data

Time data is in entered into the SAP system in a variety of different ways, but it always ends up on an infotype. The method used in Time Evaluation is to translate those infotype records into something that a payroll system can understand in order to compensate the employee. In the following sections, we'll describe the various portions of Schema TM04 dedicated to providing time data for processing. You can access the customizing tables via the IMG menu path TIME MANAGEMENT • TIME EVALUATION • TIME EVALUATION WITHOUT CLOCK TIMES • PROVIDING TIME DATA.

9.3.1 Import Work Schedules and Time Events

This section deals with a couple of different functions that are entered into the system. Based on 'if' statements in the schema, function P2011 engages for those with Time Management status of a "1" or "2." Function P2000 is typically used to import planned working time for those with a Time Management status of "9."

- ▸ **P2011** — Used to process Time Events from Infotype 2011. The entries are brought into the schema and placed in table TIP and indicators are set in table TZP.

- ▸ **P2000** — Used to process planned working times determined from the Work Schedule rule configuration. The function creates a TIP table entry for the planned working time. In addition, an entry is made in the TZP table storing a time identifier to determine how the time was created. For example, the TZP table might have a code '02,' which stands for Fill Time during planned working time.

9.3.2 Determine Breaks for Import

Breaks can also be brought into the Time Evaluation schema for processing. You can do this via functions P2011 and P2000, and then you'll have the opportunity to determine which breaks should not be imported.

In addition, personnel calculation rule TD00 can be set so that certain breaks are not brought into Time Evaluation. This rule uses the operation TFLAG to determine how breaks are processed. As delivered, the system does not import overtime breaks from Infotype 2005; however; you also have the following options:

▸ Import breaks from Infotype 2005

▸ Table T550P — Don't enter breaks from pair type 1

▸ Table T550P — Only enter breaks from pair type 1

▸ Table T550P — Don't enter breaks from pair type 2

▸ Table T550P — Only enter breaks from pair type 1

9.3.3 Provide Absence Data

Absences are imported into Time Evaluation via function P2001. The operation has various settings that can be made to alter the way in which it processes. The following are the various settings that can be made and the options under each setting. You can utilize the various settings to alter the way in which the system supplies the related information.

▸ **Parameter 1** — Helps determine under which circumstances absences should be entered.

  ▸ Blank — Only imported where the daily Work Schedule dictates it is a work day. The system uses the daily Work Schedule class that is not equal to zero and if the day type is a zero or one.

  ▸ Ever — All absences are entered regardless of the working day conditions.

▸ **Parameter 2** — Helps determine how the Time Pairs should be delimited under circumstances of overlapping Time Pairs in the TIP table.

  ▸ Blank — Existing Time Pairs remain intact.

  ▸ XY — Existing TIP entries are delimited where the pair type is listed.

The pair types can have the following meanings:

- ▶ 0 — Non-recording absence or a break has occurred.
- ▶ 1 — Employee at work and time is imported via function P2011 or P2000.
- ▶ 2 — Employee is absent with approval via function P2001.
- ▶ 3 — Employee is off-site working and time is imported via P2011 or P2002.

Every Time Pair is delimited when colliding with an entry from P2001.

- ▶ **Parameter 3** — Not used.
- ▶ **Parameter 4** — Brings forward the C1 split indicator from the substitution record in Infotype 2003. The C1 indicator stands for cost distribution.
  - ▶ Blank — No split indicators are transferred.
  - ▶ A — Split indicators are transferred but only if the absence record does not already contain a C1 split indicator.

9.3.4 Provide Attendance Data

Attendances are imported into Time Evaluation via function P2002. The operation has various settings that can be made to alter the way in which it processes when other time-related attendance may exist from other sources, such as clock time entries. As with absences, you also have various parameters for the function that can be set for attendances.

- ▶ **Parameter 1** — Not used.
- ▶ **Parameter 2** — Helps determine how the Time Pairs should be delimited under circumstances of overlapping Time Pairs in the TIP table.
  - ▶ Blank — Existing Time Pairs remain intact.
  - ▶ XY — Existing TIP entries are delimited where the pair type is listed.

The pair types can have the following meanings:

- ▶ 0 — Non-recording absence or a break has occurred.
- ▶ 1 — Employee at work and time is imported via function P2011 or P2000.
- ▶ 2 — Employee is absent with approval via function P2001.
- ▶ 3 — Employee is off-site working and time is imported via P2011 or P2002.

Every Time Pair is delimited when colliding with an entry from P2002.

▶ **Parameter 3** — Not used.

▶ **Parameter 4** — Brings forward the C1 split indicator from the substitution record in Infotype 2003. The C1 indicator stands for cost distribution.

   ▶ Blank — No split indicators are transferred.

   ▶ A — Split indicators are transferred but only if the absence record does not already contain a C1 split indicator.

9.3.5 Deduct Attendances and Absences from Generated Time Pairs

This section of the schema is processed in the TP01 subschema. This subschema is used to reduce the generated time from Work Schedules by those entries in Infotype 2002. Table V_554S_F facilitates the delivered personnel calculation rule TP06. Figure 9.3 shows the table entries.

Change View "Attendance: Time Evaluation": Overview

Expand <-> Collapse   Delimit

	PSG	A/AType	A/A type text	Start Date	End Date	Class	P/T
	01	0400	Business trip	01/01/1990	12/31/9999	01	02
	01	0420	Seminar/course/training	01/01/1990	12/31/9999	01	03
	01	0430	Vocational school/class	01/01/1990	12/31/9999	01	03
	01	0440	Active in works council	01/01/1990	12/31/9999	01	04
	01	0460	Overtime for quota hours	01/01/1990	12/31/9999	01	01
	01	0470	Actual cost distribution	01/01/1990	12/31/9999	03	

Figure 9.3 Table V_554S_F Attendance Table Entries

Like most personnel calculation rules, certain decisions are made within the rule to determine when and for who the various processing procedures should engage for. As Figure 9.4 illustrates, operation VARPRCAT makes a decision in the rule based on the class field in table V_554S_F. Those attendances with a particular class are flagged for subsequent processing in personnel calculation rule TP07. Figure 9.4 shows personnel calculation rules TP06 and TP07.

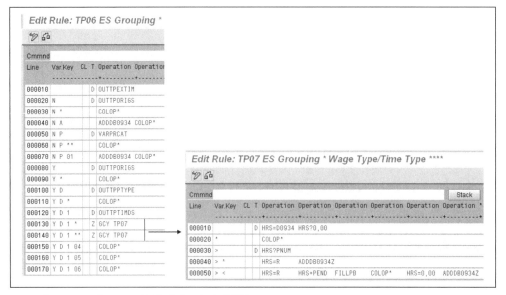

Figure 9.4 Personnel Calculation Rule TP06

9.3.6 Process Work Center Substitutions

Work center substitutions are imported into Time Evaluation via function A2003. This function imports the data from Infotype 2003. There really aren't any options other than to import the records or not. Once the records are imported, they are factored into the custom processing procedures you have defined.

9.3.7 Use Test Procedure Infotype in Time Evaluation

Infotype 0130 Test Procedures utilizes personnel calculation rule TMAP as a basis for what time-related data should be released into Time Evaluation for processing. The overall premise of this functionality is to allow a time administrator the ability to review the time information entered and enter a date on Infotype 0130. All time up to that date is allowed to process in its entirety in Time Evaluation. Personnel calculation rule TMAP has been provided as a guide and should be customized to your requirements.

9.4 Time Data Processing

After the time has been imported, it is time for the schema to conduct its processing. The following sections describe the various portions of the schema dedicated to providing time data for the schema to process. You can access the customizing table via the IMG menu path TIME MANAGEMENT • TIME EVALUATION • TIME EVALUATION WITHOUT CLOCK TIMES • TIME DATA PROCESSING.

The portion of Schema TM04 that processes the time data is broken into the following sections.

9.4.1 Assign Time Types and Processing Types

This section of the configuration and schema processing is the basic creation of Time type, linking absence and attendance types to Processing type/Time type classes and finally linking those Processing type/Time type classes to Time types.

▶ The Time types are configured in table V_T555A.

▶ Absences are linked to processing type/Time type classes via table V_554S_E.

▶ Attendances are linked to processing type/Time type classes via table V_554S_F.

▶ Assignment of processing types to Time types is done in table T555Y. These tasks do not correlate to a specific line of the Time Management schema, however, they provide the foundation on how the data is linked behind the scenes.

9.4.2 Determine Break Times

▶ Breaks from the Work Schedule are brought into Time Evaluation for processing by using function PBRKS. The data is obtained from tables T550A and T550P. The function has numerous options on how to process. If you elect to create a custom personnel calculation rule, then operation TMBRE can be used to influence how the system processes the breaks. You can also dictate the following:

▶ The sequence of the TIP table entries that are counted toward the break.

▶ The inclusion of unrecorded time that lies within the start and end times of the planned working time.

9.4.3 Determine Interim Planned Working Time

The interim planned working time is calculated using personnel calculation rule TP09. This rule sets the foundation of planned hours for the employee and is utilized in subsequent rules. TP09 does nothing more than take any TIP entry where the TIP entry has a pair type of 'S' and adds the value to Time type 0000. Time type 0000 is a delivered utility Time type and will be used in subsequent personnel calculation rule TP10.

9.4.4 Shorten Absences of Less Than One Day

This functionality utilizes the settings in the field class of table V_554S_E. The overall intent is to determine if any flextime balance has occurred as a result of absences entered into the system that are not full-day absences compare to the planned working time for the day. The functionality leverages personnel calculation rules TP10 and TP11 to conduct its analysis. The rules leverage the utility Time type time 0000 that was populated with the planned hours for the day based on the Work Schedule. The rule goes further to determine what the pair type is. If the pair type is a 2, which stands for an absence in the TIP table, and if the pair type of "S" determined along with the category defined in table V_554S_E is not equal to 02 or 03, then rule TP11 is utilized for processing flextime balances and reducing the absence by the amount of flextime hours generated.

9.4.5 Determining Overtime

The SAP system offers some baseline functionality for determining overtime for your organization. You need to customize these to your requirements. For example, in the United States, there are only a handful of states that allow for overtime processing on a daily basis. You need to customize the system such that only employees that work in these states flow through the daily overtime rules for overtime. Simple, right? Not so fast, not only do you need to figure out if they work in those states, you also need to determine what their Work Schedule is for some of the states because the daily overtime law is different for 8-hour shifts, 10-hour shifts, and 12-hour shifts for particular states. Table 9.1 outlines various overtime laws by state. This is a breakdown of the various information from the United States Department of Labor and is accurate as of 2008.

STATE	8 HR OT	10 HR OT	12 HR OT	40 HR OT	CONSECUTIVE DAYS
Alaska	X			X	
California	X	X	X	X	X
Colorado			X		
Nevada	X			X	
Puerto Rico	X			X	
Virgin Islands	X			X	X
Kentucky					X
All States				X	

Table 9.1 Overtime Laws by State

You may also want to make note of Minnesota (48 hours) and Kansas (46 hours) – not listed in the table - but where the weekly hours are higher than the federal law allows, so it is usually not used because the qualifications for a higher hour limit is normally exceeded by most businesses. Therefore, the federal law normally takes precedence and the 40 hour a week rules are used in most situations.

This section of the configuration is broken down into the following tasks:

▶ Overtime on a daily basis

▶ Overtime on a working week basis

▶ Overtime according to the number of consecutive days worked

SAP provides the following three personal calculation rules that you can reference for your requirements surrounding how overtime should be calculated.

▶ Overtime according to consecutive days worked utilizes Subschema TW10.

▶ Overtime on a daily basis utilizes Subschema TW15.

▶ Overtime on a weekly basis utilizes Subschema TW20.

The following sections discuss the various personnel calculation rules and describe what is actually happening within each rule. You will notice that the standard rules leverage delivered Time types and as such, they are noted for references purposes.

Figure 9.5 displays Subschema TW10. This is a delivered schema with the rules that shows you how to set up the system to determine how many days in a row an employee has worked and if overtime should be calculated. The schema first processes personnel calculation rule TW00 and then, based on the outcome of TW00, processes personnel calculation rule TO00.

Personnel calculation rule TW00 first determines if the employee is at work or should be. This rule leverages Time type 0905 — Sequence of Attendance Days. If the employee is not at work, indicated by an "N" in the variable key, then the condition of the rule is now false and rule TO00 will not process. If the employee is present, indicated by a "Y" in the variable key, a second decision is made. This decision is to determine if it is the seventh day of the work week by utilizing VARSTWDY 7. If it is the seventh day, again indicated by a "Y" in the variable key, then the rule is set to false. In addition, Time type 0905, which serves as a counter, is incremented by one. If the answer to the seventh-day question is no, the rule pulls in the cumulated value of the counter Time type 0905 from the previous day into the current day for processing. The rule adds one to the counter and then makes the decision on if the counter is greater than six working days. If the condition is true, the overall rule for TW00 is set to true, which means TO00 will be processed. If, at any time, a condition is set to false, the processing of this subschema stops. The next processing schema, TM04, will then commence.

Personnel calculation rule TO00 makes its first decision off of processing type. Processing types are associated with particular Time types in the system. The rule is really looking for a processing type value of 3. This means that the system is looking for all attendances because a 3 is associated with attendances. The rule then makes a decision based on pair type. If the rule finds pair types 0 or 2, then the rule just adds the current Time type through and no further processing takes place. If, however, the attendance has a pair type not equal to a 0 or 2, then the rule basically changes the processing type from an "S", which stands for planned working time, to "M", which stands for overtime. The hours are moved from the attendance Time type to a new Time type 0040 — Overtime. Time type 0040 is used to compensate overtime later during the schema processing (see Figure 9.5).

The overall goal of this subschema is to determine if the employee worked six-plus days that week and, if so, should overtime be paid. You should use this subschema and rule TO00 as an example, because not all states adhere to these calculations.

You will need to set this up specifically for California or other areas, if the business pay practices warrant such a calculation.

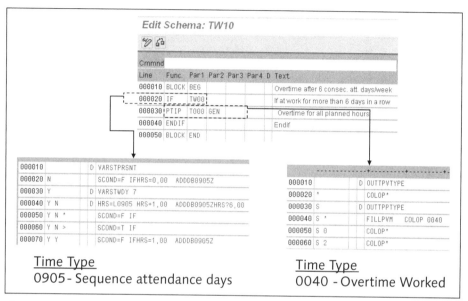

Figure 9.5 Delivered Time Management Subschema TW10 for Consecutive Days Worked

Figure 9.6 displays Subschema TW15. This subschema is utilized for processing overtime after the employee has worked X amount of hours per day. The amount of hours differs by state and only a handful of states mandate that this pay practice be followed. Subschema TW15 is broken down into two personnel calculation rules, which are described next.

Personnel calculation rule TO01 has two basic decisions within the rule. The first decision regards what is the day type of the Time type being processed. The day type is set when you configure the Work Schedule rules and the rule associated with the employee that is processing. Typically, a day type other than 0 or blank is considered a working day for the employee. According to the rule, if the answer to the day type question returns a value of a 1 or 2, then hours are added to delivered Time type 0900 — Daily Overtime After X Hours. If it is a normal working day, dictated by a 0 in the variable key to the day type question, then a second question of whether or not there are any planned hours on the daily Work Schedule.

VARSTFREE is an operation that asks the question for the planned working hours. Depending on the response to the questions, either 99 hours or 8 hours are added to Time type 0900. This concludes the processing of rule TO01. The basic goal of this rule is to establish the value of Time type 0900 so it can be leveraged in personnel calculation rule TO02.

Personnel calculation rule TO02 has four decisions within the rule that can be called. The first decision is based on the processing time of the Time type. Typically, planned time is flagged with an S; however, if you have changed the system, you might need to incorporate your custom processing types as well. The personnel calculation rule makes its second decision of what the value of the pair type is. If the values equal a 0 or 2, then the rule stops processing. All other values process through to the third decision. The third decision utilizes two Time types. The value of the current line being processed is set to the value of Time type 0904. This value is now compared against the daily value of Time type 0900, set in the previous personnel calculation rule TO01. If the value of 0904 is greater than 0900, then overtime has occurred and the processing type is changed to M for overtime and the hours are moved to Time type 0040. If the value of 0904 is less than 0900, then the final decision is made. This final process determines if the hours of 0904, plus the hours of the current Time type being processed, are now greater than the value of X hours entered on Time type 0900. If they are greater, then the rule determines how much of that is greater and only those hours are moved to the overtime Time type 0040.

Example

An employee enters two sets of time into the system. The first set is for four hours, and the second set of time is for six hours. The employee works a total of 10 hours that day. The personnel calculation rule that you customized for the applicable states where overtime on a daily basis is required determines that overtime should be based on any hours greater than eight during one working day. Time type 0900 is set to eight hours during personnel calculation rule TO01.

During personnel calculation rule TO02, the two time entries flow through the rules one at a time. The first piece of time is for four hours. The rule sets the current hours to the value of Time type 0904, which is currently equal to zero hours. Zero is less than the Time type 0900 value of eight hours so the rule then takes the value of 0904 and adds the current time entry of four to it. The total value is now four. Because four hours of time compared against eight hours of Time type 0900 is still less, there should not be any overtime calculated. The four hours are added to Time type 0904 and both 0904 and the current attendance are added through.

It's now time for the second attendance time of six hours to flow through the rule. Using the same logic, the rule checks the value of 0904 against Time type 0900. At this point, 0904 is equal to four hours from the previous time. Four hours is less than eight so no overtime is awarded. The personnel calculation rule then takes the value of 0904, which is set to four hours and adds the six hours of attendance to it. It then compares that value, which is now 10 against Time type 0900, which is still eight hours. We have finally determined that two hours of overtime should be paid. The rule continues processing by removing the two hours and placing them in Time type 0040 for overtime processing.

The preceding example is a pretty basic overtime calculation. You need to customize it to accommodate the various state requirements for 8-hour, 10-hour, and 12-hour overtime laws (see Figure 9.6).

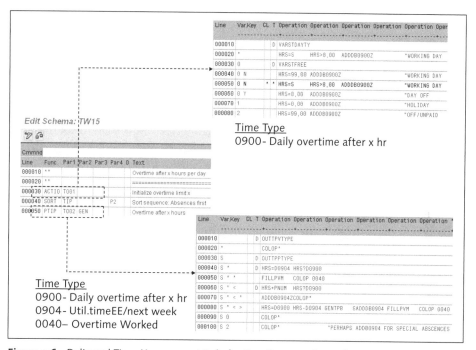

Figure 9.6 Delivered Time Management Rule for Overtime on a Particular Day

Figure 9.7 shows Subschema TW30 — weekly overtime processing. This subschema determines whether or not overtime should be paid for the week based on 40 hours. This is a larger subschema than the previous two and contains various rules that control the processing. Each of the personnel calculation rules are described as follows. Subschema TW30 is broken into two parts. The first part is for those time entries with clock times. The second is for those time entries without clock times.

Edit Schema: TW30

Line	Func.	Par1	Par2	Par3	Par4	D	Text
000010	BLOCK	BEG					Overtime calculation after x hours/week
000020	IF			WW			Working week in infotype 0007
000030	PRINT		TIP				TIP before weekly overtime analysis
000040	IF			WWTI			If clock times are defined for wk. week
000050	ACTIO	TW31					Initialize time type for weekly OT
000060	PTIP	TW32	GEN				Split if start of wk. week and OVERT
000070	ACTIO	TW33					Correct time type for weekly overtime
000080	ELSE						Working week defined without clock times
000090	ACTIO	TW34					Initialize time type for weekly OT
000100	PTIP	TW35	GEN				Overtime after prod. time in OVERT
000110	ACTIO	TW36					Correct time type for weekly overtime
000120	ENDIF						Working week with/without clock times?
000130	ENDIF						Working week in infotype 0007?
000140	BLOCK	END					

Figure 9.7 Subschema TW30

Personnel calculation rule TW31 — initialize Time types — is used to set the various values of Time types at the beginning of the processing (see Figure 9.8). Time types 0903, weekly overtime; 0904, next week time; and 0906, beginning time of working week are the three Time types that are used in this rule.

At the beginning of the rule, the value is set to the monthly value of 0903. This is pulled from the SALDO accumulation table from the B2 cluster. This value is then added to Time type 0903 and the daily balance of Time type 0904. The rule then makes a decision on whether or not it is the first day of the working week. If it is the first day of the working week, then Time type 0906 is set to the planned start time of the working week by using operation HRS=IWWEEK. If the rule determines that it is not the first day of the work week, we then need to determine if it is the last day of the work week. If it is the last day of the working week, Time type 0906 is set to the planned start time of the working week using operation HRS=IWWEEK, plus 24 hours are added to the value. If it is not the last working day of the week, Time type 0906 is set to 48 hours.

All this rule is doing is setting the baseline Time types that will be leveraged later in the subschema to determine if overtime has occurred.

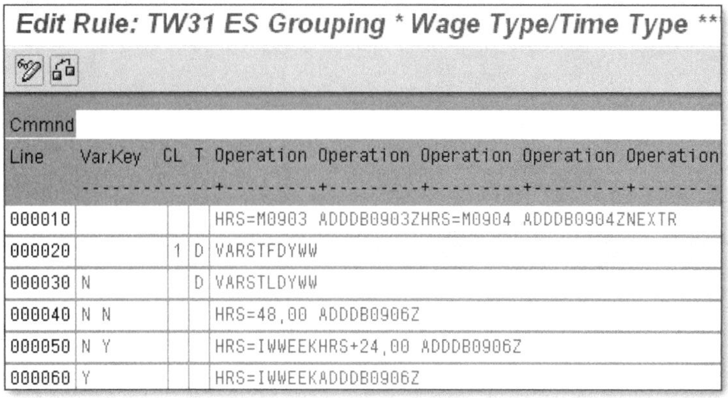

Figure 9.8 Personnel Calculation Rule TW31

Personnel calculation rule TW31 is used to determine if times exist for the Time type or if the Time type instead has lump-sum hours. Rule TW32, illustrated in Figure 9.9, determines if the start and end times have been filled. If they have not, then the rule stops processing. If the answer is yes, then personnel calculation rule TW31 branches off into personnel calculation rule TW06, where subsequent decisions and processing will occur. Similar to personnel calculation rules for daily overtime, personnel calculation rule TW06 makes a couple of decisions based on the processing type and pair type. If the system finds an attendance with the appropriate settings, then subsequent processing occurs. Personnel calculation rule TW06 determines if the start time of the Time Pair is before or after the start time that was established in Time type 0906 that was set in personnel calculation rule TW32. Based on when the Time Pair started compared to that of the beginning of the week, the rule will either add the hours to Time type 0904 or branch to a third personnel calculation rule TW04.

Personnel calculation rule TW04 has two decisions within the rule. The first decision is based on the daily bucket of time in Time type 0903 compared to a constant of 40 hours. The constant is held in table V_T511K "OVERT." If the hours are greater, then the pair type is set to M for overtime and the hours are set to Time type 0040. If the hours are less than 40, then the rule adds the current time entry to determine if that puts the balance greater than 40 hours. If the value is now greater than 40, those hours in excess are moved to the overtime Time type 0040.

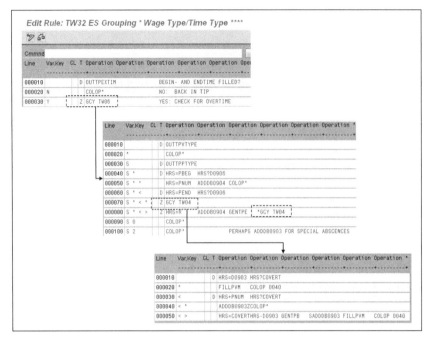

Figure 9.9 Set of Three Rules That Determine if Overtime Should Be Compensated

Personnel calculation rule TW33 — Time type Correction — is used to correct any Time type buckets that may have been altered in the previous personnel calculation rules (see Figure 9.10). The rule ensures that Time types 0903 and 0904 are reset so that future time entries have the updated buckets for their calculations.

Edit Rule: TW33 ES Grouping * Wage Type/Time

Line	Var.Key	CL	T	Operation Operation Operation Operation
000010			D	VARSTFDYWW
000020	N			HRS=D0903 HRS-M0903 ADDDB0903ZNEXTR
000030	N	1		HRS=D0904 HRS-M0904 ADDDB0904Z
000040	Y			HRS=D0904 HRS-M0903 ADDDB0903ZNEXTR
000050	Y	1		HRS=0,00 HRS-M0904 ADDDB0904Z

Figure 9.10 Personnel Calculation Rule TW33

Personnel calculation rule TW34 — Overtime Initialization — is used to initialize the Time type buckets 0903 for time entries without any clock times (see Figure

9.11). This rule determines if it is the first day of the week. If it is the first day, then the Time type 0903 is set to zero hours. If it is not the first day of the week, the daily balance of 0903 is set to the monthly balance of 0903. The monthly balance actually contains any hours of the current week for the previous days that need to count toward the 40-hour weekly overtime rules.

```
Edit Rule: TW34 ES Grouping * Wage Type/Time Type ****
Cmmnd
Line   Var.Key  CL T Operation Operation Operation Operation Operation Opera
       --------+---------+---------+---------+---------+---------+
000010         D VARSTFDYWW                   BEGIN OF NEW WORKWEEK?
000020 N         HRS=M0903 ADDDB0903Z         NO:  0903 INCL SALDO
000030 Y         HRS=0,00  ADDDB0903Z         YES: 0903 = 0
```

Figure 9.11 Personnel Calculation Rule TW34

Personnel calculation rule TW35, illustrated in Figure 9.12, is used to determine if the Time Pairs are an attendance and if personnel calculation rule TW04 should be processed. This rule makes the decisions based on pair types and processing types. You could customize this rule if you require certain absences to count toward overtime.

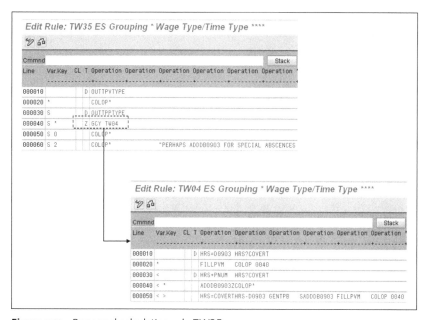

Figure 9.12 Personnel calculation rule TW35

Personnel calculation rule TW04 has two decisions within the rule. The first decision is based on the daily bucket of time in Time type 0903 compared to a constant of 40 hours. The constant is held in table V_T511K "OVERT." If the hours are greater, then the pair type is set to M for overtime and the hours are set to Time type 0040. If the hours are less than 40, then the rule adds the current time entry to determine if that puts the balance greater than 40 hours. If the value is now greater than 40, the hours in excess are moved to the overtime Time type 0040.

You will notice that this rule is also leveraged and called from other personnel calculation rules. This allows you to maintain fewer rules when functionality can be leverage for various groups of individuals. However, you should be careful when changing personnel calculation rules, it is best to determine every point in the schema that is calling the particular rule and determine if your potential change may adversely impact other processing calculations.

Personnel calculation rule TW36 —Time type Correction — is used to correct any Time type buckets that may have been altered in the previous personnel calculation rules (see Figure 9.13). This rule basically takes the daily balance of Time type 0903, subtracts the weekly balance of 0903, and adds it back to the daily balance of 0903.

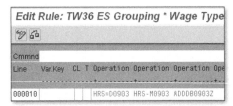

Figure 9.13 Personnel Calculation Rule TW36

9.5   Time Wage Type Selection and Overtime Compensation

Up to this point, we have entered time on absence and attendance types, generated Time types based on these entries, and those derived from planned working time and time events. It is now time to take those values and create Wage types that payroll can use to compensate employees for their time. You can access the customizing tables via the IMG menu path TIME MANAGEMENT • TIME EVALUATION • TIME EVALUATION WITHOUT CLOCK TIMES • TIME WAGE TYPE SELECTION AND OVERTIME COMPENSATION.

The configuration is broken down into the following sections.

9.5.1   Define Valuation Classes for Period Work Schedule

This section of customization allows you to associate a number with a period Work Schedule. The valuation class is just one of a few different ways you can set up the system to determine when a particular Wage type should be created. By using this functionality, you can allow the system to generate a Wage type for those that have the Work Schedule rule with the appropriate valuation class associated with the period Work Schedule. Figure 9.14 displays the configuration table.

Grpg	Period WS	Description	Start Date	End Date	Val.class for PWS
01	$XQP		01/01/1990	12/31/9999	
01	3-WK	3week Rotating Shift	01/01/1990	12/31/9999	
01	GLZ	Flextime	01/01/1990	12/31/9999	5
01	KUG	Reduced working hrs	01/01/1990	12/31/9999	
01	M3	3-shift operation 4W	01/01/1990	12/31/9999	3
01	NO	40 hours per week	01/01/1990	12/31/9999	
01	NORM	Normal shift	01/01/1990	12/31/9999	1

Figure 9.14   Table V_551C_B Valuation Class for Period Work Schedule

9.5.2   Define Groupings

Groupings for determining time Wage type selection are based on the schema function DAYMO. The groupings are associated with table entries in table T510S. If you determine there are limits to this method of associating a grouping for time Wage type selection, you can also utilize a personnel calculation rule with operation MODIF for the particular values you need. Figure 9.15 shows the groupings function DAYMO.

000540	BLOCK	BEG				Select time wage types
000550	DAYMO	01	02	02	02	Set day grouping for T510S
000560	GWT		S	DZL		Wage type selection for planned work
000570	GWT		M	ZML		Wage type selection for overtime

Figure 9.15   DAYMO Function for Table T510S Groupings

9.5.3   Define Processing Types

Processing types are used throughout Time Evaluation to further identify what kind of time the Time type really is. The main reason for such a thing is so that we know which Wage types should be generated for particular processing types. The processing types are part of the time Wage type selection rule. When Time types are processed in this section, the system validates the processing types of the Time type against the time Wage type selection rule. If the rule finds a valid processing type, and if all other conditions are successful, then the Wage type is generated. Figure 9.16 shows the configuration table for processing types.

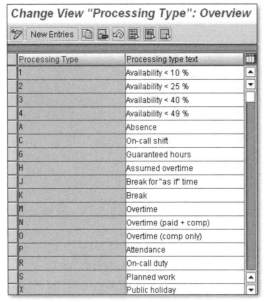

Figure 9.16   Processing Types Table V_T510V

9.5.4   Create Wage type Catalog

The Wage type catalog is one of a few locations in the IMG where you can create Wage types. It is best to find a model Wage type that is similar to what you need to create and copy it. Once you select the model Wage type, you associate the Wage type number that you want to create and the SAP system will copy all of the parameters and table entries of the model Wage type to your new Wage type.

9.5.5   Define Generation Rules

This section of the IMG is where you define the time Wage type generation rules. As previously noted, you can set up the time Wage type selection rule group via the DAYMO function or personnel calculation rule TMON utilizing operation MODIF. Figure 9.17 shows the personnel calculation rule TMON. You can use this rule to give yourself more flexibility when defining the grouping compared to the DAYMO function.

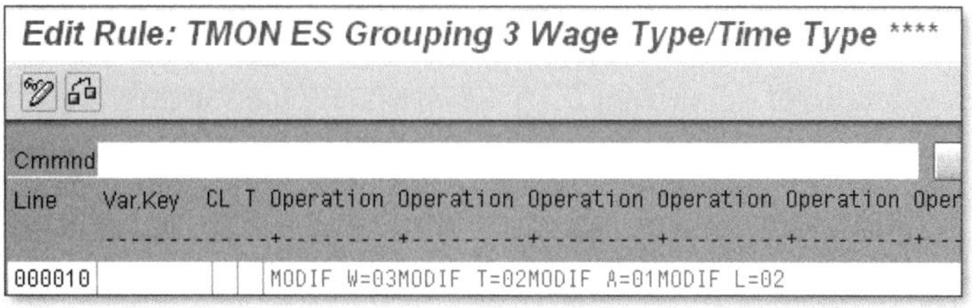

Figure 9.17 Personnel Calculation Rule TMON for Time Wage type Selection

Figure 9.18 shows what a time Wage type selection rule looks like. This is the opportunity to define when a Wage type should be generated. You have the option to be very specific as to when a Wage type should be generated. If you determine that this seems a little complex for your requirements, then you can skip this section and write a custom personnel calculation rule where you map specific Time types to Wage types.

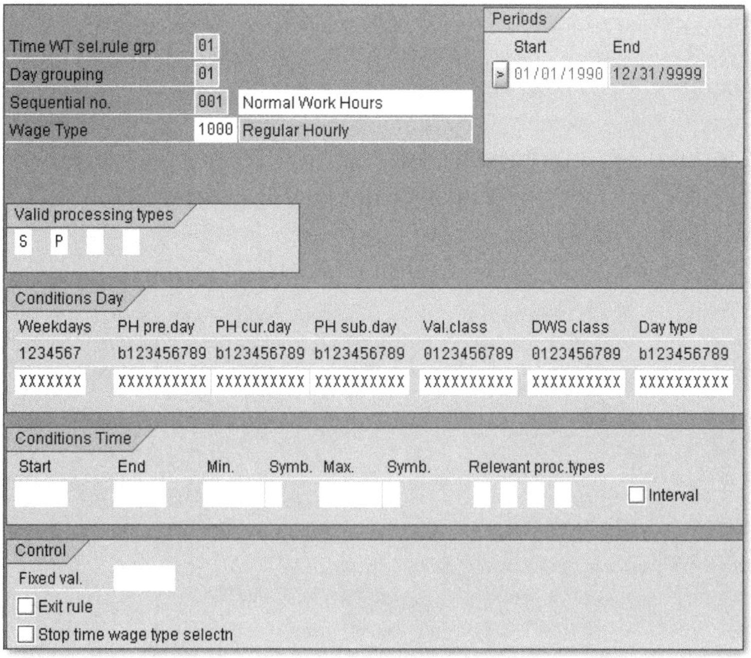

Figure 9.18 Time Wage Type Selection Rule

9.5.6   Perform Time Wage Type Selection

Now that you have set up your system with all of the various parameters to generate Wage types, you need to tell the schema which Time Pairs need to look up generation rules. Function GWT, or get Wage type, is used for this functionality. Figure 9.19 shows an example of how to set up the system. You can specify which processing types and which tables the data should be stored in.

000540	BLOCK	BEG				Select time wage types
000550	DAYMO	01	02	02	02	Set day grouping for T510S
000560	GWT		S	DZL		Wage type selection for planned work
000570	GWT		M	ZML		Wage type selection for overtime

Figure 9.19   GWT Wage Type Selection

9.5.7   Generate Higher Bonuses on a Weekly Basis

Subschema TW00 —Generate Higher Bonuses — is an example of how to compensate an employee based on the Wage type that was generated in Time Evaluation. The subschema is broken down into three personnel calculation rules. Figure 9.20 shows the placement of Subschema TW00 within Schema TM04, and also shows personnel calculation rule TW10.

Personnel calculation rule TW10 is an initialization rule that determines what to do with Time type 0901 — Weekly Overtime. If it is the first day of the week, Time type 0901 is set to zero; otherwise the amounts from the previous days in the week are accumulated and added to the daily balance of Time type 0901.

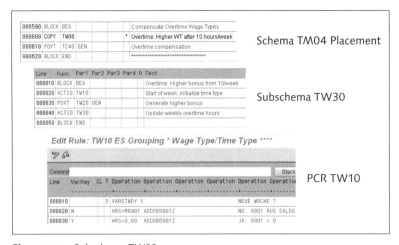

Figure 9.20   Subschema TW00

Personnel calculation rule TW20 utilizes two model Wage types that are delivered in the system. The following Wage types are referenced.

▶ MM10 — Overtime 100% plus 25%

▶ MM20 — Overtime 100% plus 50%

The personnel calculation rule first makes a decision based on Wage type. Only Wage types MM10 and MM20 are processed. Once Wage type MM10 is selected, the hours are added to Time type 0000 — utility Time type 0001. The processing sets the Wage type MM10 value to 10, and then it subtracts any amounts from the daily balance of Time type 0901. The rule then sets some minimums and maximums and ultimately adds the hours to Wage type MM20 to be compensated at a higher level. Figure 9.21 shows personnel calculation rule TW20 — generate higher payment.

Edit Rule: TW20 ES Grouping * Wage Type/Time Type ****

Line	Var.Key	CL	T	Operation Operation Operation Operation Operation Operat
000010			D	OUTOTWGTYP
000020	****			ADDOT *
000030	MM10			ADDDB0000ZHRS=10,00 HRS-D0901 HRS>0 HRS<D0000 NEXTR
000040	MM10		1	GENOWB* ADDOT MM20HRS=D0000 ADDDB0901
000050	MM20			ADDDB0901 ADDOT *

Figure 9.21 Personnel Calculation Rule TW20

The final personnel calculation rule in Subschema TW00 is TW30 — Revise Balances. This rule is designed to set Time type 0901 to the appropriate value so that it is ready for the next day's calculations (see Figure 9.22).

Edit Rule: TW30 ES Grouping * Wage Type/Time Type ****

Line	Var.Key	CL	T	Operation Operation Operation Operation Operation 0
000010				HRS=D0901 HRS-M0901 ADDDB0901Z

Figure 9.22 Personnel Calculation Rule TW30

9.5.8 Compensate Overtime

The compensation of overtime involves setting processing class 17 for particular Wage types if you want to use ratios to pay out additional overtime. If generating overtime Wage types will satisfy your requirements, then you probably do not need to bother with this configuration. This functionality is delivered with three personal calculation rules that are covered in detail next. Figure 9.23 displays the personnel calculation rule and the options that are delivered that can be linked to a Wage type via processing class 17 in table V_512W_D.

Personnel calculation rule TC40 is the first rule in the processing. The rule is based on the value of processing class 17. Based on the particular value that is linked to the Wage type, the amounts are written to other Time types, such as 0041, 0042, 0043, and 0410. The rule also branches to personnel calculation rule TC41 when processing class 17 values D, E, or F are encountered.

Personnel calculation rule TC41 makes one decision. This decision is based on the overtime compensation type. If the response is a 1, 2, or 3, the following actions occur:

▶ Amount is added to Time type 0042 and then added to the ZL table.

▶ Amount is added to Time types 0043 and 0410. The amount is also added to the ZL table under Wage types M1 and M2.

▶ Amount is added to Time type 0041. The amount is then multiplied by 12% and added to Time type 0410.

If, during the processing, the overtime compensation type is not equal to 1, 2, or 3, the personnel calculation rule TC42 is called for subsequent processing. Personnel calculation rule TC42 makes its first decision based on processing class 17. If the values are D, E, or F, then it follows the same logic as personnel calculation rule TC41 for values 1, 2, and 3.

The overall goal of this series of personnel calculation rules is to build additional Wage types based on a Wage type that was generated utilizing the time Wage type selection rules (see Figure 9.23).

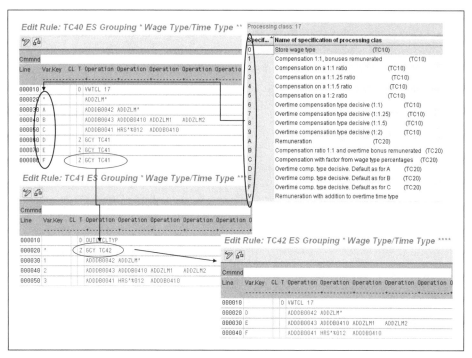

Figure 9.23 Overtime Compensation Based on Ratios

9.6 Time in Lieu

The time in lieu of overtime compensation is delivered functionality that can be leveraged and customized per your requirements. The overall premise of the functionality is to grant employees time-off quotas based on overtime worked through the year. The personnel calculations rules utilize a variety of Time types to capture time-related information, store counters of the occurrences of situations and provide the quota configuration with an amount that should be generated for a quota type.

You can access the customizing tables via the IMG menu path TIME MANAGEMENT • TIME EVALUATION • TIME EVALUATION WITHOUT CLOCK TIMES • TIME IN LIEU. SAP delivers Subschema TW40 — Time in Lieu Processing — to set up the system utilizing time in lieu of compensation. Figure 9.24 shows how the schema looks as delivered. There are a variety of personnel calculation rules that facilitate the processing. In addition, there are also a variety of Time types that facilitate the various calculations. The Time types are listed in Figure 9.24 underneath each of the personnel calculation rules that utilize them. Each of the personnel calculation rules is shown and the functionality is described under the specific figures. Some of the descriptions can be quite long, so it is best to flip back and forth from the text to the actual image of the rule. In addition, you can also write out the descriptions yourself by utilizing the F1 feature for each operation to obtain further information if you need more clarity.

Line	Func.	Par1	Par2	Par3	Par4	D	Text
000010	BLOCK	BEG					Compensation time
000020	**						- Weekly overtime analysis
000030	**						(France - model)
000040	PRINT		TIP				TIP before weekly overtime analysis
000050	PRINT		TES				TES before weekly overtime analysis
000060	ACTIO	TW40					Initialize time in lieu quota & tm.types
000070	P2012	TW42					Process time transfer
000080	IF			D01			
000090	ACTIO	TW43					Do not delete time in lieu quota
000100	ACTIO	TW41					Initialize annual overtime
000110	ENDIF						
000120	RTIPA	TW44	GEN				Process absences
000130	**						
000140	PTIP	TW45	GEN				Overtime after OVTWL hrs productive time
000150	ACTIO	TW4S					Determine wkly OT, time in lieu entitl.
000160	IF			EOM			
000170	ACTIO	TW49					Time-off entitlmnt: Remunerate remainder
000180	ENDIF						
000190	ACTIO	TW4A					Correct time type for weekly overtime
000200	PRINT		TIP				TIP after weekly overtime analysis
000210	PRINT		TES				TES after weekly overtime analysis
000220	BLOCK	END					

Rule TW40 - Time Types
0891 - Time-off entitlement
0892 - Time-off ent.: Prev.month
0893 - Tm/lieu:monthbefore last
0951 - Time in lieu
0953 - Working hours/week
Rule TW42 - Time Types
0895 - Transfer to 0893
Rule TW43 - Time Types
0891 - Time-off entitlement
0892 - Time-off ent.: Prev.month
0893 - Tm/lieu:monthbefore last
0951 - Time in lieu
0953 - Working hours/week
Rule TW41 - Time Types
0895 - Transfer to 0893
Rule TW43 - Time Types
0893 - Tm/lieu:monthbefore last
0895 - Transfer to 0893

Rule TW41 - Time Types
0952 - Overtime/year
Rule TW4D - Time Types
0891 - Time-off entitlement
0892 - Time-off ent.: Prev.month
0893 - Tm/lieu:monthbefore last
Rule TW4C - Time Types
0953 - Working hours/week
Rule TW46 - Time Types
0952 - Overtime/year
0953 - Working hours/week
Rule TW46 - Time Types
0951 - Time in lieu
0952 - Overtime/year
0953 - Working hours/week
0954 - OT/We: Counter time type

Rule TW48 - Time Types
0891 - Time-off entitlement
0951 - Time in lieu
Rule TW49 - Time Types
0951 - Time in lieu
Rule TW4A - Time Types
0891 - Time-off entitlement
0892 - Time-off ent.: Prev.month
0893 - Tm/lieu:monthbefore last
0951 - Time in lieu
0953 - Working hours/week

Figure 9.24   Schema TW40

Personnel calculation rule TW40 — Time type Balance Unitization — is the first rule in Subschema TW40. The overall premise of the rule is to establish baseline amounts for Time types 0891, Time-off entitlement; 0892, Time-off Entitlement Previous Month; 0893, Time in Lieu Month Before Last; and 0951, Time in Lieu.

Each of these Time types obtains the value of its own monthly balance and writes it to the current daily balance for each Time type. This way, the system has the latest balances to base its future calculations from. In addition, the rule checks to see if the day being processed is the first day of the week. If it is the first day, Time type 0953 is set to zero. If it is not the first day of the week, then the monthly balance from the table SALDO is brought into and saved as the daily total for the Time type. Figure 9.25 displays personnel calculation rule TW40.

Edit Rule: TW40 ES Grouping * Wage Type/Time Type ****

Line	Var.Key	CL	T	Operation	Operation	Operation	Operation	Operation	Operation	*
000010				HRS=M0891	ADDDB0891ZNEXTR			INITIALISIERUNG.		
000020		1		HRS=M0892	ADDDB0892ZNEXTR					
000030		2		HRS=M0893	ADDDB0893ZNEXTR					
000040		3		HRS=M0951	ADDDB0951ZNEXTR					
000050		4	D	VARSTWDY 1				BEGIN OF NEW WEEK?		
000060	N			HRS=M0953	ADDDB0953Z			NO: 0953 INCL SALDO		
000070	Y			HRS=0.00	ADDDB0953Z			YES: 0953 = 0		

Figure 9.25 Personnel Calculation Rule TW40

The next personnel calculation rule is very simple. All rule TW42, Time Transfer Balance Update, does is take the value entered on Infotype 2012, Time Transfer, and add it to Time type 0895. This type of time transfer from the infotype allows you to manipulate particular Time type values throughout the process. When you design rules, it is always a good idea to provide the payroll department the ability to override particular Time types, Wage types, and quota types to account for special issues that might arise. Figure 9.26 shows personnel calculation rule TW42.

Edit Rule: TW42 ES Grouping * Wage Type/Time Type 0895

Line	Var.Key	CL	T	Operation	Operation	Operation	Operation	Operation	Oper
000010				ADDDB0895Z					

Figure 9.26 Personnel Calculation Rule TW42

The next personnel calculation rule is TW43 — Update Time types. This rule sets the hours to equal the value of Time type 0895 — Transfer to 0893. Once the hours have been imported from Time type 0895, the rule checks to see what the actually value equals. If the value is greater than zero, then the hours are reset to equal the value of Time type 0893 and added to the daily balance of Time type 0893. Figure 9.27 shows personnel calculation rule TW43.

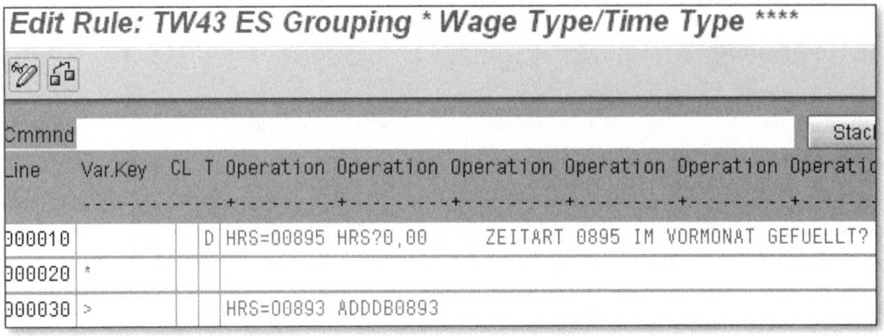
Edit Rule: TW43 ES Grouping * Wage Type/Time Type ****
Cmmnd
Stac
Line Var.Key CL T Operation Operation Operation Operation Operation Operati
000010 D HRS=00895 HRS?0,00 ZEITART 0895 IM VORMONAT GEFUELLT?
000020 *
000030 > HRS=00893 ADDDB0893

Figure 9.27 Personnel Calculation Rule TW43

The next personnel calculation rule in Subschema TW40 is TW41 — Reset Time type 0952. This rule is also a very basic personnel calculation rule. This rule determines whether or not it is the first month of the year. If the current month is January, the value of Time type 0952 is reset to equal zero. Figure 9.28 shows personnel calculation rule TW41.

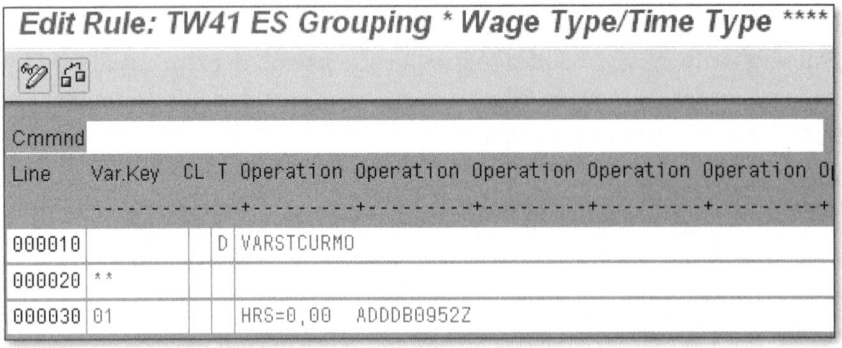
Edit Rule: TW41 ES Grouping * Wage Type/Time Type ****
Cmmnd
Line Var.Key CL T Operation Operation Operation Operation Operation O
000010 D VARSTCURMO
000020 **
000030 01 HRS=0,00 ADDDB0952Z

Figure 9.28 Personnel Calculation Rule TW41

The next two personnel calculation rules work together as rule TW4D is called directly from within rule TW44. Rule TW44 makes a series of decisions to decide whether or not rule TW4D should be processed. The decisions include determining the pair type, then determining the processing type, and finally a decision is made to determine if the absence type 0950 is currently being processed. If the system determines the absence type 0950 is used, then and only then does rule TW4D begin to process.

Personnel calculation rule TW4D utilizes a variety of Time types to conduct processing, make decisions, and update balances. The rule begins by setting the current value equal to the value of the daily balance of Time type 0891 — Time-off Entitlement. The rule then adds this value to the daily balance of Time type 0892 — Time-off Entitlement Previous Month. The rule then adds the value of the daily balance of Time type 0893 — Time in Lieu Month Before Last. You now have three Time types added together to form one balance. The rule then compares this balance against the balance of absence type 0950. If the value is less, than a message is generated and the processing of this rule stops. If the value is equal or greater, the value is now set to the value of the daily balance of Time type 0893. The rule once again checks the value of Time type 0893 against the value of absence type 0950.

If the value is equal to or greater, then the value is set back to the previous value and added to Time type 0893. The rule then stops processing. If the value is less than the value of absence type 0950, then the previous value is brought back in, Time type 0892 is added to the balance, and a decision is made to check the new balance compared to zero. If the balance is equal to or greater than zero, the value is added to Time type 0892, the hours are set to zero, and then added to Time type 0893 making the daily balance equal zero. If the result of the balance compared to zero is less than zero, the hours are added together with the daily balance of Time type 0891 and Time type 0891 is replaced with the updated value. The hours are set back to zero and added to Time types 0893 and 0892.

Wow, that is a lot to take in! The overall goal of this rule is to check a balance of one item against the value of another item. Each time the values are checked, a new variable is added to the equation. This happens a few times until the various Time types receive the balance updates that are required. Figure 9.29 shows the two personnel calculation rules.

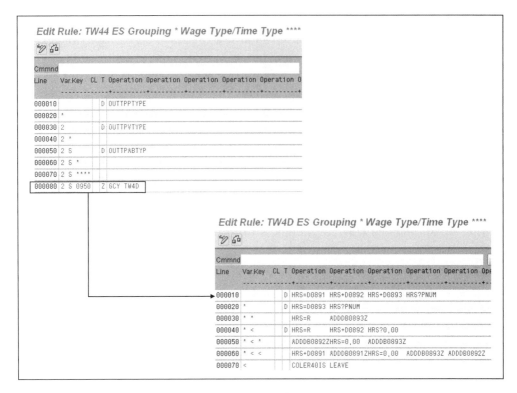

Figure 9.29 Personnel Calculation Rules TW44 and TW4D

The following two personnel calculation rules are processed next. Rule TW45 and rule TW4C are processed together. Rule TW4C is called directly from within rule TW45. Rule TW45 determines what the pair type is and what the time identifier is with the particular Time type by following the standard method of asking questions and obtaining responses. You will notice in the rule that Time Types with the identifiers 01, 02, and 03 activate rule TW4C for subsequent processing no matter where they fall in the rule.

Personnel calculation rule TW4C is going to import particular values for Time types, check them against a constant value, add a few things together, and perhaps create a few new Time types. The rule begins by importing the daily value of Time type 0953 — Working Hours/Week. The value is compared against a constant value stored in table V_T511K for the code OVTWL. If the value of Time type 0953 is greater than the constant, then the time is changed to overtime by changing the processing type to M for overtime. The hours are set back to the original value and added to Time type 0953.

If the value happens to be less than the constant, the value of Time type 0953 is added to the value of the hours that entered the rule. A comparison is again carried out against the constant value. If the value is now greater than the constant, then the hours are now set to equal the constant. Time type 0953 is subtracted from the constant value and added to Time type 0953. The Time type is then separated into two Time types, changed to overtime for one of the Time types, and added through. The hours are then reset to the original value and added back to Time type 0953 (see Figure 9.30).

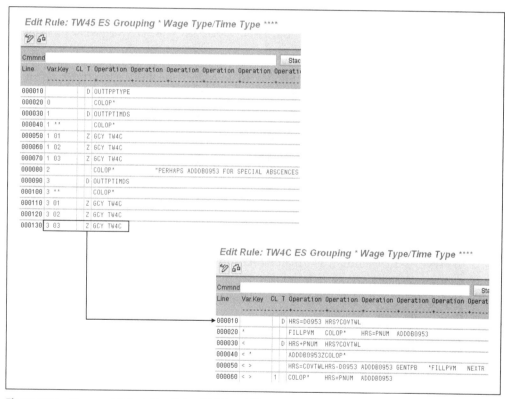

Figure 9.30 Personnel Calculation Rules TW45 and TW4C

Personnel calculation rule TW4S is utilized to branch off to three other personnel calculation rules. Rules TW46, TW47, and TW48 are the three rules that are contained within personnel calculation rule TW4S. During the rules processing a decision is made to determine if the day being processed is the seventh day of the working week. If this is true, personnel calculation rules TW46, TW47, and TW 48 are subsequently processed.

Personnel calculation rule TW46 checks to see if the value of Time type 0953 — working hours week — is greater than the overtime constant OVTWL. If the hours are greater than the constant, then the hours are set back to the original amount entering the rule. This amount is added to Time type 0952 — Overtime/Year. The hours are compared against eight hours. If the hours are greater than eight, the hours are set back to the original amount and added to Wage type MM20. The rule then sets Wage type MM10 to equal eight hours. If the original calculation amount is less than or equal to the constant, then the hours are added to Time type MM10. Compared to the previous set of rules, this one is more straightforward.

After personnel calculation rule TW46 finishes, rule TW47 is processed. Rule TW47 makes its first decision based on the value of Time type 0952 Overtime/Year. If the value is greater than zero the subsequent processing will occur, otherwise the rules processing is complete. When the amount is greater than zero, then the rule begins comparing the monthly amount of time 0952 against the constant OVTWY without taking the current day into account. Based on that outcome the rule adds the value of 0952 to Time type 0951 Time in Lieu when it is greater. If the comparison determines that the value of Time type 0952 is less than the constant, then the rule goes back and adds the daily value of 0952 to the monthly value and conducts the same comparison. Once you have the new balance, if that amount is greater than the constant, then Time type 0954 and Time type 0951 are updated with the original hours that entered the rule. The rule then sets the value of the current processing to equal the daily balance of Time type 0953. The rule then subtracts the value of 0954, and then subtracts the constant value. The remaining hours are multiplied by .50 and added to Time types 0951.

Finally, personnel calculation rule TW48 gets its turn to process. The value is set to Time type 0951 Time in Lieu. If the hours are greater than eight then the value is divided by eight, rounded, multiplied back by eight, and then added to Time types 0891 Time-off Entitlement and 0951. Figure 9.31 shows the four rules.

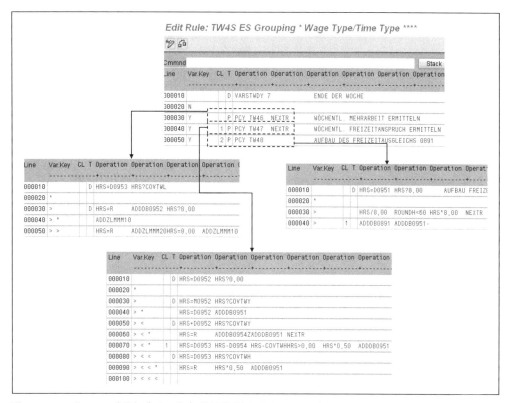

Figure 9.31 Personnel Calculation Rule TW4S, TW46, TW47, and TW48

This was a lot of information to digest and if you understand it after reading it the first four times, then perhaps writing custom rules is right up your alley. But, we still need to move on to the next personnel calculation rule of Subschema TW40, rule TW49 — End-of-Year Compensation.

Personnel calculation rule TW49 is used to compensate employees for any time remaining at the end of the year in Time type 0951 Time in lieu. During the rule processing a decision is made based on the current month. If the month happens to be the twelfth month of the year, then the processing sets the amount of hours equal to the daily balance of Time type 0951. The value of 0951 is written to Wage type MM70 in the ZL table. The hours are then cleared out of Time type 0951 and saved for the day being processed. Wage type MM70 would then be picked up in payroll and the employee would be compensated. Figure 9.32 shows personnel calculation rule TW49.

```
Edit Rule: TW49 ES Grouping * Wage Type/Time Type ****
 ✐ 🔁

Cmmnd
Line    Var.Key  CL T Operation Operation Operation Operation Operation O
        ---------+---------+---------+---------+---------+---------+
000010           D VARSTCURMO
000020  **
000030  12          HRS=D0951 ADDZLMMM7OHRS=0,00  ADDDB0951Z
```

Figure 9.32 Personnel Calculation Rule TW49

The final rule of Subschema TW40 is personnel calculation rule TW4A. This rule cor-
rects the various Time types and updates them for future processing. Each of these
Time types takes the daily balance of each Time type and subtracts the monthly balance of that Time type. Because the value cannot be negative, it is zeroed out during
the processing. Figure 9.33 shows the personnel calculation rule TW4A.

```
Edit Rule: TW4A ES Grouping * Wage Type/Time Type ****
 ✐ 🔁

Cmmnd
Line    Var.Key  CL T Operation Operation Operation Operation Operation O
        ---------+---------+---------+---------+---------+---------+
000010           HRS=D0951 HRS-M0951 ADDDB0951ZNEXTR
000020      1     HRS=D0953 HRS-M0953 ADDDB0953ZNEXTR
000030      2     HRS=D0891 HRS-M0891 ADDDB0891ZNEXTR
000040      3     HRS=D0892 HRS-M0892 ADDDB0892ZNEXTR
000050      4     HRS=D0893 HRS-M0893 ADDDB0893Z
```

Figure 9.33 Personnel Calculation Rule TW4A Updates the Various Balances

This concludes the rules that are associated with Subschema TW40. There is a lot
of detail, but the overall approach is to use various Time types to make decisions
and route the processing down different paths depending on the values of such
Time types. This takes time to learn and leveraging the system help for particular
personnel calculation rule operations is well worth your time.

9.7   Processing Balances

Now that you have processed all of the time entered into the system, generated any
necessary Wage type for Payroll to compensate, and updated Time Types throughout the schema processing, it is now time to conduct a little bit of cleanup and save

any Time types from the day's processing. This is also the time that you update any balances that are required for subsequent days processing. This includes creating new Time types, if necessary.

You can access the customizing tables via the IMG menu path TIME MANAGE-MENT • TIME EVALUATION • TIME EVALUATION WITHOUT CLOCK TIMES • PROCESSING BALANCES.

9.7.1 Form Day Balances

This personnel calculation rule adds the various balances of the Time types to other Time types to form any balance you need. These facilitate future calculations and reporting buckets that can be viewed or reported off of. Figure 9.34 shows an example of the rule for one of the Time types.

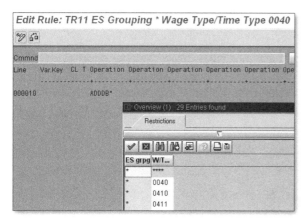

Figure 9.34 Personnel Calculation Rule TR11 — Form Time Balances

9.7.2 Total Flextime Balance, Overtime, and Productive Hours

The next personnel calculation rule is TR30 — Updates Various Balances. The following Time types are updated within the rule:

▸ 0002 — Planned Time – Add the hours

▸ 0005 — Flextime Balance Subtract the hours

▸ 0003 — Skeleton Time Add the hours from 0003 to 0005

▸ 0041 — Overtime to compensate Add Time type 0042, Overtime to Remunerate; Add Time type 0043, Overtime Basic/Time off; and then add the total to Time Type 0040, Overtime worked

► 0010 — Attendances Add hours from Time type 0030, Off-site work; add the total hours to Time types 0050, Productive hours, and 0051, Cumulative productive hours

Figure 9.35 shows personnel calculation rule TR30.

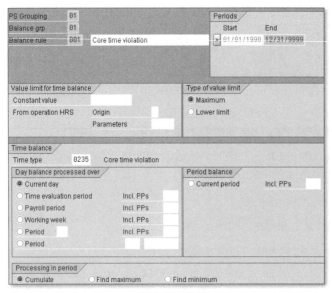

Figure 9.35 Personnel Calculation Rule TR30

9.7.3 Balance Limits

You have the opportunity to establish particular limits for Time types. This table configuration is not mandatory but may serve as a tool to satisfy your business requirements. Figure 9.36 shows the table V_T559P and the various opportunities to customize the system.

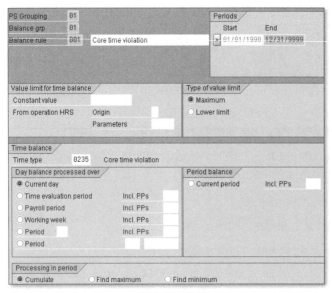

Figure 9.36 Balance Limits Table V_T559P

9.7.4 Deduct Absences from Time Balances

Personnel calculation rule TP20 allows you to deduct absences from the Time type balances. The first decision is based on the pair type of the absence type. If the value is a 2, which it normally is, then the system determines what the processing type is. If the processing type is an S, then the final decision is based on what the actual absence type is. If the absence type in this sample rule happens to be 0900 or 0910, then the particular Time types are reduced accordingly (see Figure 9.37).

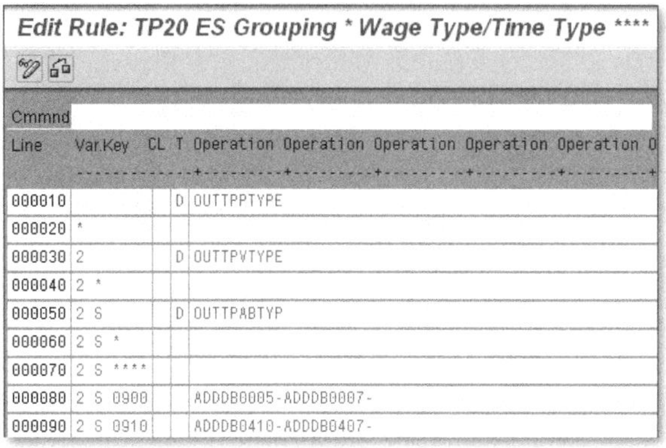

```
Edit Rule: TP20 ES Grouping * Wage Type/Time Type ****
📝 🔒
Cmmnd
Line    Var.Key  CL T Operation Operation Operation Operation Operation O
              ---------+---------+---------+---------+---------+---------+
000010              D OUTTPPTYPE
000020   *
000030   2          D OUTTPVTYPE
000040   2 *
000050   2 S        D OUTTPABTYP
000060   2 S *
000070   2 S ****
000080   2 S 0900     ADDDB0005-ADDDB0007-
000090   2 S 0910     ADDDB0410-ADDDB0407-
```

Figure 9.37 Personnel Calculation Rule TP20

9.7.5 Create Technical Wage Type from Time Balances

Personnel calculation rule TR33 — Create Technical Wage types — is a rule that is designed to create Wage types for Payroll. The rule takes the hours from the daily balance of Time type 0050 — Productive hours — and adds them to Wage type MI01. The rule then takes the hours from the daily balance of Time type 0020 — Absence and adds them to Wage type MI02. This rule is pretty simple and you can leverage the methodology anytime you need to generate Wage types based on Time type values (see Figure 9.38).

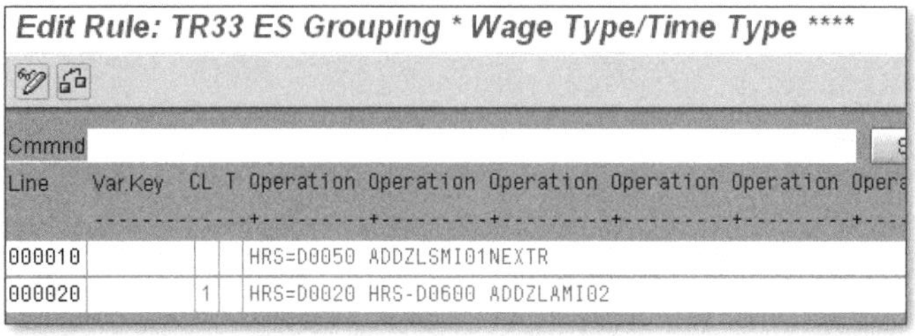

```
Edit Rule: TR33 ES Grouping * Wage Type/Time Type ****
📝 🔒
Cmmnd                                                          S
Line    Var.Key  CL T Operation Operation Operation Operation Operation Opera
              ---------+---------+---------+---------+---------+---------+
000010              HRS=D0050 ADDZLSMI01NEXTR
000020         1    HRS=D0020 HRS-D0600 ADDZLAMI02
```

Figure 9.38 Personnel Calculation Rule TR33

9.7.6 Updated Cumulated Balances

When you create Time types, you need to determine the various buckets in which the values will be stored. You have the option of saving the values to the ZES table, which stands for the daily balance or the SALDO table, which stands for the cumulative balance table. In addition, you also determine how the system brings in previously calculated values and if the values of the Time type are available for viewing via reports. Figure 9.39 shows table V_T555A.

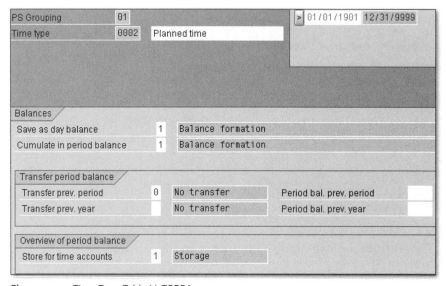

Figure 9.39 Time Type Table V_T555A

9.7.7 Time Transfer

Time transfer is the functionality in which you can enter particular codes on Info-type 2012 — Time Transfers. These entries can update one of three values when entered and are processed in Time Evaluation.

▶ Time types — Allows you to update Time types

▶ Wage types — Allows you to update Wage types

▶ Quota type — Allows you to update quota types

Each of these options is processed in the Time Management schemas via function P2012. Figure 9.40 shows the configuration tables of the three options.

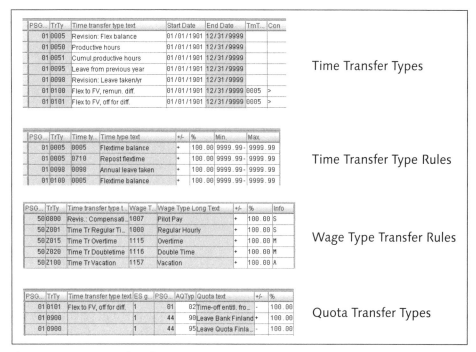

PSG...	TrTy	Time transfer type text	Start Date	End Date	TmT...	Con
01	0005	Revision: Flex balance	01/01/1901	12/31/9999		
01	0050	Productive hours	01/01/1901	12/31/9999		
01	0051	Cumul.productive hours	01/01/1901	12/31/9999		
01	0095	Leave from previous year	01/01/1901	12/31/9999		
01	0098	Revision: Leave taken/yr	01/01/1901	12/31/9999		
01	0100	Flex to FV, remun. diff.	01/01/1901	12/31/9999	0005	>
01	0101	Flex to FV, off for diff.	01/01/1901	12/31/9999	0005	>

Time Transfer Types

PSG...	TrTy	Time ty...	Time type text	+/-	%	Min.	Max.
01	0005	0005	Flextime balance	+	100.00	9999.99-	9999.99
01	0005	0710	Repost flextime	+	100.00	9999.99-	9999.99
01	0098	0098	Annual leave taken	+	100.00	9999.99-	9999.99
01	0100	0005	Flextime balance	+	100.00	9999.99-	9999.99

Time Transfer Type Rules

PSG...	TrTy	Time transfer type t...	Wage T...	Wage Type Long Text	+/-	%	Info
50	0800	Revis.: Compensati...	1007	Pilot Pay	+	100.00	S
50	Z001	Time Tr Regular Ti...	1000	Regular Hourly	+	100.00	S
50	Z015	Time Tr Overtime	1115	Overtime	+	100.00	M
50	Z020	Time Tr Doubletime	1116	Double Time	+	100.00	M
50	Z100	Time Tr Vacation	1157	Vacation	+	100.00	A

Wage Type Transfer Rules

PSG...	TrTy	Time transfer type text	ES g...	PSG...	AQTyp	Quota text	+/-	%
01	0101	Flex to FV, off for diff.	1	01	02	Time-off entitl. fro...	-	100.00
01	0900		1	44	90	Leave Bank Finland	+	100.00
01	0900		1	44	95	Leave Quota Finla...	-	100.00

Quota Transfer Types

Figure 9.40 Time Transfer Infotype 2012 Options

9.7.8 Period End Processing

Period end processing allows you one final opportunity to adjust any time balances that have been created and updated throughout the schema's processing through the various stages. Personnel calculation rules TR90 and TR91 provide examples of how you can update your particular balances.

Personnel calculation rule TR90 — Flextime Balance Transfers — utilizes two decisions. The first checks the value of the table T510S grouping. If the grouping is 01, the processing is stopped for this rule. If the value is anything other than 01, then the hours value is set to the previous day's balance of Time type 0005 — Flextime Balance for the Current Payroll Period. The daily value accumulated via the current day's processing of Time Type 0005 is also added to the balance. The total value is compared to zero. If the value equals zero, the rule stops. If the value is less than zero, a message is generated and Wage type M730 is created and Time type 0006, Flextime Excess and Time type 0005, flextime balance, are reduced. If the value is greater than zero, a different message is generated. Wage type MM00 is generated with Time types 0006 and 0005 updated. Figure 9.41 shows personnel calculation rule TR90.

Edit Rule: TR90 ES Grouping * Wage Type/Time Type **

Line	Var.Key	CL	T	Operation Operation Operation Operation Operation Operation
000010			D	VARSTMOD W
000020	**		D	HRS=X0005 HRS+D0005 HRS?0,00
000030	** *			
000040	** <			COLER41 ADDZLMM730ADDDB0006 ADDDB0005-
000050	** >			COLER42 ADDZLMMM00ADDDB0006 ADDDB0005-
000060	01			"HOURLY PAID EARNERS: REGULAR HOURS VIA T510S

Figure 9.41 Personnel Calculation Rule TR90

Personnel calculation rule TR91 also allows you to update Time type balances. Instead of looking at flextime balances, this rule utilizes Time type 0410 — Time off from Overtime (see Figure 9.42). This rule sets the current value equal to the payroll period total value of Time Type 0410. The daily value of Time type 0410 is added to the existing period value and then compared to zero. If the value is greater than zero, a message and Wage type MM00 is generated. Finally, Time type 0410 is subtracted by the value added to the Wage type.

Edit Rule: TR91 ES Grouping * Wage Type/Time Type **

Line	Var.Key	CL	T	Operation Operation Operation Operation Operation O
000010			D	HRS=X0410 HRS+D0410 HRS?0,00
000020	*			
000030	>			COLER40 ADDZLMMM00ADDDB0410-

Figure 9.42 Personnel Calculation Rule TR91 and Time Type 0410 Balances

This concludes the discussion of processing balances. Now we'll move on to how messages will be generated in the schema.

9.8 Message Output

The Message Output functionality allows you to define messages that can be associated with particular functionalities within the time schema. Message types can be called within the rules. These messages are stored for the employee and allow you to flag particular items that might warrant extra attention by an administrator.

You can access the customizing tables via the IMG menu path TIME MANAGEMENT • TIME EVALUATION • TIME EVALUATION WITHOUT CLOCK TIMES • MESSAGE OUTPUT. Figure 9.43 shows an example of the message type being called by a personnel calculation rule.

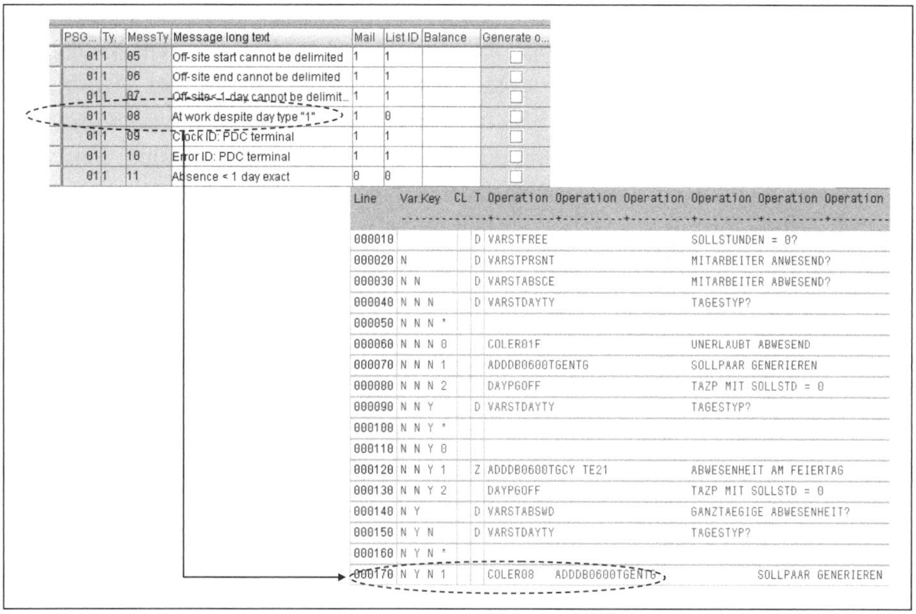

Figure 9.43 Example of an Error Message Called in a Personnel Calculation Rule

The following section is the part of the schema where you store the calculations of the current day's processing.

9.9   Storing Time Evaluation Results

You can access the customizing tables via the IMG menu path TIME MANAGEMENT • TIME EVALUATION • TIME EVALUATION WITHOUT CLOCK TIMES • STORING TIME EVALUATION RESULTS.

The final step in schema TM04 processing is to accumulate any balances and export them to the B2 Time Cluster. SAP ERP HCM delivers functions CUMBT and EXPRT that satisfy this functionality. They are one of the last functions in the schema.

9.10   Summary

In this chapter, you learned about Time Evaluation Without Clock Times utilizing Schema ZMO4. There was a lot of detail provided as we walked through the logic of the delivered personnel calculation rules and what they were doing at various stages. You also learned about the various areas of configuration within the IMG and how each item is set up, processed, and altered to accommodate your business requirements. As you begin working with Time Evaluation and customizing the personnel calculation rules, it's advantageous to always make a copy of the standard schemas and rules, and then update your copy for processing. This way, your changes will not be overridden during system updates. To really get up to speed on Time Evaluation Without Clock Times, you should spend time reviewing the delivered rules and validating what they are doing by reviewing the online help via the F1 function. There is a plethora of information available and it's next to impossible to memorize every possible option. That being said, as you become more proficient with writing rules, you will be able to write them from scratch without referencing any help screens.

In the next chapter, we'll be talking about Evaluations and the Time Management pool.

In this chapter, you'll learn about key areas to consider during the configuration of Evaluations and the Time Management Pool. At the conclusion of this chapter, you should be knowledgeable of the two approaches to setting up the Time Statement Form and the functionality offered via the Time Management Pool Interface.

10   Evaluation and Time Management Pool

The Evaluations and Time Management Pool section is comprised of two main components:

▸ Time Statement Form

▸ Time Management Pool

The Time Statement Form is an overview report that can display information concerning an employee's schedule, time worked, and balances such as quotas or other user-defined balances stored in a Time type. The report only pulls data for days that have actually run through Time Evaluation. Every employee is the target audience because they are able to view all of their time-related balances. In addition, managers are also a likely candidate so that they can keep track of particular time balances, such as regular time or overtime, for employees to prevent extra cost to the company by allowing too many work hours for one period.

The Time Management Pool is a basic interface that allows the user to branch off into different processing functionality from one central location. It is called an interface, but the overall functionality of the Time Management Pool provides the user an easy way to access data that has run through Time Evaluation by displaying various reports that can be processed from one central location. Time administrators or managers responsible for tracking Time Evaluation error messages are likely to use the Time Management Pool. In addition, the Time Management Pool allows quick access to employee time-related data that might be beneficial for managers to manage their workforce.

Key Management Decision Points – Evaluations and Time Management Pool

The following items are key decision points for the implementation of Evaluations and Time Management Pool:

▶ Determine if Time Evaluation will be processed as a fair amount of data is pulled from the output of Time Evaluation.

▶ Decide whether or not HR Forms (or the older version — the Time Management Form Editor) will be utilized. Both versions work, however, HR Forms provides greater flexibility in form design and the overall look and feel. The HR Forms Editor works in conjunction with Smart Forms, so a technical resource is required for the setup. The HR FORMs version is the better of the two versions as it allows for more flexibility and control over the look and feel of the output. You can also elect to not provide this functionality.

▶ Decide if your organization will utilize the Time Management Pool Interface via Transaction code PT40, or if the employees will use the various transaction codes for the functionality individually. A decision to use the interface may require multiple variants to be set up for each program. The effort is minimal, but required nonetheless.

Evaluations and Time Management Pool can be found in the Implementation Guide (IMG) under the menu path TIME MANAGEMENT • TIME EVALUATION • EVALUATIONS AND THE TIME MANAGEMENT POOL. Next we'll take a look at Time Statements.

10.1 Time Statements

Time Statements are forms that can be set up within the SAP system and made available to employees, managers, and administrators so that they can see the results of Time Evaluations. You can customize these forms to particular groups or individuals so that they can be informed of all time-related balances. For example, let's say you have a benefits program that tracks a bucket of hours, including regular time and overtime, to determine if the employee may be eligible for a bonus at the end of the year. If an employee works more than 2,200 hours in one year, they will receive the year-end bonus. Toward the end of the year, employees will be curious about how close they are to the target qualifying hours and can use this information to work extra shifts if they are close. But do you really want them calling the payroll department each week? If not, why not put the data in the hands of the employees so they can manage their time without putting a resource burden on the payroll department.

By setting up a Time Statement Form and linking the balance of hours that you created via Time Evaluation, an employee would have real-time data at his disposal through the portal. This allows him to manage whether he will be able to receive a bonus by working extra hours. "That's great," you say, "but we haven't implemented the portal yet." Good news, the form can be run and sent out to managers directly. In addition, you can also run a Time Evaluation report specifically for that bucket of hours and email those to the managers.

Let's have a look at one of the tools used to set up the form.

10.1.1 Time Statement via Forms Editor

There are a few ways you can set up the form. The first method is called the Forms Editor. The second method is called HR Forms. Let's start by looking at the Forms Editor as seen in Figure 10.1.

```
                        Time statement list
                        ====================
Accounting period:   200801 From 01/01/2008 - 01/31/2008      WS rule:  10X7REG

                        Individual results
                        ==================
Day Text          BTer ETer  BTime ETime  rec.  SkelTime Flex   CViol OTime  DWS

01  New Years             Employee not at wor 0.00    0.00   0.00   0.00  D 10
    off

02                        Employee not at wor 0.00    0.00   0.00   0.00  D 10

03                        Employee not at wor 0.00    0.00   0.00   0.00  D 10

04  Regular Time                              0.00    0.00   0.00   0.00  D 10

                        Totals overview
                        ===============
Type                    Working time          Overtime

Previous month's           0.00                 0.00
Planned time               0.00
Working time               0.00
Revision                   0.00                 0.00
Balance                    0.00                 0.00
Excess/deficit             0.00
Remaining leave            0.00

                        Time wage types
                        ===============
Day Wage type                        Number  M/S/A (M=overtime)

01  1000 Regular Hourly              10.00
01  1000 Regular Hourly              10.00
```

Figure 10.1 Time Statement Form via the Forms Editor

The Time Statement is a customizable form that allows you to display time-related data to the employees or time administrators. The forms are customized via the Forms Editor (Transaction code PE50). This book does not detail all aspects of the Forms Editor; however, the following examples are some of the types of data that can be placed on the form. The system offers more options for placing particular pieces of master data on the form, but this list gives you an idea of the types of data available at your disposal.

- Employee Master Data
  - Infotype 0001 - Organizational Assignment
  - Infotype 0002 — Address
- Period Information
  - Start and end of the current period
  - Current period
- Key Words
  - Page-related Information
  - Current Date
  - Absence and Attendance Quotas
  - Leave Information
  - Weekdays
- Other Information
  - System Date
  - User name
- Work Pay/Basic Pay–related Information
  - Daily Hours
  - Work Contract
  - Dynamic Daily Work Schedule
  - Action and Reason Codes
  - Enterprises Structure–related Information
  - Infotype 0008 — Payscale Information

▶ Time-related Information from the following tables:

- ▶ AB — Absences
- ▶ ABK — Absence Quotas
- ▶ ALP — Different Payments
- ▶ ANK — Attendance Quotas
- ▶ ANWES — Attendances
- ▶ C1 — Cost Center Assignments
- ▶ CVS — Cumulative Variable Balances
- ▶ FEH — Errors
- ▶ MEHR — Overtime
- ▶ PSP — Monthly Work Schedule
- ▶ PT — Time Pairs
- ▶ RUFB — On-call Duty
- ▶ SALDO — Time Period Balances
- ▶ SKO — Time Transfer Specifications
- ▶ T001 — Company Codes
- ▶ T001P — Personnel Subareas
- ▶ T500P — Personnel Areas
- ▶ T501T — Employee Group Text
- ▶ T503T — Employee Subgroup Text
- ▶ T512T — Wage Type Text
- ▶ T554T — Absence and Attendance Texts
- ▶ T555F — Time Evaluation Error Text
- ▶ T555Q — Balance Revision Texts
- ▶ T556B — Absence Quota Text
- ▶ T556Q — Attendance Quota Text
- ▶ T557T — Availability Type Text
- ▶ TEXT — Text Conversions

- ▶ THOLT — Public Holiday Text
- ▶ TP — Time Pairs for an Exact Day
- ▶ VS — Variable Balances
- ▶ ZED — Time Balances
- ▶ ZL — Time Wage Types

By reviewing some of the data available, you can quickly gauge the types of benefits your company might receive by setting up the Forms Editor and allowing employees and managers access to the information.

Now let's learn how to call the Time Statement form from Time Evaluation. Figure 10.2 shows the Time Evaluation program RPTIME00 and where you can pull the form from within Time Evaluation processing.

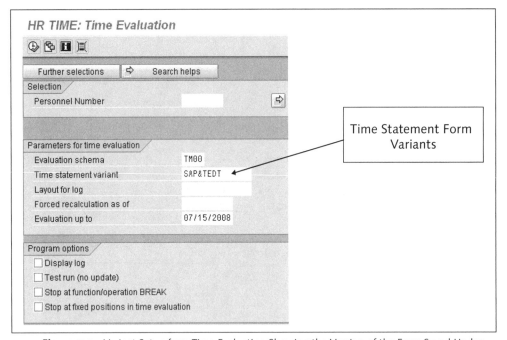

Figure 10.2 Variant Setup from Time Evaluation Showing the Version of the Form Saved Under the Variant

The variants setup can be selected directly from the Time Evaluation program via Transaction code PT60. In addition, the user can select the form of their choice at the point of processing. Because the program allows you to define which form is processed, you could utilize this to set up various versions of the form from the same program. This might be beneficial if you were only running a simulation of Time Evaluation where the system will not actually update anything. By placing a particular form on the screen, you could quickly review the results of the simulation without having to drill down into the various Time Evaluation tables to see the details. This is beneficial in troubleshooting production issues or testing new personnel calculation rules that have been set up, where you are not sure of their impact to existing data in the system.

The next section shows the actual output of the form from the Time Evaluation program. The output is displayed by employee. Figure 10.3 shows the output of Time Evaluation based on the form selected.

Day	Text	ITer	OTer	Start End	rec.	Plnd	Skel.	Flex	OTime	DWS
			Individual results							
01	Labor Day			EE not at work		0.00	0.00	0.00	0.00	D 10
	Day off									
02	Regular Time					0.00	0.00	0.00	0.00	D 10
	Regular Hourly				10.00					
03	Regular Time					0.00	0.00	0.00	0.00	D 10
	Regular Hourly				10.00					
04	Regular Time					0.00	0.00	0.00	0.00	D 10
	Regular Hourly				10.00					
05	Regular Time					0.00	0.00	0.00	0.00	D 10
	Regular Hourly				10.00					
	Weekly total					0.00	0.00	0.00	0.00	
06	Vacation					0.00	0.00	0.00	0.00	D 10 A

Figure 10.3 Output in the Time Evaluation Log

As you can see in Figure 10.3, the days are listed down the left side with the various buckets of time set up as columns. Some of the columns listed, such as PLND or SKEL, are Time type buckets whereas the column DWS is the daily Work Schedule used for that employee on a specific day. If you do not plan to use such items, you can always customize the form to show the exact data that your business would find beneficial.

Next we'll look at an additional method for creating the Time Statement — HR Forms.

10.2 HR Forms

HR Forms are a separate piece of functionality used to set up and display time-related data. This method of setting up the form can also be utilized in the Employee Self-Service (ESS) function, and by calling it from a standard report also processed through Time Evaluation.

If you want to print the HR FORM version of the timesheet, then use Transaction code PC00_M99_HRF_CALL. This allows you to process the form output without having to use the portal.

Due to the complexity of HR Forms, we will not cover every aspect of the setup in detail; however, we will provide a baseline of knowledge so that you will be familiar with what is possible, how the tool looks when setting up a form, how to process the form, and how the output might look different from the Forms Editor version.

Figure 10.4 shows the HR Forms Editor screen. All of the data that is available in the Forms Editor will also be available in the HR Forms editor. There is one main difference between the two versions of setting up the Time Statement. The Forms Editor allows you to define the layout of the report whereas HR Forms is a place where you define which information is available.

There is a second step, called Smart Forms, where you can build the actual layout of the form based on the data established in HR Forms. What advantage is there to maintaining the form in two different locations? This approach is beneficial in that you can define all of the data that is available for the form. You can then link that data to a Smart Form. Let's say your business has two different locations, each with a requirement to have a different layout of the form. Would you really want to define the exact same data twice because you have two different layouts? Probably not. Instead, you can define the data that is available to all forms, then, within the Smart Forms setup, you can pick and choose which data should be displayed, and the overall layout of the form for each businesses requirement.

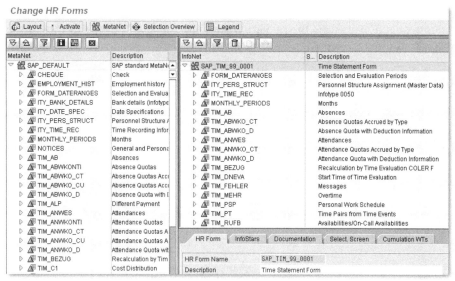

Figure 10.4 Setup of the Data for the Form, which Will Then Be Called By a Smart Form

Now that you've seen the HR Forms setup, let's have a look at the second step, which is to set up the Smart FORM. Figure 10.5 shows the initial screen to set up the form.

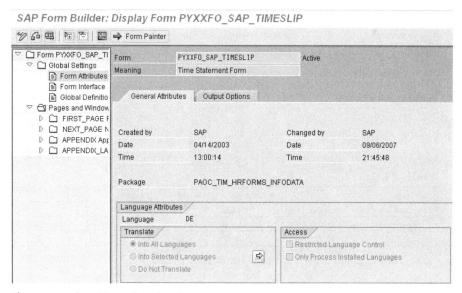

Figure 10.5 Smart Form Overview Screen

On the Smart FORM screen, you set up a form name and link the form back to the HR Forms name. This way, the two are linked and the layout of the form will use the data you established within the HR FORM.

So now we've seen two instances of using the HR FORM Time Statement methodology. Now let's have a look at the output. Figure 10.6 shows the actual output of the form. You'll notice this looks a lot more robust than the output of the Forms Editor version.

Figure 10.6 Sample Output of the Smart Form within the SAP System

Another main difference between the Forms Editor and HR Forms is the ability to add formatting, such as bold, shading, etc. When deciding which method to use, the overall look and feel of the Forms Editor is now perceived as antiquated and not the image a business wants end users to see as users are used to seeing forms that have a lot of formatting to make them easier to read.

Now let's show you how the form can be called from within Time Evaluation. Figure 10.7 shows you how to call the HR Forms version to display the Time Evaluation results.

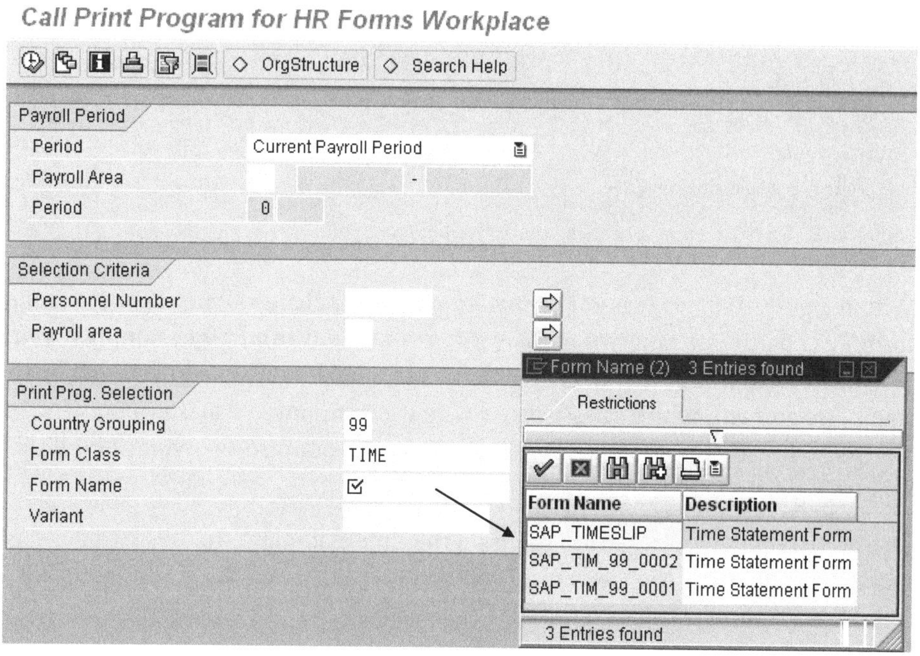

Figure 10.7 Initial Screen from Transaction PC00_M99_HRF_CALL

As you can see in Figure 10.7, you can run the form for a particular payroll area; however, the priority is to select the HR FORM name you intend to process in the Print Prog. Selection section.

There is one final step to running the Time Statement Form and it is shown in Figure 10.8. This is the last screen you use prior to running the program and the form producing the output.

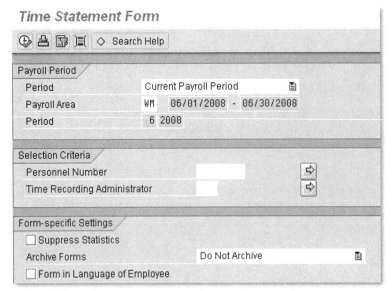

Figure 10.8 Final Screen in Processing the Time Statement Form

Within Figure 10.8, you can make any last parameter changes, such as running the form for a particular range of employees or running it from Time Administrator. The Time Recording Administrator link is from a field in Infotype 0001 Organizational Assignment, which is associated with each employee's master data. This is an optional field, but you may find it beneficial to set up so that you can call this report by the time administrator.

That wraps up the various ways to create the time statement, so let's switch gears and discuss the Time Management Pool.

10.3 Time Management Pool

The Time Management Pool is a comprehensive interface containing links to information necessary in the processing and maintenance of employee time data. Although it is not a required piece of functionality, it does provide a convenient way to access data for employees from one location. If you are using Time Manager's Workplace (TMW), similar functionality exists under that processing workbench and therefore the Time Management Pool is not necessary. You may use this functionality if you are not utilizing TMW and want to provide your time administrators with a tool to manage employee time-related data. Instead of having to find each report in the Time Management menu path, this one transaction can be utilized so they have one location to administer time data.

The Time Management Pool has the following features:

- Review — Display time data that has been entered and processed.
- Maintenance —
  - Process error messages from Time Evaluation
  - Process Time Events, Absences, Attendances, Absence and Attendance Quotas
  - Substitutions
  - Availability
  - Overtime
  - Remuneration Information
  - Time Transfer Specifications
  - Process Time Evaluation
- Special — Email functionality to notify time administrator.
- Subsystem Connection — A quick link to Transaction PT80 used for processing personnel Time Events from third-party time collection subsystems.

Figure 10.9 shows the initial screen of the Time Management Pool and the layout of the interface.

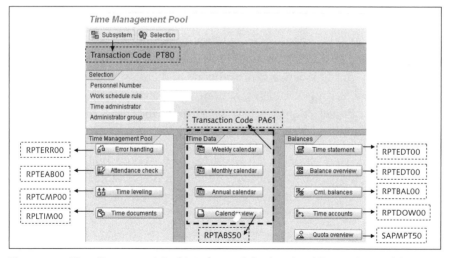

Figure 10.9 Time Management Pool Interface and the Associated Transactions and Programs

There are numerous processes and reports that can be run. Each of the buttons is covered in more detail in the following sections, but you can see in Figure 10.9 that the functionality is laid out in logical sections, including the Time Management Pool, Time Data, and Balances. One other benefit is located in the upper left-hand portion of the screen — the Subsystem button. This is a useful link for those supporting the system because once it's selected, it shows statistical information related to a connection to another system. For example, let's say you are using a third-party time-keeping system. How do you know the interface between that system and the SAP system has processed? The Subsystem button provides you with data to help manage the interface between the two systems.

Now let's take a look at the first report — Error Handling.

10.3.1 Error Handling

The Error Handling functionality is used when errors are detected while uploading time data into the SAP system. Errors can be a direct result of poor data attempting to enter the SAP system from the Time Collection system or internally from the SAP Logistics component. This processing is found under the Time Management Pool menu path of Transaction code PT40.

You may be asking yourself, "Because there are variations of the reports that are linked to the Time Management Pool, how do I define which version of the report I want the system to use?" To answer that question, SAP offers a feature called LLREP.

All of the various reports are based on variants that store the reporting parameters to be used. Once a variant is created, you can then link the variant to the program via Feature LLREP. Features can be accessed via Transaction code PE03. After you've set up this link between the program and the variant of the program, the Time Management Pool executes each report. This saves you time because you don't have to enter the selection parameters each and every time you run a report. Figure 10.10 shows Feature LLREP.

Within the feature, you can define a variant for each of the variable key entries listed in the Variable key. Each of the rows defined in the Variable Key can have a linked variant; however, it's not required that all have a variant.

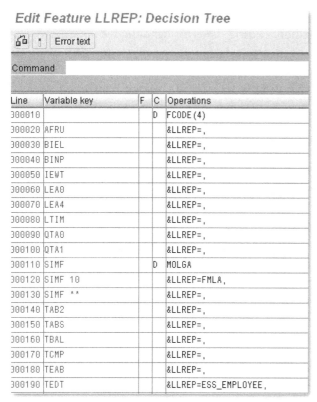

Figure 10.10 Feature LLREP and How the Variants Can Be Set Up for Each Program Class

Let's take a look at the Error Handling report seen in Figure 10.11.

Figure 10.11 Error Handling Output

The Plant data Collection (PDC) Error Handling functionality detects errors during the processing of Time Evaluation. During the error handling resolution process, an administrator can correct the incorrect data on the relative infotype records, or create entirely new records. PDC Error Handling also displays messages that can be configured in Time Evaluation to generate for any reason. This report is very useful in determining what may or may not have happened in Time Evaluation processing.

For example, let's say Time Evaluation has been executed and an employee was missing a required piece of master data or, based on the time entered, the employee received too much overtime due to a time entry error. You can set up Time Evaluation so that error messages are generated in the case of missing master data. You can also set up messages that won't stop Time Evaluation from processing for an employee, but they will generate a message that will be stored and can be reported from. Using the overtime example, you could have set up Time Evaluation to generate a message if the total overtime in a work week is greater than 25. When the time administrator reviews the errors and messages, they would quickly determine there might be an issue with time entry and then can drill down into that individual's time records to determine if there are any issues.

Time Evaluation can be rerun for the employees after the data has been resolved to ensure the error message has been resolved.

The next section is about the Attendance Check report, as shown in Figure 10.12.

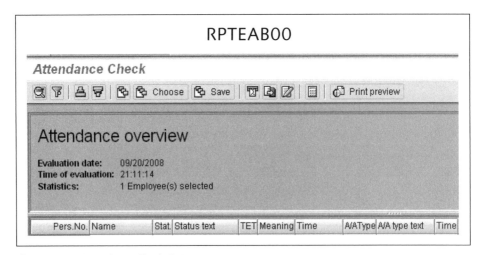

Figure 10.12 Attendance Check Output

This report determines, at the point of Time Evaluation, which employees are either present at work, tardy or, if an absence was entered in advance, which employees may be out for the day. The data is gathered from Infotypes 2001, Absences; 2002, Attendances; and 2011, Time Events. If you're using a third-party time collection system, your time has to be uploaded from those systems in order to get an accurate reflection of current data. This might be useful, for example, if you've set up the system to transfer time-related data throughout the morning and then process Time Evaluation multiple times and during periodic increments. By doing so, time administrators can determine who has clocked in for work, or if there may be any resource issues, such as a no-show that might cause a production line to be understaffed.

Now let's look at the output of the Time Leveling report shown in Figure 10.13.

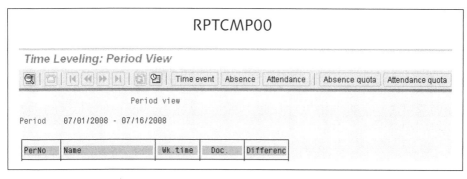

Figure 10.13 Time Leveling Output

The Time Leveling report is utilized to validate the employee's entered time against those times documented within the Incentive Wage functionality. The report outputs the working time against the documented time and shows the difference between the two. The setup to determine which data is pulled into the report and the different time criteria is done within the variant of the report itself. The variant is then linked via feature LLREP to default from the Time Management Pool interface.

The data is pulled from a variety of sources, such as Time Evaluation results, Infotypes 2001, 2002, and 2010, Employee Remuneration, based on the status field of Infotype 0007 Planned Working Time Management Status field.

From within the report, you can branch out to create the following:

▶ Time Events — Infotype 2011

▶ Substitutions — Infotype 2003

▶ Absences — Infotype 2001

▶ Attendances — Infotype 2002

▶ Absence Quotas — Infotype 2006

▶ Attendence Quotas — Infotype2007

▶ Availability — Infotype 2004

▶ Overtime — Infotype 2005

▶ Remuneration Information — Infotype 2010

▶ Time Transfer Specifications — Infotype 2012

▶ Time Tickets — Incentive Wages

This report might be useful during the setup of the variant, because you could set up the report so that it shows any employees who have worked less than their target hours for a given work day. Then only those employees would show up in the report. So if employees are entering a time of four hours per day and their target is eight, they would show up on the report and you could make the decision if further action is required.

The last report shows under the left side of the Time Management Pool screen in Figure 10.14 is the Time Documents report.

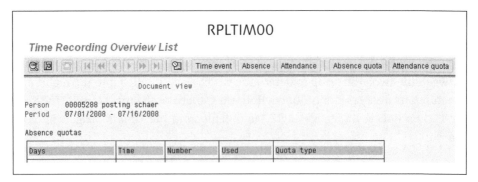

Figure 10.14 Time Documents Output for Time Recording

This program gathers all of the time from the infotypes for a personnel number and displays it on one report. Not only does the report display the various infotypes, but like report RPTCMP00, you can create the various time pieces as well. The data is pulled from the following infotypes:

▶ Infotype 2001 — Absences

▶ Infotype 2002 — Attendances

▶ Infotype 2003 — Substitutions

▶ Infotype 2004 — Availability

▶ Infotype 2005 — Overtime

▶ Infotype 2006 — Absence Quotas

▶ Infotype 2007 — Attendance Quotas

▶ Infotype 2010 — Employee Remuneration Information

▶ Infotype 2012 — Time Transfer Specifications

Continuing with our example of the employee who had 25 hours of ovetime generated, we know who the employee is, so now we need to review their time-related information. This report provides you one platform to branch to the various time-related master data to make any necessary changes.

This concludes our coverage of the various reports for the Time Management Pool, so let's explore the reports in Time Data next, beginning with the Weekly Calendar (see Figure 10.15).

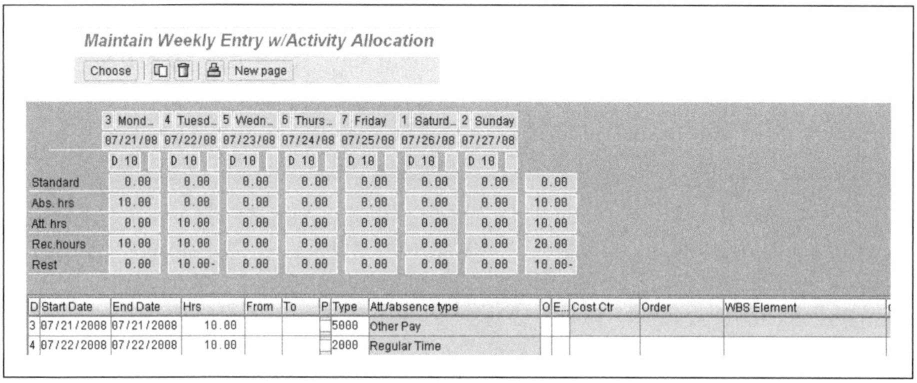

Figure 10.15 Weekly Calendar View for Time Data Maintenance

The weekly view of the employee calendar displays attendances and absences already entered into the system. This view allows the user to quickly enter or change time-related data in the system. The view also allows for activity allocation changes to new and existing records where applicable. You can also maintain master data via Transaction code PA30, but this methodology is a little more efficient because the data is displayed for the particular week.

The second report under time data is the Monthly Calendar (see Figure 10.16).

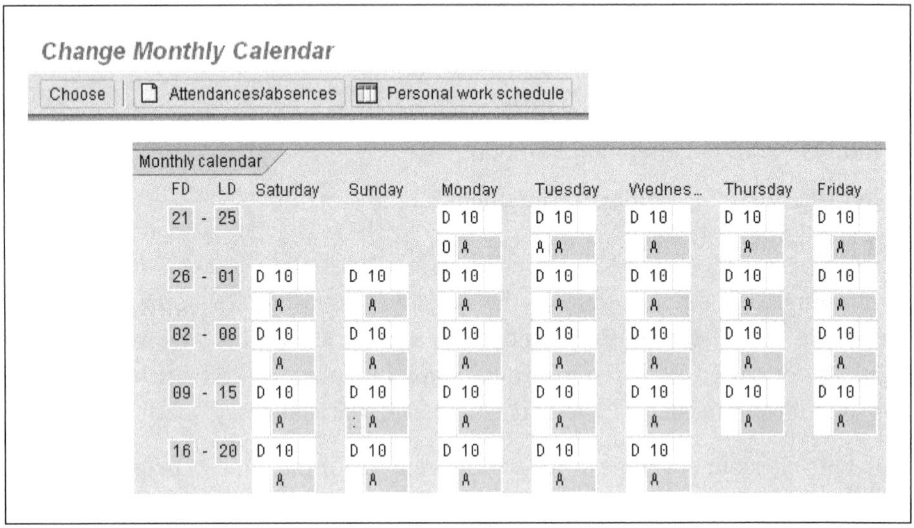

Figure 10.16 Monthly Calendar View for Time Data Maintenance

The monthly view of the calendar displays each of the daily Work Schedules, or the variants thereof, associated with a particular day. These daily Work Schedules can be changed on this screen. The changes are reflected on an Infotype 2003 substitution record that is automatically created behind the scenes. The view displays any absence that has been entered and allows the user to enter full-day absences for a particular day by selecting an absence/attendance category. This type of entry has a code linked to an attendance or absence type and automatically creates a full-day's record for that day. In addition, time-related infotypes can also be accessed, changed, created, or deleted via this report.

The third report under the time data section is for the Annual Calendar as seen in Figure 10.17.

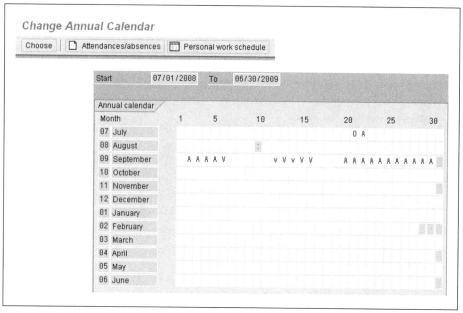

Figure 10.17 Annual Calendar View for Time Data Maintenance

The annual view displays an entire year starting from the beginning date selected. The screen breaks the data down into three basics data types:

▶ The periods are an indicator of a scheduled day off according to the daily Work Schedule.

▶ The blanks or empty boxes represent days that should be worked according to the daily Work Schedule.

▶ The other various codes represent the attendances and absences that are linked to those codes.

You can double-click on any existing fields that are not blank to drill down into the various master data records behind the scenes. You can also create additional records for any day by selecting the value associated for an absence or attendance on a particular day. After you save, the infotype record linked to the code you selected is created for a full day. For example, in Figure 10.17 you will notice the letters A and V on particular days. These represent absence and attendance codes. If the letter A was set up to dictate an unpaid absence, you could select the value of A and the absence type for unpaid absence would be automatically created upon savings.

What would happen though if you decided to run the reports listed next to the buttons in Figure 10.17? Using the Calendar View, let's have a look at what would show up on the initial screen. Figure 10.18 shows the initial screen for report RPTABS50.

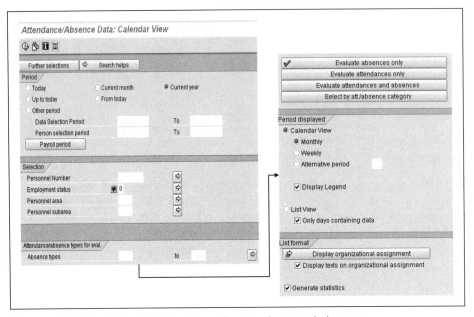

Figure 10.18 Calendar View Selection Screen for Attendances and Absences

As you can see in Figure 10.18, you have numerous options to vary data while processing. Once you decide on the data you need, you can execute the report. Figure 10.19 shows the results from the report RPTABS50.

The Calendar View is merely a report that allows the user to display data for a specific time period. The user has some flexibility on the types of data entered, as illustrated in Figure 10.18. Figure 10.19, for example, was set up to show all absences and attendances.

This concludes the Time Data Reporting section. Now let's move on to look at how the Time Management Pool allows you to report from various Time Evaluation balances. The first report is called Time Statement. This is the same type of statement we discussed at the beginning of the chapter. Figure 10.20 shows the Time Statement output.

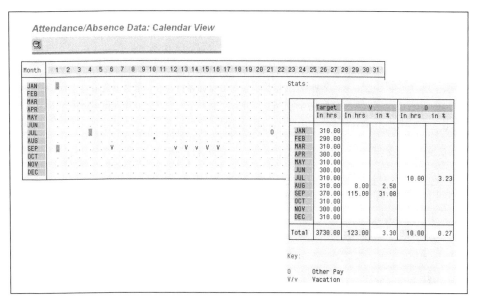

Attendance/Absence Data: Calendar View

Month	1 2 3 4 5 6 7 8 9 10 11 12 13 14 15 16 17 18 19 20 21 22 23 24 25 26 27 28 29 30 31	Stats:

Stats:

	Target In hrs	V In hrs	V in %	O In hrs	O in %
JAN	310.00				
FEB	290.00				
MAR	310.00				
APR	300.00				
MAY	310.00				
JUN	300.00				
JUL	310.00			10.00	3.23
AUG	310.00	8.00	2.58		
SEP	370.00	115.00	31.08		
OCT	310.00				
NOV	300.00				
DEC	310.00				
Total	3730.00	123.00	3.30	10.00	0.27

Key:

O   Other Pay
V/v   Vacation

Figure 10.19   Results from the Report RPTABS50

RPTEDT00

Time statement list
====================

Individual results
==================

Day	Text	BTer ETer	BTime ETime	rec.	SkelTime Flex	CViol	OTime	DWS
01			Employee not at wor	0.00	0.00	0.00	0.00	D 10
02			Employee not at wor	0.00	0.00	0.00	0.00	D 10
03			Employee not at wor	0.00	0.00	0.00	0.00	D 10
04	Independen off		Employee not at wor	0.00	0.00	0.00	0.00	D 10
07			Employee not at wor	0.00	0.00	0.00	0.00	D 10
08			Employee not at wor	0.00	0.00	0.00	0.00	D 10
09			Employee not at wor	0.00	0.00	0.00	0.00	D 10
10			Employee not at wor	0.00	0.00	0.00	0.00	D 10

Figure 10.20   Time Statement Output

The Time Statement is a basic overview of all time-related activities that have been linked to a particular form. This form is called via the program RPTEDT00 by means of a variant established in the Feature LLREP. The report is useful for employees to validate their time data, any balances that are tracked, or accumulators that the business may track for whatever reason. This is the same type of report that can be run when running Time Evaluation to validate simulations by reviewing the simulation results on the form.

Now let's look at the Balance Overview report as seen in Figure 10.21.

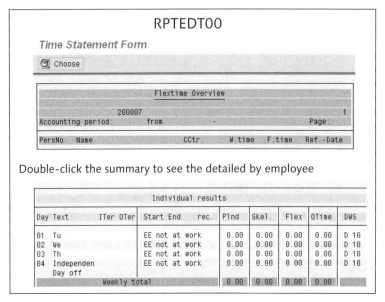

Figure 10.21 Balance Overview of the Time Evaluation Results

> **Note**
>
> You can access the details of the summary by double-clicking on the Employee Line.

This report displays the summary overview of each of the data points linked to the Time Statement. The user can double-click on the summary items to receive the details. This report is used if, for example, you were interested in the total amount of particular Time types and not the pieces of time that made up the total. Overtime is a good example in that you may just need to know how much total overtime for the period has occurred versus which particular days of the week it happened.

The next report is a very useful report that managers, time administrators, and even those who support the Time Management function frequently process — Cumulated Balances — as seen in Figure 10.22.

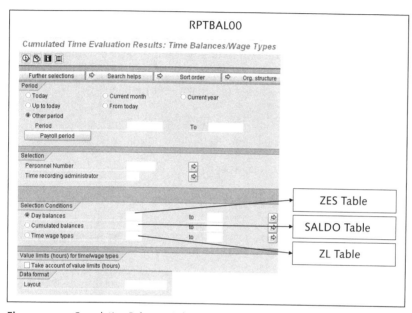

Figure 10.22 Cumulative Balances Selection Screen

This report is very useful for extracting results from the Time Evaluation clusters. As illustrated in Figure 10.22, you can extract data from the clusters to obtain, daily, summarized time data, or the Wage types that will pass to payroll on the ZL table. These reports can be run for individual employees or for a certain group of people or location.

The next report is for Time Accounts (see Figure 10.23).

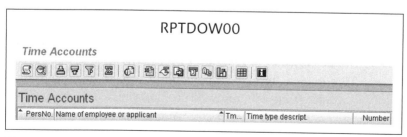

Figure 10.23 Time Accounts Overview

This report shows any Time type buckets that have been set up on table V_T555A — Field Store for Time Accounts. This report allows you to quickly run the summarized data, download it, and send it out to employees electronically. These are also typically the balances that are displayed on a third-party time collection subsystem screen. We have discussed throughout the chapter the ability to provide managers certain balances of time that employees have accumulated. This report is a good tool to provide such data such as total overtime worked or, as a previous example cited, how many hours an employee has already worked toward the minimum hours for an annual bonus that the benefits department manages.

The final report is for Quota Overview (see Figure 10.24).

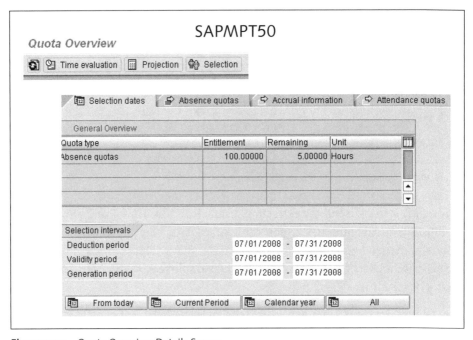

Figure 10.24 Quota Overview Details Screen

The Quota Overview report takes you to Transaction code PT50. This overview screen allows you to select date ranges, quotas on Infotype 2006, any quota amounts that may have accrued, the particular amounts of such accruals, and attendance quotas. Why would a time administrator use this transaction versus going directly to Infotype 2006 Absence Quotas or 2007 Attendance Quotas? One advantage would be the Accrual Information tab. If you are processing quotas through

Time Evaluation, an employee may be awarded eight hours of vacation for each month worked. The Accrual Information tab shows you each eight-hour segment awarded as the month was processed.

Let's take a look at the various tabs listed in program SAPMPT50 — Quota Overview — as seen in Figure 10.25.

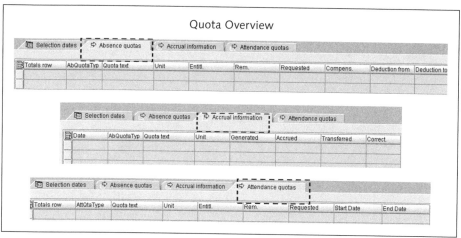

Figure 10.25 Details of Program SAPMPT50

This report shows all of the information related to quotas. The report can also be accessed directly from Transaction code PT50. The various tabs show the quotas in a variety of ways. The Absence Quota tab shows the total amount of the quota whether or not it was front loaded, created manually, or was created via an accrual. The accrual information tab will show the individual accrual amounts that make the total. Also on this tab, you can create quota corrections Infotype 2013 for those quotas that are configured via an accrual. The final tab is for attendance quotas and displays information similar to that of the Absences Quotas tab.

This report allows you to display, create, change, or delete any of the quota information necessary.

10.4   Summary

In this chapter, you learned about the concepts regarding two methodologies for how to set up the Time Statement and the functionality related to the Time Management Pool. The Time Statement usually takes the most time to set up as it is more technical in nature and the customization is heavily dependent upon the Time types used to store relevant time information that will be displayed on the Time Statement. In addition, you learned about the Time Management Pool and how the interface to the various programs to administer Time Management infotypes may be utilized at your organization. If you're interested in the Time Management Pool, then you may want to read the next chapter on the Time Manager's Workplace (TMW), which was designed to replace the Time Management Pool. In the next chapter we'll explain the functionality surrounding TMW.

In this chapter, you'll learn about key areas to consider during the configuration of the Time Manager's Workplace (TMW). At the conclusion of this chapter, you should be knowledgeable of the concepts and configuration sets of the Implementation Guide (IMG) for the TMW.

11   Time Manager's Workplace

The TMW is a Time Management workbench that can be utilized to enter, maintain, and administer time in a distributed environment. The workbench interfaces to all time-related infotypes to bring relative information to your attention in one location. The workbench is accessed via Transaction code PTMW. You may want to consider using this functionality if you have dedicated time managers that are allocated to a set amount of employees. These time administrators ensure all data is entered correctly, and as part of their responsibility, they would review, correct, and ensure that the data is accurate so Payroll can compensate the employees. This functionality is similar to that of Time Management Pool in Chapter 10; however, this functionality was designed to replace the Time Management Pool. As we proceed through this chapter, we will first discuss what data is available and how the overall workplace looks to an end user. We'll then follow the IMG and review the available configuration settings, so that you can tailor the functionality and the overall look and feel of TMW to the time administrators that utilize the system to administer time.

The workbench has two basic views that a time administrator can see:

▶ Employee View

▶ Message View

When you set up the system, you can define which administrator gets which view, or both views. For example, you may have a business requirement whereby certain time administrators are only allowed to view the messages and report to the manager any fixes that need to occur. If this were the case, you would just provide the message view. The employee view can be set up to provide all of the time-related infotype master data for the administrator to maintain. The message view shows any messages that may have been generated within Time Evaluation.

From within TMW, you can navigate to the following functionalities. Each of these can be found on the TMW menu bar.

▸ **Run Time Evaluation** — Allows you to process Time Evaluation within the workplace to ensure your changes to time data produce the desired effect.

▸ **Display the Time Statement Form** — Shows the results of Time Evaluation run in a report.

▸ **Call the Employee** — Allows you to directly contact an employee if you have any questions regarding an entered time.

▸ **Insert Employees Temporarily** — As an administrator, you may have certain employees that you're responsible for. There may be times where you need to help other administrators process their employees. You can insert other personnel numbers that do not report directly to you.

▸ **Link to Display Master Data Transaction** — This allows you to view the infotype data.

▸ **Link to Maintain Master Data Transaction** — This allows you to maintain the infotype data.

If you elect to allow a time administrator to change the entries that an employee has made, the following infotypes can be set up so that they are available within the workplace for maintenance. Depending on which infotype your organization utilizes, you can customize the data within the workplace to show only the infotypes that need to be maintained. By doing so, you make the screen that is used by the time administrator easier to navigate and reduce the amount of data that is displayed so that they can concentrate on specific tasks.

The following infotypes can be maintained. Each of these infotypes was described in Chapter 4, "Master Data."

▸ Infotype 2001 — Absences

▸ Infotype 2002 — Attendances

▸ Infotype 2003 — Substitutions

▸ Infotype 2004 — Availability

▸ Infotype 2007 — Attendance Quota

▸ Infotype 2010 — Employee Remuneration

▸ Infotype 2012 — Time Transfer Specifications

Now that we have discussed the kinds of data that can be displayed, how can we customize the TMW so that only your business requirements are available? Let's begin our discussion with the employee view.

11.1 Employee View

As we discussed, there are two basic views that can be tailored to your requirements. Figure 11.1 shows the standard employee view. In this section, we will review each section and explain how it can be customized by following the IMG configuration section for TMW.

As you can see from Figure 11.1, the employee view has three tabs. The overall approach of the tabs is to break the data that can be displayed and maintained into logical sections. Within each tab, the configuration is delivered so that specific master data maintenance can occur. We'll cover each of these sections:

▸ **Time Data** — Utilizes data from Infotype 2001 and 2002 — Absences and Attendances

▸ **Time Events** — Utilizes data from Infotype 2011 — Time Events

▸ **Calendar** — Displays all of the related infotypes by person or group

The TMW also provides a couple of different options to view data for employees. The main screen of the workplace has the following views:

▸ **Multi-day view** — You can see multiple days' worth of details

▸ **Multi-person view** — You can view the time data for more than one employee at a time

▸ **One-day view** — You can limit the displayed time data so that only one day of time data is shown

▸ **Team View** — You can view all you are responsible for administering time related data for

Let's have a look at how all of this looks within the system. Figure 11.1 shows you what the TMW looks like.

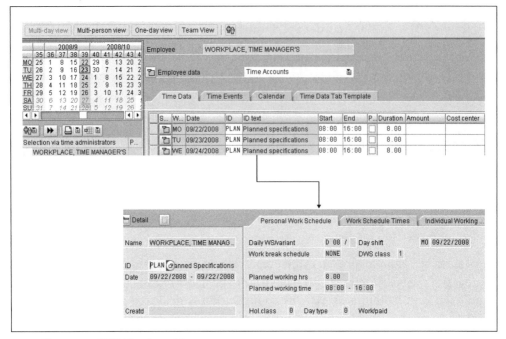

Figure 11.1 TMW Employee View

Let's take a closer look at each of the tabs so you can learn what they are used for and how using them can work in your own processes.

11.1.1 Time Data Tab

The first tab is the Time Data tab. This tab shows basic time-related data that pertains to the employees. Specifically, you should notice in Figure 11.1 that each day of the week is displayed on a row. Within that row, you can see that the employee's planned working time from Infotype 0007 is populated for the start and end times. Next you can see the total hours the employee is supposed to work. The remainder of the fields toward the right on each row are fields that can be populated for a time record. For example, if there was a cost center override for a particular day, where the employee worked in a different department, then the cost center could be maintained on this field. What if we don't actually utilize every field on the Time Data tab? Can we change it? The short answer is yes, and we will cover it during the configuration of the TMW.

Let's have another look at Figure 11.1. What else do you notice about the screen? If you were to double-click on a particular row, additional tabs will show up that have data that can be maintained. Let's explore this further.

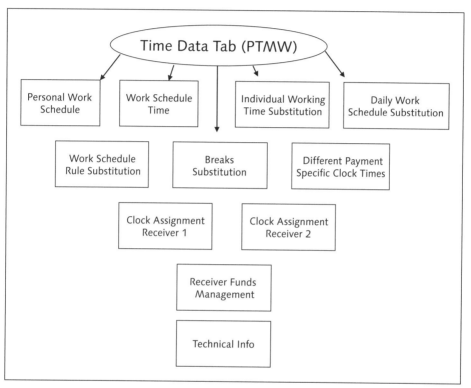

Figure 11.2 Time Data Functionality Tabs

The Time Data tab has the following subtabs whereby certain functionality is available to be maintained or displayed. What does this mean? For example, let's say an employee has requested to work a different shift that will be 10 hours. As you can see in Figure 11.1, you can select the Personal Work Schedule tab, and then change the daily work hours and the start and end times so that it shows 10 hours. As a follow up to our example, each and every tab shows data that is logically grouped together. You select the tab for the data you want to maintain and update the fields. Even though Figure 11.1 only shows a few tabs, there are others that are listed under the Time Data tab but not captured in Figure 11.1 due to screen size limitations. Figure 11.2 shows all of the delivered subtabs under the standard Time Data tab. Just as we discussed with the Time Data tab, you can also customize the subtabs to show the information the time administrator works with on a daily basis and hide everything else. You can even set up the tabs so that one administrator sees one set of data, while another administrator might have a totally different screen layout.

Chapter 4 discussed Infotype 2003 Substitutions. Some subtabs listed in Figure 11.2 allow you to create the substitutions through the TMW. Let's discuss what some of the various fields are under the standard delivered subtabs. (Each of the fields was discussed in Chapter 4 and Chapter 5.) So now you may be asking yourself, why would I ever need to use this? Under what situations is a substitution required? You basically need to take a detailed assessment of how you have set up your system. By this, we mean you need to understand how detailed your Work Schedules have been configured and how, if at all, is the business using them to help pay employees correctly. Each of these particular fields listed under the subtabs can have implications during Time Evaluation processing. These implications dictate how Wage types are generated or how various time buckets are created. At the end of the day, the substitution is a temporary change to master data to what the employee is normally assigned, and by making a substitution you may impact which Time Evaluation personnel calculation rules are processed for a particular employee. The following text provides a more detailed view of the fields delivered within each subtab.

► **Individual Working Time Substitution**
  Under this tab, you can select the substitution type, change the start and end times of the work day, change the daily Work Schedule class, change the day type, and mark the time to be credited toward the previous day.

► **Daily Work Schedule Substitution**
  Under this tab, you can select a substitution type, a daily Work Schedule variant, or change the particular day type.

► **Work Schedule Rule Substitution**
  Under this tab, you can select the substitution type, the Personnel Subarea grouping for Work Schedules, Employee Subgroup grouping for Work Schedules, the holiday calendar ID, or the Work Schedule rule.

► **Break Substitution**
  Under this tab, you can select the substitution type, whether or not breaks are calculated, and whether the breaks are paid or unpaid.

▸ **Different Payment for Specfic Clock Times**

Under this tab, you can assign a different position or a work center in conjunction with a start and end time. This means the position or work center is only relevant between the times you have entered.

▸ **Clock Assignment Receiver 1**

Under this tab, you can assign various costing elements to the time entry for that particular day. For example, you can assign a company code, business area, cost center, order, cost object, or Work Breakdown Structure (WBS) element.

▸ **Clock Assignment Receiver 2**

This tab allows you to assign various activity elements to the time entry for that particular day. For example, you can assign a network, an activity, a sales order, a sales order item, a business procedure, a service type, or a service category. Each of the terms are elements that are pulled from other SAP components. Chapter 3 provides some insight into some of these fields.

Now that we have covered the Time Data tab, let's have a look at the Time Events tab.

11.1.2 Time Events Tab

The Time Events tab is utilized when you have clock-in and clock-out time entries. The entries are pulled into TMW from Infotype 2011. When would you use this tab? Let's explore that thought for a moment. Let's say you have a third-party time-keeping system that collects all of the various swipe-card entries for employees throughout the day. The system takes those entries and determines how many hours the entries added up to. Those entries are then passed via an interface to the Cross-Application Time Sheet (CATS), where they are approved and sent to Infotype 2001 and Infotype 2002. At this point, should you use the Time Events tab? The answer is no. You'd only use this tab if you are receiving unevaluated time from a time collection system, and Time Evaluation with Clock Times is processing each night. The Time Events tab shows all of the various entries made when the employees swiped in and out through the day. The Time Events tab is illustrated in Figure 11.3. You'll notice a similar layout to that of the Time Data tab; however, some of the fields in the columns are different. For example, instead of planned time, you might see the actual clock time and the time even types, such as P01, associated with that time.

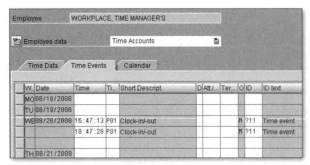

Figure 11.3 Time Events Screen

As we discussed under the Time Data tab, you can also set up the system so that various subtypes are available for master data changes to a Time Event. Figure 11.4 shows the various subtabs that are delivered in the standard system. The process is pretty much the same as how you utilize the tabs to enter subsequent information for the day's time record. As always, if you're not happy with the data on the tabs, they can be changed via configuration, which is discussed later in the chapter.

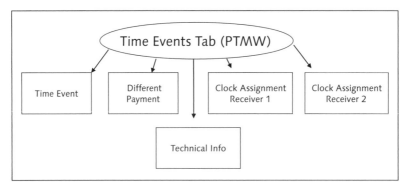

Figure 11.4 Time Events Functionality Tabs

We've now covered two ways to view data. The first tab was for Time Data, and the second tab was for Time Events. The third tab, which we'll cover next, is the Calendar tab.

11.1.3 Calendar Tab

The Calendar tab allows a time administrator a different view of the various time-related entries, in a manner that may be easier to see. As Figure 11.5 shows, the particular entries per day are listed, and the time administrator has the ability to see the entries based on a daily view, a weekly view, a monthly view, and also a calendar view. Figure 11.5 shows the weekly view of the calendar. Within the calendar, you have the same drill-down capabilities to view and maintain the subtab information that you did with the previous two tabs.

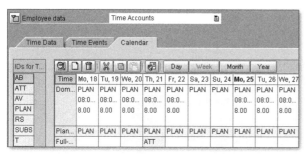

Figure 11.5 Calendar Tab

Just like the Time Data and Time Events tabs, the Calendar tab also has the ability to view and maintain data on subtabs. Figure 11.6 shows the subtabs with the calendar view.

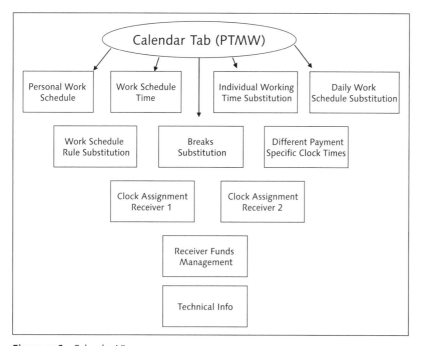

Figure 11.6 Calendar View

This gives you a general understanding of the employee view for TMW. As you saw, there are various tabs and related data that can be maintained under each; however, the TMW has two views. Let's take a look at the second view, the messages view, in the next section.

11.2 Messages View

The second view is called the messages view. This view allows the time administrator to view and process messages that might have been created during the Time Evaluation schema processing. In Chapters 8 and 9, which are both about Time Evaluation, you probably noticed that we discussed certain sections of the schema that generate messages. Those messages are stored in the B2 cluster of the Time Evaluation results. The TMW selects those messages and presents them to the time administrator so that he can view and react to the messages by correcting whatever issues may have resulted from incorrect master data. For example, an employee may have failed to clock out at the end of a shift. Time Evaluation can generate a message notifying the administrator of the failed clock-out entry. After viewing this message, the administrator can contact the employee to determine the actual clock-out time, and then update the employee's time master data record for the actual clock-out record. Figure 11.7 shows an example of the TMW with the message view displayed.

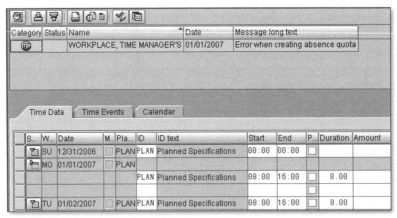

Figure 11.7 Messages Display

You have now had the opportunity to view how the TMW looks and how the data is presented. You may not be 100% satisfied with the overall layout of the data, and might want to make a few changes. The following section shows you how to configure the IMG tasks related to the TMW.

11.3 System Setup

The functionality that drives what the user sees via the TMW can be customized to alter the look and feel of the screens. The configuration for the TMW can be found in the IMG under menu path TIME MANAGEMENT • TIME MANAGER'S WORKPLACE.

The setup for TMW is broken down into six areas:

▶ **Menu Design** — This section allows you to select the fields that are used in the profiles, the general screen menu functions, and the activation of functionalities utilized by the toolbar.

▶ **Basic Settings** — This section is for general settings.

▶ **IDs for Time Data** — This section is for setting up the system so that different administrators can see different information, if necessary.

▶ **Screen Areas** — This section allows you to customize the screen areas.

▶ **Employee Selection** — This section is the basis for how employees are pulled into the workplace so that time administrators can process their time data.

▶ **Profiles** — This section is the definition of profiles that reside on an administrator's user profile. By setting up a profile and linking that profile to an administrator, you can control which screens they see and the data they maintain.

Figure 11.8 shows the various sections of configuration in the IMG related to the TMW.

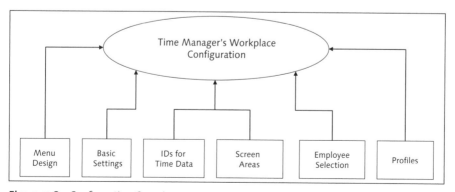

Figure 11.8 Configuration Overview

The first section of configuration we'll discuss is the overall menu design. We'll then move on to setting up the menus that will be available for the administrators once they enter the TMW.

11.3.1   Menu Design

The overall menu design takes into account the following areas of configuration. As we saw in Figure 11.1, this is the section where you begin to define the overall layout of initial screen.

▸ Definition of the particular tasks that are available. Under these tasks, you have two options. You can offer either Maintain time data or Process messages, or you can assign both. The screen area is defined under code TSK for task selection.

▸ Definition of task views allows you to select which views are available. You have four options, which can include any combination of the four under a particular view. You can select from multi-day, multi-person, one-day, or team view. The screen area is defined under code VTD for views for time data maintenance task. A visual representation can be found in Figure 11.9.

▸ Menu functions allow you to customize which functionality is ultimately assigned to the profile. The screen area is defined under code MEN for menu functions. A visual representation can be found in Figure 11.10.

Figure 11.9 shows an overview of the task selection.

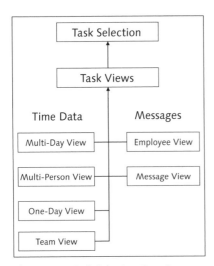

Figure 11.9   Task Selection Overview

The next section of configuration is to define the particular functionality that is available to the time administrators under the TMW menu.

Menu functions control which time administrator can process which functionality within the workplace. Figure 11.10 shows the functionalities available within the workplace. You can customize the menus so that different time administrators see different options for processing. For example, if you want to prevent certain time administrators from running Time Evaluation, you would create a menu and assign all of the pieces of functionality except time evaluation. When the time administrator enters the transaction for TMW, they will see Time Evaluation on the menu path, however, it will be grayed out and unavailable for processing. Using this example, you can set up as many different variations as your business might need.

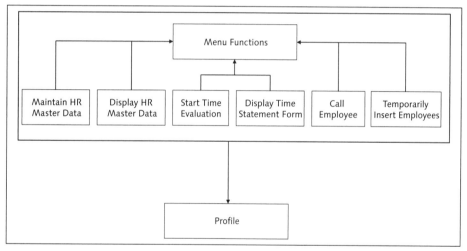

Figure 11.10 Menu Design

Now let's take a look at the next section of the IMG — basic settings.

11.3.2 Basic Settings

The basic settings for the workbench are broken down into five different areas, which are illustrated in Figure 11.11. Within this section, we continue with the options that are available to customize not only the layout of the workplace but also the data that the workplace will display.

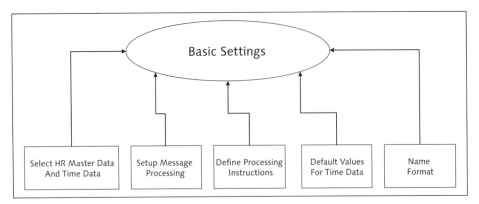

Figure 11.11 Basic Settings Configuration Components

Select HR Master Data and Time Data

Have you wondered how the various infotype-related fields are pulled into the workplace and how you might change the way the standard system imports the various fields? This is the section of the IMG for setting up the Human Resouces (HR) master and time data. Within this step, you can define which master data fields can be pulled into the initial workplace screen. Within the configuration, there are numerous options for master data available. If you don't see a particular piece of master data that your requirements dictate should show up on the initial screen, then in this step you define an object, which is just a description, link an infotype, and then select which field(s) you want to add. Figure 11.12 illustrates this configuration. As you can see, the Standard objects button has been highlighted with the various delivered fields shown in the dropdown. If you don't see a particular field when you are setting up the system, in Figure 11.12 you'll notice a display object called TMW_TIMSPEC_BLOP_R and a field from Infotype 2010 called STDAZ. This is the configuration you need to conduct if the fields in the standard display objects don't meet your business requirements.

In addition to defining specific fields on infotypes that you may want included in TMW, the next step is to define which time accounts, such as quota information, should be displayed.

In this step, you first need to define a reporting quota type, which is nothing more than a descriptive field that has the various quota type–related information linked. This field is then linked to a display object.

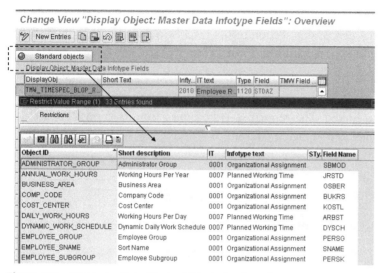

Figure 11.12 HR Master Data Display Objects Configuration

Figure 11.13 shows the time accounts used to display quota-related information. Here, you can see an example of how the Reporting Quota Type 00000001 has multiple absence quotas linked. The reporting quota type is then linked to an object type, also illustrated at the bottom of Figure 11.13

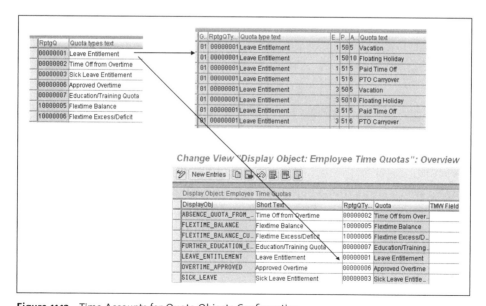

Figure 11.13 Time Accounts for Quota Objects Configuration

We have now defined how to import master data and quota-related information. The third and final part of this section of the IMG is to define which time-related information should appear within the workplace.

The employee time and labor section of the IMG allows you to define reporting Time types that can have either absences and attendances, Time types, or Wage type–related data linked. The reporting Time type accounts are assigned to an object type as illustrated in Figure 11.14.

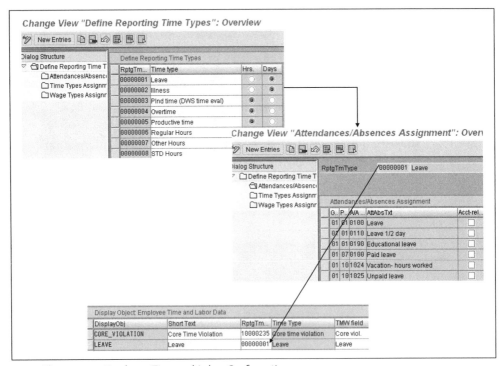

Figure 11.14 Employee Time and Labor Configuration

Why do we create all of the object types for these three areas? These object types are used during the set up of the overall screen layout. By linking the object types to various layouts, the data assigned is pulled into the various screens you have defined for the administrator.

Let's look at the next section of configuration under the basic settings, setup of message processing.

Setup of Message Processing

During the setup of message processing, you have the opportunity to decide which messages should be displayed, how they are displayed, and who they are displayed for. Figure 11.15 shows all of the various configuration tables related to message processing. Within Figure 11.15, you'll see the letters A, B, and C. Using these letters, we'll explain the figure.

▶ **Letter A** — The first step is to define functional areas that process similar messages. As you can see in Figure 11.5, the functional area of CUST has been created. We'll follow this functional area throughout this example. After you create the functional area, you will notice that you can assign that functional area to all of the various messages that were created as part of the Time Evaluation configuration from Chapters 8 and 9. At this point, you have a functional area and linked the various messages to the functional area.

▶ **Letter B** — The second section of this configuration has to do with building a processing method first. This is just a code with a description that enables you to group like messages together to make life easier for the administrator. As you can see in Figure 11.15, your next step is to create groups of display objects that contain contextual information for the various error messages. Finally, in the third step, you merge the previous two steps together. As you can see, you link the processing method to the group of display objects.

▶ **Letter C** — The final section of Figure 11.15 illustrates how you link the functional areas created as the first step of Figure 11.15 to the processing methods that were described in Letter B. The next and final step is to merge the processing methods to the message types.

This configuration may seem confusing, however, with a little bit of time spent in the IMG, you should be up and running pretty quickly. The benefit of this configuration is that it is defined in such a way so that the messages display in a manner that not only allows your administrators to understand them, but also lets them quickly review and process the list in an organized fashion.

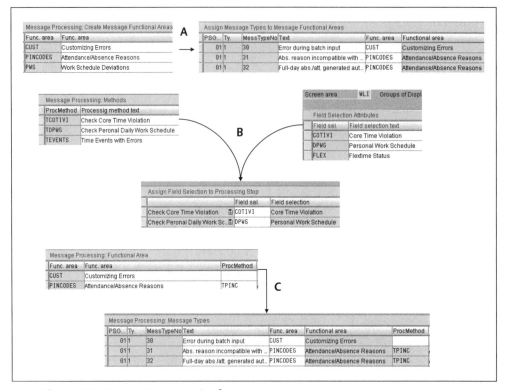

Figure 11.15 Message Processing Configuration

Let's move on to the next section of configuration under the basic settings section, which is to define processing instructions.

Define Processing Instructions

What are processing settings? Processing settings are used to help expedite the time data maintenance of repetitive tasks. Let's walk through an example. Let's say the administrator needs to add a time bonus of four hours for each employee. Instead of going into each employee and entering an attendance time of four hours, is there a quicker way? This section of configuration allows you to define specific processing that expedites the master data entry of creating the end result of four hours. So what does that mean, and how does it work? First of all, this functionality utilizes Infotype 2012, which was covered in Chapter 4 and Chapters 8 and 9. Basically, you can set up the system so that an administrator can select a checkbox. The checkbox is configured to create an Infotype 2012 entry that is processed in Time Evaluation. During the processing of Time Evaluation, you've written a custom personnel calculation rule that takes the Infotype 2012 entry and converts it into a four-hour bonus. This piece of custom code could prove to be a huge time-saver for those that administer time data for a large number of employees.

Now let's look at the next section under the basic settings — Default Values for Time Data.

Default Values for Time Data

The IMG task of configuring default values for time data is very simple. The configuration deals with Feature VTART, which allows you to default which substitution type will be used if you create a particular substitution from within the TMW.

The final section under the basic settings is to define how you want the employees' names to appear on the initial screen's employee list and within the multi-person list. Let's take a quick look at that section next.

Name Format

Under the name format IMG task, you define which order you want names to appear. For example: first name, last name; or last name, first name.

This concludes the basic settings configuration within the TMW configuration. We are almost halfway done with the IMG configuration. Now let's move on to the next section of configuration — Define IDs for Time Data.

11.3.3 IDs for Time Data

The IDs for time data allow you to customize the screens so that the administrators can select a particular ID that is linked to an infotype. By selecting and saving the data, the infotype record is automatically created without having to go directly to maintain the particular record. The IDs for time data are broken down into the following configuration areas. Figure 11.16 shows the IMG configuration steps.

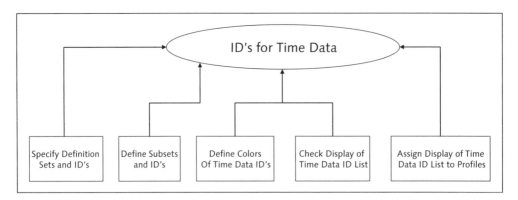

Figure 11.16 IDs for Time Data Configuration

Let's have a closer look at the configuration.

The first section of configuration is to specify definition sets and IDs. This customization allows you to define definition sets that are utilized to group like IDs together. Within the definition set, you create an ID. This becomes the key to the table where the remainder of the setup can be conducted. The time IDs have the following tabs that can be customized to default specific values, such as the following examples:

▶ Absences

▶ Attendances

▶ Planned Specifications Substitution

▶ Availability

▶ Attendance Approval

▶ Remuneration Information

▶ Transfer Specifications

▶ Time Pairs

▶ Status Information

▶ Time Events

Figure 11.17 shows the configuration for definition sets and IDs. Here, you can see how to link absences and attendances to time data IDs. Let's say you have two company codes. Company code 0001 only has one unpaid absence type that resides in Infotype 2001. Company code 0002 has a couple of different absences that would reside on Infotype 2001. For company code 0001, you create the ID AB and link the absence type to the ID. For company 0002, you create the ID AC, but you leave the absence type blank. When the time administrator of the company code selects AB, the information defaults, creating the absence record.

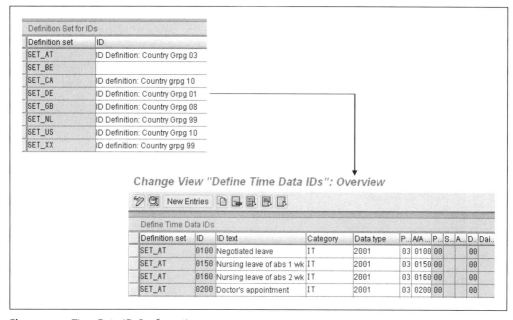

Figure 11.17 Time Data ID Configuration

The next section of configuration under the IDs for Time Management is called defining subsets and IDs. Within this section of configuration, you can establish a further breakdown of the definition sets you just configured. You can then pick and choose which IDs a time administrator can select to help expedite the data entry. If all of your administrators use the exact same absence and attendance codes, then you really only need one subset; otherwise, you may need to create as many subsets as your requirements dictate, linking the specific IDs to the applicable subsets. Figure 11.18 shows two different subsets and the various IDs that are linked to both.

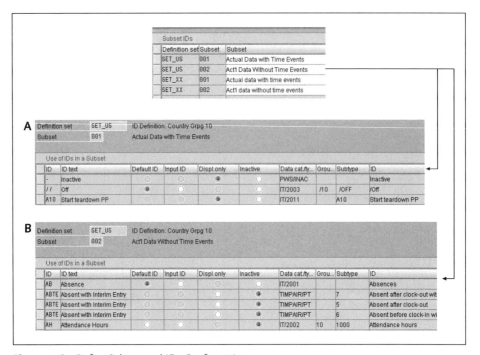

Figure 11.18 Define Subsets and IDs Configuration

After you have set up the IDs in the configuration, what does this look like in the TMW? Figure 11.19 shows an example of where on the screen the data is shown and a dropdown of eligible IDs available to this particular time administrator.

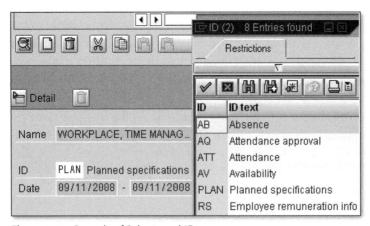

Figure 11.19 Example of Subsets and IDs

The next section of configuration under the IDs for time data supports the colors that the administrator sees on their screen.

Define Colors of the Time Data IDs

Customization of time data ID's allows you to define the color layouts for each definition set. Within each definition set, you can set up each applicable ID with the following color options. Figure 11.20 shows an example of how to set up the colors assigned to particular IDs. In this example, we flagged absence as red and attendance as green. The following colors are your options when customizing this section:

▶ Background color — Dependent on the GUI

▶ Gray-blue — Titles

▶ Light gray — Normal

▶ Blue-green — Key fields

▶ Green — Positive threshold

▶ Red — Negative threshold value

▶ Violet — Groups

Within each of these color selections, you can also specify whether or not the color will be normal, intense (makes it darker), or inverted (lighter shade).

Definition set	SET_XX	ID definition: Country grpg 99		
Set Colors of Time Data IDs for Calendar View				
ID	Short text	Color	Intense	Inverse
/ /	Off	Gray-blue (titles dependent... 🖹	☐	☐
AB	Absence	Red (negative threshold val... 🖹	☐	☐
ATT	Attendance	Green (positive threshold v... 🖹	☐	☐

Figure 11.20 Time Data List Color Definition

The next section of configuration under the IDs for time data is to establish if the IDs should be displayed, and if so, what data should be displayed. For example, we used the code AB for absence in previous examples. Would you want to show just AB? Perhaps you want to provide additional data so the administrator knows which ID to select. Within this customization, you can identify additional fields to help define the IDs the administrator will select. You can choose to hide the IDs, display the data IDs, or even display the text of the data IDs.

The final step of this section is to associate the time data ID list to a profile. The configuration task takes the display settings you configured in the previous step and links those to a profile. The profile will eventually be associated with a time administrator.

This concludes this section of the IMG configuration for setting up IDs for time data. All of these configuration items allow you to customize the TMW so that each administrator can enter and maintain data more efficiently.

The next section of the IMG configuration is to define the screen areas.

11.3.4 Screen Areas

The screen area of customization allows you to define how the screen will look and feel. You specify what data is displayed, what can be maintained, etc. Screen areas are broken up into the areas shown in Figure 11.21.

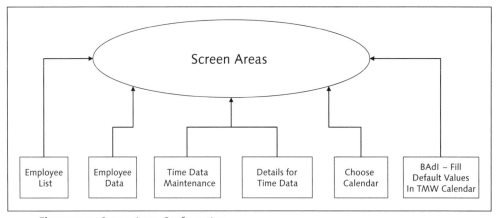

Figure 11.21 Screen Areas Configuration

Before we review the configuration for the various screen areas, let's have a look at Figure 11.22, which shows exactly which section you're setting up. That way, you can visualize what your changes will do to the overall look and feel of TMW.

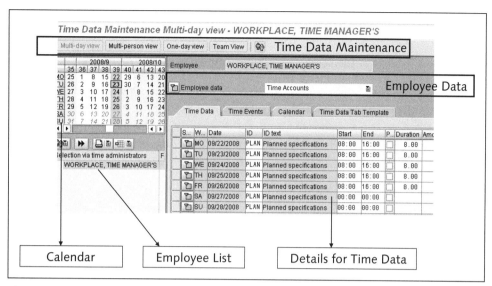

Figure 11.22 TMW Screen Layout

Let's review the configuration tables for the screen areas.

Under the Employee List, this customization allows you to define the field selections that display on the screen. For example, in Figure 11.22, the employee section shows the employee name, personnel number, and work schedule rule. If you don't want the Work Schedule rule, or perhaps you want additional data, you can set up the appropriate fields to display for the Employee List. As we've seen numerous times throughout the configuration, we first assign the fields we want to a particular code, and then link that code to a profile. For each of the fields, you have some flexibility in the settings that are applied. For example, you can set the following parameters for each field that you want to display in the Employee List.

- Display type (display value, display text for value, display icon)
- Update checkbox — specifies whether or not the field value is updated after every change you make
- Sort field
- Sort descending checkbox
- Add — adds the values of the column
- Hide column

373

▶ Alternative field label — allows you to customize the actual label of the field if you think the field is too vague

The next section of the screen area is the Employee Data screen area.

The Employee Data screen area customization allows you to define the layout for employee data based on objects configured within the basic settings section of the configuration. This is the section just above the data tabs, where time data maintenance occurs. Based on the employee data options, you can define what kinds of master data are displayed. This section is comprised of three steps:

▶ Define the layout for employee data

▶ Add the layout to the Employee Data screen area

▶ Assign the layout selection to the profiles

The layout for employee data allows you to select up to six fields of master data that will display. The fields listed in Table 11.1 are available for selection.

Field	Field	Field	Field
Administrator group	Working hours per year	Business area	Company code
Working hours per day	Dynamic daily Work Schedule	Employee name	Employee group
Sort name	Employee subgroup	Employment percentage	Job
Legal person	Working hours per month	Organizational assignment	Part-time employee
Payroll administrator	Payroll area	Pay scale group	Pay scale level
Personnel administrator	Personnel Area	Personnel Subarea	Position
USA social security number	Supervisor area	Time administrator	Time management status

Table 11.1 List of Master Data Fields Available

Field	Field	Field	Field
Weekly work days	Working hours per week	Work Schedule rule	Working week
Personnel number	Flextime excess/deficit	Education/training Quota	Approved overtime
Sick leave entitlement	Vacation	Core time violation	Productive hours
Illness time	Skeleton time	Unapproved overtime	Leave
Leave entitlement	Flextime balance	Time off from overtime	Planned hours
Overtime	Cost center		

Table 11.1 List of Master Data Fields Available (Cont.)

The next step is to add the layout to the employee data selection area.

▸ Add layout to employee data screen area

After defining the layout of the employee data by linking up to six objects, you can then add the layout to the data screen area so that the field label will be eligible for selection once assigned to a profile.

The last step is to assign the layout selections to the profiles.

▸ Assign layout selections to profiles

This is the final area of configuration for employee data where you assign the profile ID that is assigned to the time administrator to a layout selection.

We'll now move on to the Time Data Maintenance screen area.

The Time Data Maintenance customization allows you to define how the data is presented under various views. As Figure 11.22 shows, the views include the multi-day, multi-person, one-day, and team views. Each view can be configured to display the fields you are interested in giving the time administrator access to. Table 11.2 lists the fields that are delivered for time data. The Time Events tab also shares some of the same fields.

Field	Field	Field	Field
Activity allocation text	Activity number	Activity type	Attendance or absence type
Attendance quota type	Availability distribution key	Availability subtype	Business area
Business process	Calendar week number	Calendar week year	Commitment item
Controlling area	Cost center	Cost object	Currency key
Current date	Daily Work Schedule	Daily Work Schedule abbreviation	Daily Work Schedule class
Daily Work Schedule text	Daily Work Schedule variant	Day type	Deduction of employee time quota
Dominant	Duration of time data record in hours	Employee = Active	Employee subgroup grouping for Work Schedules
Employee time transfer type	End date	End of break	End time
Evaluation type for attendances/ absences	External application record	External document number	Extra pay indicator
Functional area	Fund	Funds center	Grant
Infotype text	Item number in sales order	Item number of purchasing document	Lock indicator for HR master data record
More time data exists	Multi-day indicator	Network number for account assignment	Number per employee time quota
Number per time unit for EE remuneration info	Object ID	Object type	Order number
Overtime compensation type	Paid break period	Pay scale group	Pay scale level

Table 11.2 Time Data Maintenance Fields

Field	Field	Field	Field
Personnel Subarea grouping for daily Work Schedules	Personnel Subarea grouping for Work Schedule	Premium indicator	Premium number
Previous day indicator	Productive hours on current day	Public holiday calendar	Public holiday class
Purchasing document number	Quota deduction to	Quota transaction unit	Quota transactions on current day
Receiver company code	Record is for full day	Sales order number	Sender business area
Sender company code	Sender cost center	Sender fund	Sender grant
Sender functional area	Service category	Service number	Service type
Several items of additional info for Time Pair	Show/Hide button	Start date	Start date for quota deduction
Start of break	Start time	Substitution type	Subtype text
Text for overtime compensation type	Time data ID text	Time data ID type	Time data text exists
Time/measurement unit text	Unpaid break period	User-defined hours	User-defined processing instructions
User-defined text field	Valuation basis for different payment	Wage type	Wage type amount for payments
Weekday ID	Work break schedule	WBS element	Work Schedule rule
Work tax area			

Table 11.2 Time Data Maintenance Fields (Cont.)

The next section of the configuration screen areas is for the display of the time data details screen. Figure 11.22 shows the screen for time data details.

The details for time data customization allows you to define which tabs are displayed for the time data ID type that is created. This functionality allows you to identify specific fields that can or should be entered based on the data ID type. The fields are presented on the tabs that have been authorized based on the time

377

administrator's profile. The basic goal of this configuration is to limit the number of information fields that the time administrator needs to maintain for a particular activity. In the absence of configuration specifying the particular fields that should be displayed, all fields are presented on the tabs for the user to maintain.

The detailed tabs are broken into the following sections. The Cs represent the tab strips, while the Ds represent the field selections.

▶ C01 – Absences (Infotype 2001)

▶ C02 – Attendances (Infotype 2002)

▶ C03 – Substitutions (Infotype 2003)

▶ C04 – Availability (Infotype 2004)

▶ C07 – Attendance Quota (Infotype 2007)

▶ C10 – Employee Remuneration (Infotype 2010)

▶ C11 – Time Eevents (Infotype 2011)

▶ C12 – Time Transfer Specifications (Infotype 2012)

▶ CWS – Personnel Work Schedule

▶ D01 – Absences (Infotype 2001)

▶ D02 – Attendances (Infotype 2002)

▶ D03 – Substitutions (Infotype 2003)

▶ D04 – Availability (Infotype 2004)

▶ D07 – Attendance Quota (Infotype 2007)

▶ D10 – Employee Remuneration (Infotype 2010)

▶ D11 – Time Events (Infotype 2011)

▶ D12 – Time Transfer Specifications (Infotype 2012)

▶ DWS – Personnel Work Schedule

The next section screen area is for the calendar. The following section describes this basic setup.

The Calendar customization has the following options:

▶ A simple calendar – CL_PT_GUI_TMW_CALENDAR

▶ Enhanced navigation calendar – CL_PT_GUI_TMW_CALENDAR2

The main difference is that the enhanced navigation calendar offers functionality to quickly maneuver to the period of time you are going to make updates in.

There is one final piece of configuration under the Details for Time Data section. This configuration has to do with utilizing a Business Add-in (BAdI) for defaulting particular days for processing. For example, you could have the BAdI populate the dates for the previous week if the current day is a Monday. This way, you are reviewing the time data that will be processed during the current week's payroll.

There are two sections left in the IMG for TMW configuration: Employee selection and the final definition of profiles. In the next section, we'll discuss employee selection.

11.3.5   Employee Selection

The employee selection functionality offer flexibility for time administrators to select which employees in which time will be maintained. You can customize the employee selection under three main areas of the profile:

▶ User specific

▶ Multi-user selections

▶ Interactive selections

Each of these options base their selections off of configuration from the definition of selection IDs and HR infosets from ADHOC Query or SAP Query. They are then associated with a group that is definable and then linked to the selection profile in the final step. Figure 11.23 shows the configuration steps for defining employee selection.

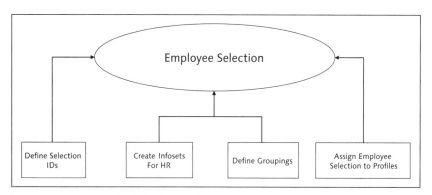

Figure 11.23   Options for Selecting Employees

Figure 11.24 shows where the employee selection parameters are linked to a profile.

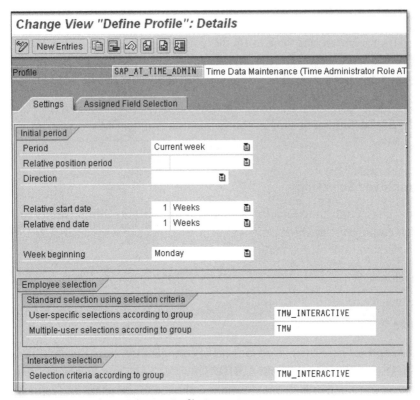

Figure 11.24 Employee Selection Profile Parameters

The final section of the configuration is where you link all of the configurations from the previous sections to a profile. This is the place that determines administrator X sees a different TMW screen than employee Y.

11.3.6 Profiles

Entry into the TMW begins with a profile. A profile can be stored in the user's own data under parameter PT_TMW_PROFILR and is utilized each time upon entering Transaction PTMW. All of the configurations that were set up in the previous sections are linked to a profile. This allows you to heavily customize the time manager's workbench per your requirements and per the individuals executing time administration. Each profile can be defined under the following structures and is shown in Figure 11.25.

▶ Menu Format Assignment

▶ Employee List Assignment

▶ Employee Data Assignment

▶ Multi-Day Assignment

▶ Multi-Person Assignment

▶ One-Day Assignment

▶ Team View Assignment

▶ Detailed Screens Assignment

▶ Degree of Detail Assignment

▶ Processing Instructions Assignment

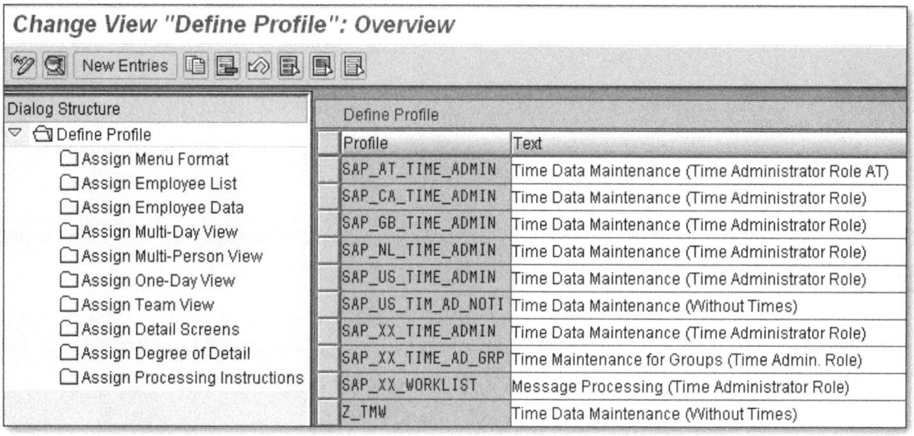

Figure 11.25 TMW Profile Definitions

In Figure 11.25, you can see folders down the left side. Within each profile, you have the opportunity to configure step by step through the various folders and customize the way the workplace will be used for that particular profile. All of the various items you have configured under each of their respective steps will be available for selection. It is up to you to combine them in such a manner to satisfy your business requirements.

11.4 Summary

The TMW functionality is geared toward a distributed time administration environment. The user interfaces in which the time administrators conduct their activities can be heavily customized to allow a variety of different functionality per group and the overall look and feel of the screens for master data maintenance can be tailored as necessary. This chapter introduced you to the core concepts and provided an overview of what may be possible to customize. If you elect to implement this functionality, you need to review each section of configuration to determine the exact fields that are available for each tab and have a firm grasp of how the setup should work prior to conducting your blueprint. The next chapter on Shift Planning provides you with an overview of the functionality available within the SAP system.

In this chapter, you'll learn about key areas to consider during the configuration of Shift Planning. At the conclusion of this chapter, you should be knowledgeable of the concepts, setup, and processing capabilities of Shift Planning.

12   Shift Planning

Shift Planning is a subcomponent within the ERP HCM Time Management functionality. The functionality enables the business to schedule their employees to enable proper planning regarding shift times, locations, the number of employees required, and the actual scheduled employees. Its capability enables you to utilize your workforce as effectively as possible.

Shift Planning can be integrated with a variety of areas. Those areas include the Logistics component, the Human Resources (HR) component, and the portal. This chapter explains how the Shift Planning component can be used, the areas of the IMG that support the component, and examples of how you can leverage this functionality for your business. The following are some of the data integration points.

▶ **Logistics** — Capacity planning and distribution requirements to determine availability based on an employee's Work Schedule.

▶ **Human Resources**

  ▶ Time Management Infotypes — Creates Infotype 2003 — Substitutions.

  ▶ Time Evaluation — You can run Time Evaluation from within Shift Planning.

  ▶ Payroll — Shift plans impact employees' personal shift plans, which can impact payroll proration rules for salary amounts or month-end accrual calculations.

  ▶ Organizational Structure–Related Data — Utilizes the organizational units or whichever component within the organizational structure you configure for the profile. The profile is explained later within the configuration section in Figure 12.13.

> ▸ Qualifications — Used to determine if an employee is qualified to work a particular shift. For example, you could set up a shift that has a particular requirement to be eligible for that shift. If the employee isn't qualified, then they won't be able to work the shift.

▸ **Internet Applications**

▸ **Key Management** — Shift Planning.

Shift Planning can provide your organization with a lot of functionality and flexibility surrounding the management of your labor force. You need to decide if this functionality is something that should be implemented. You should also ensure that those that receive this functionality are willing and able to use the tool to schedule their employees.

Shift planning utilizes organizational units to build a shift plan. This is how it's delivered. If the organizational units structure that was, or will be, established during blueprinting allows you to have the appropriated level for managers to plan their labor force. For example, when you first begin the Shift Planning process, the functionality requests an organizational unit to determine which employees should be selected for the Shift Planning process. You must select an organizational unit or you can't enter the Shift Planning component. If your manager was planning out their labor force, you'd want an organizational unit that selects the employees that the manager is responsible for instead of a larger population, which is a little overwhelming to manage. This may cause some problems selecting employees if your organizational units are not aligned with those that administer the shifts. Luckily, during the profile setup, you're not locked into using the organizational unit and can instead select one of many different options for selecting employees.

You must determine if the groupings that have been established for Personnel Area/Subarea combinations for daily Work Schedule, attendance and absence type groupings, and substitution/availability type groupings offer the flexibility you need to set up shift plans for employees.

The Shift Planning component has various features to help you in scheduling your labor force. Figure 12.1 provides an overview of the features that are provided within Shift Planning.

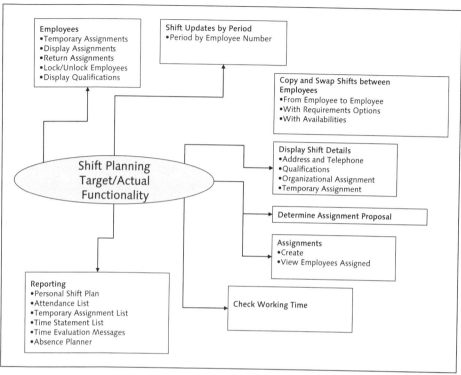

Figure 12.1 Overview of Shift Planning Functionality

This chapter is divided into two parts. In the first part, we'll show you the front-end transaction that you'd use to set up your organizational unit shift plan. In the second part, we'll provide an overview of the IMG configuration and the various parameters that can be set up to customize the Shift Planning component.

Let's begin with how you can use the Shift Planning component.

12.1   Processing Overview

As we discussed earlier in the chapter, when beginning the processing for Shift Planning, you'll need to select an organizational unit. Organizational units are defined during the blueprinting stage of the project and are maintained by those in charge of the organizational structure for your company. Specifically, an organizational unit is a unit of your enterprise. It's a vague description because each company defines what it means for their business. Examples of an organizational unit might include a payroll department, a distribution center, a specific piece of a distribution center, etc. It can be as granular as you need it to be.

Upon selecting this organizational unit, you need to associate a shift group to the organizational unit. A shift group is defined in the configuration and allows you to group values, such as shift abbreviations, requirement types, and general color formatting (which is discussed later in this chapter), that enable them to be pulled into the Shift Planning component. You can utilize shift groups to customize the functionality for every organizational unit that is using shift planning. After you select a shift group, you can begin creating your target plan for whatever period of time your resource plan dictates.

Let's address a couple of items regarding the two types of plans that you see upon entering the transaction.

▶ Target Plan — Utilized for medium or long-term planning. You need to create a target plan prior to creating the actual plan.

▶ Actual Plan — Utilized for short-term plans or alterations to existing plans. The target plan must exist before you can change an Actual plan.

What does the initial Shift Planning screen look like? Figure 12.2 shows the initial screen upon entering the transaction.

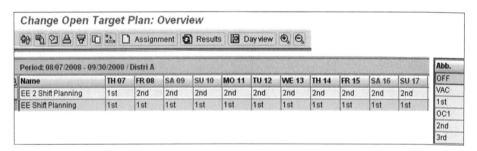

Figure 12.2 Overview Screen for Shift Planning

In Figure 12.2, you will notice a couple of employees with Work Schedules that have been assigned from Infotype 0007 Planned Working Time. The data is pulled in from their Work Schedule rule. Infotype 0007 were discussed in Chapter 4, and Work Schedule rules were discussed in Chapter 5. You will notice that each day of the week is listed, and the Work Schedules for the employees are shown under each date.

In addition to what you see on the initial screen, there are other features of the Shift Planning component that are available to the manager. What are these features? Let's begin by double-clicking on a particular day for a particular employee. Figure 12.3 shows the pop-up window that appears. The first tab, called Working Time, defaults.

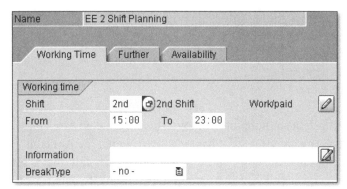

Figure 12.3 Overview of the Working Time Tab

In Figure 12.3, you can change any of the parameters on the screen. If you change the times, the shift displaying 2nd would show a # or whatever indicator that you have configured to display, which we will discuss during the configuration of Shift Planning. This lets you know that a change has been made to the existing shift. Changing the actual shift to a different shift or adding a break type displays the shift as selected.

The pop-up screen used to edit a particular shift for a single employee has three tabs. Let's discuss the kinds of information available on the second tab, called Further. The Further tab enables you to assign an employee to a different organizational unit so that their working time can be scheduled. At the beginning of the chapter, we discussed the importance of organizational units. If, for example, an employee is temporarily working in another organizational unit, you can reassign them so that they can be scheduled with all of the employees of that other organizational unit. You can also assign the employee to a different cost center to track costs and a different position to receive a different compensation level if they are performing a position in a different pay grade. Figure 12.4 shows the Further tab.

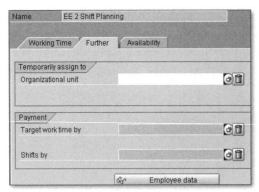

Figure 12.4 Overview of the Further Tab

There is one more tab in the edit shift pop-up window. This tab is called Availability. In previous chapters, such as Chapter 3 and Chapter 5, we covered the Availability functionality in the system. This tab allows you to select a particular shift that is set up to allow other components within the SAP system to determine if you are available or not. You also have the opportunity to further define such availability based on start and end times for that shift. Figure 12.5 shows the Availability tab.

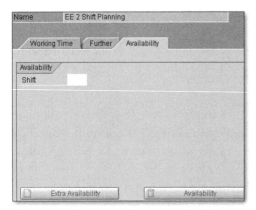

Figure 12.5 Overview of the Availability Tab

Now that we have covered how to edit a particular shift, let's have a look at how to change an employee from one shift to another shift.

Another feature of Shift Planning is to allow the manager to quickly change an employee's shift. For example, you might decide to change an employee's shift from first shift to second shift to correlate to a spike in production where you need extra resources. Figure 12.6 shows the screen to change an employee's shift.

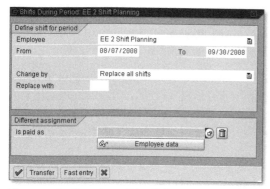

Figure 12.6 Overview of the Shift Swap Screen

Next, we'll discuss how you can quickly swap schedules between two employees.

Let's say, for example, you have two employee's walk into your office. One of them has a doctor's appointment during his scheduled shift and would like to swap out his shift with another employee. By utilizing the Copy Shifts feature, you can quickly make the change in the system. You can also use this feature to copy shifts, copy availabilities associated with those shifts, and swap those availabilities. Figure 12.7 shows the Copy Shifts during the period functionality. Depending on which processing type you select, you can conduct the items we just discussed between employees.

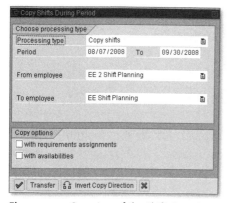

Figure 12.7 Overview of the Shift Copy Screen

In the following section, let's take a look at how a manager could quickly assign shifts to employees. Figure 12.8 shows the steps that a manager would take to complete this process. As shown in Figure 12.8, the manager would highlight the employees and the days he wanted to change. He would then select the appropriate shift abbreviation, and the highlighted areas would automatically change. Upon saving, those changes generate an Infotype 2003 substitution record.

What are the shift abbreviations, and how does the system know which abbreviations are available? During the configuration of the Shift Planning component, you have the opportunity to define those abbreviations and the types of substitution records that are automatically created in Infotype 2003. We will discuss the configuration in the second part of this chapter.

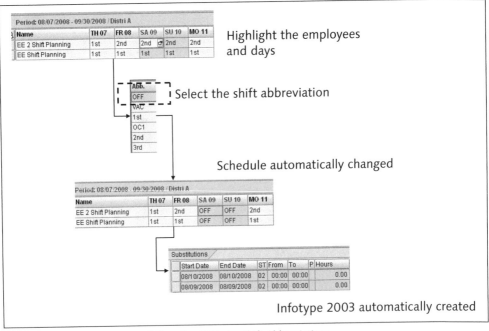

Figure 12.8 Overview of Changing Shifts by Shift Abbreviations

We have covered some of the ways in which you can utilize shift planning to build your resource allocations for a specific period of time. Let's now switch gears and review the configuration that supports Shift Planning.

12.2 Configuration

Now let's move on to some areas of the configuration that you can set up, including, Table T77SU — Various Settings Available. The configuration for Shift Planning can be found in the IMG under the menu path TIME MANAGEMENT • SHIFT PLANNING.

If you're reading this book in order, you've learned about the Time Manager's Workplace (TMW) and the customizations that you can set up so that the overall screen can look different based on groups of employees. Within Shift Planning, your options on what you can change are somewhat limited.

Another major difference in the IMG for Shift Planning and that of the other components is that the configuration for Shift Planning is not driven by specific table entries, but instead by placing certain values in table T77S0 – System Table, which drives the processing of the Shift Planning component. In this section, we will list the various configuration tables and where they apply. Most of the IMG nodes take you directly to table T77S0, so, to prevent a lot of table images, we have consolidated the various items you can configure into tables that are easier to read.

Let's proceed with the configuration.

As noted earlier, all of the IMG nodes related to the table entries made in table T77S0 have been extracted and placed in a table. The table shown in Figure 12.9 shows the first list of parameters you can change. All of the entries are switches of functionality that you can activate and, with some of them, define the default information they would use.

How do you interpret the data in the tables in the following sections? The table lists four different columns of data, which we will explain here:

▶ Group — This is delivered from SAP and represents a grouping of switches for a particular part of functionality.

▶ Semantic Abbreviation — With a group, you have a variation of entries called semantic abbreviations. The combination of Group and Semantic Abbreviation is used by the standard system's programs to process data and features as SAP intended them to.

▶ Value — This is the only field you can update. For each group and Semantic Abbreviation combination, you have only one opportunity to enter a value. What do the values mean? By going to the table, some of the values have a dropdown that allows you to select from different options — some of the value fields do not. The various nodes with the IMG may provide additional documentation on what may or may not be allowed as a value for the combination of Group and Semantic Abbreviation. Another option for help is in the table in Figure 12.9.

▶ Description — A high-level description of what the switch is used for.

Let's take a look at one of the groups from Figure 12.9.

GROUP	SEMANTIC ABBREVIA	VALUE	DESCRIPTION	NOTES
PEINS	VARTI	5	Substitution type for shifts in the actual plan (s	Used to default which substitution type utilized on the actual plan of shift planning will generate a substitution infotype 2003
PEINS	VARTS	2	Substitution type for shifts in the target plan (s	Used to default which substitution type utilized on the target plan of shift planning will generate a substitution infotype 2003
PEINS	VARWI	6	Substitution type for working time preferences (se	Used to default which substitution type will be created on infotype 2003 Substitution if working time preferences are utilized
PEINS	SCEME		Report variant for time evaluation	The variant of Time Evaluation should be setup here
PEINS	AWART		Attendance type of assignments for simulation	You can assign an attendance type that will be utilized during a time evaluation simulation to a shift or a defined requirement
PEINS	VARIA		2. Report variant for calling time evaluation	You can assign a Time Evaluation variant that has been setup as a simulation to test an employee's assignment to a shift or a defined requirement
PEINS	PZTEF	X	Org. employee status from Time Management	This will determine which time management status should be used for the simulation
PEINS	TIM_V	#	Shift abbreviation for time substitution in plan	This is to define what will be displayed in the shift plan for a shift that is different than their normal planned working time
PEINS	GROUP	STANDARD	Default value for shift group of Shift Planning	The entry here will be proposed when assigning an Organizational Unit to a shift group
PEINS	MOABW	1	Personnel subarea grouping for absence/attendance	Default value proposed when creating a new shift group for absences and attendances
PEINS	MOTPR	1	Personnel subarea grouping for daily work schedule	Default value proposed when creating a new shift group for daily work schedules
PEINS	MOVER	1	Personnel subarea grouping for substitution/availa	Default value proposed when creating a new shift group for Personnel Subarea grouping for substitutions
PEINS	CALID	1	Calendar ID of the Shift Planning factory calendar	Defaults the Factory Calendar ID in the absence of one associated with infotype 1027 Site Dependent Information. Using infotype 1027, you can assign different factory calendars to different Organizational Units

Figure 12.9 Groups and Descriptions for Table T77S0 Entries

392

Look at the very first entry in the table. You can see the entry under the group called PEINS with a Semantic abbreviation of VARTI. As you read the description, you see that this switch allows you to default a particular substitution type on Infotype 2003. To find the various values available, you can go directly to table T77S0, find the combination of Group and Semantic abbreviation and conduct a dropdown on the value field. Here you'll see a variety of options available for you to choose as the default. Remember, you can default one value only so you can't default 05 for one group of managers and 06 for a different group.

Figure 12.9 shows the first table of switches and Figure 12.10 shows additional switches and the functionality they support.

GROUP	SEMANTIC ABBREVIA	VALUE	DESCRIPTION	NOTES
PEINS	RULE	SAP_1	Strategy for automatic assignment proposal	Used to determine automated employee proposals for particular requirements
PEINS	SMUCD		Assignment Proposal Only on Days with Changes	Used to setup the system to make proposals only on days where changes were made
PEINS	SMUDR		Period for Assignment Proposal	Used in conjunction with the assignment proposal only on days with changes functionality
PEINS	RULE2	SAP_2	Strategy for automatic assignment if plan changes	Used to specify the specify strategy the system should used when assigning employees to requirements
PEINS	DBSEL	SAP_ WFP	Selection view to restrict employee selection	Used to define which view should be used when selecting employees
PEINS	VTART	X	Change of substitution type in shift plan active	
PEINS	MJOB	I	Error message for different job	Enables a message to be displayed if the employee is assigned to a different job than normal
PEINS	MORG	I	Error message for different organizational object	Enables a message to be displayed if the employee is assigned to a different Organiational Unit than normal
PEINS	ARBPL		Save work center substitute schedule	Determines if a substitution due to a temporary assignment should be evaluated in Time Management as a substitution
PEINS	DCUST		Detail Dialog Box: Allow Subscreen Selection	Enter an X to define the actual screens that will show. They will need to be setup via the next step in this node

Figure 12.10 Groups and Descriptions for Table T77S0 Entries, continued

Continuing with our list of switches, Figure 12.11 shows additional switches and the functionality they support.

GROUP	SEMANTIC ABBREVIA	VALUE	DESCRIPTION	NOTES
PEINS	PLSTE	2	Different payment (position) active	Here you can determine if payment from a different position is possible
PEINS	LOCK	X	Activate lock for employee in shift plan	Allows you to lock the time master data to prevent updates during the maintenance of a shift schedule
PEINS	PSESK		Get Shift Abbreviation	Determines whether or not to use the original shift abbreviation or the one closest to the clock time when a change is made to the times of the start and end times
PEINS	RFRSH		Refresh Time Data and Temp. Assignments When Save	Allows you to see the updates made to temporary assignments without the need of existing and reentering the plan
PEINS	TASSA		Temporary Assignment Despite Attendance or Absence	Allows you to assign temporary assignments even though there might be absences or attendances for tha t period already entered in the system
PEINS	EXBDA	PSRM1MAC	Name of MS Excel Print Macro for Requirmnt Matchup	Enables the requirement match up to be printed with EXCEL
PEINS	EXCDR	0	Automatic Printout of Shift Plan via MS Excel	Determines if the shift should automatically be printed or be viewed prior to print
PEINS	EXCFV	VORLAGE	Name of MS Excel Style for Shift Plan	Used to identify a template used in EXCEL to format the data
PEINS	EXCMA	WDPDDMAC	Name of MS Excel Print Macro for Shift Plan	Used to identify the print macro when using EXCEL
PEINS	EXCME		Environment for Path of MS Excel Macro	Used to store the path where the macro is stored

Figure 12.11 Groups and Descriptions for Table T77S0 Entries, continued

Figure 12.12 shows the final switches and the functionality they support.

GROUP	SEMANTIC ABBREVIA	VALUE	DESCRIPTION	NOTES	IMG Node	Subnode
PEINS	TTYP1	8	Time type for output of shift plan via MS EXCEL	Describes the time type from table T555A	Connecting to Microsoft EXCEL	Define Time Types for Connecting to
PEINS	TTYP2	5	Time type for output of shift plan via MS EXCEL	Describes the time type from table T555A	Connecting to Microsoft EXCEL	Define Time Types for Connecting to
PEINS	TTYP3	6	Time type for output of shift plan via MS EXCEL	Describes the time type from table T555A	Connecting to Microsoft EXCEL	Define Time Types for Connecting to
PEINS	TTYP4	40	Time type for output of shift plan via MS EXCEL	Describes the time type from table T555A	Connecting to Microsoft EXCEL	Define Time Types for Connecting to

Figure 12.12 Groups and Descriptions for Table T77S0 Entries, continued

This concludes the list of switches that can be set up. There are, however, some configuration tables in the IMG for Shift Planning. Let's take a look at how to set up a profile.

12.2.1 Profile Setup

During the profile setup, you have the following options when establishing the profile that will be linked to the employee's master record that plans the Shift Schedule. These allow you to customize how employees are pulled into the Shift Planning employee selection processing. Figure 12.13 shows the following options:

▶ Employee Selection

▶ Removal of Employees from Selection

▶ Employee Assigned Elsewhere

▶ Requirements Source for Entry Objects

The selection is based on defining evaluation paths. Evaluation paths are used to select employees, and you'll need to work with the individual that is in charge of setting these up to determine which ones you can use. You'll also notice in Figure 12.13 that the letter O for organizational unit is listed. You can change this option to one that works for you. For example, you can change this to Personnel Subarea or profit center. Let's have a look at the profile configuration tables in Figure 12.13

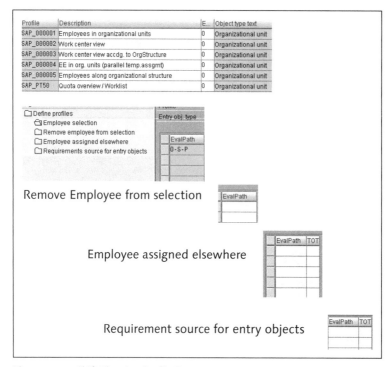

Figure 12.13 Shift Planning Profile Setup

The next section of IMG configuration for Shift Planning is the definition of the abbreviation we discussed earlier in the chapter that allows you to quickly change the shift an employee is assigned to. Figure 12.8 was your first exposure to this concept. Let's revisit shift abbreviations now.

12.2.2 Shift Abbreviation

Shift abbreviations are linked to shift groups and are a core component of Shift Planning. The abbreviations are the foundation that allows you to select various daily Work Schedules and the supporting configuration that is linked to them. After selecting the shift abbreviation, you can further alter the information contained on the edit shift pop-up screen we previously reviewed.

The shift abbreviation has the following functionality:

▶ Assign Daily Work Schedule

▶ Assign Daily Work Schedule Variants

- ▶ Assign Start and End Times

- ▶ Assign Absences

- ▶ Assign Attendances

- ▶ Assign Availability

- ▶ Assign Colors to the Shift

- ▶ Assign Formatting including Highlights, Inverse the Colors, Bold, Italics, and Underlining

Shift groups can also have requirement types assigned to the group. The overall look and feel of the screen can be customized to show various color settings.

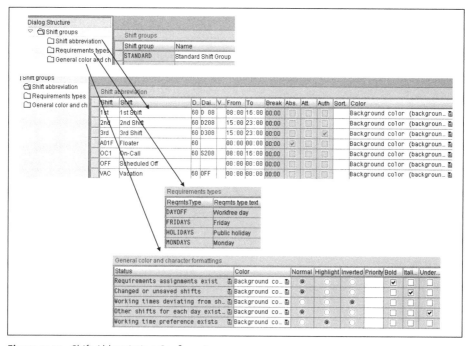

Figure 12.14 Shift Abbreviation Configuration

Figure 12.14 shows where you set up shift groups. You can then further assign the shift abbreviations, any requirement types you feel are necessary, and set up the Shift Planning screens to display various colors for particular conditions. Let's take a look at Figure 12.14. As you can see from the figure, you assign particular abbreviations to specific daily Work Schedules. For example, the abbreviation

1st is linked to daily Work Schedule D 08. If you want, you can associate the 1st abbreviation with a color that would show on the screen anytime somebody was on the first shift.

If you've set up the system with particular shifts and requirements to limit who can be on that shift, is there a way to quickly determine who might be eligible for that shift? There's good news. You can, and we'll discuss how to propose employees for shifts in the next section.

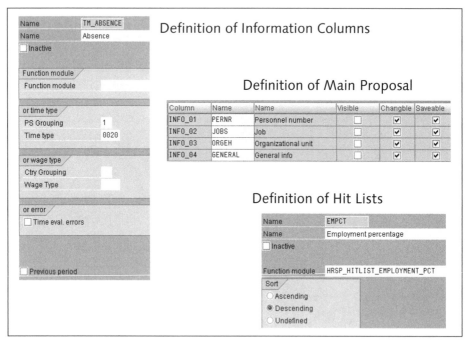

Figure 12.15 Columns and Proposal Setup

12.2.3 Proposal Determination

This section of the configuration allows you to customize what data is displayed for employees during the proposal processes. Figure 12.15 shows the configuration table where you can set up a column to pull information from a function module, a Time Type, a Wage type, or a from a Time Evaluation error. A function module is standard SAP code that is used to extract information. When defining the layout, you specify the column number and the name of the information column established in the previous step. The final step is to define how the system is going to propose the hit list of available candidates. In this example, the hit list is based on the employee percentage from Infotype 0007.

Figure 12.15 shows the screen that allows you to customize the look of the information columns and the initial setup for defining how the system will propose employees that are available for a particular shift.

The next figure shows how to set up the automatic proposal to find employees for particular conditions. The SAP system calls these strategies as the automatic proposal is customized to how you want to find eligible employees. As you can see from Figure 12.16, there are numerous settings you can make to tailor your strategy. The defined hit list and our example of employee percentage can be linked to the priority field. You can link multiple hit lists in the priority of your requirements. Let's have a look at Figure 12.16.

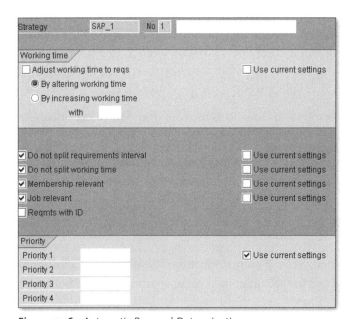

Figure 12.16 Automatic Proposal Determination

Figure 12.16 provides a further look into the strategy definitions that can be made during the system setup when determining the proposals.

This concludes our review of the configuration for Shift Planning. In the next section, we'll look at a practical example of utilizing Shift Planning.

12.3 Practical Example

Shift Planning can be used in a variety of ways for different organizational structures. The drivers for setting up the screen included the following:

▶ Organizational Structure

▶ Daily Work Schedule groupings

▶ Absence and Attendance type groupings

▶ Substitution and Availability type groupings

One reason to implement Shift Planning and to utilize the Shift Planning functionality might stem from your decision-making process for the Work Schedule set up for the company. As you've learned, Work Schedule set up and maintenance can be a daunting task to configure and accurately maintain for employees. The following high-level steps are defined to offer you a possible solution to minimize Work Schedule creation and maintenance, yet offer visibility to accurately maintained Work Schedules for work force planning and compensation rules.

How can we set up the system to accommodate the following business requirements?

▶ How do we pay employees that work multiple shifts with shift differentials on various days of the week, yet minimize the amount of Work Schedules required to do so?

▶ How do we allow employees to enter absences if their defined Work Schedule lists a day off?

▶ How do we ensure that month-end accrual functionality in payroll is accommodated for and that the basis for calculations is using accurate working hours per period and not calendar days?

▶ If we use generic Work Schedules, how can we prorate based on hours worked for new hires, mid-period terminations, etc.

There are probably other business requirements, but these should illustrate the point.

Let's assume you have decided not to set up very detailed Work Schedules and instead have decided on the following:

- You have the following defined shifts
    - 8-hour Days
    - 10-hour Days
    - 12-hour Days
- Employees work first, second, and third shift with shift differential payments due for hours worked on those shifts. Your exempt or salary population also works a variety of shifts to manage the labor force and the peaks in demand due to seasonal conditions.
- You have defined that employees work a variety of schedules depending on business demands and that a third-party time-keeping system is out of scope.
- How can you set up the system to accommodate all of your requirements?

Even though we're discussing Shift Planning in this chapter, this example explains how you can use Shift Planning to accommodate your Time Management requirement to pay employees correctly by knowing what Work Schedules they are on. Instead of creating thousands of Work Schedules for every possible combination, you can leverage Shift Planning. Also take note of Appendix D, which lists various combinations of Work Schedules, if you need a refresher on the various combinations that employees might work. How, may you ask, can we leverage Shift Planning to reduce our number of work schedules?

The rest of this example will explain detailed parts of the Work Schedule configuration. You can utilize Shift Planning by setting up the system with the following Work Schedule rule configuration. In Chapter 5, we discussed how to set up a Work Schedule. One of the components of a Work Schedule is a daily Work Schedule, which is all of the parameters that an employee works for a given day. In our example, we will provide configuration for the Work Schedule rules.

- Daily Work Schedules — Set up the daily Work Schedules so that you know which schedule is described by the amount of hours per day. The following daily Work Schedule lets you know which employees are working 8-hour, 10-hour, and 12-hour shifts. It can also tell you if there are any shift differentials due to an employee.

- ▸ D108 = Daily 8 Hours 1st Shift
- ▸ D208 = Daily 8 Hours 2nd Shift
- ▸ D308 = Daily 8 Hours 3rd Shift
- ▸ D110 = Daily 8 Hours 1st Shift
- ▸ D210 = Daily 8 Hours 2nd Shift
- ▸ D310 = Daily 8 Hours 3rd Shift
- ▸ D112 = Daily 8 Hours 1st Shift
- ▸ D212 = Daily 8 Hours 2nd Shift
- ▸ D312 = Daily 8 Hours 3rd Shift
- ▸ Off = Scheduled Day Off
- ▸ OC01 = On-Call 1st Shift
- ▸ OC02 = On-Call 2nd Shift
- ▸ OC03 = On-Call 3rd Shift
- ▸ ** Add any others that you may need.

We know from Chapter 5 that daily Work Schedules make up period Work Schedules. For our example, we will create generic period Work Schedules. Notice that we only have nine possible entries. If you take a look at Appendix D, you'll notice that there are 127 possible combinations. Keep that in mind for later.

- ▸ Period Work Schedules — Set up one period Work Schedule per variation of daily Work Schedule:
  - ▸ D108 = Monday through Sunday daily Work Schedules are set to D108
  - ▸ D208 = Monday through Sunday daily Work Schedules are set to D208
  - ▸ D308 = Monday through Sunday daily Work Schedules are set to D308
  - ▸ D110 = Monday through Sunday daily Work Schedules are set to D110
  - ▸ D210 = Monday through Sunday daily Work Schedules are set to D210
  - ▸ D310 = Monday through Sunday daily Work Schedules are set to D310
  - ▸ D112 = Monday through Sunday daily Work Schedules are set to D110
  - ▸ D212 = Monday through Sunday daily Work Schedules are set to D210
  - ▸ D312 = Monday through Sunday daily Work Schedules are set to D310

Now that you've set up the period Work Schedule, you have to create the Work Schedule rule. For this example, we will create the following Work Schedule rules. Notice that there are only 9 work schedules that allow you to identify employees working 8-, 10-, and 12-hour shifts. You can also determine if they are on first, second, or third shift based on our naming conventions, which means we can determine if any shift differentials should be paid.

Take a few minutes to review the following Work Schedule naming conventions.

▶ Work Schedule rules — Set up one Work Schedule rule per period Work Schedule.

  ▶ 0000108 — 8-hour normal shift

  ▶ 0000208 — 8-hour second shift with shift differential

  ▶ 0000308 — 8-hour third shift with shift differential

  ▶ 0000110 — 10-hour normal shift

  ▶ 0000210 — 10-hour second shift with shift differential

  ▶ 0000310 — 10-hour third shift with shift differential

  ▶ 0000112 — 12-hour normal shift

  ▶ 0000212 — 12-hour second shift with shift differential

  ▶ 0000312 — 12-hour third shift with shift differential

Why did we set these Work Schedule rules up in this fashion? Let's explain.

You have two options:

1. Set up very detailed Work Schedules in the configuration to accommodate every possibility that the business is aware of, and perhaps even those that they aren't aware of.

2. Streamline the Work Schedule configuration so that enough configurations are made available to the Shift Planning component that managers can build their own combinations of Work Schedules.

You have set up very generic Work Schedules residing in Infotype 0007 that are 8-, 10-, and 12-hour days, 7 days a week. The variety of daily Work Schedules can be used by the individuals that plan their organizational unit's employee Work Schedules as daily Work Schedules are an integration point with Shift Planning. Using just the basic daily Work Schedules, the schedules can be customized as needed, using Shift Planning, without the need for new configurations or new Work Schedules. As long as all of the necessary daily Work Schedules appear in Shift Planning, the shift plans can be allocated to the employees' schedules as needed.

The updates that are done via Shift Planning create an Infotype 2003 substitution record automatically. Once the record is on Infotype 2003, the information also adjusts the working times in the time applications timesheet. The employee's Infotype 0007 no longer needs to be maintained directly, but is now the default Work Schedule in the absence of a Shift Planning schedule.

The naming convention of the daily Work Schedules allow you to have the appropriate criteria to drive overtime and shift-related hours generation for regular time entered from within the Time Evaluation processing covered in Chapters 8 and 9. In addition to compensation, the personnel shift plan, which the month-end accruals functionality in payroll uses to determine working hours for the cost percentage allocation to accounting, use the updated daily Work Schedules to determine which days are working days and which days aren't. The updated total hours in the payroll period are utilized in the calculations instead of the generic Work Schedule on Infotype 0007, which showed the employee working seven days a week.

The overall design, if set up correctly, allows the shift planner to create custom schedules per group or individual employee. It also provides the flexibility to adapt to changing business requirements, while allowing administration of compensation rules to be set up in Time Evaluation.

12.4 Summary

In this chapter, you learned about the functionality included in Shift Planning. This included an overview of the overall functionality, processing of custom shifts, configuration setup, and an example of how you could utilize the functionality as part of the great landscape of Time Management. The following chapter on Incentive Wages provides you with an overview of the functionality available within the SAP system.

In this chapter, you'll learn about the various Time Entry options for Time Management. At the conclusion of this chapter, you should have a solid understanding of the various methods for entering time data into Time Management.

13 Time Entry Options in SAP ERP HCM Time Management

There are a variety of methodologies related to the entry of time-related data into the SAP system. The following options are available and any and all can be used by themselves or in conjunction with one another. We will discuss each of them in this chapter.

- SAP Portal Touch Screen
- SAP Portal Time Sheet
- HR Plant Data Collection (PDC) Time Entry
- Cross-Application Time Sheet (CATS)
- Third-party Time Collection System
- Direct Entry of Infotypes 2001, 2002, 2003, and 2010
- Time Manager's Workplace (TMW)

Before we review the various components of time entry, Figures 13.1, 13.2, and 13.3 provide an overview of the time entry options that can be used for entering time data into the SAP system and a process flow for where the data resides and is processed. Let's first have a look at Figure 13.1, which shows the various entry options.

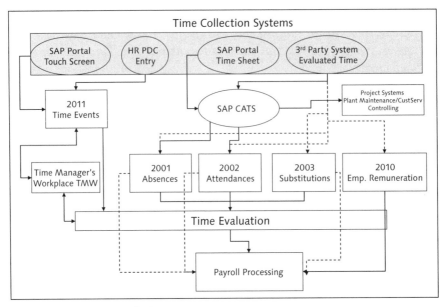

Figure 13.1 Various Entry Options

Figure 13.2 illustrates the data flow for the SAP functionality and that of a third-party collection system.

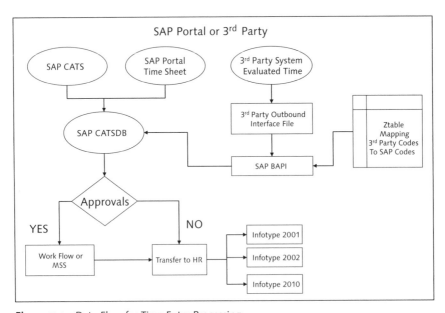

Figure 13.2 Data Flow for Time Entry Processing

Figure 13.3 illustrates the data flow for the SAP Portal functionality and that of a third-party collection system for clock times.

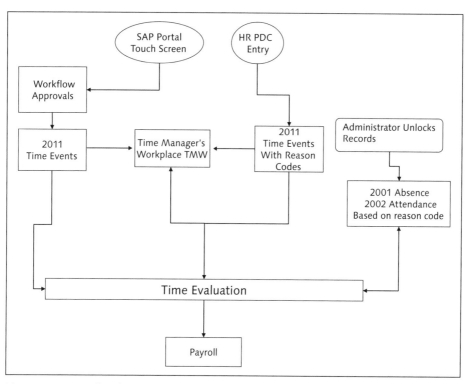

Figure 13.3 Data Flow for SAP Portal Touch Screen and the HR PDC Entry

Each of the options discussed in this chapter have some similar traits, such as the following:

▸ Regardless of how they enter the system, they are stored on various infotypes.

▸ Once the infotypes are updated, they can all process through Time Evaluation, with the exception of Infotype 2010 — Employee Remuneration.

▸ They can be set up for approvals.

▸ The final results are passed to Payroll for processing.

Let's have a look at the options in more detail.

13.1 SAP Portal Touch Screen

The first area of time entry is a variation of time entry provided in the portal. This time entry method is a clock-in/clock-out method where you simply push a button for the Time Pair. The Time Pair is captured in Infotype 2011 Time Events and then processed to payroll. This functionality is rather limited, because it merely captures the core clock times. Figure 13.4 shows the portal screen.

Figure 13.4   Clock-in/Clock-out Correction Details

Let's also have a look at the clock-in/clock-out corrections overview in Figure 13.5. The clock-in/clock-out overview screen allows you to adjust any previous clock entries.

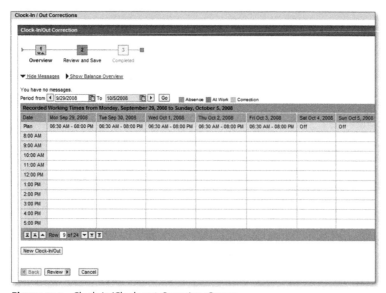

Figure 13.5   Clock-in/Clock-out Overview Screen

13.2   SAP Portal Time Sheet

One of the more heavily utilized time entry options of late is the time sheet via the portal (Figure 13.6). The SAP Portal Time Sheet is basically a web-based version of CATS. All of the entries captured in the portal are directed toward the CATS database. The entries exist in the CATS database as if they had been entered directly in the SAP CATS Classic version of the time sheet. You can use the normal approval process by utilizing Transaction CATS_APPR_LITE or Portal approval via Manager's Self Service (MSS). Once approved, the time can be transferred directly from the approval or by utilizing Transaction CAT6. These approved and transferred records are kept in Infotypes 2001, Absences; 2002, Attendances; and 2010, Employee Remuneration.

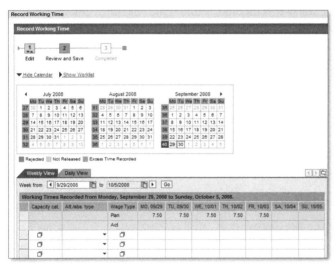

Figure 13.6   Portal Time Sheet

This option is more robust compared to the portal clock-in/clock-out screen in that this option allows you to enter specific codes to track absence or attendance types. Users can either enter total hours by type or enter start and end times, depending on which profile they have been assigned for time entry. In addition, there are numerous other fields that can be set up for the users to track time against. For example, they can allocate their time against the Project System's related fields or use a different cost center for an entry of time that they work in another department.

13.3   HR PDC Time Entry

This method of time entry is based on utilizing other SAP components, such as production planning, Plant Maintenance, or Project Systems, to capture the time and import the data into the Time Management via time events. The data does not reside within the CATS database but instead is imported into the infotypes directly. (Chapter 3 went into more detail regarding how the information is passed to Time Management.)

13.4   CATS

CATS is used to enter all time-related information, just as the portal time sheet is. The only difference between them really boils down to who uses them. Users that normally work with the SAP system utilize this method, while those that don't utilize the portal version. One other difference is that the CATS functionality with the SAP system offers additional opportunities for customization through user exits compared to that of the portal. CATS has multiple user interfaces, but we'll only review three options for recording time: CATS Classic, CATS Service Providers, and CATS Notebook.

13.4.1   CATS Classic

CATS classic is the traditional time sheet and utilizes Transaction code CAT2 to enter time into the system (Figure 13.7).

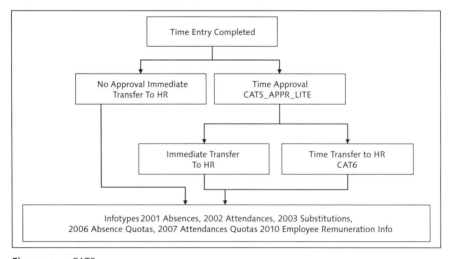

Figure 13.7   CATS

Let's turn to the next section of CATS for service providers.

13.4.2 CATS Service Providers

CATS service providers is an alternative method of time entry normally utilized for those that may be entering billable time. Transaction code CATSXT is utilized for those entering their own time, and Transaction code CATSXT_ADMIN is utilized for those in positions to enter data on behalf of those employees. The time entered can be associated with activity types and task levels. You can also use Wage types or statistical key figures when recording quantities or units. In addition, travel expense entry is also possible within the transaction.

The next section of CATS is for notebook.

13.4.3 CATS Notebook

CATS notebook is an alternative method of time entry utilized by those working remotely and connecting from their laptops to enter time-related data. This methodology is sometime referred to as the Mobile Time Sheet and does not require a connection to the SAP system when entering the data. The data is synchronized with the SAP system to upload the data. As noted in Figure 13.8 the business process for approving and transferring time follows the same path as those entered through CATS classic and CATS service providers.

Once the time is entered, it is sent to the employee infotypes. Figure 13.8 shows the dataflow, including the approval process for all of the CATS options.

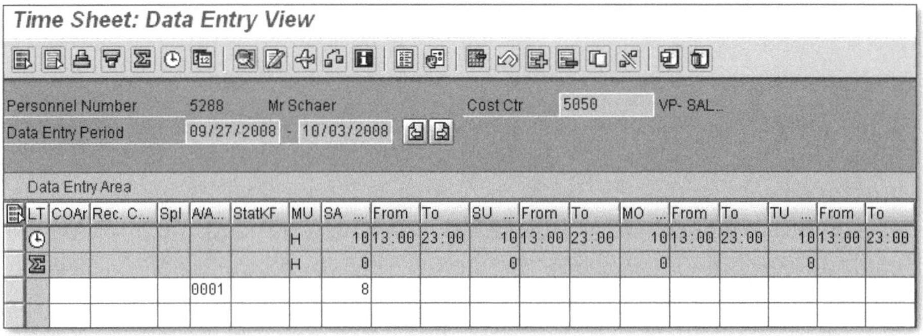

Figure 13.8 Approval Process Flow for the CATS Sheet

The next section of time entry is for third-party time collection systems that interface with the SAP system.

13.5   Third-Party Time Collection System

There are many different vendors that provide time collection systems that can be integrated with the SAP system. Each vendor has their pros and cons, and their own look and feel to the user screens. Third-party collection systems are those bolt-on time entry systems that offer similar functionality to the SAP system but are utilized for one reason or another. There are many different service providers, and SAP offers a certification program for their interfaces. However, it is usually not a simple install to get the systems up and running. Depending on how much evaluation of the time data is conducted by the outside time system determines how much you need to set up the SAP system. The information is brought into the SAP system and contained in the same CATS database tables as if the time was entered directly into the SAP system. There is one exception in that some external time-keeping systems can create a substitution that will be imported into table PTEX2003 and transferred to Infotype 2003 Substitutions. Once inside, the time follows the normal path in the SAP system as the CATS data entered.

There is one final note on third-party collection systems. SAP has partnered with Microsoft to create what is called SAP DUET. This allows users to utilize Microsoft Outlook and an interface within it to allow the user to enter their time and expenses.

The next section is about direct entry of the infotype screens with the SAP system.

13.6   Direct Entry of Infotypes 2001, 2002, 2003, and 2010

There may be situations where, even though you have various methodologies and solutions to enter time into the SAP system, you want to manually create the records on the infotypes. Perhaps the employee is going on a leave of absence and the service center, as part of the leave of absence action, enters the absence type and the duration.

The next time entry option is the Time Manager's Workplace (TMW).

13.7 Time Manager's Workplace

TMW was covered in detail in Chapter 11, but as a reminder, you should remember that it offers the functionality to enter and maintain time data, enter or maintain time events, and view the employee's calendar of time entered. The time that is entered on the various infotypes is pulled into the workplace and can be changed as needed. In addition, the time can be associated with various tracking items, such as cost centers, positions, and functional areas, etc.

This concludes our review of the time entry options.

13.8 Summary

In this chapter, we introduced various ways time can be captured and processed in the SAP system. There are many different options and many vendors that have bolt-on time-keeping solutions that can be utilized to capture time prior to sending it to the SAP system. It should be noted that based on your investment in SAP, it's usually advisable to leverage SAP to its fullest and minimize the amount of dual effort that would be needed if you decide to leverage a third-party bolt-on system. This means you need to decide which system will hold the quota calculations and overtime calculations, etc. In the end, your final solution should have the goal of being relatively easy to maintain, support, and provide accurate data to Payroll. The final chapter covers a few advanced topics and provides additional data that can be used for reference material as needed.

This chapter is not intended to provide every configuration step but to point out the main tables within each section. With this overview, you should be able to determine if you need the functionality of the covered areas.

14 Advanced Configuration Topics

In this chapter, we will cover some of the more advanced configuration topics, including incentive wages, the configuration for Web applications, concurrent employment, and the Time Management transaction codes and authorization objects delivered in SAP ERP HCM. Let's begin with incentive wages.

14.1 Incentive Wages

Incentive wages are payments to employees for obtaining certain goals. These payments are used to increase employee efficiency during the creation of particular items. For example, let's say you have certain production goals on the assembly line to produce 10,000 widgets within the next month. Historically, your production line has only created 9,000 per month. Within the production assembly line, there are times that you have to set up equipment and break it down in order to build the parts that comprise the widget. You need a way to excite your workforce in order to reach your production goals.

One proven method to improve employee efficiency is to throw money into the mix. But do you just give employees the money upfront? How do you figure out the formula to compensate employees? You basically have two options. You can set up your software system to track the widgets created and compensate employees accordingly, or you can figure out the amounts owed to the employees manually, and then load those additional payments into the SAP system. We will focus on the first option — setting up the system to pay employees for performance-based work.

Let's have a look at the configuration settings for incentive wages.

The Incentive Wages configuration is broken into five sections in the Implementation Guide (IMG). The configuration is located under the menu path TIME MANAGEMENT • INCENTIVE WAGES.

We will cover the following configuration sections in detail:

▶ Default Settings

▶ Groups

▶ Time Ticket Types

▶ Premium Formulas

▶ Integration with Logistics

14.1.1 Default Settings

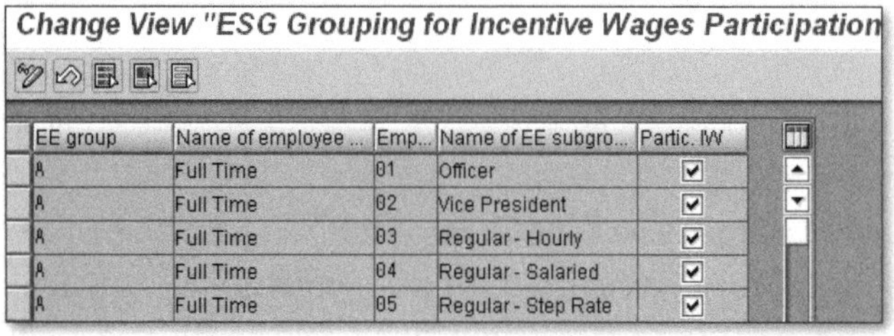

Figure 14.1 Employee Subgroups for Participation in Incentive Wages

The next IMG task gives you the opportunity to answer the "when" question. You can establish the earliest date you want the system to begin processing incentives. Feature TIMMO can be updated to help determine what the earliest date a recalculation can occur for incentive wages (see Figure 14.2).

The next IMG task, Maintain Parameters for Incentive Wages, provides an answer to the "what" question. The configuration set under this task is very simple. You have two checkboxes to select or deselect. The Daily work schedule checkbox allows you to take into account any Work Schedule rule for break times that are associated with the employee. The second checkbox is for the Daily cumulations, which allow you to define whether or not the system will display daily and period overviews of all cumulations. In addition, this checkbox provides an overview of the incentive wage results for individuals and the groups that you will define later in the configuration. If you elect to not select the checkbox, you will only see the period basis information and not the daily.

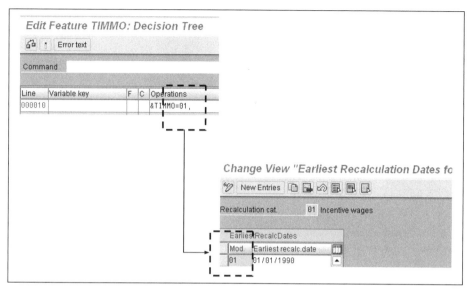

Figure 14.2 Settings for Earliest Calculation Date

Figure 14.3 shows the checkboxes you can select.

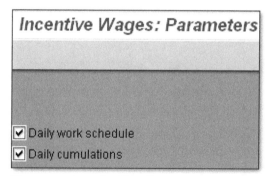

Figure 14.3 Incentive Wage Parameters

Finally, in the last section of this configuration, we answer the question of "how." Incentives are processed via three transaction codes. Transaction codes PW01, PW02, and PW03 let you record, display, and maintain incentives respectably. These transactions are how you maintain data related to incentives, so let's have a look at one. Figure 14.4 shows Transaction PW03, which is used to record incentive wages.

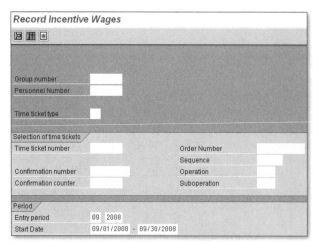

Figure 14.4 Transaction PW03 — Record Incentives

The configuration step in Figure 14.5 shows the settings that are available for customizing the screen shown in Figure 14.4. As you can see in Figure 14.5, the transaction status allows you to change transactions PW01, PW02, and PW03 to Maintain, Display, or Create Transaction. The next section of Figure 14.5 defines what period should be used to display the incentive wage–related data.

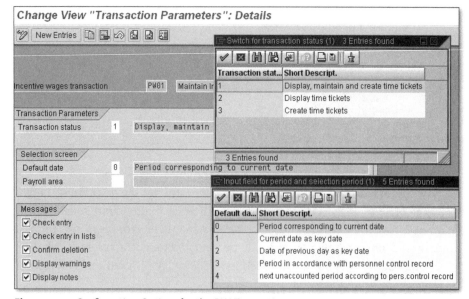

Figure 14.5 Configuration Options for the PW Transactions

The next section of the IMG is called Groups. The Groups configuration allows you to define how a group is validated when incentive Time Tickets are entered for groups of employees. You can also define which groups are available for a premium formula by linking the group to the formula. It seems a little premature to link a premium formula if you haven't established it yet, but nonetheless, this is where it is linked. The premium formulas are defined in the fourth section of the IMG configuration later in this chapter. Let's have a look at Figure 14.6, which shows the entire configuration under the Groups IMG section.

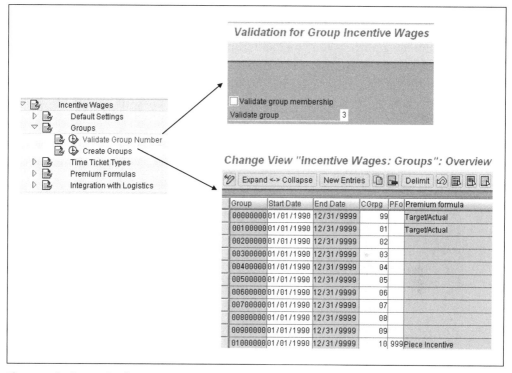

Figure 14.6 Groups Configuration

In the next section of the IMG, we get to set up the various Time Tickets used in the incentive payments.

14.1.2 Time Ticket Types

The first section of this IMG is creating Time Ticket types. A Time Ticket type can be defined as a descriptive code used to process different types of premiums. For example, in the standard system, there are a couple of different Time Ticket types defined. For instance, there are Time Ticket types defined as premium tickets, quantity tickets, person tickets, time-related tickets, and foreman tickets. When you define a Time Ticket type, there are multiple configuration options for you to choose from.

Figure 14.7 shows the fields that you can customize for a Time Ticket type. The first two checkboxes determine if the group number or the personnel number will be required data when you enter an incentive wage. The third checkbox lets you determine if the Time Ticket will have its own labor utilization rate that will be used in the premium formula. The final checkbox, if selected, enables the fields Confirmation Number and Order or Sequence Number to display on the Incentive Entry screen.

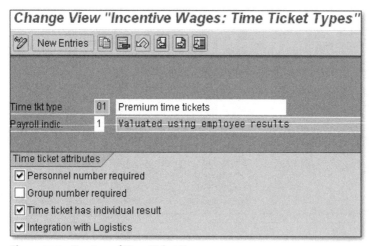

Figure 14.7 Creation of Time Ticket Types

The next configuration IMG task of the Time Ticket types section is to define the entry screens for the incentive premiums. The Time Ticket types created in Figure 14.7 can now be linked to screens for data entry. Figure 14.8 shows the configuration table. SAP offers a tool called Screen Painter that allows you to create your own screen. If you elect to build your own screen for your business requirements, you can then link that screen to your custom time ticket type.

Screen	Screen...	Screen type	PersNo	GrpNo	Time tkt type	Time ticket type
0100		Initial screen	☐	☐		
0101	0	Full screen	☑	☐	01	Premium time ti
0160	9	Internal usage	☑	☑		
0201	0	Full screen	☐	☑	02	Quantity time tick
0301	0	Full screen	☑	☑	03	Person time tick
0305	5	Employees in group	☑	☑		
0330	9	Internal usage	☑	☑		
0331	9	Internal usage	☑	☑		
0332	9	Internal usage	☑	☑		
0333	9	Internal usage	☑	☑		
0334	9	Internal usage	☑	☑		
0335	9	Internal usage	☑	☑		
0336	9	Internal usage	☑	☑		
0401	0	Full screen	☑	☐	04	Time-related tim
0501	0	Full screen	☑	☑	05	Foreman time ti
0800	9	Internal usage	☑	☑		

The above table appears within the window titled *Change View "Incentive Wages: Entry Screen Data": Overview* with a *New Entries* toolbar.

Figure 14.8 Configuration Linking Time Ticket Types to Data Entry Screens

So where do these settings come into play? Figure 14.9 shows Transaction code PW01. Under the menu path of the screen, you can see how the configuration steps in Figures 14.8 to 14.10 come into play for the incentive wages transaction codes.

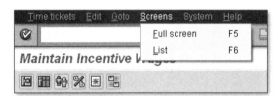

Figure 14.9 Shows the Screens on the Incentive Maintenance Screen

Let's continue with the IMG configuration steps. The following step is to define the list screens. As you saw in Figure 14.9, the list screen is part of the menu bar. Figure 14.10 shows you an example of a list screen. Have a look at the figure and then we'll see where those fields come from in the configuration.

Figure 14.10 List Screen

Now that you have seen what a list screen looks like, you may have noticed that this screen has fields that will facilitate the creation of incentive wages for employees. Figure 14.11 shows the configuration table where you can change the layout of the screens. Compare what you see in Figure 14.11 to that in Figure 14.10. You can see that Figure 14.10 matches Figure 14.11. If you want to change the layout, the configuration steps of List Screen are where that change occurs.

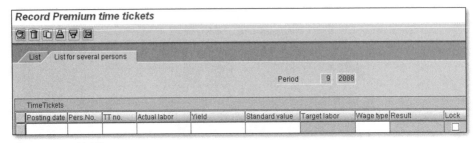

Field Name	Field Label	Disp.lngth	Input
BUDAT	Posting date	10	☑
RUCKR	Time ticket number	8	☑
RUW01	Confirmation Value	13	☑
LMNGR	Yield	13	☑
VGW01	Standard value	13	☑
LOARR	Wage type	8	☑
LOGRR	Pay Scale Group	8	☑
LGRAD	Result of calculation rule for premium formula	13	☐
SPERR	Lock: Time ticket locked for Payroll	5	☑

Figure 14.11 List Screen Configuration Field Options

The next IMG step within the Time Ticket types section is to create the Wage type that compensates the employees. This step allows you to create the Wage types. All Wage types are assigned to a Wage type group. For incentive wages, you need to use group 0LL1. If you ever create a Wage type, it is best to copy an existing Wage type. By doing so, all of your required parameters will be copied; including the fact that your new Wage type will be in group 0LL1. There is one main setting that the Wage type must have in order to process correctly. That setting is processing class 46. We have now branched into SAP Payroll language in that a Wage type has numerous processing classes that control how a Wage type is processed during payroll.

Once you create a Wage type, are you done? Not yet. The next step is to assign those Wage types to the very first step of this section, which was Ticket types. Figure 14.12 shows the table where you link the two values.

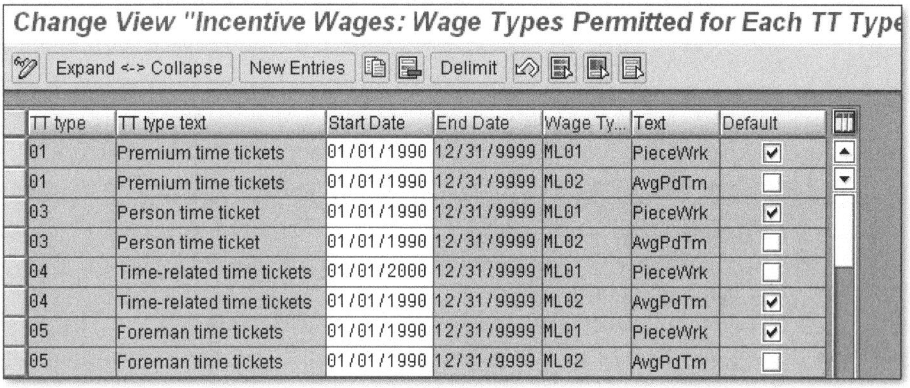

Figure 14.12 Link Wage Types to Time Ticket Types

The fourth section of the IMG configuration is called Premium Formulas.

14.1.3 Premium Formulas

Premium formulas are the calculations that you define in the system to compensate individual employees or groups of employees for incentive pay. The first step of this section of the IMG is to set some initial parameters, including value limits for the formula. Figure 14.13 shows the configuration table.

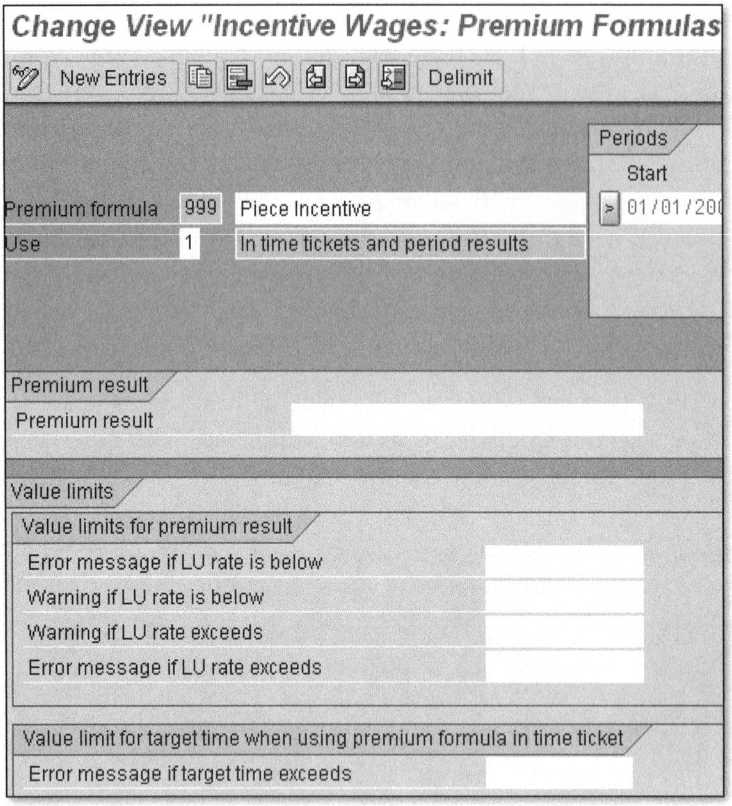

Figure 14.13 Premium Formula Definitions

The following configuration step is Define Cumulation rules for both individual employees and groups of employees. Figure 14.14 shows an example of the individual settings; however, the same fields are available for the groups. In this step, you define which cumulations to store. For example, you can see on Figure 14.14 that you can cumulate actual labor, actual setup, and actual tear down and the target times for those three categories of time. The result types, which are displayed on the screen by codes DSCHN and LEIST, can be defined and set up in a cumulation rule as Figure 14.14 shows.

The next IMG configuration item is to Define Parameters. Parameters are codes you define that the premium formula can take into account. For example, in Figure 14.15 we created an example called parameter 1 and included the value of 15. You can use these additional parameters in your calculations.

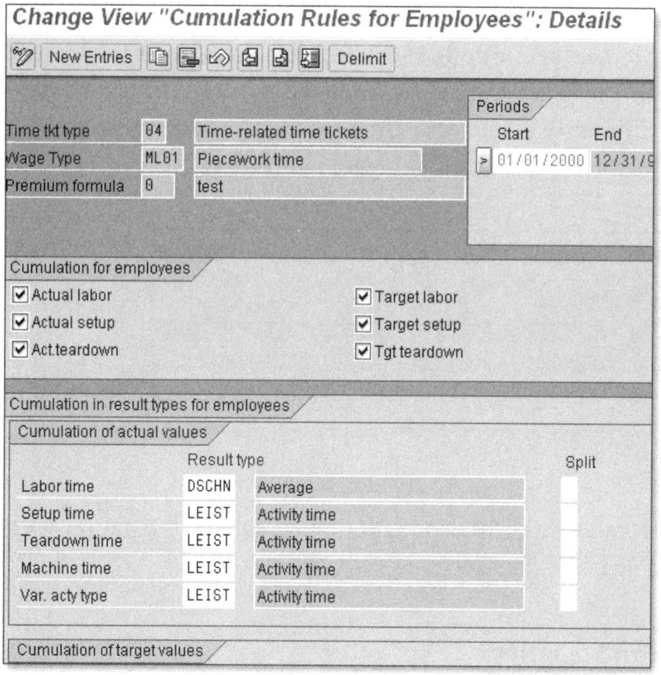

Figure 14.14 Definition of Cumulation Rules for Individuals

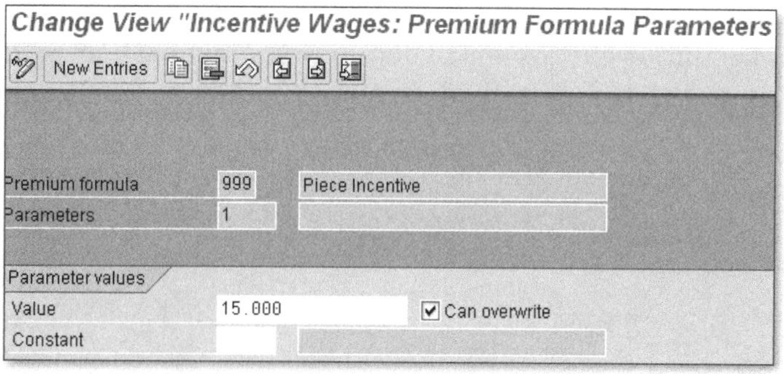

Figure 14.15 Additional Premium Formula Parameters

The next step is to define the actual premium calculation formulas. We provided a very basic example in Figure 14.16 and explained what those values mean. When developing your formula, it's recommend to utilize the standard SAP help, which provides all of the value parameters for premium formulas. In our example, you can't simply take 5 x 15 to make 45. That is not what we are talking about when we discuss formulas. We are looking at target versus actual times it took to complete a job. In our example, we take code SOW01, which stands for target time for an accumulated group, and subtract Transaction code RUW01, which is the actual time for the group. The difference is sent on a Time Ticket type to be compensated in a manner you develop. Let's have a look at Figure 14.16.

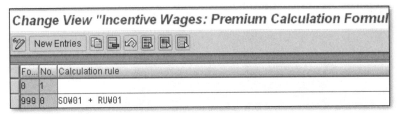

Figure 14.16 Example Formula

The final step of the incentive pay IMG configuration is called Integration with Logistics. Let's have a look at the final section.

14.1.4 Integration with Logistics

This is the last section of configuration for incentive wages. This is where you can specify how the data is received into incentive wages from Logistics. There's not much to it. There are three simple checkboxes that you can activate. When pulling information from Logistics, you have the option to read order data, retrieve confirmations, and maintain Plant Data Collection (PDC) Time Tickets (see Figure 14.17).

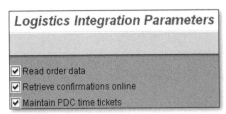

Figure 14.17 Integration Checkbox Configuration for Logistics

This concludes our review of the configuration tables. The overall goal of incentive wages is to utilize recorded time information against specific tasks, such as tearing down a piece of equipment, and comparing that time against what management thought it might take. Additional compensation can be made in Payroll, if the formulas you establish determine the employee or group of employees should be awarded for their efficiency.

In the next section, we'll discuss the concept of configuring Time Management for Web applications.

14.2   Time Management Web Application Settings

Most companies who implement the SAP system also install a portal that allows employees to conduct business activities, such as entering time via the Internet. SAP delivers a portal and functionality called Employee Self-Service (ESS) and Manager Self–Service (MSS). These items in the portal allow employees to maintain their own master data, such as home address, banking information, etc. Manager's can also utilize tools to conduct their activities for the workforce they manage. In addition, the Web applications utilize SAP Workflows to move data to where it needs to be. For example, in a leave request, you submit a request to go on vacation. That request is sent to your supervisor so they can approve or deny your request. The process by which the supervisor was notified is an example of workflow. So if you plan to implement the Web applications, you have different setting opportunities for Time Management. Let's look at some of the key configuration tables you can maintain.

The settings for Time Management can be found in the IMG under the menu path: PERSONNEL MANAGEMENT EMPLOYEE SELF-SERVICE • SERVICE-SPECIFIC SETTINGS • WORKING TIME.

Once you follow that menu path, you will notice there are a few areas in which you can set up Time Management–related information. Figure 14.18 shows the areas related to Time Management.

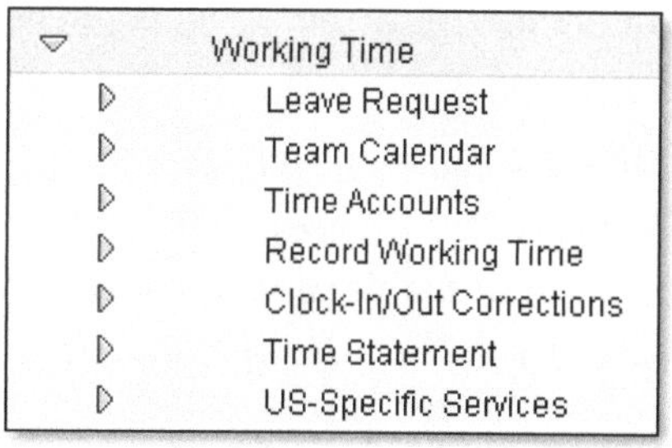

Figure 14.18   Time Management ESS IMG Tasks

Within each of these items of configuration, you can specify groups of individuals via a feature that utilizes the same values. Figure 14.19 shows the grouping table and the Feature WEBMO that utilizes it. As we proceed through the value items of configuration in each IMG node, the rule group is usually the first node defined.

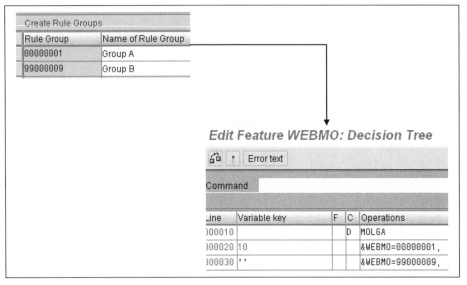

Figure 14.19 Time Management Web Applications Rule Groups

Let's discuss the first area — Leave Request.

14.2.1 Leave Request

The Leave Request functionality allows employees to request time off via the portal. This section of configuration is used to define which leave requests are allowed, and how the system should react to the requests. In this section, we will first define what kinds of leave are available, and then explore the layout configuration changes that are possible.

The leave request utilizes absence types that we reviewed in Chapter 4, "Master Data." In particular, we are talking about Infotype 2001 Absences. Figure 14.20 shows a particular Absence type. The configuration in this table supports how this absence type is displayed on other portal screens, such as the team calendar, overview of leave, and clock-in and clock-out correction screens.

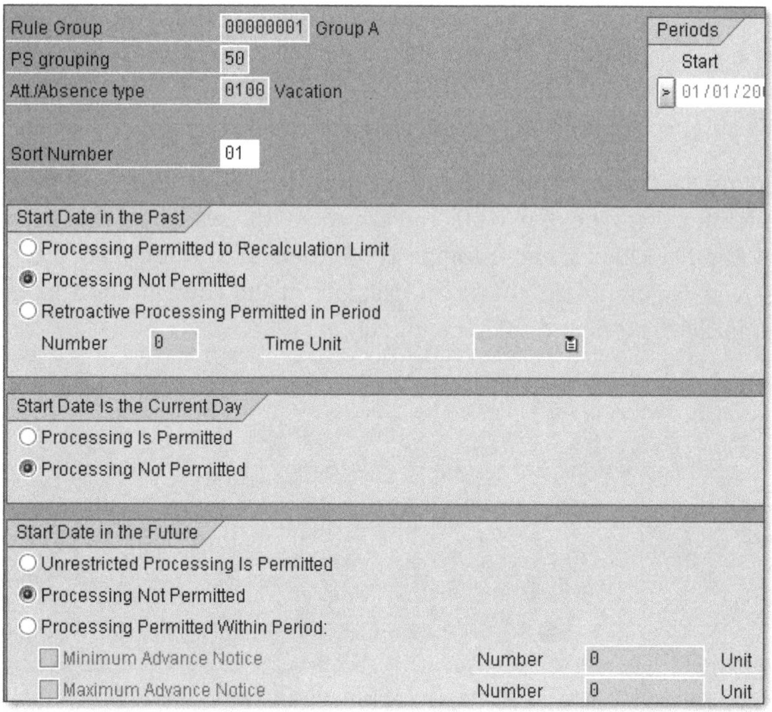

Rule Group	00000001 Group A	Periods
PS grouping	50	Start
Att./Absence type	0100 Vacation	≽ 01/01/20(
Sort Number	01	

Start Date in the Past
- ○ Processing Permitted to Recalculation Limit
- ◉ Processing Not Permitted
- ○ Retroactive Processing Permitted in Period
   - Number 0 Time Unit 📄

Start Date Is the Current Day
- ○ Processing Is Permitted
- ◉ Processing Not Permitted

Start Date in the Future
- ○ Unrestricted Processing Is Permitted
- ◉ Processing Not Permitted
- ○ Processing Permitted Within Period:
   - ☐ Minimum Advance Notice   Number 0   Unit
   - ☐ Maximum Advance Notice   Number 0   Unit

Figure 14.20 Leave Request Absence Processing

The next section of configuration for Leave Requests is to define messages that are output on the portal screens. This setup allows you to enter, alter, or suppress standard messages delivered from the SAP system that a user would see under certain conditions, such as a failure to enter a required field. Figure 14.21 shows the message configuration table.

Rule Group	00000001						
Configure Output of Messages							
Application Area	Message Type	Message	Message Text	Do Not Display M...	Application Area (User)	Message Type (User)	Message Numbe...
	📄			☐		📄	

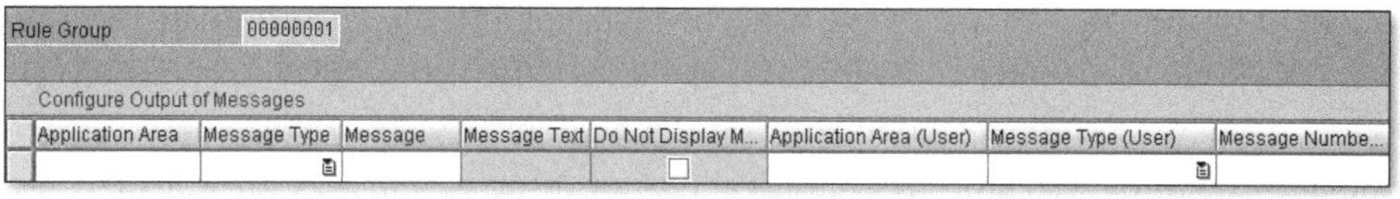

Figure 14.21 Message Configuration Table

The next section of configuration deals with how the data for leave requests are displayed on the screen. For example, you can display how far back the screen displays absences or what particular color the leave request shows on the screen. Other functionality that is available is that you can define master data fields to show up on the leave requests screen. But what if you want specific master data to show up for one leave request type, but not another. The good news is that functionality is available. You define the additional fields you want shown and then link them to an absence type.

When an employee wants to request a day off, it's nice to know if they have enough quota left for that type of day off. You can set up the system so that from Infotype 2006 Absence Quotas, and Infotype 2007 Attendance Quotas, are available on the screen. Figure 14.22 shows an example of the configuration table where you can make changes to display the quotas.

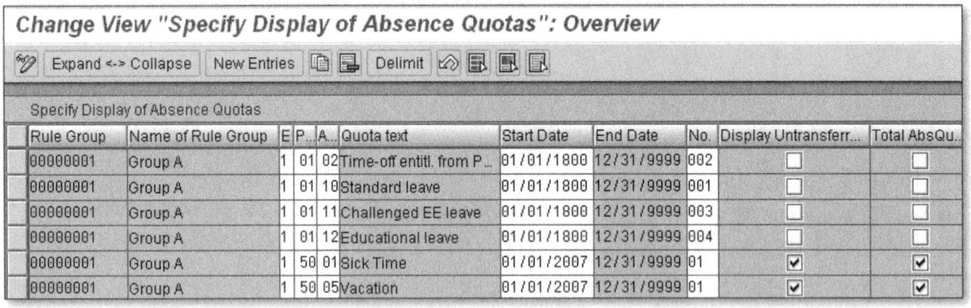
Change View "Specify Display of Absence Quotas": Overview

Expand <-> Collapse | New Entries | Delimit

Specify Display of Absence Quotas

Rule Group	Name of Rule Group	E	P...	A...	Quota text	Start Date	End Date	No.	Display Untransferr...	Total AbsQu...
00000001	Group A	1	01	02	Time-off entitl. from P...	01/01/1800	12/31/9999	002	☐	☐
00000001	Group A	1	01	10	Standard leave	01/01/1800	12/31/9999	001	☐	☐
00000001	Group A	1	01	11	Challenged EE leave	01/01/1800	12/31/9999	003	☐	☐
00000001	Group A	1	01	12	Educational leave	01/01/1800	12/31/9999	004	☐	☐
00000001	Group A	1	50	01	Sick Time	01/01/2007	12/31/9999	01	☑	☑
00000001	Group A	1	50	05	Vacation	01/01/2007	12/31/9999	01	☑	☑

Figure 14.22 Configuration for Displaying Quotas on Leave Accrual Screens

The next area of functionality is called the Team Calendar.

14.2.2 Team Calendar

The Team Calendar is a tool in the portal in which managers can view all of their employees' attendances and absences on a calendar-like screen. The configuration for the Team Calendar is very similar to that of the Leave Request. By this we mean the functionality shares the same established groupings and sets using Feature WEBMO. One piece of configuration that is different, however, is the ability to set up which employee is pulled into your calendar view. Figure 14.23 shows the configuration screen where you can set up how employees are selected for team calendars. In this table, you will notice the rule groups that all of the Time Management functions share. You will also notice a field called Mode. Under this field, there are various options delivered such as Approval Mode, Request Mode, Team View Mode, etc. By having different modes, you can customize the setup so that the different modes can pull in different employees. For example, if you were under the approval mode, you might need greater access to employees than somebody under the team view mode.

Rule Group	Name of Rule Group	Start Date	End Date	Mode	View/Grp.	Group of Organiz...	Group
00000001	Group A	01/01/1800	12/31/9999	Approval Mode	View Gr...	MSS_LEA_EE	
00000001	Group A	01/01/1800	12/31/9999	CATS Approval	View Gr...	MSS_LCA_EE	
00000001	Group A	01/01/1800	12/31/9999	Attendance Overview	View Gr...	MSS_LAV_EE	
00000001	Group A	01/01/1800	12/31/9999	Request Mode	View Gr...	ESS_LEA_EE	
00000001	Group A	01/01/1800	12/31/9999	Team View Mode	View Gr...	MSS_LTV_EE	

Figure 14.23 Team Calendar Employee Selection

As far as the definition for the layout of the Team Calendar, your only real option for customizing is to define how many lines are displayed on a page, and if the data you are viewing remain static, or if an employee makes a change to their absence while you are in the Team Calendar, should that change be brought into your calendar during the next refresh of the screen data.

Now let's move on to Time Accounts.

14.2.3 Time Accounts

The Time Accounts functionality allows you to determine what kind of data is displayed to an employee. In particular, we are talking about absence and attendance quota information. Within the time accounts, you can determine how much quota you have remaining. You have the option to configure the system to take into account any leave request that has not been processed by your supervisor. Figure 14.24 shows an example of the portal screen.

Absence Quota

Entitlement Type: All Types ▼   On Key Date 9/24/2008   Display

Time Account	Deductible from	Deductible to	Entitlement	Remainder
		Table is empty		

Figure 14.24 Time Accounts Absence Display Screen

Within the time accounts portal screen, you can also run Time Evaluation into the future to determine if you will have any more quota accrued so that you can make decisions for future time off. The quotas have to accrue within the Time Evaluation processing for this functionality to work.

The next section of the customization is for a category called Record Working Time.

14.2.4 Record Working Time

The configuration to support employees who record working time is very similar to that of setting up the Cross-Application Time Sheet (CATS). You have to define profile that stores parameters that are used to control formatting and functionality on the screen where you enter time. Figure 14.25 shows you a few of the field selections that you can customize.

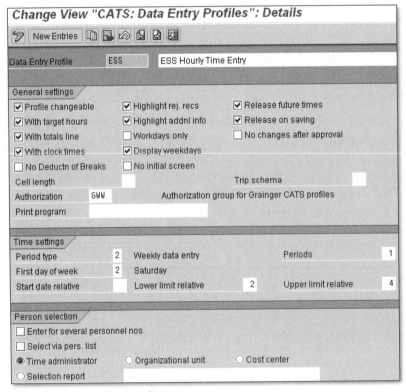

Figure 14.25 Time Sheet Profile Setup

Let's say you have 10 different absence types, but you only want a few of them to display on the Portal time sheet. Figure 14.26 shows you the configuration table where you can select which absences or attendances to display.

Change View "ESS: Deactivation of attendance/absence types"

	PSG	A/AType	A/A type text	End Date	Deact	
	1	0100	Leave	12/31/1998	✔	▲
	1	0100	Leave	12/31/9999	✔	▼
	1	0101	Leave IT0005	12/31/9999	✔	
	1	0110	Leave 1/2 day	12/31/1998	✔	
	1	0110	Leave 1/2 day	12/31/9999	✔	
	1	0190	Educational leave	12/31/9999	✔	
	1	0200	Illness with certificate	12/31/9999	✔	
	1	0210	Illness w/o certificate	12/31/9999	✔	
	1	0220	Health spa	12/31/9999	✔	
	1	0221	Health spa, reduced pay	12/31/1998	✔	
	1	0222	Spa, full pay for leave	12/31/1998	✔	

Figure 14.26 Configuration Settings to Control Portal Absence and Attendance Display

After an employee enters a time, in most organizations that time needs to be approved by a manager. The next section shows some of the tables related to approving employee times. One of the first steps of this section is to define the approval process. In this step, you define which fields a manager would see related to the time entered. You can establish that the field can be seen in two different views. View one is for the detail screen. View two is for the individual record view. Once you have established which fields you want the manager to see, you link them to a view that is assigned to the manager. In Figure 14.27, you can see the field selection parameters SLIN and SLIN1. These entries have the fields you defined for the manager to see.

In the next section, we are going to move away from one method of recording time and show the configuration tables that you would use if you had employee's recording clock times via swipe cards or through the portal touch screen for time entry that captures clock times.

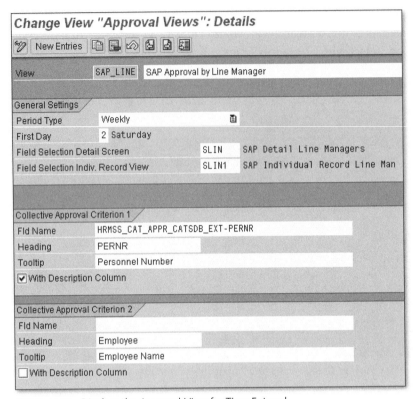

Figure 14.27 Displays the Approval View for Time Entered

14.2.5 Clock-in/Clock-out Corrections

Clock-in/Clock-out Corrections provide an opportunity for employees to correct any time data related to clock times that may be incorrect. The configuration that supports this area of functionality is very similar to the other Time Management Web application configuration. This area shares the same groups allocated in Feature WEBMO defined back in Figure 14.19. In addition, this area also shares some of the same configurations already defined back in Figure 14.20. So let's look at a few tables specific to the Clock-in/Clock-out Corrections setup.

The first IMG node is called Section Processing Processes. Within this part is an opportunity for you to define which periods are displayed for employees when they enter the portal screen. Figure 14.28 shows the configuration table.

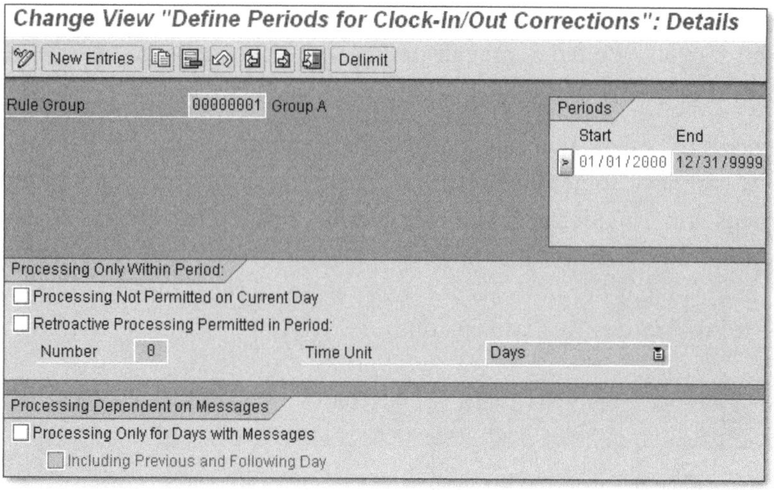

Figure 14.28 Clock-in/Clock-out Period Definitions

The next IMG task within this section relates to the definition of processing processes. In this step, you can define whether the corrections are subject to an approval process. You can also define if workflow will be used in the process for approvals. Figure 14.29 shows the configuration screen.

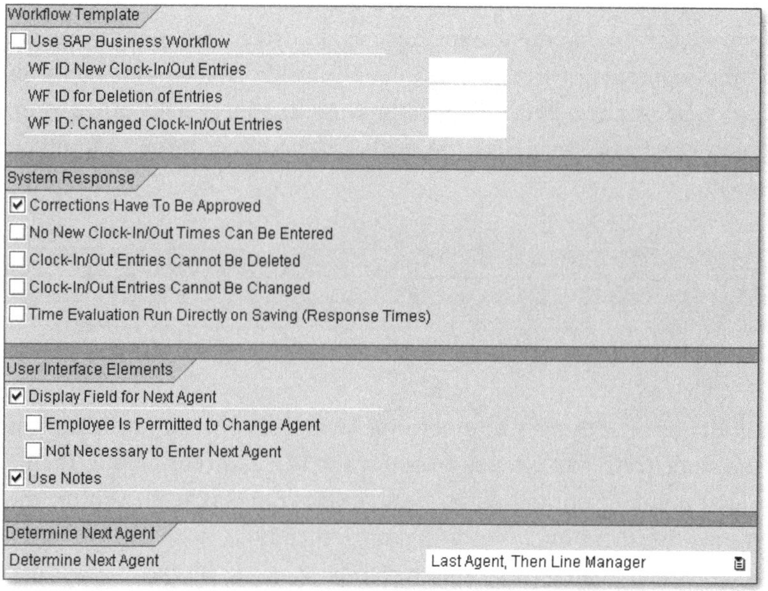

Figure 14.29 Clock-in/Clock-out Corrections Approvals and Workflow

The second section of configuration is listed under Section Layout of Web Application. Within this section, you have some flexibility with how you want the screen to look for the end user. The first task is to define the calendar.

Figure 14.30 shows the calendar configuration table. As you can see from the configuration table, you have some flexibility with the screen layout. Depending on how many groups you have defined, you may also have different versions of the screen per group. You can also see that the start date of the week, how many rows are displayed, and whether or not to display time pairs or absence and attendance types are a few of the options you can customize.

Clock-In/Out Corrections: Calendar								
Rule Group	First Day of Week	Cal. Scale	Time Frame Type	1st Time	No. Rows	Time Pair	Att/Abs
	Sunday		Fixed Time Frame			☐	☐
	Sunday		Fixed Time Frame			☐	☐
	Sunday		Fixed Time Frame			☐	☐
	Sunday		Fixed Time Frame			☐	☐
	Sunday		Fixed Time Frame			☐	☐

Figure 14.30 Clock Time Corrections Calendar Configuration Table

Now that we have seen the calendar configuration, let's have a look at how you can set up the screens to show different fields. The IMG step Define Field Selection allows you to determine which fields you want presented on the screen. As you can see in Figure 14.31, the groups once again drive how you can set up screens for specific segments of the population. Within the screen you establish which time event type, such as P10 for Clock-in Time to a Field Selection group. The Field Selection group TMP contains the fields that you determined should be on the Portal screen.

Assign Time Event Types to Field Selection								
Rule Gro...	Name of Rule Group	T...	Ti...	Short Descript.	Start Date	End Date	Field sel.	Field selection
00000001	Group A	01	P10	Clock-In	01/01/2000	12/31/9999	TMP	

Figure 14.31 Clock Time Correction Field Definitions

The next section of configuration is to determine which absences or attendances to display on the screen. As you can see from Figure 14.32, a reoccurring theme continues as your original grouping plays a role in this table as well. Within the group, you can make settings by absence or attendance type, such as if changes are actually allowed, or if changes to a day which happens to be the current day is allowed.

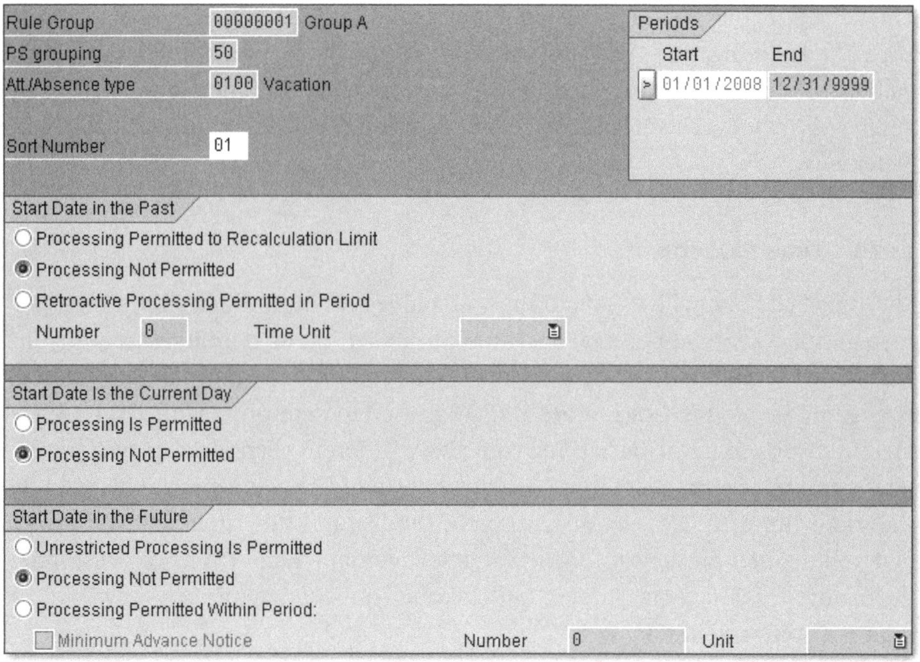

Rule Group	00000001 Group A	Periods	
PS grouping	50	Start	End
Att./Absence type	0100 Vacation	> 01/01/2008	12/31/9999
Sort Number	01		

Start Date in the Past
○ Processing Permitted to Recalculation Limit
◉ Processing Not Permitted
○ Retroactive Processing Permitted in Period
   Number   0   Time Unit   ▤

Start Date Is the Current Day
○ Processing Is Permitted
◉ Processing Not Permitted

Start Date in the Future
○ Unrestricted Processing Is Permitted
◉ Processing Not Permitted
○ Processing Permitted Within Period:
   ☐ Minimum Advance Notice   Number   0   Unit   ▤

Figure 14.32

In the following section of configuration, called specify display of Partial-Day Absences, you can define whether the partial days should be displayed in Hours and Clock Times, Hours, or Clock Times. Figure 14.33 shows the configuration table.

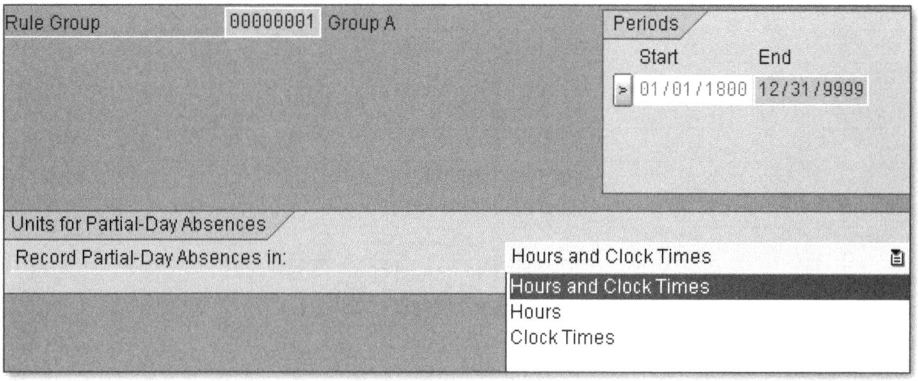

Rule Group	00000001 Group A	Periods	
		Start	End
		> 01/01/1800	12/31/9999

Units for Partial-Day Absences

Record Partial-Day Absences in:	Hours and Clock Times ▤
	Hours and Clock Times
	Hours
	Clock Times

Figure 14.33 Partial Day Absence Configuration

This concludes our section of configuration tables for Clock-in/Clock-out functionality. The last section of Web applications for Time Management relates to a Time Statement. Chapter 10 provided an overview of what the Time Statement is, so here we'll review the single area of configuration for Web applications for Time Statements.

14.2.6 Time Statement

The Time Statement allows you to show employees their time-related information, such as hours worked per day, overtime calculated, quota entitlements available, etc. that was generated during the Time Evaluation process. Within this section of configuration, we see that Feature HRFOR is used to determine which Time Statement is displayed in the portal. You could have different versions displayed for different groups of employees, but typically you should only have one. Figure 14.34 shows Feature HRFOR. As you can see in the feature, the Time Statement form that you defined can be set for the variable key that equals T. You can customize the feature for you requirements so that your Time Statements are shown to the required groups of employees.

Edit Feature HRFOR: Decision Tree

Error text

Command

Line	Variable key	F	C	Operations
000010			D	RCLAS(01)
000020	C		D	MOLGA
000030	C 01			&HRFOR=SAP_PAYSLIP_DE,
000040	C 10			&HRFOR=$CEDT$, 'ZSAP_PAYSLIP_CHQ,
000050	C **		D	RCLAS+01 (03)
000060	C ** ESS			&HRFOR=&CEDT&,
000070	C ** ***			&HRFOR=SAP_PAYSLIP,
000080	T		D	RCLAS+01 (03)
000090	T ESD			&HRFOR=SAP_TIMESLIP,
000100	T ESP			&HRFOR=SAP_TIMESLIP,
000110	T TMW			&HRFOR=SAP_TIMESLIP,
000120	T ***			&HRFOR=,

Figure 14.34 Feature HRFOR Time Statement Portal Display

Of course the IMG has other tables that you need to review; however, we have reviewed some of the key tables that you will utilize. The next section is about the various settings available for Time Management Concurrent Employment.

14.3   Concurrent Employment

Concurrent employment is where employees can be assigned to multiple positions throughout the day and compensated differently based on those positions. An employee can only have a single Infotype 0001 organizational assignment at any given time; however, some industries allow their employees to work multiple jobs throughout the day.

Example

You have been hired by a studio to help them with one of their movie productions. As part of your interview, you reach an agreement with the studio that your expertise goes further than a single skill set and your skills can be utilized across a couple of different positions that are open. After leaving the interview, your business card now reads writer, stunt double, and production assistant. On any given day, you may be called upon to conduct duties under any or all of the three positions. Each of these positions is regulated by unions and therefore you should receive certain benefits and compensation for the hours you work within each position. How in the world is the studio going to get your pay check correct with all of these moving parts. SAP offers functionality called Concurrent Employment where your master data is set up to track all three positions. Where appropriate, you will have a single infotype, such as which bank you want your pay check deposited, that all three of your employment positions will utilize. You will also have certain master data tracked that is specific to the various roles you are holding. For example, you might have three different types of pay rates.

In this example, you need to work closely with your other team members when reviewing whether or not concurrent employment is right for your organization, and if it is, how the overall design is going to be laid out.

How does this example impact Time Management? Let's say that all three positions are hourly. If you work 45 hours a week between all of the positions, you should be entitled to 5 hours of overtime. How is the system going to know that you worked 5 hours over 40 if each position is showing hours less than 40? If the system did know that you worked 5 hours overtime and you had different rates of pay for the three positions, which pay rate should be used for the overtime? This is where Time Evaluation Concurrent Employment comes into play.

The Time Management configuration for concurrent employment allows you to define the particular pieces of master data that an employee might share across positions and combine them into one bucket for calculation purposes. To continue our example, if you worked 20 hours on the first job, 15 on the second, and 10 on the third, you can set up Time Evaluation to combine all of these hours to determine.

Let's have a look at some of the configuration tables.

The IMG menu path for the configuration is located under PAYROLL • PAYROLL INTERNATIONAL • DAY PROCESSING OF TIME DATA • CONCURRENT EMPLOYMENT IN DAY PROCESSING OF TIME DATA.

The configuration for Time Management Concurrent Employment is broken into four IMG nodes, which we will cover in the following sections. Time Evaluation for Concurrent Employment utilizes the program RPTIME01 instead of RPTIME00. Schema TM0C is delivered and should be customized.

▶ Business subjects of Time Evaluation

▶ Check rule for Determining Output Data

▶ Business rules of Time Evaluation

▶ Set up Time Evaluation using RPTIME01

Let's start with the business subjects of Time Evaluation.

14.3.1 Business Subject of Time Evaluation

A Time Evaluation business subject is used to define a Time Management calculation or task. Business subjects can be assigned to Time types, message types, Wage types, and Quota types. By defining business subjects, you can use our example regarding overtime and create a business subject that will conduct overtime calculations for an employee's various positions. Figure 14.35 is divided into two areas. The first area, designated with the letter A, is where you would create the business subject and assign it to a group reason. The business subject is freely definable. The group reason is utilized across all components, such as Payroll or Benefits. The reason is what would group our sample employee that works three different jobs for the studio. In our configuration table, you can see we have linked our custom overtime business subject to the grouping reason Personnel Assignment.

Section B of Figure 14.35 shows the four areas that can be assigned to your business subject. Utilizing the Time type example, Time Evaluation would look for all Time type 0040 — Overtime — for each position the employee has for the particular payroll period. Once it had the total hours, then overtime rules would determine if overtime should be awarded.

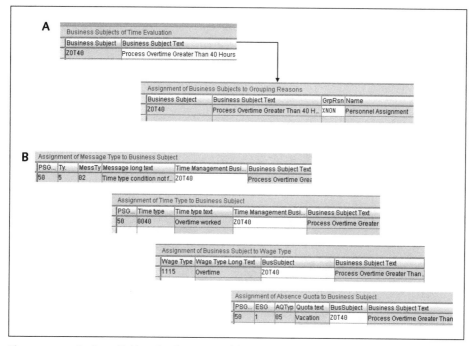

Figure 14.35 Business Subject Configuration Tables

The next section within the concurrent time evaluation configuration is for checking rules for determining output data.

14.3.2 Check Rules for Determining Output Data

Time Evaluation for concurrent employment utilizes the same methodology and overall setup as in Chapters 8 and 9. As you recall, you can establish groupings for employees so that they utilize the same configuration tables. You also reviewed, throughout the course of this book, the tables that are accessible from this part of the IMG. The configuration within this section takes you to the Time types configuration table V_T555A, the messages table V_T555E, the attendance quota table V_T556P, Wage type selection table V_T510S, and absence quotas table V_T559L.

Let's move on to the third section of the IMG for Time Evaluation for concurrent employment — business rules of Time Evaluation.

14.3.3 Business Rules of Time Evaluation

This section of the IMG allows you to define rules for processing and assign them to your custom business subjects. This is the main section that you establish where in Time Evaluation an employee's multiple assignments should be treated as one for calculation purposes. Figure 14.36 shows all of the tables for this section listed A through E.

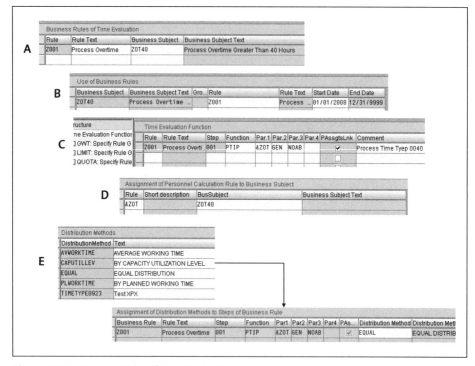

Figure 14.36 Business Rules of Time Evaluation

Within Figure 14.36, there are letters associated with each table. The following describes what each of the letters mean.

- A — This table allows you to define the name of a particular rule and associate it with your custom business subject. In our example, we created rule Z001 and linked it to our business subject ZOT40.

- B — Your next configuration table is to take the link and establish which dates the rule will be used.

- C — The next configuration step let's you to associate rule Z001 with specific Time Evaluation functions and personnel calculation rules that should process your employee's multiple assignments as if they were one. You can select the checkbox for processing personnel assignments together.

- D — Within this table, you need to associate your custom personnel calculation rule with your business subject.

- E — Finally the last set of tables enable you to determine how the results of the calculations are distributed across the multiple assignments. In our example, there were five hours of overtime, therefore those five hours will be distributed across all three positions.

This concludes our section on various tables related to concurrent employment processing. The next section provides you a list of authorization objects and time management transaction codes.

14.4 Time Management Authorization Objects and Transaction Code References

In this section, you will learn about the various authorization objects and transaction codes for Time Management. SAP ERP HCM Security and Authorizations is such a complex area to set up and establish correctly for an organization a complete book could be written on the subject. But in this chapter we'll only focus on listing the authorization objects and transaction codes, so that as you begin to work with the team in charge of security, you'll have an idea of the particular transactions you might what to enable for your users. At the conclusion of this chapter, you should be knowledgeable of the various delivered security objects and transaction codes related to Time Management.

SAP ERP HCM provides authorization functionality that allows you to control which employees can process specific transactions for particular groups.

The SAP ERP HCM Time Management solution offers two methodologies for setting up the system:

- Structural Authorizations
  - Utilizes the HR hierarchical structure to define the authorizations.
- General Authorization Check
  - Utilizes a concept of Roles that is defined as certain business processing tasks that an employee would perform as part of their job. These roles are assigned to profiles that are assigned to the employees.

14.4.1 Human Resources and Time Management Authorization Objects

Time Management utilizes the authorization objects of Personnel Management. Authorization objects are an element within the SAP R/3 system that allows your security administrator to define 10 or less authorization fields and the level of access granted. All authorization objects listed in Table 14.1 can be found using Transaction code SU21.

Authorization Object	Description	Notes
P_RCF_WL	Access to Worklists Authorization Object	RCF_WL_ID — Identifier of Worklist
P_RCF_ACT	Activities in E-Recruiting	ACTVT – Activity RCF_A_PROC — Process RCF_A_TYPE — Activity Type
P_RCF_APPL	Applications in E-Recruiting	RCF_APPL — Application in E-Recruiting
P_HAP_DOC	Appraisal Systems: Appraisal	ACTVT – Activity PLVAR — Plan Version HAP_CAT_G — Appraisal Category Group ID HAP_CAT — Appraisal Category ID HAP_TEMPL — Appraisal Template PROFL — Authorization Profile

Table 14.1 Authorization Objects Using Transaction Code SU21

Authorization Object	Description	Notes
P_DRL_COST	Authorization for drilldown reporting	KOKRS — Controlling Area KOSTL — Cost Center PROJECT_ID — Project name AUFART — Order Type PROFIT_CTR — Profit Center
P_LSO_FOUP	Authorization Object for Participation Follow-Up	LSO_FOUP — LSO: Authorization to Follow Up Participation
P_LSO_TU	Authorization for LSO Content Management	LSO_TU — LSO: Activity for Course Content
P_ASRCONT	Authorization for Process Content	ASRCONTYPE — Content Type ASRCONTGRP — Content Group ASRACTVT — Activities ASROBJSCOP — Authorization Sc
S_MWB_FCOD	BC-BMT-OM: Allowed Function Codes for Manager's Desktop	MWBFCODE — Function Code
P_ES_PA_OK	Check auth.codes for function codes allowed fr Spain PA data	INFTY — Infotype SUBTY — Subtype PES_SPRPS — Lock Indicator for HR Master Data Re PES_FCODE — Function Code ACTVT — Activity
P_RCF_VIEW	Data Overview in E-Recruiting	RCF_VIEW — Data Overview
P_DEL_PERN	Deletion of Personnel Numbers in Live Systems	PAYDELROLE — Role Definition for Deleting Personnel Nos.
P_RCF_POOL	Direct Access to Talent Pool	RCF_POOL Permitted Type of Access to Talent

Table 14.1 Authorization Objects Using Transaction Code SU21 (Cont.)

Authorization Object	Description	Notes
P_B2A	HR-B2A: B2A Manager	MOLGA — Country Grouping B2A_WERKS — HR-B2A: Authorization Check - Personnel A B2A_BTRTL — HR-B2A: Authorization Check - Personnel S SAGRP — Area DOCTY — HR-B2A: Document Class B2A_ACTIO — HR-B2A: Authorization Check — Action
P_CH_PK	HR-CH: Pension Fund: Account Access	KONNR — Individual PF account number AUTGR — HR-CH: Authorization group for PF accounts PKKLV — HR-CH: Pension fund: Authorization level for account
P_DE_BW	HR-DE: Statements SAPScript	BEWID — Statement Identifier BSUBJ — Functional Area ID for Statements BACT — Activities for Statements in Authorization
P_DK_PBS	HR-DK: Authorization Check for Access to PBS Company	PBSFIRMA HR_DK: Company used for PBS
P_RU_PKMN	HR-RU: Authority to check HR_RU_PF DMS — Package Manager	HR_RU_EVNT — Count Parameters HR_RU_PKID — Package Type HR_RU_REGN — Registration number HR_RU_USER — Name of Person Who Changed Object
P_RU_0294C	HR-RU: Authority to check records of Infotype 0294	AUTHC — Authorization level
P_OCWBENCH	HR: Activities in the Off-Cycle Workbench	P_OCTYP Type of off-cycle activity

Table 14.1 Authorization Objects Using Transaction Code SU21 (Cont.)

Authorization Object	Description	Notes
P_APPL	HR: Applicants	INFTY — Infotype SUBTY — Subtype AUTHC — Authorization Level PERSA — Personnel Area APGRP — Applicant Group APTYP — Applicant Range VDSK1 — Organizational Key RESRF — Personnel officer responsible for application
P_HRF_INFO	HR: Authorization Check Infodata Maintenance for HR Forms	MOLGA — Country Grouping P_HRF_INET — HR Forms: InfoNet Name ACTVT — Activity
P_HRF_META	HR: Authorization Check Metadata Maintenance for HR Forms	P_HRF_TYP — HR Forms: Object Type MOLGA — Country Grouping P_HRF_MOBJ — HR Forms: Object Name for Metadata ACTVT — Activity
P_NL_LA06	HR: Authorization Object for Wage Return 2006	JUPER — Legal Person ACTVT — Activity
P_PE02	HR: Authorization for Personnel Calculation Rule	P_AUTHPE02 — Personnel Calculation Rule: Authorization
P_PE01	HR: Authorization for Personnel Calculation Schemas	P_AUTHPE01 — HR-schema: Authorization
P_NL_AEDM	HR: Authorization object for Day-one-announcement	JUPER — Legal Person ACTVT — Activity
P_BEN	HR: Benefit Area	PBEN_AREA — Benefit area ACTVT — Activity

Table 14.1 Authorization Objects Using Transaction Code SU21 (Cont.)

Authorization Object	Description	Notes
P_PCLX	HR: Clusters	RELID — Area identifier for cluster in tables PCLx AUTHC — Authorization level
P_DBAU_SKV	HR: DBAU: Construction pay in Germany — social funds proceed.	REPID — ABAP Program Name ZVKAS — SI fund RZNUM — Data Processing Center Number for Constr.Ind.SI Fund ACTVT — Activity
P_ORGIN	HR: Master Data	INFTY — Infotype SUBTY — Subtype AUTHC — Authorization Level PERSA — Personnel Area PERSG — Employee Group PERSK — Employee Subgroup VDSK1 — Organizational Key
P_ORGXX	HR: Master Data — Extended Check	INFTY — Infotype SUBTY — Subtype AUTHC — Authorization level SACHA — Payroll Administrator SACHP — Administrator for HR Master Data SACHZ — Administrator for Time Recording SBMOD — Administrator Group
P_ORGXXCON	HR: Master Data — Extended Check with Context	INFTY — Infotype SUBTY — Subtype AUTHC — Authorization Level SACHA — Payroll Administrator SACHP — Administrator for HR Master Data SACHZ — Administrator for Time Recording SBMOD — Administrator Group PROFL — Authorization Profile

Table 14.1 Authorization Objects Using Transaction Code SU21 (Cont.)

Authorization Object	Description	Notes
P_PERNR	HR: Master Data — Personnel Number Check	AUTHC — Authorization level PSIGN — Interpretation of assigned personnel number INFTY — Infotype SUBTY — Subtype
P_ORGINCON	HR: Master Data with Context	INFTY — Infotype SUBTY — Subtype AUTHC — Authorization level PERSA — Personnel Area PERSG — Employee Group PERSK — Employee Subgroup VDSK1 — Organizational Key PROFL — Authorization Profile
P_ENGINE	HR: PBC — Authorization for Automatic Commitment Creation	ACTVT — Activity
P_FINADM	HR: PBC — Changes in the Financing Past	EXTENDED — Changes in the Past Allowed
P_EXMGRP	HR: PBC — Exceptions for Financing Rules	HRFPMEXGRP — Grouping of Check Exceptions
P_ENCTYPE	HR: PBC — Financing	ENCTYPE — Earmarked Funds Category ACTVT — Activity
P_PCR	HR: Payroll Control Record	ABRKS — Payroll Area ACTVT — Activity
P_PYEVDOC	HR: Posting Document	BUKRS — Company Code ACTVT — Activity
P_PYEVRUN	HR: Posting Run	P_EVTYP — Run type P_EVSIMU — Posting run: Simulation indicator ACTVT — Activity

Table 14.1 Authorization Objects Using Transaction Code SU21 (Cont.)

Authorization Object	Description	Notes
P_ABAP	HR: Reporting	REPID — ABAP Program Name
		COARS — Degree of simplification for authorization check
P_CERTIF	HR: Statements	MOLGA — Country Grouping
		BESNR — Statement number
		AUTHC — Authorization level
P_CATSXT	HR: Time Sheet for Service Providers Type/ Level Check	CATS_AUTHP — Personnel Number Check
		TASKLEVEL — Task Level
		TASKTYPE — Activity Type
		BUKRS — Company Code
		PERSA — Personnel Area
		KOSTL — Cost Center
		PERSG — Employee Group
		PERSK — Employee Subgroup
		ORGEH — Organizational Unit
		ACTVT - Activity
P_TCODE	HR: Transaction codes	TCD — Transaction Code
P_USTR	HR: US Tax Reporter	ACTVT — Activity
		PERSA — Personnel Area
		BTRTL — Personnel Subarea
P_RCF_STAT	Object Status in E-Recruiting	OTYPE — Object Type
		RCF_STATUS — Generic Object Status
P_NL_PKEV	P_NL_PKEV	KASSE — Pension fund
		EVENT
		PKELV
P_NL_PKFKT	P_NL_PKFKT	PKNL_PKFKT — PF function
P_NL_PKFXV	P_NL_PKFXV	KASSE — Pension fund
		PKNL_FXVIE — Fund function view
P_PBSFRDBT	P_PBSFRDBT	ACTVT — Activity
		DECRE
		TYPEDEC

Table 14.1 Authorization Objects Using Transaction Code SU21 (Cont.)

Authorization Object	Description	Notes
P_PBSFRDST	P_PBSFRDST	STATUSDEC DECRE TYPEDEC
P_PBSFRDVL	P_PBSFRDVL	VALIDERDEC DECRE TYPEDEC
PLOG	Personnel Planning	PLVAR — Plan Version OTYPE — Object Type INFOTYP — Infotype SUBTYP — Subtype ISTAT — Planning Status PPFCODE — Function Code
PLOG_CON	Personnel Planning with Context	PLVAR — Plan Version OTYPE — Object Type INFOTYP — Infotype SUBTYP — Subtype ISTAT — Planning Status PPFCODE — Function Code PROFL — Authorization Profile
P_PBSPWE	Process Workbench Engine (PWE) authorization	REQTYPE — Business Scenario PRSCN — Process Scenario PROCSCEN — Sub Process Scenario PROCTSK — Process tasks ACTVT — Activity
P_PEPSVAR	Shift Planning: User-Independent Sort Variants	P_PEPSVAR — Authorization for User-Independent Sort Variants
P_TNMSNAPH	Training need management: authorization object for snapshot	TPSTATS — Status ACTVT — Activity

Table 14.1 Authorization Objects Using Transaction Code SU21 (Cont.)

The notes section in Table 14.1 describes the various fields delivered for authorization checks within the profile. Within each field, you may be able to further define the authorization.

The following is an example of the field AUTHC and the various ways you can further define the authorization.

Field AUTHC contains the following:

R — Read access

M — Matchcode for read access help

W — Write access

E — Create and change lock records (Asymmetrical Double Verification Principle)

D — Change the locked indicator (Asymmetrical Double Verification Principle)

S — Write access (Symmetric Verification Principle)

14.4.2 Time Management Transaction Codes

Table 14.2 is a list of commonly used transaction codes for Time Management.

Transaction Code	Description
ACTEXP_APPR	Approve Working Times and Trips
ACTEXP_APPR_LITE	Approve Working Times and Trips
CAC1	Time Sheet: Maintain Profiles
CAC2	Time Sheet: Field Selection
CAC3	Time Sheet: Rejection Reasons
CAC4	CATS: Profile Authorization Groups
CAC5	Define Customer Fields
CAC6	Allowed Print Reports
CAC7	Number Range Maintenance: CATS
CAC8	Number Range Maintenance: CATS_INTRN
CADE	CATS: Delete Transaction Data
CADO	Time Sheet: Display Data

Table 14.2 Transaction Codes for Time Management

Transaction Code	Description
CAOR	Display Report (Structure-Related)
CAPP	CATS: Object-related Approval
CAT2	Time Sheet: Maintain Times
CAT2_ISCR	CATS: Maintain Times (Init. Screen)
CAT3	Time Sheet: Display Times
CAT3_ISCR	CATS: Display Times (Initial Screen)
CAT5	Data Transfer CATS -> PS
CAT6	Transfer to Human Resources
CAT7	CATS: Transfer Data to CO
CAT8	Time Sheet: Document Display
CAT9	Data Transfer CATS -> PM/CS
CATA	Transfer All Components
CATC	Time Sheet: Time Leveling
CATM	Selection From Time Recording
CATR	Reorganize Interface Tables
CATS_APPR	Approve Working Times (Power user)
CATS_APPR_LITE	Approve Working Times
CATS_DA	Display Working Times
CATSARCH	Archiving Time Sheet Data
CATSWF	CATS Workflow
CATSXT	CATS for Service Providers
CATSXT_ADMIN	CATS for Service Providers (Admin.)
CATSXT_DA	Display Working Times and Tasks
CATSXT_DTL	Working Times and Task: Display Details
CATW	Record Working Time
CN30	Postprocessing Confirmations
COFC	Postprocesing Actual Costs
COGI	Postprocessing Goods Movements
IW46	Postprocessing Confirmations

Table 14.2 Transaction Codes for Time Management (Cont.)

Transaction Code	Description
PA20	Display HR Master Data
PA51	Display Time Data
PA53	Display Time Data
PA61	Maintain Time Data
PA62	List Entry of Additional Data
PA63	Maintain Time Data
PA64	Calendar Entry
PA71	Fast Entry of Time Data
PC00_M99_CLSTPC	Absences — International
PC00_M99_TLEA	Annual leave listing — International
PC00_M99_TLEA30	Annual leave update — International
PE01	Maintain Schemas
PE02	Maintain Personnel Calculation Rules
PE03	Maintain Features
PE04	Functions/Operations
PE50	Form Editor
PEPM	Profile Matchup
PP01	Detailed Maintenance
PP60	Display Temporary Assignment List
PP61	Change Shift Plan
PP62	Display Requirements
PP63	Change Requirements
PP64	Choose Plan Version
PP65	Simple Maintenance
PP66	Choose Profile
PP67	Create Requirements
PP6A	Display Personal Shift Plan
PP6B	Display Attendance List
PP6C	Undo Completed Target Plan

Table 14.2 Transaction Codes for Time Management (Cont.)

Transaction Code	Description
PP6I	Display Temporary Assignment List
PPOME	Change Organization and Staffing
PPPD	Display Profile
PPPM	Change Profile
PT_55400	Find Attendance/Absence
PT_ABS20_ATT	Attendance/Absence Data: Overview
PT_BAL00	Cumulated Time Evaluation Results
PT_BPC00	Generate Personal Calendar
PT_BPC10	Leave Accrual and Quota Deduction
PT_CLSTB1	Temp. Time Eval. Results (ClusterB1)
PT_CLSTB2	Display Time Evaluation Results Cluster (B2)
PT_CLSTG1	Display Group Incentive Wages (Cluster G1)
PT_CLSTL1	Display Individual Incentive Wages (Cluster L1)
PT_CLSTPC	Display Personal Calendar (Cluster PC)
PT_DOW00	Time Accounts
PT_DSH20	Daily Work Schedule
PT_EDT_TEDT	Time Statement
PT_EDT_TELU	Time Balances Overview
PT_ERL00	Time Evaluation Messages: Analysis
PT_ILVA00	Leave Accrual
PT_LEA40_ABS	Att./Absences: Graphical Overview
PT_LEA40_ATT	Att./Absences: Graphical Overview
PT_LEACONV	Transfer Remaining Leave from IT0005
PT_QABS	Absences: List
PT_QATT	Attendances: List
PT_QREM	Employee Remuneration Information
PT_QTA00	Generate Absence Quotas
PT_QTA10	Absence Quota Information
PT_QTAL	Employee Time and Labor

Table 14.2 Transaction Codes for Time Management (Cont.)

Transaction Code	Description
PT_REOPC	Personal Calendar Reorganization (Cluster PC)
PT_SHF00	Generation of Work Schedules
PT_UPD00	Recalculate Attendance/Absence Record
PT_UTPR00	Revaluate Daily Work Schedules
PT_UWSH00	Revaluate Planned Working Time IT
PT01	Work Schedule Create
PT02	Change Work Schedule
PT03	Work Schedule Display
PT40	Time Management Pool
PT41	Customizing CC1 Communication Param.
PT42	Supply Personnel Data
PT43	Supply Master Data
PT44	Upload Request
PT45	Post Person Time Events
PT46	Post Working Time Events
PT50	Quota Overview
PT60	Time Evaluation
PT60_NON_CE	Time Evaluation (RPTIME00)
PT61	Time Statement
PT62	Attendance List
PT63	Personal Work Schedule
PT64	Attendance/Absence Data Overview
PT65	Attendance/Absence Overview Graphic
PT66	Display Cluster B2
PT67	Third-Party Payroll
PT68	Activity Allocation
PT69	Multiple Time Recording
PT70	Time Management Info System
PT71	Tool Selection for Time Management

Table 14.2 Transaction Codes for Time Management (Cont.)

Transaction Code	Description
PT80	Subsystem Connection
PT90	Absence Data: Calendar View
PT90_ATT	Attendance Data: Calendar View
PT91	Absence Data: Multiple Employee View
PT91_ATT	Attendances: For Multiple Employees
PTARQ	Test Environment for Leave Request
PTCCX	Test Environment
PTE1	Generate Batch Input Session
PTE2	Process Batch Input Session
PTE3	Reorganize Interface File
PTFMLA	FMLA Workbench
PTFMLA_PROF	FMLA Workbench
PTME	Time Manager's Workplace
PTME_PROF	Time Manager's Workplace
PTMW	Time Manager's Workplace
PTMW	Time Manager's Workplace
PTMW_PROF	Time Manager's Workplace
PTMW_TIME_ADMIN	Maintain Time Data
PTMW_TIME_ADMIN_GRP	Maintain Time Data for Group
PTMW_WORKLIST	Process Messages
PU03	Change Payroll Status
PU12	Third- Party Payroll
PU22	HR Archiving
PW_CEDTX0_AFTER	After Gross Pay
PW_CEDTX0_BEFORE	Before Gross Pay
PW01	Time Tickets Maintain
PW02	Time Tickets Display
PW03	Time Tickets Record
PW61	Time Leveling

Table 14.2 Transaction Codes for Time Management (Cont.)

Transaction Code	Description
PW62	Working Times of Time and Incentive Wage Earners
PW63	Reassignment Proposals for Wage Groups
PW70	Individual Incentive Wages
PW71	Group Incentive Wages
PW72	Withdrawal from Group
PZ04	Time Statement
PZ04_OLD	Time Statement
PZ09	Time Accounts
PZ17_OLD	Work Schedule
PZ34	ESS Time Management
S_AHR_61004980	Maintain Shift Group Infotype for Organizational Unit
S_AHR_61004989	Specify Shift Groups
S_AHR_61005002	Define Time Types for Connecting to Microsoft Excel
S_AHR_61008856	Earliest Recalculation for Pair Formation
S_AHR_61009123	Create Evaluation Periods
S_AHR_61010096	Earliest Recalculation for Incentive Wages
S_AHR_61010745	Earliest Recalculation for the Time Statement
S_AHR_61018652	Time Leveling
S_AHR_61018653	Time Leveling
S_AHR_61018654	Remuneration Statements
S_AHR_61018655	Remuneration Statements
S_AHR_61018656	Remuneration Statements
S_AHR_61018657	Att./Absences: Graphical Overview
S_AHR_61018658	Att./Absences: Graphical Overview
S_AHR_61018659	Attendance/Absence Data: Overview
S_AHR_61018660	Att./Absence Data: Calendar View
S_AHR_61018661	Display Temporary Assignment List

Table 14.2 Transaction Codes for Time Management (Cont.)

Transaction Code	Description
S_PH0_48000380	Transfer Remaining Leave from IT0005
S_PH0_48000381	Generate Absence Quotas
S_PH9_46000588	Time Evaluation Messages Display
SCAL	Holiday Calendar
SQ01	SAP Query
WS01000109	Cancel Leave Request
WS01000109M	Dummy for Authorization for Canc. WF
WS04200009	Leave Request
WS04200009M	Approve Leave Request
WS12400005	Cancel Leave Request
WS12400005M	Dummy for Authorization for Canc. WF
WS20000081	Leave Request
WS20000081M	Approve Leave Request

Table 14.2   Transaction Codes for Time Management (Cont.)

14.5   Summary

This chapter covered some of the configuration tables related to Incentive Wages, the Web applications for Time Management, Concurrent Employment for Time Evaluation, and the various authorization objects and transaction codes. This information, and all of the other chapters in the book, should give you a detailed overview of the possibilities that these areas provide for your business, and can be used as a reference as you design your own system setup.

Appendices

A   Infotypes

This appendix lists all of the fields for the master data infotypes covered in this book. This appendix will prove invaluable whenever you need to reference particular fields, their field lengths, etc., while developing interfaces or completing requirements documents for custom programming.

A.1   Infotype Technical Fields

The following master data sections are broken down by infotype and list each infotype's technical details of the available fields according to the database tables. This section can be referenced during the blueprinting phase, when conducting data-mapping exercises from the legacy systems to the SAP system for data conversions, for developing custom programs, and for interface development. Each of these infotypes can be referenced directly in the SAP system by using Transaction code SE11 • PAXXXX, where XXXX represents the infotype number.

Ref	Field	Key Field	Initial Values	Data Element	Data Type	Length	Decimals	Description
1	MANDT	X	X	MANDT	CLNT	3	0	Client
2	.INCLUDE	X	X	PAKEY	STRU	0	0	Key for HR Master Data
3	PERNR	X	X	PERSNO	NUMC	8	0	Personnel number
4	SUBTY	X	X	SUBTY	CHAR	4	0	Subtype
5	OBJPS	X	X	OBJPS	CHAR	2	0	Object Identification
6	SPRPS	X	X	SPRPS	CHAR	1	0	Lock Indicator for HR Master Data Record
7	ENDDA	X	X	ENDDA	DATS	8	0	End Date
8	BEGDA	X	X	BEGDA	DATS	8	0	Start Date
9	SEQNR	X	X	SEQNR	NUMC	3	0	Number of Infotype Record with Same Key
10	.INCLUDE			PSHD1	STRU	0	0	HR Master Record: Control Field
11	AEDTM			AEDAT	DATS	8	0	Changed On
12	UNAME			AENAM	CHAR	12	0	Name of Person Who Changed Object
13	HISTO			HISTO	CHAR	1	0	Historical Record Flag
14	ITXEX			ITXEX	CHAR	1	0	Text Exists for Infotype
15	REFEX			PRFEX	CHAR	1	0	Reference Fields Exist (Primary/Secondary Costs)
16	ORDEX			ORDEX	CHAR	1	0	Confirmation Fields Exist
17	ITBLD			ITBLD	CHAR	2	0	Infotype Screen Control
18	PREAS			PREAS	CHAR	2	0	Reason for Changing Master Data
19	FLAG1			NUSED	CHAR	1	0	Reserved Field/Unused Field
20	FLAG2			NUSED	CHAR	1	0	Reserved Field/Unused Field
21	FLAG3			NUSED	CHAR	1	0	Reserved Field/Unused Field
22	FLAG4			NUSED	CHAR	1	0	Reserved Field/Unused Field
23	RESE1			NUSED2	CHAR	2	0	Reserved Field/Unused Field of Length 2
24	RESE2			NUSED2	CHAR	2	0	Reserved Field/Unused Field of Length 2

Figure A.1   Infotype 0005 — Leave Entitlement

Ref	Field	Key Field	Initial Values	Data Element	Data Type	Length	Decimals	Description
26	.INCLUDE			PS0005	STRU	0	0	HR Master Record: Infotype 0005 (Leave Entitlement)
27	URLJJ			URLJJ	NUMC	4	0	Leave year
28	URBEG			URBEG	DATS	8	0	Start of leave
29	UREND			UREND	DATS	8	0	End of leave
30	UAR01			URART	CHAR	2	0	Leave type
31	UAN01			PTM_HENTITLE	DEC	10	5	Leave entitlement
32	UBE01			URBEG	DATS	8	0	Start of leave
33	UEN01			UREND	DATS	8	0	End of leave
34	UAB01			PTM_HACCOUNTED	DEC	10	5	Leave accounted
35	UAR02			URART	CHAR	2	0	Leave type
36	UAN02			PTM_HENTITLE	DEC	10	5	Leave entitlement
37	UBE02			URBEG	DATS	8	0	Start of leave
38	UEN02			UREND	DATS	8	0	End of leave
39	UAB02			PTM_HACCOUNTED	DEC	10	5	Leave accounted
40	UAR03			URART	CHAR	2	0	Leave type
41	UAN03			PTM_HENTITLE	DEC	10	5	Leave entitlement
42	UBE03			URBEG	DATS	8	0	Start of leave
43	UEN03			UREND	DATS	8	0	End of leave
44	UAB03			PTM_HACCOUNTED	DEC	10	5	Leave accounted
45	UAR04			URART	CHAR	2	0	Leave type
46	UAN04			PTM_HENTITLE	DEC	10	5	Leave entitlement
47	UBE04			URBEG	DATS	8	0	Start of leave
48	UEN04			UREND	DATS	8	0	End of leave
49	UAB04			PTM_HACCOUNTED	DEC	10	5	Leave accounted

Figure A.2 Infotype 0005 — Leave Entitlement, continued

Ref	Field	Key Field	Initial Values	Data Element	Data Type	Length	Decimals	Description
50	UAR05			URART	CHAR	2	0	Leave type
51	UAN05			PTM_HENTITLE	DEC	10	5	Leave entitlement
52	UBE05			URBEG	DATS	8	0	Start of leave
53	UEN05			UREND	DATS	8	0	End of leave
54	UAB05			PTM_HACCOUNTED	DEC	10	5	Leave accounted
55	UAR06			URART	CHAR	2	0	Leave type
56	UAN06			PTM_HENTITLE	DEC	10	5	Leave entitlement
57	UBE06			URBEG	DATS	8	0	Start of leave
58	UEN06			UREND	DATS	8	0	End of leave
59	UAB06			PTM_HACCOUNTED	DEC	10	5	Leave accounted
60	.INCLUDE			CI_P0005	STRU	0	0	

Figure A.3 Infotype 0005 — Leave Entitlement, continued

Ref	Field	Key Field	Initial Values	Data Element	Data Type	Length	Decimals	Description
1	MANDT	X	X	MANDT	CLNT	3	0	Client
2	.INCLUDE	X	X	PAKEY	STRU	0	0	Key for HR Master Data
3	PERNR	X	X	PERSNO	NUMC	8	0	Personnel number
4	SUBTY	X	X	SUBTY	CHAR	4	0	Subtype
5	OBJPS	X	X	OBJPS	CHAR	2	0	Object Identification
6	SPRPS	X	X	SPRPS	CHAR	1	0	Lock Indicator for HR Master Data Record
7	ENDDA	X	X	ENDDA	DATS	8	0	End Date
8	BEGDA	X	X	BEGDA	DATS	8	0	Start Date
9	SEQNR	X	X	SEQNR	NUMC	3	0	Number of Infotype Record with Same Key
10	.INCLUDE			PSHD1	STRU	0	0	HR Master Record: Control Field
11	AEDTM			AEDAT	DATS	8	0	Changed On
12	UNAME			AENAM	CHAR	12	0	Name of Person Who Changed Object
13	HISTO			HISTO	CHAR	1	0	Historical Record Flag
14	ITXEX			ITXEX	CHAR	1	0	Text Exists for Infotype
15	REFEX			PRFEX	CHAR	1	0	Reference Fields Exist (Primary/Secondary Costs)
16	ORDEX			ORDEX	CHAR	1	0	Confirmation Fields Exist
17	ITBLD			ITBLD	CHAR	2	0	Infotype Screen Control
18	PREAS			PREAS	CHAR	2	0	Reason for Changing Master Data
19	FLAG1			NUSED	CHAR	1	0	Reserved Field/Unused Field
20	FLAG2			NUSED	CHAR	1	0	Reserved Field/Unused Field
21	FLAG3			NUSED	CHAR	1	0	Reserved Field/Unused Field
22	FLAG4			NUSED	CHAR	1	0	Reserved Field/Unused Field
23	RESE1			NUSED2	CHAR	2	0	Reserved Field/Unused Field of Length 2
24	RESE2			NUSED2	CHAR	2	0	Reserved Field/Unused Field of Length 2
25	GRPVL			PCCE_G PVAL	CHAR	4	0	Grouping Value for Personnel Assignments

Figure A.4 Infotype 0007 — Planned Working Time

465

Ref	Field	Key Field	Initial Values	Data Element	Data Type	Length	Decimals	Description
26	.INCLUDE			PS0007	STRU	0	0	HR Master Record: Infotype 0007 (Planned Working Time)
27	SCHKZ			SCHKN	CHAR	8	0	Work Schedule Rule
28	ZTERF			PT_ZTERF	NUMC	1	0	Employee Time Management Status
29	EMPCT			EMPCT	DEC	5	2	Employment percentage
30	MOSTD			MOSTD	DEC	5	2	Monthly hours
31	WOSTD			WOSTD	DEC	5	2	Hours per week
32	ARBST			STDTG	DEC	5	2	Daily Working Hours
33	WKWDY			WARST	DEC	4	2	Weekly Workdays
34	JRSTD			JRSTD	DEC	7	2	Annual working hours
35	TEILK			TEILK	CHAR	1	0	Indicator Part-Time Employee
36	MINTA			MINTA	DEC	5	2	Minimum number of work hours per day
37	MAXTA			MAXTA	DEC	5	2	Maximum number of work hours per day
38	MINWO			MINWO	DEC	5	2	Minimum weekly working hours
39	MAXWO			MAXWO	DEC	5	2	Maximum number of work hours per week
40	MINMO			MINMO	DEC	5	2	Minimum number of work hours per month
41	MAXMO			MAXMO	DEC	5	2	Maximum number of work hours per month
42	MINJA			MINJA	DEC	7	2	Minimum annual working hours
43	MAXJA			MAXJA	DEC	7	2	Maximum Number of Working Hours Per Year
44	DYSCH			DYSCH	CHAR	1	0	Create Daily Work Schedule Dynamically
45	KZTIM			KZTIM	CHAR	2	0	Additional indicator for time management
46	WWEEK			WWEEK	CHAR	2	0	Working week
47	AWTYP			AWTYP	CHAR	5	0	Reference Transaction
48	.INCLUDE			CI_P0007	STRU	0	0	

Figure A.5 Figure A.5 Infotype 0007 — Planned Working Time, continued

466

Ref	Field	Key Field	Initial Values	Data Element	Data Type	Length	Decimals	Description
1	MANDT	X	X	MANDT	CLNT	3	0	Client
2	.INCLUDE	X	X	PAKEY	STRU	0	0	Key for HR Master Data
3	PERNR	X	X	PERSNO	NUMC	8	0	Personnel number
4	SUBTY	X	X	SUBTY	CHAR	4	0	Subtype
5	OBJPS	X	X	OBJPS	CHAR	2	0	Object Identification
6	SPRPS	X	X	SPRPS	CHAR	1	0	Lock Indicator for HR Master Data Record
7	ENDDA	X	X	ENDDA	DATS	8	0	End Date
8	BEGDA	X	X	BEGDA	DATS	8	0	Start Date
9	SEQNR	X	X	SEQNR	NUMC	3	0	Number of Infotype Record with Same Key
10	.INCLUDE			PSHD1	STRU	0	0	HR Master Record: Control Field
11	AEDTM			AEDAT	DATS	8	0	Changed On
12	UNAME			AENAM	CHAR	12	0	Name of Person Who Changed Object
13	HISTO			HISTO	CHAR	1	0	Historical Record Flag
14	ITXEX			ITXEX	CHAR	1	0	Text Exists for Infotype
15	REFEX			PRFEX	CHAR	1	0	Reference Fields Exist (Primary/Secondary Costs)
16	ORDEX			ORDEX	CHAR	1	0	Confirmation Fields Exist
17	ITBLD			ITBLD	CHAR	2	0	Infotype Screen Control
18	PREAS			PREAS	CHAR	2	0	Reason for Changing Master Data
19	FLAG1			NUSED	CHAR	1	0	Reserved Field/Unused Field
20	FLAG2			NUSED	CHAR	1	0	Reserved Field/Unused Field
21	FLAG3			NUSED	CHAR	1	0	Reserved Field/Unused Field
22	FLAG4			NUSED	CHAR	1	0	Reserved Field/Unused Field
23	RESE1			NUSED2	CHAR	2	0	Reserved Field/Unused Field of Length 2
24	RESE2			NUSED2	CHAR	2	0	Reserved Field/Unused Field of Length 2

Figure A.6 Infotype 0008 — Basic Pay

Ref	Field	Key Field	Initial Values	Data Element	Data Type	Length	Decimals	Description
25	GRPVL			PCCE_GPVAL	CHAR	4	0	Grouping Value for Personnel Assignments
26	.INCLUDE			PS0008	STRU	0	0	HR Master Record: Infotype 0008 (Basic Pay)
27	TRFAR			TRFAR	CHAR	2	0	Pay scale type
28	TRFGB			TRFGB	CHAR	2	0	Pay Scale Area
29	TRFGR			TRFGR	CHAR	8	0	Pay Scale Group
30	TRFST			TRFST	CHAR	2	0	Pay Scale Level
31	STVOR			STVOR	DATS	8	0	Date of Next Increase
32	ORZST			ORTZS	CHAR	2	0	Cost of Living Allowance Level
33	PARTN			PARTN	CHAR	2	0	Partnership
34	WAERS			WAERS	CUKY	5	0	Currency Key
35	VGLTA			VGLTA	CHAR	2	0	Comparison pay scale type
36	VGLGB			VGLGB	CHAR	2	0	Comparison pay scale area
37	VGLGR			VGLTG	CHAR	8	0	Comparison pay scale group
38	VGLST			VGLST	CHAR	2	0	Comparison pay scale level
39	VGLSV			STVOR	DATS	8	0	Date of Next Increase
40	BSGRD			BSGRD	DEC	5	2	Capacity Utilization Level
41	DIVGV			DIVGV	DEC	5	2	Working Hours per Payroll Period
42	ANSAL			ANSAL_15	CURR	15	2	Annual salary
43	FALGK			FALGK	CHAR	10	0	Case group catalog
44	FALGR			FALGR	CHAR	6	0	Case group
45	LGA01			LGART	CHAR	4	0	Wage Type
46	BET01			PAD_AMT7S	CURR	13	2	Wage Type Amount for Payments
47	ANZ01			ANZHL	DEC	7	2	Number
48	EIN01			PT_ZEINH	CHAR	3	0	Time/Measurement Unit
49	OPK01			OPKEN	CHAR	1	0	Operation Indicator for Wage Types
50	LGA02			LGART	CHAR	4	0	Wage Type

Figure A.7 Infotype 0008 — Basic Pay, continued

Ref	Field	Key Field	Initial Values	Data Element	Data Type	Length	Decimals	Description
51	BET02			PAD_AMT7S	CURR	13	2	Wage Type Amount for Payments
52	ANZ02			ANZHL	DEC	7	2	Number
53	EIN02			PT_ZEINH	CHAR	3	0	Time/Measurement Unit
54	OPK02			OPKEN	CHAR	1	0	Operation Indicator for Wage Types
55	LGA03			LGART	CHAR	4	0	Wage Type
56	BET03			PAD_AMT7S	CURR	13	2	Wage Type Amount for Payments
57	ANZ03			ANZHL	DEC	7	2	Number
58	EIN03			PT_ZEINH	CHAR	3	0	Time/Measurement Unit
59	OPK03			OPKEN	CHAR	1	0	Operation Indicator for Wage Types
60	LGA04			LGART	CHAR	4	0	Wage Type
61	BET04			PAD_AMT7S	CURR	13	2	Wage Type Amount for Payments
62	ANZ04			ANZHL	DEC	7	2	Number
63	EIN04			PT_ZEINH	CHAR	3	0	Time/Measurement Unit
64	OPK04			OPKEN	CHAR	1	0	Operation Indicator for Wage Types
65	IND01			INDBW	CHAR	1	0	Indicator for indirect valuation
66	IND02			INDBW	CHAR	1	0	Indicator for indirect valuation
67	IND03			INDBW	CHAR	1	0	Indicator for indirect valuation
68	IND04			INDBW	CHAR	1	0	Indicator for indirect valuation
69	ANCUR			ANCUR	CUKY	5	0	Currency Key for Annual Salary
70	CPIND			P_CPIND	CHAR	1	0	Planned compensation type
71	FLAGA			FLAG	CHAR	1	0	General Flag
72	.INCLUDE			CI_P0008	STRU	0	0	

Figure A.8 Infotype 0008 — Basic Pay, continued

Ref	Field	Key Field	Initial Values	Data Element	Data Type	Length	Decimals	Description
1	MANDT	X	X	MANDT	CLNT	3	0	Client
2	.INCLUDE	X	X	PAKEY	STRU	0	0	Key for HR Master Data
3	PERNR	X	X	PERSNO	NUMC	8	0	Personnel number
4	SUBTY	X	X	SUBTY	CHAR	4	0	Subtype
5	OBJPS	X	X	OBJPS	CHAR	2	0	Object Identification
6	SPRPS	X	X	SPRPS	CHAR	1	0	Lock Indicator for HR Master Data Record
7	ENDDA	X	X	ENDDA	DATS	8	0	End Date
8	BEGDA	X	X	BEGDA	DATS	8	0	Start Date
9	SEQNR	X	X	SEQNR	NUMC	3	0	Number of Infotype Record with Same Key
10	.INCLUDE			PSHD1	STRU	0	0	HR Master Record: Control Field
11	AEDTM			AEDAT	DATS	8	0	Changed On
12	UNAME			AENAM	CHAR	12	0	Name of Person Who Changed Object
13	HISTO			HISTO	CHAR	1	0	Historical Record Flag
14	ITXEX			ITXEX	CHAR	1	0	Text Exists for Infotype
15	REFEX			PRFEX	CHAR	1	0	Reference Fields Exist (Primary/Secondary Costs)
16	ORDEX			ORDEX	CHAR	1	0	Confirmation Fields Exist
17	ITBLD			ITBLD	CHAR	2	0	Infotype Screen Control
18	PREAS			PREAS	CHAR	2	0	Reason for Changing Master Data
19	FLAG1			NUSED	CHAR	1	0	Reserved Field/Unused Field
20	FLAG2			NUSED	CHAR	1	0	Reserved Field/Unused Field
21	FLAG3			NUSED	CHAR	1	0	Reserved Field/Unused Field
22	FLAG4			NUSED	CHAR	1	0	Reserved Field/Unused Field
23	RESE1			NUSED2	CHAR	2	0	Reserved Field/Unused Field of Length 2

Figure A.9 Infotype 0050 — Time Recording Info

Ref	Field	Key Field	Initial Values	Data Element	Data Type	Length	Decimals	Description
24	RESE2			NUSED2	CHAR	2	0	Reserved Field/Unused Field of Length 2
25	GRPVL			PCCE_G PVAL	CHAR	4	0	Grouping Value for Personnel Assignments
26	.INCLUDE			PS0050	STRU	0	0	HR Master Record: Infotype 0050 (Time Recording Info.)
27	ZAUSW			DZAUSW	NUMC	8	0	Time Recording ID Number
28	ZAUVE			DZAUVE	CHAR	1	0	ID version
29	ZABAR			DZABAR	CHAR	1	0	Employee grouping for the time evaluation rule
30	BDEGR			BDEGR	CHAR	3	0	Grouping for Connection to Subsystem
31	ZANBE			DZANBE	CHAR	2	0	Access control group
32	ZDGBE			DZDGBE	CHAR	1	0	Off-site work authorization
33	ZMAIL			DZMAIL	CHAR	1	0	Mail indicator
34	ZPINC			DZPINC	CHAR	4	0	Personal code
35	GLMAX			GLMAX	DEC	5	2	Flextime maximum
36	GLMIN			GLMIN	DEC	5	2	Flextime minimum
37	ZTZUA			DZTZUA	DEC	5	2	Time Bonus/Deduction
38	ZMGEN			DZMGEN	CHAR	1	0	Standard overtime
39	ZUSKZ			DZUSKZ	CHAR	1	0	Additional indicator
40	PMBDE			PMBDE	NUMC	2	0	Work time event type group
41	GRAWG			GRAWG	CHAR	3	0	Grouping of Attendance/Absence Reasons
42	GRELG			GRELG	CHAR	3	0	Grouping for Employee Expenses
43	.INCLUDE			CI_P0050	STRU	0	0	

Figure A.10   Infotype 0050 — Time Recording Info, continued

Ref	Field	Key Field	Initial Values	Data Element	Data Type	Length	Decimals	Description
1	MANDT	X	X	MANDT	CLNT	3	0	Client
2	.INCLUDE	X	X	PAKEY	STRU	0	0	Key for HR Master Data
3	PERNR	X	X	PERSNO	NUMC	8	0	Personnel number
4	SUBTY	X	X	SUBTY	CHAR	4	0	Subtype
5	OBJPS	X	X	OBJPS	CHAR	2	0	Object Identification
6	SPRPS	X	X	SPRPS	CHAR	1	0	Lock Indicator for HR Master Data Record
7	ENDDA	X	X	ENDDA	DATS	8	0	End Date
8	BEGDA	X	X	BEGDA	DATS	8	0	Start Date
9	SEQNR			SEQNR	NUMC	3	0	Number of Infotype Record with Same Key
10	.INCLUDE			PSHD1	STRU	0	0	HR Master Record: Control Field
11	AEDTM			AEDAT	DATS	8	0	Changed On
12	UNAME			AENAM	CHAR	12	0	Name of Person Who Changed Object
13	HISTO			HISTO	CHAR	1	0	Historical Record Flag
14	ITXEX			ITXEX	CHAR	1	0	Text Exists for Infotype
15	REFEX			PRFEX	CHAR	1	0	Reference Fields Exist (Primary/Secondary Costs)
16	ORDEX			ORDEX	CHAR	1	0	Confirmation Fields Exist
17	ITBLD			ITBLD	CHAR	2	0	Infotype Screen Control
18	PREAS			PREAS	CHAR	2	0	Reason for Changing Master Data
19	FLAG1			NUSED	CHAR	1	0	Reserved Field/Unused Field
20	FLAG2			NUSED	CHAR	1	0	Reserved Field/Unused Field
21	FLAG3			NUSED	CHAR	1	0	Reserved Field/Unused Field

Figure A.11 Infotype 0082 — Additional Absence Data

Ref	Field	Key Field	Initial Values	Data Element	Data Type	Length	Decimals	Description
22	FLAG4			NUSED	CHAR	1	0	Reserved Field/Unused Field
23	RESE1			NUSED2	CHAR	2	0	Reserved Field/Unused Field of Length 2
24	RESE2			NUSED2	CHAR	2	0	Reserved Field/Unused Field of Length 2
25	GRPVL			PCCE_GP VAL	CHAR	4	0	Grouping Value for Personnel Assignments
26	.INCLUDE			PS0082	STRU	0	0	HR Master Record: Infotype 0082 (Additional Absence Data)
27	CASNO			CASNO	CHAR	10	0	Case number
28	DESCR			TEXT40	CHAR	40	0	Text, 40 Characters Long
29	RDATE			RDAT1	DATS	8	0	Reported on
30	RTIME			RTIM1	TIMS	6	0	Time reported
31	IDATE			IDAT1	DATS	8	0	Date of illness
32	ITIME			ITIME	TIMS	6	0	Time of illness
33	TCOST			TCOST	CURR	9	2	Estimated costs
34	OCD01			OCCCD	CHAR	2	0	Event indicator
35	ODT01			OCDAT	DATS	8	0	Event date
36	OTM01			OCTIM	TIMS	6	0	Time of event
37	OCD02			OCCCD	CHAR	2	0	Event indicator
38	ODT02			OCDAT	DATS	8	0	Event date
39	OTM02			OCTIM	TIMS	6	0	Time of event
40	OCD03			OCCCD	CHAR	2	0	Event indicator
41	ODT03			OCDAT	DATS	8	0	Event date
42	OTM03			OCTIM	TIMS	6	0	Time of event
43	VDT01			OCEND	DATS	8	0	End of event
44	JNF01			JNFLD	CHAR	1	0	Yes/No field for internal medical service

Figure A.12 Infotype 0082 — Additional Absence Data, continued

473

Ref	Field	Key Field	Initial Values	Data Element	Data Type	Length	Decimals	Description
45	RCD01			REMCD	CHAR	2	0	Description indicator
46	REM01			REMAR	CHAR	20	0	Event remark
47	VDT02			OCEND	DATS	8	0	End of event
48	JNF02			JNFLD	CHAR	1	0	Yes/No field for internal medical service
49	RCD02			REMCD	CHAR	2	0	Description indicator
50	REM02			REMAR	CHAR	20	0	Event remark
51	VDT03			OCEND	DATS	8	0	End of event
52	JNF03			JNFLD	CHAR	1	0	Yes/No field for internal medical service
53	RCD03			REMCD	CHAR	2	0	Description indicator
54	REM03			REMAR	CHAR	20	0	Event remark
55	WAERS			WAERS	CUKY	5	0	Currency Key
56	EVTAR			EVTAR	CHAR	4	0	Event Location
57	EVTSR			EVTSR	CHAR	4	0	Personal subarea of the event
58	.INCLUDE			CI_P0082	STRU	0	0	

Figure A.13 Infotype 0082 — Additional Absence Data, continued

Ref	Field	Key Field	Initial Values	Data Element	Data Type	Length	Decimals	Description
1	MANDT	X	X	MANDT	CLNT	3	0	Client
2	.INCLUDE	X	X	PAKEY	STRU	0	0	Key for HR Master Data
3	PERNR	X	X	PERSNO	NUMC	8	0	Personnel number
4	SUBTY	X	X	SUBTY	CHAR	4	0	Subtype
5	OBJPS	X	X	OBJPS	CHAR	2	0	Object Identification
6	SPRPS	X	X	SPRPS	CHAR	1	0	Lock Indicator for HR Master Data Record
7	ENDDA	X	X	ENDDA	DATS	8	0	End Date
8	BEGDA	X	X	BEGDA	DATS	8	0	Start Date
9	SEQNR	X	X	SEQNR	NUMC	3	0	Number of Infotype Record with Same Key
10	.INCLUDE			PSHD1	STRU	0	0	HR Master Record: Control Field
11	AEDTM			AEDAT	DATS	8	0	Changed On
12	UNAME			AENAM	CHAR	12	0	Name of Person Who Changed Object
13	HISTO			HISTO	CHAR	1	0	Historical Record Flag
14	ITXEX			ITXEX	CHAR	1	0	Text Exists for Infotype
15	REFEX			PRFEX	CHAR	1	0	Reference Fields Exist (Primary/Secondary Costs)
16	ORDEX			ORDEX	CHAR	1	0	Confirmation Fields Exist
17	ITBLD			ITBLD	CHAR	2	0	Infotype Screen Control
18	PREAS			PREAS	CHAR	2	0	Reason for Changing Master Data
19	FLAG1			NUSED	CHAR	1	0	Reserved Field/Unused Field
20	FLAG2			NUSED	CHAR	1	0	Reserved Field/Unused Field

Figure A.14 Infotype 0130 — Test Procedures Time Evaluation

Ref	Field	Key Field	Initial Values	Data Element	Data Type	Length	Decimals	Description
21	FLAG3			NUSED	CHAR	1	0	Reserved Field/Unused Field
22	FLAG4			NUSED	CHAR	1	0	Reserved Field/Unused Field
23	RESE1			NUSED2	CHAR	2	0	Reserved Field/Unused Field of Length 2
24	RESE2			NUSED2	CHAR	2	0	Reserved Field/Unused Field of Length 2
25	GRPVL			PCCE_GPVAL	CHAR	4	0	Grouping Value for Personnel Assignments
26	.INCLUDE			PS0130	STRU	0	0	HR Master Record: Infotype 0130 (Checking Procedures)
27	CKTYP			CKTYP	CHAR	4	0	Infotypes to be tested
28	RELDT			RELDT	DATS	8	0	Release date
29	CKREP			CKREP	CHAR	8	0	Test report
30	CKTIM			CKTIM	TIMS	6	0	Last tested at
31	.INCLUDE			CI_P0130	STRU	0	0	

Figure A.15   Infotype 0130 — Test Procedures Time Evaluation, continued

Ref	Field	Key Field	Initial Values	Data Element	Data Type	Length	Decimals	Description
1	MANDT	X	X	MANDT	CLNT	3	0	Client
2	.INCLUDE	X	X	PAKEY	STRU	0	0	Key for HR Master Data
3	PERNR	X	X	PERSNO	NUMC	8	0	Personnel number
4	SUBTY	X	X	SUBTY	CHAR	4	0	Subtype
5	OBJPS	X	X	OBJPS	CHAR	2	0	Object Identification
6	SPRPS	X	X	SPRPS	CHAR	1	0	Lock Indicator for HR Master Data Record
7	ENDDA	X	X	ENDDA	DATS	8	0	End Date
8	BEGDA	X	X	BEGDA	DATS	8	0	Start Date
9	SEQNR	X	X	SEQNR	NUMC	3	0	Number of Infotype Record with Same Key
10	.INCLUDE			PSHD1	STRU	0	0	HR Master Record: Control Field
11	AEDTM			AEDAT	DATS	8	0	Changed On
12	UNAME			AENAM	CHAR	12	0	Name of Person Who Changed Object
13	HISTO			HISTO	CHAR	1	0	Historical Record Flag
14	ITXEX			ITXEX	CHAR	1	0	Text Exists for Infotype
15	REFEX			PRFEX	CHAR	1	0	Reference Fields Exist (Primary/Secondary Costs)
16	ORDEX			ORDEX	CHAR	1	0	Confirmation Fields Exist
17	ITBLD			ITBLD	CHAR	2	0	Infotype Screen Control
18	PREAS			PREAS	CHAR	2	0	Reason for Changing Master Data
19	FLAG1			NUSED	CHAR	1	0	Reserved Field/Unused Field
20	FLAG2			NUSED	CHAR	1	0	Reserved Field/Unused Field

Figure A.16   Infotype 0315 — Time Sheet Defaults

Ref	Field	Key Field	Initial Values	Data Element	Data Type	Length	Decimals	Description
21	FLAG3			NUSED	CHAR	1	0	Reserved Field/Unused Field
22	FLAG4			NUSED	CHAR	1	0	Reserved Field/Unused Field
23	RESE1			NUSED2	CHAR	2	0	Reserved Field/Unused Field of Length 2
24	RESE2			NUSED2	CHAR	2	0	Reserved Field/Unused Field of Length 2
25	GRPVL			PCCE_GPVAL	CHAR	4	0	Grouping Value for Personnel Assignments
26	.INCLUDE			PS0315	STRU	0	0	CATS: Sender Information
27	KOSTL			SKOSTL	CHAR	10	0	Sender Cost Center
28	LSTAR			LSTAR	CHAR	6	0	Activity Type
29	PLSTA			PLSTA	CHAR	6	0	Master activity type
30	WERKS			WERKS_D	CHAR	4	0	Plant
31	LIFNR			ELIFN	CHAR	10	0	Vendor Account Number
32	EBELN			SEBELN	CHAR	10	0	Sending purchase order
33	EBELP			SEBELP	NUMC	5	0	Sending purchase order item
34	LSTNR			ASNUM	CHAR	18	0	Activity Number
35	SPRZNR			CO_PRZNR	CHAR	12	0	Business Process
36	ACCNT			CATSACCNT	CHAR	1	0	Required Time Recording in Time Sheet
37	.INCLUDE			CI_P0315	STRU	0	0	

Figure A.17 Infotype 0315 — Time Sheet Defaults, continued

Ref	Field	Key Field	Initial Values	Data Element	Data Type	Length	Decimals	Description
1	MANDT	X	X	MANDT	CLNT	3	0	Client
2	.INCLUDE	X	X	PAKEY	STRU	0	0	Key for HR Master Data
3	PERNR	X	X	PERSNO	NUMC	8	0	Personnel number
4	SUBTY	X	X	SUBTY	CHAR	4	0	Subtype
5	OBJPS	X	X	OBJPS	CHAR	2	0	Object Identification
6	SPRPS	X	X	SPRPS	CHAR	1	0	Lock Indicator for HR Master Data Record
7	ENDDA	X	X	ENDDA	DATS	8	0	End Date
8	BEGDA	X	X	BEGDA	DATS	8	0	Start Date
9	SEQNR	X	X	SEQNR	NUMC	3	0	Number of Infotype Record with Same Key
10	.INCLUDE			PSHD1	STRU	0	0	HR Master Record: Control Field
11	AEDTM			AEDAT	DATS	8	0	Changed On
12	UNAME			AENAM	CHAR	12	0	Name of Person Who Changed Object
13	HISTO			HISTO	CHAR	1	0	Historical Record Flag
14	ITXEX			ITXEX	CHAR	1	0	Text Exists for Infotype
15	REFEX			PRFEX	CHAR	1	0	Reference Fields Exist (Primary/Secondary Costs)
16	ORDEX			ORDEX	CHAR	1	0	Confirmation Fields Exist
17	ITBLD			ITBLD	CHAR	2	0	Infotype Screen Control
18	PREAS			PREAS	CHAR	2	0	Reason for Changing Master Data
19	FLAG1			NUSED	CHAR	1	0	Reserved Field/Unused Field
20	FLAG2			NUSED	CHAR	1	0	Reserved Field/Unused Field
21	FLAG3			NUSED	CHAR	1	0	Reserved Field/Unused Field
22	FLAG4			NUSED	CHAR	1	0	Reserved Field/Unused Field

Figure A.18 Infotype 0416 — Time Quota Compensation

Ref	Field	Key Field	Initial Values	Data Element	Data Type	Length	Decimals	Description
23	RESE1			NUSED2	CHAR	2	0	Reserved Field/Unused Field of Length 2
24	RESE2			NUSED2	CHAR	2	0	Reserved Field/Unused Field of Length 2
25	GRPVL			PCCE_GPVAL	CHAR	4	0	Grouping Value for Personnel Assignments
26	.INCLUDE			PS0416	STRU	0	0	Time Quota Compensation Infotype
27	QCTYP			TIM_QCTYP	CHAR	4	0	Time Quota compensation method
28	STYPE			QTYPE	CHAR	1	0	Quota type (attendance/absence quota)
29	WAERS			WAERS	CUKY	5	0	Currency Key
30	QTYPE			ABWKO	NUMC	2	0	Absence Quota Type
31	SRULE			DEDRG	NUMC	3	0	Rule for deduction sequence of quotas
32	NUMBR			PTM_QSETTLED	DEC	10	5	Quota Number Compensated
33	AMONT			ABBTR	CURR	9	2	Amount for time quota compensation
34	WGTYP			LGART	CHAR	4	0	Wage Type
35	QUONR			PTM_QUONR	NUMC	20	0	Counter for time quotas
36	DOCSY			PTM_DOCSY	CHAR	10	0	Logical system for document (personnel time)
37	DOCNR			PTM_DOCNR	NUMC	20	0	Document number for time data
38	NOPAY			NOLCOMP	CHAR	1	0	Do Not Account
39	.INCLUDE			CI_P0416	STRU	0	0	

Figure A.19 Infotype 0416 — Time Quota Compensation, continued

Ref	Field	Key Field	Initial Values	Data Element	Data Type	Length	Decimals	Description
1	MANDT			MANDT	CLNT	3	0	Client
2	.INCLUDE			PAKEY	STRU	0	0	Key for HR Master Data
3	PERNR			PERSNO	NUMC	8	0	Personnel number
4	SUBTY			SUBTY	CHAR	4	0	Subtype
5	OBJPS			OBJPS	CHAR	2	0	Object Identification
6	SPRPS			SPRPS	CHAR	1	0	Lock Indicator for HR Master Data Record
7	ENDDA			ENDDA	DATS	8	0	End Date
8	BEGDA			BEGDA	DATS	8	0	Start Date
9	SEQNR			SEQNR	NUMC	3	0	Number of Infotype Record with Same Key
10	.INCLUDE			PSHD1	STRU	0	0	HR Master Record: Control Field
11	AEDTM			AEDAT	DATS	8	0	Changed On
12	UNAME			AENAM	CHAR	12	0	Name of Person Who Changed Object
13	HISTO			HISTO	CHAR	1	0	Historical Record Flag
14	ITXEX			ITXEX	CHAR	1	0	Text Exists for Infotype
15	REFEX			PRFEX	CHAR	1	0	Reference Fields Exist (Primary/Secondary Costs)
16	ORDEX			ORDEX	CHAR	1	0	Confirmation Fields Exist
17	ITBLD			ITBLD	CHAR	2	0	Infotype Screen Control
18	PREAS			PREAS	CHAR	2	0	Reason for Changing Master Data
19	FLAG1			NUSED	CHAR	1	0	Reserved Field/Unused Field
20	FLAG2			NUSED	CHAR	1	0	Reserved Field/Unused Field
21	FLAG3			NUSED	CHAR	1	0	Reserved Field/Unused Field
22	FLAG4			NUSED	CHAR	1	0	Reserved Field/Unused Field
23	RESE1			NUSED2	CHAR	2	0	Reserved Field/Unused Field of Length 2
24	RESE2			NUSED2	CHAR	2	0	Reserved Field/Unused Field of Length 2
25	GRPVL			PCCE_GPVAL	CHAR	4	0	Grouping Value for Personnel Assignments

Figure A.20 Infotype 0672 — FLMA Event Screen

477

Ref	Field	Key Field	Initial Values	Data Element	Data Type	Length	Decimals	Description
26	.INCLUDE			PS0672	STRU	0	0	FMLA Event Infotype
27	FMLAR			PT_FMLAR	NUMC	3	0	FMLA Rule
28	REASN			PT_FMLA_REASON	CHAR	5	0	FMLA Reason
29	FMLAN			PT_FMLA_REQNR	NUMC	12	0	FMLA Request Number
30	STATU			PT_FMLA_STATUS	CHAR	1	0	Approval Status
31	CONFL			PT_FMLA_CONFL	CHAR	1	0	Continuity Indicator
32	INTHR			PT_FMLA_INTHR	DEC	7	2	Planned Hours for Intermittent FMLA
33	MEDCF			PT_FMLA_MEDCF	CHAR	1	0	Indicator: Medical Certificate Submitted
34	RQDAY			PT_FMLA_RQDAY	DATS	8	0	Date Request Made
35	DEROL			PT_FMLA_DEROL	DEC	3	0	Length of Rolling Deduction Interval
36	DEBEG			PT_FMLA_DEBEG	DATS	8	0	Deduction from
37	DEEND			PT_FMLA_DEEND	DATS	8	0	Deduction to
38	WCONV			PT_FMLA	DEC	8	4	Week Converter
39	ELIFL			PT_FMLA_ELIFL	CHAR	1	0	Eligibility Indicator
40	ELHRS			PT_FMLA_ELHRS	DEC	9	4	Creditable Hours from Eligibility Check
41	ELMTH			PT_FMLA_ELMTH	NUMC	3	0	Creditable Length of Service in Months
42	ELDTE			PT_FMLA_ELDTE	DATS	8	0	Reference Date for Eligibility Check
43	OELHR			PT_FMLA_OELHR	DEC	9	4	Creditable Hours from First Eligibility Check
44	OELMT			PT_FMLA_OELMT	NUMC	3	0	Creditable Length of Service (Months) from First Elig. Check
45	OELDT			PT_FMLA_OELDT	DATS	8	0	Date of First Eligibility Check
46	DOCNR			PT_FMLA_DOCNR	NUMC	20	0	Number for FMLA Events
47	DOCSY			PTM_DOCSY	CHAR	10	0	Logical system for document (personnel time)
48	SENLM			PT_FMLA_SENIO	NUMC	3	0	Seniority Threshold for Eligibility
49	WKHLM			PT_FMLA_WKHRS	DEC	7	2	Actual Working Hours Threshold for Eligibility
50	ENTIT			PT_FMLA_ENTIT	DEC	5	2	FMLA Entitlement in Weeks
51	REMAN			PT_FMLA_REMAN				FMLA Remainder in Weeks

Figure A.21 Infotype 0672 — FMLA Event, continued

Ref	Field	Key Field	Initial Values	Data Element	Data Type	Length	Decimals	Description
1	MANDT	X	X	MANDT	CLNT	3	0	Client
2	.INCLUDE	X	X	PAKEY	STRU	0	0	Key for HR Master Data
3	PERNR	X	X	PERSNO	NUMC	8	0	Personnel number
4	SUBTY	X	X	SUBTY	CHAR	4	0	Subtype
5	OBJPS	X	X	OBJPS	CHAR	2	0	Object Identification
6	SPRPS	X	X	SPRPS	CHAR	1	0	Lock Indicator for HR Master Data Record
7	ENDDA	X	X	ENDDA	DATS	8	0	End Date
8	BEGDA	X	X	BEGDA	DATS	8	0	Start Date
9	SEQNR	X	X	SEQNR	NUMC	3	0	Number of Infotype Record with Same Key
10	.INCLUDE			PSHD1	STRU	0	0	HR Master Record: Control Field
11	AEDTM			AEDAT	DATS	8	0	Changed On
12	UNAME			AENAM	CHAR	12	0	Name of Person Who Changed Object
13	HISTO			HISTO	CHAR	1	0	Historical Record Flag
14	ITXEX			ITXEX	CHAR	1	0	Text Exists for Infotype
15	REFEX			PRFEX	CHAR	1	0	Reference Fields Exist (Primary/Secondary Costs)
16	ORDEX			ORDEX	CHAR	1	0	Confirmation Fields Exist
17	ITBLD			ITBLD	CHAR	2	0	Infotype Screen Control
18	PREAS			PREAS	CHAR	2	0	Reason for Changing Master Data
19	FLAG1			NUSED	CHAR	1	0	Reserved Field/Unused Field
20	FLAG2			NUSED	CHAR	1	0	Reserved Field/Unused Field
21	FLAG3			NUSED	CHAR	1	0	Reserved Field/Unused Field
22	FLAG4			NUSED	CHAR	1	0	Reserved Field/Unused Field

Figure A.22 Infotype 2001 — Absences

Ref	Field	Key Field	Initial Values	Data Element	Data Type	Length	Decimals	Description
23	RESE1			NUSED2	CHAR	2	0	Reserved Field/Unused Field of Length 2
24	RESE2			NUSED2	CHAR	2	0	Reserved Field/Unused Field of Length 2
25	GRPVL			PCCE_GPVAL	CHAR	4	0	Grouping Value for Personnel Assignments
26	.INCLUDE			PS2001	STRU	0	0	Personnel Time Record: Infotype 2001 (Absences)
27	BEGUZ			BEGTI	TIMS	6	0	Start Time
28	ENDUZ			ENDTI	TIMS	6	0	End Time
29	VTKEN			VTKEN	CHAR	1	0	Previous Day Indicator
30	AWART			AWART	CHAR	4	0	Attendance or Absence Type
31	ABWTG			ABWTG	DEC	6	2	Attendance and Absence Days
32	STDAZ			ABSTD	DEC	7	2	Absence hours
33	ABRTG			ABRTG	DEC	6	2	Payroll days
34	ABRST			ABRST	DEC	7	2	Payroll hours
35	ANRTG			ANRTG	DEC	6	2	Days credited for continued pay
36	LFZED			LFZED	DATS	8	0	End of continued pay
37	KRGED			KRGED	DATS	8	0	End of sick pay
38	KBBEG			KBBEG	DATS	8	0	Certified start of sickness
39	RMDDA			RMDDA	DATS	8	0	Date on which illness was confirmed
40	KENN1			KENN1	DEC	2	0	Indicator for Subsequent Illness
41	KENN2			KENN2	DEC	2	0	Indicator for repeated illness
42	KALTG			KALTG	DEC	6	2	Calendar days
43	URMAN			URMAN	CHAR	1	0	Indicator for manual leave deduction
44	BEGVA			BEGVA	NUMC	4	0	Start year for leave deduction
45	BWGRL			PTM_VBAS7S	CURR	13	2	Valuation Basis for Different Payment
46	AUFKZ			AUFKN	CHAR	1	0	Extra Pay Indicator
47	TRFGR			TRFGR	CHAR	8	0	Pay Scale Group
48	TRFST			TRFST	CHAR	2	0	Pay Scale Level

Figure A.23 Infotype 2001 — Absences, continued

Ref	Field	Key Field	Initial Values	Data Element	Data Type	Length	Decimals	Description
49	PRAKN			PRAKN	CHAR	2	0	Premium Number
50	PRAKZ			PRAKZ	NUMC	4	0	Premium Indicator
51	OTYPE			OTYPE	CHAR	2	0	Object Type
52	PLANS			PLANS	NUMC	8	0	Position
53	MLDDA			MLDDA	DATS	8	0	Reported on
54	MLDUZ			MLDUZ	TIMS	6	0	Reported at
55	RMDUZ			RMDUZ	TIMS	6	0	Sickness confirmed at
56	VORGS			VORGS	CHAR	15	0	Superior Out Sick (Illness)
57	UMSKD			UMSKD	CHAR	6	0	Code for description of illness
58	UMSCH			UMSCH	CHAR	20	0	Description of illness
59	REFNR			RFNUM	CHAR	8	0	Reference number
60	UNFAL			UNFAL	CHAR	1	0	Absent due to accident?
61	STKRV			STKRV	CHAR	4	0	Subtype for sickness tracking
62	STUND			STUND	CHAR	4	0	Subtype for accident data
63	PSARB			PSARB	DEC	4	2	Work capacity percentage
64	AINFT			AINFT	CHAR	4	0	Infotype that maintains 2001
65	GENER			PGENER	CHAR	1	0	Generation flag
66	HRSIF			HRS_INPFL	CHAR	1	0	Set number of hours
67	ALLDF			ALLDF	CHAR	1	0	Record is for Full Day
68	WAERS			WAERS	CUKY	5	0	Currency Key
69	LOGSYS			LOGSYS	CHAR	10	0	Logical system
70	AWTYP			AWTYP	CHAR	5	0	Reference Transaction
71	AWREF			AWREF	CHAR	10	0	Reference Document Number
72	AWORG			AWORG	CHAR	10	0	Reference Organizational Units
73	DOCSY			PTM_DOCSY	CHAR	10	0	Logical system for document (personnel time)
74	DOCNR			PTM_DOCNR	NUMC	20	0	Document number for time data

Figure A.24 Infotype 2001 — Absences, continued

Ref	Field	Key Field	Initial Values	Data Element	Data Type	Length	Decimals	Description
75	PAYTY			PAYTY	CHAR	1	0	Payroll type
76	PAYID			PAYID	CHAR	1	0	Payroll Identifier
77	BONDT			BONDT	DATS	8	0	Off-cycle payroll payment date
78	OCRSN			PAY_OCRSN	CHAR	4	0	Reason for Off-Cycle Payroll
79	SPPE1			SPPEG	DATS	8	0	End date for continued pay
80	SPPE2			SPPEG	DATS	8	0	End date for continued pay
81	SPPE3			SPPEG	DATS	8	0	End date for continued pay
82	SPPIN			SPPIN	CHAR	1	0	Indicator for manual modifications
83	ZKMKT			P05_ZKMKT	CHAR	1	0	Status of Sickness Notification
84	FAPRS			FAPRS	CHAR	2	0	Evaluation Type for Attendances/Absences
85	.INCLUDE			TMW_TDT_FIELDS	STRU	0	0	Infotype Fields Relevant for Short Descriptions
86	TDLANGU			TMW_TDLANGU	CHAR	10	0	Definition Set for IDs
87	TDSUBLA			TMW_TDSUBLA	CHAR	3	0	Definition Subset for IDs
88	TDTYPE			TDTYPE	CHAR	4	0	Time Data ID Type
89	NXDFL			PTM_NXDFL	CHAR	1	0	Next Day Indicator

Figure A.25 Infotype 2001 — Absences, continued

Ref	Field	Key Field	Initial Values	Data Element	Data Type	Length	Decimals	Description
1	.INCLUDE			PSKEY		0	0	Keys for HR Master Data
2	PERNR			PERNR_D	NUMC	8	0	Personnel Number
3	INFTY			INFTY	CHAR	4	0	Infotype
4	SUBTY			SUBTY	CHAR	4	0	Subtype
5	OBJPS			OBJPS	CHAR	2	0	Object Identification
6	SPRPS			SPRPS	CHAR	1	0	Lock Indicator for HR Master Data Record
7	ENDDA			ENDDA	DATS	8	0	End Date
8	BEGDA			BEGDA	DATS	8	0	Start Date
9	SEQNR			SEQNR	NUMC	3	0	Number of Infotype Record with Same Key
10	.INCLUDE			PSREF		0	0	Assignment Values for HR Objects
11	BUKRS			BUKRS	CHAR	4	0	Company Code
12	GSBER			GSBER	CHAR	4	0	Business Area
13	KOKRS			KOKRS	CHAR	4	0	Controlling Area
14	KOSTL			KOSTL	CHAR	10	0	Cost Center
15	AUFNR			AUFNR	CHAR	12	0	Order Number
16	KSTRG			KSTRG	CHAR	12	0	Cost Object
17	POSNR			PS_PSP_PNR	NUMC	8	0	Work Breakdown Structure Element (WBS Element)
18	NPLNR			NPLNR	CHAR	12	0	Network Number for Account Assignment
19	VORNR			VORNR	CHAR	4	0	Operation/Activity Number
20	KDAUF			KDAUF	CHAR	10	0	Sales Order Number

Figure A.26 Info type 2001/2002 — Additional Information

Ref	Field	Key Field	Initial Values	Data Element	Data Type	Length	Decimals	Description
21	KDPOS			KDPOS	NUMC	6	0	Item Number in Sales Order
22	PAOBJNR			RKEOBJNR	NUMC	10	0	Profitability Segment Number (CO-PA)
23	PRZNR			CO_PRZNR	CHAR	12	0	Business Process
24	FISTL			FISTL	CHAR	16	0	Funds Center
25	FIPOS			FIPOS	CHAR	14	0	Commitment Item
26	GEBER			BP_GEBER	CHAR	10	0	Fund
27	EBELN			EBELN	CHAR	10	0	Purchasing Document Number
28	EBELP			EBELP	NUMC	5	0	Item Number of Purchasing Document
29	LSTNR			ASNUM	CHAR	18	0	Activity Number
30	LTLST			LSTAR	CHAR	6	0	Activity Type
31	SBUKR			BUKRS	CHAR	4	0	Company Code
32	SGSBR			GSBER	CHAR	4	0	Business Area
33	SKOST			KOSTL	CHAR	10	0	Cost Center
34	LSTAR			LSTAR	CHAR	6	0	Activity Type
35	EXBEL			HR_ZUONR	CHAR	18	0	Assignment number
36	MWSKZ			MWSKZ	CHAR	2	0	Sales Tax Code
37	OTYPE			OTYPE	CHAR	2	0	Object Type
38	STELL			STELL	NUMC	8	0	Job
39	POHRS			POHRS	DEC	7	2	Number of Hours for Activity Allocation/External Services
40	DART			DART	CHAR	2	0	Service Type (Public Service Germany)

Figure A.27 Infotype 2001/2002 — Additional Information, continued

Ref	Field	Key Field	Initial Values	Data Element	Data Type	Length	Decimals	Description
41	UDART			UDART	CHAR	2	0	Service Category (Public Service Germany)
42	SGTXT			SGTXT	CHAR	50	0	Item Text
43	TXJCD			TXJCD	CHAR	15	0	Tax Jurisdiction
44	FIPEX			FM_FIPEX	CHAR	24	0	Commitment Item
45	FKBER			FKBER	CHAR	16	0	Functional Area
46	GRANT_NBR			GM_GRANT_NBR	CHAR	20	0	Grant
47	SGEBER			FM_SFONDS	CHAR	10	0	Sender fund
48	SFKBER			SFKTBER	CHAR	16	0	Sending Functional Area
49	SGRANT_NBR			GM_GRANT_SENDER	CHAR	20	0	Sender Grant
50	SEGMENT			FB_SEGMENT	CHAR	10	0	Segment for Segmental Reporting
51	SSEGMENT			FB_SEGMENT	CHAR	10	0	Segment for Segmental Reporting

Figure A.28 Infotype 2001/2002 — Additional Information, continued

Ref	Field	Key Field	Initial Values	Data Element	Data Type	Length	Decimals	Description
1	MANDT	X	X	MANDT	CLNT	3	0	Client
2	.INCLUDE	X	X	PAKEY	STRU	0	0	Key for HR Master Data
3	PERNR	X	X	PERSNO	NUMC	8	0	Personnel number
4	SUBTY	X	X	SUBTY	CHAR	4	0	Subtype
5	OBJPS	X	X	OBJPS	CHAR	2	0	Object Identification
6	SPRPS	X	X	SPRPS	CHAR	1	0	Lock Indicator for HR Master Data Record
7	ENDDA	X	X	ENDDA	DATS	8	0	End Date
8	BEGDA	X	X	BEGDA	DATS	8	0	Start Date
9	SEQNR	X	X	SEQNR	NUMC	3	0	Number of Infotype Record with Same Key
10	.INCLUDE			PSHD1	STRU	0	0	HR Master Record: Control Field
11	AEDTM			AEDAT	DATS	8	0	Changed On
12	UNAME			AENAM	CHAR	12	0	Name of Person Who Changed Object
13	HISTO			HISTO	CHAR	1	0	Historical Record Flag
14	ITXEX			ITXEX	CHAR	1	0	Text Exists for Infotype
15	REFEX			PRFEX	CHAR	1	0	Reference Fields Exist (Primary/Secondary Costs)
16	ORDEX			ORDEX	CHAR	1	0	Confirmation Fields Exist
17	ITBLD			ITBLD	CHAR	2	0	Infotype Screen Control
18	PREAS			PREAS	CHAR	2	0	Reason for Changing Master Data
19	FLAG1			NUSED	CHAR	1	0	Reserved Field/Unused Field
20	FLAG2			NUSED	CHAR	1	0	Reserved Field/Unused Field

Figure A.29 Infotype 2002 — Attendances

Ref	Field	Key Field	Initial Values	Data Element	Data Type	Length	Decimals	Description
21	FLAG3			NUSED	CHAR	1	0	Reserved Field/Unused Field
22	FLAG4			NUSED	CHAR	1	0	Reserved Field/Unused Field
23	RESE1			NUSED2	CHAR	2	0	Reserved Field/Unused Field of Length 2
24	RESE2			NUSED2	CHAR	2	0	Reserved Field/Unused Field of Length 2
25	GRPVL			PCCE_GPVAL	CHAR	4	0	Grouping Value for Personnel Assignments
26	.INCLUDE			PS2002	STRU	0	0	HR Time Record: Infotype 2002 (Attendances)
27	BEGUZ			BEGTI	TIMS	6	0	Start Time
28	ENDUZ			ENDTI	TIMS	6	0	End Time
29	VTKEN			VTKEN	CHAR	1	0	Previous Day Indicator
30	AWART			AWART	CHAR	4	0	Attendance or Absence Type
31	ABWTG			ABWTG	DEC	6	2	Attendance and Absence Days
32	ABRTG			ABRTG	DEC	6	2	Payroll days
33	ABRST			ABRST	DEC	7	2	Payroll hours
34	KALTG			KALTG	DEC	6	2	Calendar days
35	STDAZ			ATTHR	DEC	7	2	Attendance hours
36	LGART			LGART	CHAR	4	0	Wage Type
37	BWGRL			PTM_VBAS7S	CURR	13	2	Valuation Basis for Different Payment
38	AUFKZ			AUFKN	CHAR	1	0	Extra Pay Indicator
39	VERSL			VRSCH	CHAR	1	0	Overtime Compensation Type
40	TRFGR			TRFGR	CHAR	8	0	Pay Scale Group

Figure A.30 Infotype 2002 — Attendances, continued

Ref	Field	Key Field	Initial Values	Data Element	Data Type	Length	Decimals	Description
41	TRFST			TRFST	CHAR	2	0	Pay Scale Level
42	PRAKN			PRAKN	CHAR	2	0	Premium Number
43	PRAKZ			PRAKZ	NUMC	4	0	Premium Indicator
44	OTYPE			OTYPE	CHAR	2	0	Object Type
45	PLANS			PLANS	NUMC	8	0	Position
46	GENER			PGENER	CHAR	1	0	Generation flag
47	EXBEL			EXBEL	CHAR	8	0	External Document Number
48	HRSIF			HRS_INPFL	CHAR	1	0	Set number of hours
49	ALLDF			ALLDF	CHAR	1	0	Record is for Full Day
50	WAERS			WAERS	CUKY	5	0	Currency Key
51	LOGSYS			LOGSYS	CHAR	10	0	Logical system
52	AWTYP			AWTYP	CHAR	5	0	Reference Transaction
53	AWREF			AWREF	CHAR	10	0	Reference Document Number
54	AWORG			AWORG	CHAR	10	0	Reference Organizational Units
55	DOCSY			PTM_DOCSY	CHAR	10	0	Logical system for document (personnel time)
56	DOCNR			PTM_DOCNR	NUMC	20	0	Document number for time data
57	WTART			WTART	CHAR	4	0	Work tax area
58	FAPRS			FAPRS	CHAR	2	0	Evaluation Type for Attendances/Absences
59	.INCLUDE			TMW_TDT_FIELDS	STRU	0	0	Infotype Fields Relevant for Short Descriptions
60	TDLANGU			TMW_TDLANGU	CHAR	10	0	Definition Set for IDs

Figure A.31 Infotype 2002 — Attendances, continued

Ref	Field	Key Field	Initial Values	Data Element	Data Type	Length	Decimals	Description
61	TDSUBLA			TMW_TD SUBLA	CHAR	3	0	Definition Subset for IDs
62	TDTYPE			TDTYPE	CHAR	4	0	Time Data ID Type
63	.INCLUDE			HRTIM_ATT_BREAKS	STRU	0	0	Breaks During Attendances
64	KEPAU			TIM_KEPAU	CHAR	1	0	No break
65	EXPAU			TIM_EXPAU	CHAR	1	0	Breaks Specified Explicitly
66	.INCLUDE			HRTIM_BREAKS	STRU	0	0	Breaks
67	PBEG1			PDBEG	TIMS	6	0	Start of Break
68	PEND1			PDEND	TIMS	6	0	End of Break
69	PBEZ1			PDBEZ	DEC	4	2	Paid Break Period
70	PUNB1			PDUNB	DEC	4	2	Unpaid Break Period
71	PBEG2			PDBEG	TIMS	6	0	Start of Break
72	PEND2			PDEND	TIMS	6	0	End of Break
73	PBEZ2			PDBEZ	DEC	4	2	Paid Break Period
74	PUNB2			PDUNB	DEC	4	2	Unpaid Break Period
75	NXDFL			PTM_NXDFL	CHAR	1	0	Next Day Indicator

Figure A.32 Infotype 2002 — Attendances, continued

Ref	Field	Key Field	Initial Values	Data Element	Data Type	Length	Decimals	Description
1	MANDT	X	X	MANDT	CLNT	3	0	Client
2	.INCLUDE	X	X	PAKEY	STRU	0	0	Key for HR Master Data
3	PERNR	X	X	PERSNO	NUMC	8	0	Personnel number
4	SUBTY	X	X	SUBTY	CHAR	4	0	Subtype
5	OBJPS	X	X	OBJPS	CHAR	2	0	Object Identification
6	SPRPS	X	X	SPRPS	CHAR	1	0	Lock Indicator for HR Master Data Record
7	ENDDA	X	X	ENDDA	DATS	8	0	End Date
8	BEGDA	X	X	BEGDA	DATS	8	0	Start Date
9	SEQNR	X	X	SEQNR	NUMC	3	0	Number of Infotype Record with Same Key
10	.INCLUDE			PSHD1	STRU	0	0	HR Master Record: Control Field
11	AEDTM			AEDAT	DATS	8	0	Changed On
12	UNAME			AENAM	CHAR	12	0	Name of Person Who Changed Object
13	HISTO			HISTO	CHAR	1	0	Historical Record Flag
14	ITXEX			ITXEX	CHAR	1	0	Text Exists for Infotype
15	REFEX			PRFEX	CHAR	1	0	Reference Fields Exist (Primary/Secondary Costs)
16	ORDEX			ORDEX	CHAR	1	0	Confirmation Fields Exist
17	ITBLD			ITBLD	CHAR	2	0	Infotype Screen Control
18	PREAS			PREAS	CHAR	2	0	Reason for Changing Master Data
19	FLAG1			NUSED	CHAR	1	0	Reserved Field/Unused Field
20	FLAG2			NUSED	CHAR	1	0	Reserved Field/Unused Field

Figure A.33 Infotype 2003 — Substitutions

Ref	Field	Key Field	Initial Values	Data Element	Data Type	Length	Decimals	Description
21	FLAG3			NUSED	CHAR	1	0	Reserved Field/Unused Field
22	FLAG4			NUSED	CHAR	1	0	Reserved Field/Unused Field
23	RESE1			NUSED2	CHAR	2	0	Reserved Field/Unused Field of Length 2
24	RESE2			NUSED2	CHAR	2	0	Reserved Field/Unused Field of Length 2
25	GRPVL			PCCE_GPVAL	CHAR	4	0	Grouping Value for Personnel Assignments
26	.INCLUDE			PS2003	STRU	0	0	HR Time Record: Infotype 2003 (Substitutions)
27	BEGUZ			BEGUZ	TIMS	6	0	Start Time
28	ENDUZ			ENDUZ	TIMS	6	0	End Time
29	VTKEN			VTKEN	CHAR	1	0	Previous Day Indicator
30	VTART			VTART	CHAR	2	0	Substitution Type
31	STDAZ			VTSTD	DEC	7	2	Substitution hours
32	PAMOD			PAMOD	CHAR	4	0	Work Break Schedule
33	PBEG1			PDBEG	TIMS	6	0	Start of Break
34	PEND1			PDEND	TIMS	6	0	End of Break
35	PBEZ1			PDBEZ	DEC	4	2	Paid Break Period
36	PUNB1			PDUNB	DEC	4	2	Unpaid Break Period
37	PBEG2			PDBEG	TIMS	6	0	Start of Break
38	PEND2			PDEND	TIMS	6	0	End of Break
39	PBEZ2			PDBEZ	DEC	4	2	Paid Break Period
40	PUNB2			PDUNB	DEC	4	2	Unpaid Break Period

Figure A.34 Infotype 2003 — Substitutions, continued

Ref	Field	Key Field	Initial Values	Data Element	Data Type	Length	Decimals	Description
41	ZEITY			DZEITY	CHAR	1	0	Employee Subgroup Grouping for Work Schedules
42	MOFID			HIDENT	CHAR	2	0	Public Holiday Calendar
43	MOSID			MOSID	NUMC	2	0	Personnel Subarea Grouping for Work Schedules
44	SCHKZ			SCHKN	CHAR	8	0	Work Schedule Rule
45	MOTPR			MOTPR	NUMC	2	0	Personnel Subarea Grouping for Daily Work Schedules
46	TPROG			TPROG	CHAR	4	0	Daily Work Schedule
47	VARIA			VARIA	CHAR	1	0	Daily Work Schedule Variant
48	TAGTY			TAGTY	CHAR	1	0	Day Type
49	TPKLA			TPKLA	CHAR	1	0	Daily Work Schedule Class
50	VPERN			VPERN	NUMC	8	0	Substitute Personnel Number
51	AUFKZ			AUFKN	CHAR	1	0	Extra Pay Indicator
52	BWGRL			PTM_VBAS7S	CURR	13	2	Valuation Basis for Different Payment
53	TRFGR			TRFGR	CHAR	8	0	Pay Scale Group
54	TRFST			TRFST	CHAR	2	0	Pay Scale Level
55	PRAKN			PRAKN	CHAR	2	0	Premium Number
56	PRAKZ			PRAKZ	NUMC	4	0	Premium Indicator
57	OTYPE			OTYPE	CHAR	2	0	Object Type
58	PLANS			PLANS	NUMC	8	0	Position
59	EXBEL			EXBEL	CHAR	8	0	External Document Number
60	WAERS			WAERS	CUKY	5	0	Currency Key

Figure A.35 Infotype 2003 — Substitutions, continued

Ref	Field	Key Field	Initial Values	Data Element	Data Type	Length	Decimals	Description
61	WTART			WTART	CHAR	4	0	Work tax area
62	.INCLUDE			TMW_TDT_FIELDS	STRU	0	0	Infotype Fields Relevant for Short Descriptions
63	TDLANGU			TMW_TDLANGU	CHAR	10	0	Definition Set for IDs
64	TDSUBLA			TMW_TDSUBLA	CHAR	3	0	Definition Subset for IDs
65	TDTYPE			TDTYPE	CHAR	4	0	Time Data ID Type
66	LOGSYS			LOGSYS	CHAR	10	0	Logical system
67	AWTYP			AWTYP	CHAR	5	0	Reference Transaction
68	AWREF			AWREF	CHAR	10	0	Reference Document Number
69	AWORG			AWORG	CHAR	10	0	Reference Organizational Units
70	NXDFL			PTM_NXDFL	CHAR	1	0	Next Day Indicator

Figure A.36 Infotype 2003 — Substitutions, continued

485

Ref	Field	Key Field	Initial Values	Data Element	Data Type	Length	Decimals	Description
1	MANDT	X	X	MANDT	CLNT	3	0	Client
2	.INCLUDE	X	X	PAKEY	STRU	0	0	Key for HR Master Data
3	PERNR	X	X	PERSNO	NUMC	8	0	Personnel number
4	SUBTY	X	X	SUBTY	CHAR	4	0	Subtype
5	OBJPS	X	X	OBJPS	CHAR	2	0	Object Identification
6	SPRPS	X	X	SPRPS	CHAR	1	0	Lock Indicator for HR Master Data Record
7	ENDDA	X	X	ENDDA	DATS	8	0	End Date
8	BEGDA	X	X	BEGDA	DATS	8	0	Start Date
9	SEQNR	X	X	SEQNR	NUMC	3	0	Number of Infotype Record with Same Key
10	.INCLUDE			PSHD1	STRU	0	0	HR Master Record: Control Field
11	AEDTM			AEDAT	DATS	8	0	Changed On
12	UNAME			AENAM	CHAR	12	0	Name of Person Who Changed Object
13	HISTO			HISTO	CHAR	1	0	Historical Record Flag
14	ITXEX			ITXEX	CHAR	1	0	Text Exists for Infotype
15	REFEX			PRFEX	CHAR	1	0	Reference Fields Exist (Primary/Secondary Costs)
16	ORDEX			ORDEX	CHAR	1	0	Confirmation Fields Exist
17	ITBLD			ITBLD	CHAR	2	0	Infotype Screen Control
18	PREAS			PREAS	CHAR	2	0	Reason for Changing Master Data
19	FLAG1			NUSED	CHAR	1	0	Reserved Field/Unused Field
20	FLAG2			NUSED	CHAR	1	0	Reserved Field/Unused Field

Figure A.37 Infotype 2004 — Availability

Ref	Field	Key Field	Initial Values	Data Element	Data Type	Length	Decimals	Description
21	FLAG3			NUSED	CHAR	1	0	Reserved Field/Unused Field
22	FLAG4			NUSED	CHAR	1	0	Reserved Field/Unused Field
23	RESE1			NUSED2	CHAR	2	0	Reserved Field/Unused Field of Length 2
24	RESE2			NUSED2	CHAR	2	0	Reserved Field/Unused Field of Length 2
25	GRPVL			PCCE_GPVAL	CHAR	4	0	Grouping Value for Personnel Assignments
26	.INCLUDE			PS2004	STRU	0	0	HR Time Record: Infotype 2004 (Availability)
27	BEGUZ			BEGUZ	TIMS	6	0	Start Time
28	ENDUZ			ENDUZ	TIMS	6	0	End Time
29	VTKEN			VTKEN	CHAR	1	0	Previous Day Indicator
30	STNBY			STNBY	CHAR	2	0	Availability Subtype
31	ZEITY			DZEITY	CHAR	1	0	Employee Subgroup Grouping for Work Schedules
32	MOFID			HIDENT	CHAR	2	0	Public Holiday Calendar
33	MOSID			MOSID	NUMC	2	0	Personnel Subarea Grouping for Work Schedules
34	SCHKZ			SCHKN	CHAR	8	0	Work Schedule Rule
35	MOTPR			MOTPR	NUMC	2	0	Personnel Subarea Grouping for Daily Work Schedules
36	TPROG			TPROG	CHAR	4	0	Daily Work Schedule
37	VARIA			VARIA	CHAR	1	0	Daily Work Schedule Variant
38	AUFKZ			AUFKN	CHAR	1	0	Extra Pay Indicator
39	BWGRL			PTM_VBAS7S	CURR	13	2	Valuation Basis for Different Payment

Figure A.38 Infotype 2004 — Availability, continued

Ref	Field	Key Field	Initial Values	Data Element	Data Type	Length	Decimals	Description
40	TRFGR			TRFGR	CHAR	8	0	Pay Scale Group
41	TRFST			TRFST	CHAR	2	0	Pay Scale Level
42	PRAKN			PRAKN	CHAR	2	0	Premium Number
43	PRAKZ			PRAKZ	NUMC	4	0	Premium Indicator
44	OTYPE			OTYPE	CHAR	2	0	Object Type
45	PLANS			PLANS	NUMC	8	0	Position
46	EXBEL			EXBEL	CHAR	8	0	External Document Number
47	WAERS			WAERS	CUKY	5	0	Currency Key
48	WTART			WTART	CHAR	4	0	Work tax area
49	ADPER			TIM_AVAIL_DIST_PERC	DEC	5	2	Availability Distribution Key (currently not functional)
50	.INCLUDE			TMW_TDT_FIELDS	STRU	0	0	Infotype Fields Relevant for Short Descriptions
51	TDLANGU			TMW_TDLANGU	CHAR	10	0	Definition Set for IDs
52	TDSUBLA			TMW_TDSUBLA	CHAR	3	0	Definition Subset for IDs
53	TDTYPE			TDTYPE	CHAR	4	0	Time Data ID Type

Figure A.39   Infotype 2004 — Availability, continued

Ref	Field	Key Field	Initial Values	Data Element	Data Type	Length	Decimals	Description
1	MANDT	X	X	MANDT	CLNT	3	0	Client
2	.INCLUDE	X	X	PAKEY	STRU	0	0	Key for HR Master Data
3	PERNR	X	X	PERSNO	NUMC	8	0	Personnel number
4	SUBTY	X	X	SUBTY	CHAR	4	0	Subtype
5	OBJPS	X	X	OBJPS	CHAR	2	0	Object Identification
6	SPRPS	X	X	SPRPS	CHAR	1	0	Lock Indicator for HR Master Data Record
7	ENDDA	X	X	ENDDA	DATS	8	0	End Date
8	BEGDA	X	X	BEGDA	DATS	8	0	Start Date
9	SEQNR	X	X	SEQNR	NUMC	3	0	Number of Infotype Record with Same Key
10	.INCLUDE			PSHD1	STRU	0	0	HR Master Record: Control Field
11	AEDTM			AEDAT	DATS	8	0	Changed On
12	UNAME			AENAM	CHAR	12	0	Name of Person Who Changed Object
13	HISTO			HISTO	CHAR	1	0	Historical Record Flag
14	ITXEX			ITXEX	CHAR	1	0	Text Exists for Infotype
15	REFEX			PRFEX	CHAR	1	0	Reference Fields Exist (Primary/Secondary Costs)
16	ORDEX			ORDEX	CHAR	1	0	Confirmation Fields Exist
17	ITBLD			ITBLD	CHAR	2	0	Infotype Screen Control
18	PREAS			PREAS	CHAR	2	0	Reason for Changing Master Data
19	FLAG1			NUSED	CHAR	1	0	Reserved Field/Unused Field
20	FLAG2			NUSED	CHAR	1	0	Reserved Field/Unused Field
21	FLAG3			NUSED	CHAR	1	0	Reserved Field/Unused Field
22	FLAG4			NUSED	CHAR	1	0	Reserved Field/Unused Field

Figure A.40   Infotype 2005 — Overtime

Ref	Field	Key Field	Initial Values	Data Element	Data Type	Length	Decimals	Description
23	RESE1			NUSED2	CHAR	2	0	Reserved Field/Unused Field of Length 2
24	RESE2			NUSED2	CHAR	2	0	Reserved Field/Unused Field of Length 2
25	GRPVL			PCCE_GPVAL	CHAR	4	0	Grouping Value for Personnel Assignments
26	.INCLUDE			PS2005	STRU	0	0	HR Time Record: Infotype 2005 (Overtime)
27	BEGUZ			BEGTI	TIMS	6	0	Start Time
28	ENDUZ			ENDTI	TIMS	6	0	End Time
29	VTKEN			VTKEN	CHAR	1	0	Previous Day Indicator
30	STDAZ			MESTD	DEC	7	2	Overtime hours
31	PBEG1			PDBEG	TIMS	6	0	Start of Break
32	PEND1			PDEND	TIMS	6	0	End of Break
33	PBEZ1			PDBEZ	DEC	4	2	Paid Break Period
34	PUNB1			PDUNB	DEC	4	2	Unpaid Break Period
35	PBEG2			PDBEG	TIMS	6	0	Start of Break
36	PEND2			PDEND	TIMS	6	0	End of Break
37	PBEZ2			PDBEZ	DEC	4	2	Paid Break Period
38	PUNB2			PDUNB	DEC	4	2	Unpaid Break Period
39	PBEG3			PDBEG	TIMS	6	0	Start of Break
40	PEND3			PDEND	TIMS	6	0	End of Break
41	PBEZ3			PDBEZ	DEC	4	2	Paid Break Period
42	PUNB3			PDUNB	DEC	4	2	Unpaid Break Period
43	PBEG4			PDBEG	TIMS	6	0	Start of Break
44	PEND4			PDEND	TIMS	6	0	End of Break

Figure A.41 Infotype 2005 — Overtime, continued

Ref	Field	Key Field	Initial Values	Data Element	Data Type	Length	Decimals	Description
45	PBEZ4			PDBEZ	DEC	4	2	Paid Break Period
46	PUNB4			PDUNB	DEC	4	2	Unpaid Break Period
47	VERSL			VRSCH	CHAR	1	0	Overtime Compensation Type
48	AUFKZ			AUFKN	CHAR	1	0	Extra Pay Indicator
49	BWGRL			PTM_VBAS7S	CURR	13	2	Valuation Basis for Different Payment
50	TRFGR			TRFGR	CHAR	8	0	Pay Scale Group
51	TRFST			TRFST	CHAR	2	0	Pay Scale Level
52	PRAKN			PRAKN	CHAR	2	0	Premium Number
53	PRAKZ			PRAKZ	NUMC	4	0	Premium Indicator
54	OTYPE			OTYPE	CHAR	2	0	Object Type
55	PLANS			PLANS	NUMC	8	0	Position
56	EXBEL			EXBEL	CHAR	8	0	External Document Number
57	HRSIF			HRS_INPFL	CHAR	1	0	Set number of hours
58	WAERS			WAERS	CUKY	5	0	Currency Key
59	WTART			WTART	CHAR	4	0	Work tax area
60	.INCLUDE			TMW_TDT_FIELDS	STRU	0	0	Infotype Fields Relevant for Short Descriptions
61	TDLANGU			TMW_TDLANGU	CHAR	10	0	Definition Set for IDs
62	TDSUBLA			TMW_TDSUBLA	CHAR	3	0	Definition Subset for IDs
63	TDTYPE			TDTYPE	CHAR	4	0	Time Data ID Type

Figure A.42 Infotype 2005 — Overtime, continued

Ref	Field	Key Field	Initial Values	Data Element	Data Type	Length	Decimals	Description
1	MANDT	X	X	MANDT	CLNT	3	0	Client
2	.INCLUDE	X	X	PAKEY	STRU	0	0	Key for HR Master Data
3	PERNR	X	X	PERSNO	NUMC	8	0	Personnel number
4	SUBTY	X	X	SUBTY	CHAR	4	0	Subtype
5	OBJPS	X	X	OBJPS	CHAR	2	0	Object Identification
6	SPRPS	X	X	SPRPS	CHAR	1	0	Lock Indicator for HR Master Data Record
7	ENDDA	X	X	ENDDA	DATS	8	0	End Date
8	BEGDA	X	X	BEGDA	DATS	8	0	Start Date
9	SEQNR	X	X	SEQNR	NUMC	3	0	Number of Infotype Record with Same Key
10	.INCLUDE			PSHD1	STRU	0	0	HR Master Record: Control Field
11	AEDTM			AEDAT	DATS	8	0	Changed On
12	UNAME			AENAM	CHAR	12	0	Name of Person Who Changed Object
13	HISTO			HISTO	CHAR	1	0	Historical Record Flag
14	ITXEX			ITXEX	CHAR	1	0	Text Exists for Infotype
15	REFEX			PRFEX	CHAR	1	0	Reference Fields Exist (Primary/Secondary Costs)
16	ORDEX			ORDEX	CHAR	1	0	Confirmation Fields Exist
17	ITBLD			ITBLD	CHAR	2	0	Infotype Screen Control
18	PREAS			PREAS	CHAR	2	0	Reason for Changing Master Data
19	FLAG1			NUSED	CHAR	1	0	Reserved Field/Unused Field
20	FLAG2			NUSED	CHAR	1	0	Reserved Field/Unused Field

Figure A.43 Infotype 2006 — Absences Quotas

Ref	Field	Key Field	Initial Values	Data Element	Data Type	Length	Decimals	Description
21	FLAG3			NUSED	CHAR	1	0	Reserved Field/Unused Field
22	FLAG4			NUSED	CHAR	1	0	Reserved Field/Unused Field
23	RESE1			NUSED2	CHAR	2	0	Reserved Field/Unused Field of Length 2
24	RESE2			NUSED2	CHAR	2	0	Reserved Field/Unused Field of Length 2
25	GRPVL			PCCE_GPVAL	CHAR	4	0	Grouping Value for Personnel Assignments
26	.INCLUDE			PS2006	STRU	0	0	HR Time Record: Infotype 2006 (Absence Quotas)
27	BEGUZ			BEGTI	TIMS	6	0	Start Time
28	ENDUZ			ENDTI	TIMS	6	0	End Time
29	VTKEN			VTKEN	CHAR	1	0	Previous Day Indicator
30	KTART			ABWKO	NUMC	2	0	Absence Quota Type
31	ANZHL			PTM_QUONUM	DEC	10	5	Number of Employee Time Quota
32	KVERB			PTM_QUODED	DEC	10	5	Deduction of Employee Time Quota
33	QUONR			PTM_QUONR	NUMC	20	0	Counter for time quotas
34	DESTA			PTM_DEDSTART	DATS	8	0	Start Date for Quota Deduction
35	DEEND			PTM_DEDEND	DATS	8	0	Quota Deduction to
36	QUOSY			PTM_DOCSY	CHAR	10	0	Logical system for document (personnel time)
37	.INCLUDE			TMW_TDT_FIELDS	STRU	0	0	Infotype Fields Relevant for Short Descriptions
38	TDLANGU			TMW_TDLANGU	CHAR	10	0	Definition Set for IDs
39	TDSUBLA			TMW_TDSUBLA	CHAR	3	0	Definition Subset for IDs
40	TDTYPE			TDTYPE	CHAR	4	0	Time Data ID Type

Figure A.44 Infotype 2006 — Absences Quotas, continued

489

Ref	Field	Key Field	Initial Values	Data Element	Data Type	Length	Decimals	Description
1	MANDT	X	X	MANDT	CLNT	3	0	Client
2	.INCLUDE	X	X	PAKEY	STRU	0	0	Key for HR Master Data
3	PERNR	X	X	PERSNO	NUMC	8	0	Personnel number
4	SUBTY	X	X	SUBTY	CHAR	4	0	Subtype
5	OBJPS	X	X	OBJPS	CHAR	2	0	Object Identification
6	SPRPS	X	X	SPRPS	CHAR	1	0	Lock Indicator for HR Master Data Record
7	ENDDA	X	X	ENDDA	DATS	8	0	End Date
8	BEGDA	X	X	BEGDA	DATS	8	0	Start Date
9	SEQNR	X	X	SEQNR	NUMC	3	0	Number of Infotype Record with Same Key
10	.INCLUDE			PSHD1	STRU	0	0	HR Master Record: Control Field
11	AEDTM			AEDAT	DATS	8	0	Changed On
12	UNAME			AENAM	CHAR	12	0	Name of Person Who Changed Object
13	HISTO			HISTO	CHAR	1	0	Historical Record Flag
14	ITXEX			ITXEX	CHAR	1	0	Text Exists for Infotype
15	REFEX			PRFEX	CHAR	1	0	Reference Fields Exist (Primary/Secondary Costs)
16	ORDEX			ORDEX	CHAR	1	0	Confirmation Fields Exist
17	ITBLD			ITBLD	CHAR	2	0	Infotype Screen Control
18	PREAS			PREAS	CHAR	2	0	Reason for Changing Master Data
19	FLAG1			NUSED	CHAR	1	0	Reserved Field/Unused Field
20	FLAG2			NUSED	CHAR	1	0	Reserved Field/Unused Field
21	FLAG3			NUSED	CHAR	1	0	Reserved Field/Unused Field
22	FLAG4			NUSED	CHAR	1	0	Reserved Field/Unused Field
23	RESE1			NUSED2	CHAR	2	0	Reserved Field/Unused Field of Length 2

Figure A.45 Infotype 2007 — Overtime Quota

Ref	Field	Key Field	Initial Values	Data Element	Data Type	Length	Decimals	Description
24	RESE2			NUSED2	CHAR	2	0	Reserved Field/Unused Field of Length 2
25	GRPVL			PCCE_GPVAL	CHAR	4	0	Grouping Value for Personnel Assignments
26	.INCLUDE			PS2007	STRU	0	0	HR Time Record: Infotype 2007 (Attendance Quotas)
27	BEGUZ			BEGTI	TIMS	6	0	Start Time
28	ENDUZ			ENDTI	TIMS	6	0	End Time
29	VTKEN			VTKEN	CHAR	1	0	Previous Day Indicator
30	KTART			ANWKO	NUMC	2	0	Attendance Quota Type
31	ANZHL			PTM_QUONUM	DEC	10	5	Number of Employee Time Quota
32	VERSL			VRSCH	CHAR	1	0	Overtime Compensation Type
33	KVERB			PTM_QUODED	DEC	10	5	Deduction of Employee Time Quota
34	BWTIM			BWTIM	CHAR	1	0	Approval only before working time
35	AWTIM			AWTIM	CHAR	1	0	Approval only after working time
36	TTIME			TTIME	CHAR	1	0	Full-day approval
37	QUONR			PTM_QUONR	NUMC	20	0	Counter for time quotas
38	DESTA			PTM_DEDSTART	DATS	8	0	Start Date for Quota Deduction
39	DEEND			PTM_DEDEND	DATS	8	0	Quota Deduction to
40	QUOSY			PTM_DOCSY	CHAR	10	0	Logical system for document (personnel time)
41	.INCLUDE			TMW_TDT_FIELDS	STRU	0	0	Infotype Fields Relevant for Short Descriptions
42	TDLANGU			TMW_TDLANGU	CHAR	10	0	Definition Set for IDs
43	TDSUBLA			TMW_TDSUBLA	CHAR	3	0	Definition Subset for IDs
44	TDTYPE			TDTYPE	CHAR	4	0	Time Data ID Type

Figure A.46 Infotype 2007 — Overtime Quotas, continued

Ref	Field	Key Field	Initial Values	Data Element	Data Type	Length	Decimals	Description
1	MANDT	X	X	MANDT	CLNT	3	0	Client
2	.INCLUDE	X	X	PAKEY	STRU	0	0	Key for HR Master Data
3	PERNR	X	X	PERSNO	NUMC	8	0	Personnel number
4	SUBTY	X	X	SUBTY	CHAR	4	0	Subtype
5	OBJPS	X	X	OBJPS	CHAR	2	0	Object Identification
6	SPRPS	X	X	SPRPS	CHAR	1	0	Lock Indicator for HR Master Data Record
7	ENDDA	X	X	ENDDA	DATS	8	0	End Date
8	BEGDA	X	X	BEGDA	DATS	8	0	Start Date
9	SEQNR	X	X	SEQNR	NUMC	3	0	Number of Infotype Record with Same Key
10	.INCLUDE			PSHD1	STRU	0	0	HR Master Record: Control Field
11	AEDTM			AEDAT	DATS	8	0	Changed On
12	UNAME			AENAM	CHAR	12	0	Name of Person Who Changed Object
13	HISTO			HISTO	CHAR	1	0	Historical Record Flag
14	ITXEX			ITXEX	CHAR	1	0	Text Exists for Infotype
15	REFEX			PRFEX	CHAR	1	0	Reference Fields Exist (Primary/Secondary Costs)
16	ORDEX			ORDEX	CHAR	1	0	Confirmation Fields Exist
17	ITBLD			ITBLD	CHAR	2	0	Infotype Screen Control
18	PREAS			PREAS	CHAR	2	0	Reason for Changing Master Data
19	FLAG1			NUSED	CHAR	1	0	Reserved Field/Unused Field
20	FLAG2			NUSED	CHAR	1	0	Reserved Field/Unused Field

Figure A.47　Infotype 2010 — Employee Remuneration Information

Ref	Field	Key Field	Initial Values	Data Element	Data Type	Length	Decimals	Description
21	FLAG3			NUSED	CHAR	1	0	Reserved Field/Unused Field
22	FLAG4			NUSED	CHAR	1	0	Reserved Field/Unused Field
23	RESE1			NUSED2	CHAR	2	0	Reserved Field/Unused Field of Length 2
24	RESE2			NUSED2	CHAR	2	0	Reserved Field/Unused Field of Length 2
25	GRPVL			PCCE_GPVAL	CHAR	4	0	Grouping Value for Personnel Assignments
26	.INCLUDE			PS2010	STRU	0	0	HR Time Record: Infotype 2010 (Employee Remuneration Info.)
27	BEGUZ			BEGTI	TIMS	6	0	Start Time
28	ENDUZ			ENDTI	TIMS	6	0	End Time
29	VTKEN			VTKEN	CHAR	1	0	Previous Day Indicator
30	STDAZ			ENSTD	DEC	7	2	No.of hours for remuneration info.
31	LGART			LGART	CHAR	4	0	Wage Type
32	ANZHL			ENANZ	DEC	7	2	Number per Time Unit for EE Remuneration Info
33	ZEINH			PT_ZEINH	CHAR	3	0	Time/Measurement Unit
34	BWGRL			PTM_VBAS7S	CURR	13	2	Valuation Basis for Different Payment
35	AUFKZ			AUFKN	CHAR	1	0	Extra Pay Indicator
36	BETRG			PAD_AMT7S	CURR	13	2	Wage Type Amount for Payments
37	ENDOF			ENDOF	CHAR	1	0	Indicator for final confirmation
38	UFLD1			USFLD	CHAR	1	0	User field
39	UFLD2			USFLD	CHAR	1	0	User field
40	UFLD3			USFLD	CHAR	1	0	User field

Figure A.48　Infotype 2010 — Employee Remuneration Information, continued

491

Ref	Field	Key Field	Initial Values	Data Element	Data Type	Length	Decimals	Description
41	KEYPR			KEYPR	CHAR	3	0	Number of Infotype Record with Identical Key
42	TRFGR			TRFGR	CHAR	8	0	Pay Scale Group
43	TRFST			TRFST	CHAR	2	0	Pay Scale Level
44	PRAKN			PRAKN	CHAR	2	0	Premium Number
45	PRAKZ			PRAKZ	NUMC	4	0	Premium Indicator
46	OTYPE			OTYPE	CHAR	2	0	Object Type
47	PLANS			PLANS	NUMC	8	0	Position
48	VERSL			VRSCH	CHAR	1	0	Overtime Compensation Type
49	EXBEL			EXBEL	CHAR	8	0	External Document Number
50	WAERS			WAERS	CUKY	5	0	Currency Key
51	LOGSYS			LOGSYS	CHAR	10	0	Logical system
52	AWTYP			AWTYP	CHAR	5	0	Reference Transaction
53	AWREF			AWREF	CHAR	10	0	Reference Document Number
54	AWORG			AWORG	CHAR	10	0	Reference Organizational Units
55	WTART			WTART	CHAR	4	0	Work tax area
56	.INCLUDE			TMW_TDT_FIELDS	STRU	0	0	Infotype Fields Relevant for Short Descriptions
57	TDLANGU			TMW_TDLANGU	CHAR	10	0	Definition Set for IDs
58	TDSUBLA			TMW_TDSUBLA	CHAR	3	0	Definition Subset for IDs
59	TDTYPE			TDTYPE	CHAR	4	0	Time Data ID Type

Figure A.49 Infotype 2010 — Employee Remuneration Information, continued

Ref	Field	Key Field	Initial Values	Data Element	Data Type	Length	Decimals	Description
	Note structure P2011							
1	.INCLUDE			PSHDR		0	0	Headers for Infotype Records
2	.INCLUDE			PSKEY		0	0	Keys for HR Master Data
3	PERNR			PERNR_D	NUMC	8	0	Personnel Number
4	INFTY			INFTY	CHAR	4	0	Infotype
5	SUBTY			SUBTY	CHAR	4	0	Subtype
6	OBJPS			OBJPS	CHAR	2	0	Object Identification
7	SPRPS			SPRPS	CHAR	1	0	Lock Indicator for HR Master Data Record
8	ENDDA			ENDDA	DATS	8	0	End Date
9	BEGDA			BEGDA	DATS	8	0	Start Date
10	SEQNR			SEQNR	NUMC	3	0	Number of Infotype Record with Same Key
11	.INCLUDE			PSHD1		0	0	HR Master Record: Control Field
12	AEDTM			AEDAT	DATS	8	0	Changed On
13	UNAME			AENAM	CHAR	12	0	Name of Person Who Changed Object
14	HISTO			HISTO	CHAR	1	0	Historical Record Flag
15	ITXEX			ITXEX	CHAR	1	0	Text Exists for Infotype
16	REFEX			PRFEX	CHAR	1	0	Reference Fields Exist (Primary/Secondary Costs)
17	ORDEX			ORDEX	CHAR	1	0	Confirmation Fields Exist
18	ITBLD			ITBLD	CHAR	2	0	Infotype Screen Control
19	PREAS			PREAS	CHAR	2	0	Reason for Changing Master Data
20	FLAG1			NUSED	CHAR	1	0	Reserved Field/Unused Field
21	FLAG2			NUSED	CHAR	1	0	Reserved Field/Unused Field
22	FLAG3			NUSED	CHAR	1	0	Reserved Field/Unused Field

Figure A.50 Infotype 2011 — Employee Time Events

Ref	Field	Key Field	Initial Values	Data Element	Data Type	Length	Decimals	Description
23	FLAG4			NUSED	CHAR	1	0	Reserved Field/Unused Field
24	RESE1			NUSED2	CHAR	2	0	Reserved Field/Unused Field of Length 2
25	RESE2			NUSED2	CHAR	2	0	Reserved Field/Unused Field of Length 2
26	GRPVL			PCCE_GPVAL	CHAR	4	0	Grouping Value for Personnel Assignments
27	.INCLUDE			PS2011		0	0	HR Time Record: Infotype 2011 (Time Events)
28	BEGUZ			BEGUZ	TIMS	6	0	Start Time
29	ENDUZ			ENDUZ	TIMS	6	0	End Time
30	VTKEN			VTKEN	CHAR	1	0	Previous Day Indicator
31	PDSNR			PDSNR_D	NUMC	12	0	Sequential number for PDC messages
32	.INCLUDE			PDEVE		0	0	Time Event Data for Input Interface to Analysis Module
33	LDATE			LDATE	DATS	8	0	Logical Date
34	LTIME			LTIME	TIMS	6	0	Logical time
35	ERDAT			PHDAT	DATS	8	0	Created on
36	ERTIM			PHTIM	TIMS	6	0	Created at
37	SATZA			RETYP	CHAR	3	0	Time Event Type
38	TERID			TERID	CHAR	4	0	Terminal ID
39	ABWGR			ABWGR	CHAR	4	0	Attendance/Absence Reason
40	EXLGA			EXLGA	CHAR	4	0	Employee Expenditures
41	ZEINH			PT_ZEINH	CHAR	3	0	Time/Measurement Unit
42	HRAZL			HRAZL	DEC	7	2	Number
43	HRBET			HRBET	CURR	9	2	Amount for remuneration information

Figure A.51 Infotype 2011 — Employee Time Events, continued

Ref	Field	Key Field	Initial Values	Data Element	Data Type	Length	Decimals	Description
44	ORIGF			ORIGF	CHAR	1	0	Origin Indicator of PDC Message
45	DALLF			DALLF	CHAR	1	0	Day assignment
46	PDC_OTYPE			OTYPE	CHAR	2	0	Object Type
47	PDC_PLANS			PLANS	NUMC	8	0	Position
48	OTYPE			OTYPE	CHAR	2	0	Object Type
49	PLANS			PLANS	NUMC	8	0	Position
50	PDC_USRUP			PDC_USRUP	CHAR	20	0	Customer-Specific Field
51	USER2			HR_USRFLD	CHAR	40	0	Customer-Specific Field
52	ABWEX			ABWEX	CHAR	1	0	Fields for alternative payment are filled
53	.INCLUDE			TEVEN_APL		0	0	Different Payment (for Time Events)
54	TRFGR			TRFGR	CHAR	8	0	Pay Scale Group
55	TRFST			TRFST	CHAR	2	0	Pay Scale Level
56	PRAKN			PRAKN	CHAR	2	0	Premium Number
57	PRAKZ			PRAKZ	NUMC	4	0	Premium Indicator
58	AUFKZ			AUFKN	CHAR	1	0	Extra Pay Indicator
59	BWGRL			PTM_VBAS7S	CURR	13	2	Valuation Basis for Different Payment
60	WAERS			WAERS	CUKY	5	0	Currency Key

Figure A.52 Infotype 2011 — Employee Time Events, continued

Ref	Field	Key Field	Initial Values	Data Element	Data Type	Length	Decimals	Description
1	MANDT	X	X	MANDT	CLNT	3	0	Client
2	.INCLUDE	X	X	PAKEY	STRU	0	0	Key for HR Master Data
3	PERNR	X	X	PERSNO	NUMC	8	0	Personnel number
4	SUBTY	X	X	SUBTY	CHAR	4	0	Subtype
5	OBJPS	X	X	OBJPS	CHAR	2	0	Object Identification
6	SPRPS	X	X	SPRPS	CHAR	1	0	Lock Indicator for HR Master Data Record
7	ENDDA	X	X	ENDDA	DATS	8	0	End Date
8	BEGDA	X	X	BEGDA	DATS	8	0	Start Date
9	SEQNR	X	X	SEQNR	NUMC	3	0	Number of Infotype Record with Same Key
10	.INCLUDE			PSHD1	STRU	0	0	HR Master Record: Control Field
11	AEDTM			AEDAT	DATS	8	0	Changed On
12	UNAME			AENAM	CHAR	12	0	Name of Person Who Changed Object
13	HISTO			HISTO	CHAR	1	0	Historical Record Flag
14	ITXEX			ITXEX	CHAR	1	0	Text Exists for Infotype
15	REFEX			PRFEX	CHAR	1	0	Reference Fields Exist (Primary/Secondary Costs)
16	ORDEX			ORDEX	CHAR	1	0	Confirmation Fields Exist
17	ITBLD			ITBLD	CHAR	2	0	Infotype Screen Control
18	PREAS			PREAS	CHAR	2	0	Reason for Changing Master Data
19	FLAG1			NUSED	CHAR	1	0	Reserved Field/Unused Field
20	FLAG2			NUSED	CHAR	1	0	Reserved Field/Unused Field

Figure A.53 Infotype 2012 — Time Transfer Specifications

Ref	Field	Key Field	Initial Values	Data Element	Data Type	Length	Decimals	Description
21	FLAG3			NUSED	CHAR	1	0	Reserved Field/Unused Field
22	FLAG4			NUSED	CHAR	1	0	Reserved Field/Unused Field
23	RESE1			NUSED2	CHAR	2	0	Reserved Field/Unused Field of Length 2
24	RESE2			NUSED2	CHAR	2	0	Reserved Field/Unused Field of Length 2
25	GRPVL			PCCE_GPVAL	CHAR	4	0	Grouping Value for Personnel Assignments
26	.INCLUDE			PS2012	STRU	0	0	HR Time Record: Infotype 2012 (Time Transfer Specifications)
27	BEGUZ			BEGUZ	TIMS	6	0	Start Time
28	ENDUZ			ENDUZ	TIMS	6	0	End Time
29	VTKEN			VTKEN	CHAR	1	0	Previous Day Indicator
30	ZTART			SALKO	CHAR	4	0	Employee Time Transfer Type
31	ANZHL			THOUR	DEC	7	2	Number of hours in a time type
32	ATIME			ATIME	CHAR	6	0	Time point for time evaluation
33	.INCLUDE			TMW_TDT_FIELDS	STRU	0	0	Infotype Fields Relevant for Short Descriptions
34	TDLANGU			TMW_TDLANGU	CHAR	10	0	Definition Set for IDs
35	TDSUBLA			TMW_TDSUBLA	CHAR	3	0	Definition Subset for IDs
36	TDTYPE			TDTYPE	CHAR	4	0	Time Data ID Type

Figure A.54 Infotype 2012 — Time Transfer Specifications, continued

Ref	Field	Key Field	Initial Values	Data Element	Data Type	Length	Decimals	Description
1	MANDT	X	X	MANDT	CLNT	3	0	Client
2	.INCLUDE	X	X	PAKEY	STRU	0	0	Key for HR Master Data
3	PERNR	X	X	PERSNO	NUMC	8	0	Personnel number
4	SUBTY	X	X	SUBTY	CHAR	4	0	Subtype
5	OBJPS	X	X	OBJPS	CHAR	2	0	Object Identification
6	SPRPS	X	X	SPRPS	CHAR	1	0	Lock Indicator for HR Master Data Record
7	ENDDA	X	X	ENDDA	DATS	8	0	End Date
8	BEGDA	X	X	BEGDA	DATS	8	0	Start Date
9	SEQNR	X	X	SEQNR	NUMC	3	0	Number of Infotype Record with Same Key
10	.INCLUDE			PSHD1	STRU	0	0	HR Master Record: Control Field
11	AEDTM			AEDAT	DATS	8	0	Changed On
12	UNAME			AENAM	CHAR	12	0	Name of Person Who Changed Object
13	HISTO			HISTO	CHAR	1	0	Historical Record Flag
14	ITXEX			ITXEX	CHAR	1	0	Text Exists for Infotype
15	REFEX			PRFEX	CHAR	1	0	Reference Fields Exist (Primary/Secondary Costs)
16	ORDEX			ORDEX	CHAR	1	0	Confirmation Fields Exist
17	ITBLD			ITBLD	CHAR	2	0	Infotype Screen Control
18	PREAS			PREAS	CHAR	2	0	Reason for Changing Master Data
19	FLAG1			NUSED	CHAR	1	0	Reserved Field/Unused Field
20	FLAG2			NUSED	CHAR	1	0	Reserved Field/Unused Field

Figure A.55 Infotype 2013 — Quota Corrections

Ref	Field	Key Field	Initial Values	Data Element	Data Type	Length	Decimals	Description
21	FLAG3			NUSED	CHAR	1	0	Reserved Field/Unused Field
22	FLAG4			NUSED	CHAR	1	0	Reserved Field/Unused Field
23	RESE1			NUSED2	CHAR	2	0	Reserved Field/Unused Field of Length 2
24	RESE2			NUSED2	CHAR	2	0	Reserved Field/Unused Field of Length 2
25	GRPVL			PCCE_GPVAL	CHAR	4	0	Grouping Value for Personnel Assignments
26	.INCLUDE			PS2013	STRU	0	0	HR Time Record: Infotype 2013 (Quota Corrections)
27	BEGUZ			BEGUZ	TIMS	6	0	Start Time
28	ENDUZ			ENDUZ	TIMS	6	0	End Time
29	VTKEN			VTKEN	CHAR	1	0	Previous Day Indicator
30	KTART			ABWKO	NUMC	2	0	Absence Quota Type
31	ACCNU			PTM_QUONUM	DEC	10	5	Number of Employee Time Quota
32	ACCOP			ACCOP	CHAR	1	0	Operation Indicators for Automatic Accrual of Absence Quotas
33	ACCTR			ACCTR	CHAR	1	0	Transfer Accrued Entitlement

Figure A.56 Infotype 2013 — Quota Corrections, continued

Ref	Field	Key Field	Initial Values	Data Element	Data Type	Length	Decimals	Description
1	.INCLUDE			PSHDR		0	0	Headers for Infotype Records
2	.INCLUDE			PSKEY		0	0	Keys for HR Master Data
3	PERNR			PERNR_D	NUMC	8	0	Personnel Number
4	INFTY			INFTY	CHAR	4	0	Infotype
5	SUBTY			SUBTY	CHAR	4	0	Subtype
6	OBJPS			OBJPS	CHAR	2	0	Object Identification
7	SPRPS			SPRPS	CHAR	1	0	Lock Indicator for HR Master Data Record
8	ENDDA			ENDDA	DATS	8	0	End Date
9	BEGDA			BEGDA	DATS	8	0	Start Date
10	SEQNR			SEQNR	NUMC	3	0	Number of Infotype Record with Same Key
11	.INCLUDE			PSHD1		0	0	HR Master Record: Control Field
12	AEDTM			AEDAT	DATS	8	0	Changed On
13	UNAME			AENAM	CHAR	12	0	Name of Person Who Changed Object
14	HISTO			HISTO	CHAR	1	0	Historical Record Flag
15	ITXEX			ITXEX	CHAR	1	0	Text Exists for Infotype
16	REFEX			PRFEX	CHAR	1	0	Reference Fields Exist (Primary/Secondary Costs)
17	ORDEX			ORDEX	CHAR	1	0	Confirmation Fields Exist
18	ITBLD			ITBLD	CHAR	2	0	Infotype Screen Control
19	PREAS			PREAS	CHAR	2	0	Reason for Changing Master Data
20	FLAG1			NUSED	CHAR	1	0	Reserved Field/Unused Field
21	FLAG2			NUSED	CHAR	1	0	Reserved Field/Unused Field

Figure A.57 Infotype 2050 — Annual Calendar

Ref	Field	Key Field	Initial Values	Data Element	Data Type	Length	Decimals	Description
22	FLAG3			NUSED	CHAR	1	0	Reserved Field/Unused Field
23	FLAG4			NUSED	CHAR	1	0	Reserved Field/Unused Field
24	RESE1			NUSED2	CHAR	2	0	Reserved Field/Unused Field of Length 2
25	RESE2			NUSED2	CHAR	2	0	Reserved Field/Unused Field of Length 2
26	GRPVL			PCCE_GPVAL	CHAR	4	0	Grouping Value for Personnel Assignments
27	BEGUZ			BEGUZ	TIMS	6	0	Start Time
28	ENDUZ			ENDUZ	TIMS	6	0	End Time
29	VTKEN			VTKEN	CHAR	1	0	Previous Day Indicator
30	MONAT			MONTH	NUMC	2	0	Month
31	TAG01			ABSTP	CHAR	1	0	Absence/attendance category
32	TAG02			ABSTP	CHAR	1	0	Absence/attendance category
33	TAG03			ABSTP	CHAR	1	0	Absence/attendance category
34	TAG04			ABSTP	CHAR	1	0	Absence/attendance category
35	TAG05			ABSTP	CHAR	1	0	Absence/attendance category
36	TAG06			ABSTP	CHAR	1	0	Absence/attendance category
37	TAG07			ABSTP	CHAR	1	0	Absence/attendance category
38	TAG08			ABSTP	CHAR	1	0	Absence/attendance category
39	TAG09			ABSTP	CHAR	1	0	Absence/attendance category
40	TAG10			ABSTP	CHAR	1	0	Absence/attendance category
41	TAG11			ABSTP	CHAR	1	0	Absence/attendance category
42	TAG12			ABSTP	CHAR	1	0	Absence/attendance category

Figure A.58 Infotype 2050 —Annual Calendar, continued

Ref	Field	Key Field	Initial Values	Data Element	Data Type	Length	Decimals	Description
43	TAG13			ABSTP	CHAR	1	0	Absence/attendance category
44	TAG14			ABSTP	CHAR	1	0	Absence/attendance category
45	TAG15			ABSTP	CHAR	1	0	Absence/attendance category
46	TAG16			ABSTP	CHAR	1	0	Absence/attendance category
47	TAG17			ABSTP	CHAR	1	0	Absence/attendance category
48	TAG18			ABSTP	CHAR	1	0	Absence/attendance category
49	TAG19			ABSTP	CHAR	1	0	Absence/attendance category
50	TAG20			ABSTP	CHAR	1	0	Absence/attendance category
51	TAG21			ABSTP	CHAR	1	0	Absence/attendance category
52	TAG22			ABSTP	CHAR	1	0	Absence/attendance category
53	TAG23			ABSTP	CHAR	1	0	Absence/attendance category
54	TAG24			ABSTP	CHAR	1	0	Absence/attendance category
55	TAG25			ABSTP	CHAR	1	0	Absence/attendance category
56	TAG26			ABSTP	CHAR	1	0	Absence/attendance category
57	TAG27			ABSTP	CHAR	1	0	Absence/attendance category
58	TAG28			ABSTP	CHAR	1	0	Absence/attendance category
59	TAG29			ABSTP	CHAR	1	0	Absence/attendance category
60	TAG30			ABSTP	CHAR	1	0	Absence/attendance category
61	TAG31			ABSTP	CHAR	1	0	Absence/attendance category

Figure A.59 Infotype 2050 — Annual Calendar, continued

Ref	Field	Key Field	Initial Values	Data Element	Data Type	Length	Decimals	Description
1	.INCLUDE			PSHDR		0	0	Headers for Infotype Records
2	.INCLUDE			PSKEY		0	0	Keys for HR Master Data
3	PERNR			PERNR_D	NUMC	8	0	Personnel Number
4	INFTY			INFTY	CHAR	4	0	Infotype
5	SUBTY			SUBTY	CHAR	4	0	Subtype
6	OBJPS			OBJPS	CHAR	2	0	Object Identification
7	SPRPS			SPRPS	CHAR	1	0	Lock Indicator for HR Master Data Record
8	ENDDA			ENDDA	DATS	8	0	End Date
9	BEGDA			BEGDA	DATS	8	0	Start Date
10	SEQNR			SEQNR	NUMC	3	0	Number of Infotype Record with Same Key
11	.INCLUDE			PSHD1		0	0	HR Master Record: Control Field
12	AEDTM			AEDAT	DATS	8	0	Changed On
13	UNAME			AENAM	CHAR	12	0	Name of Person Who Changed Object
14	HISTO			HISTO	CHAR	1	0	Historical Record Flag
15	ITXEX			ITXEX	CHAR	1	0	Text Exists for Infotype
16	REFEX			PRFEX	CHAR	1	0	Reference Fields Exist (Primary/Secondary Costs)
17	ORDEX			ORDEX	CHAR	1	0	Confirmation Fields Exist
18	ITBLD			ITBLD	CHAR	2	0	Infotype Screen Control
19	PREAS			PREAS	CHAR	2	0	Reason for Changing Master Data
20	FLAG1			NUSED	CHAR	1	0	Reserved Field/Unused Field
21	FLAG2			NUSED	CHAR	1	0	Reserved Field/Unused Field

Figure A.60 Infotype 2051 — Monthly Calendar

Ref	Field	Key Field	Initial Values	Data Element	Data Type	Length	Decimals	Description
22	FLAG3			NUSED	CHAR	1	0	Reserved Field/Unused Field
23	FLAG4			NUSED	CHAR	1	0	Reserved Field/Unused Field
24	RESE1			NUSED2	CHAR	2	0	Reserved Field/Unused Field of Length 2
25	RESE2			NUSED2	CHAR	2	0	Reserved Field/Unused Field of Length 2
26	GRPVL			PCCE_GPVAL	CHAR	4	0	Grouping Value for Personnel Assignments
27	BEGUZ			BEGTI	TIMS	6	0	Start Time
28	ENDUZ			ENDTI	TIMS	6	0	End Time
29	VTKEN			VTKEN	CHAR	1	0	Previous Day Indicator
30	WEEKN			WEEKN	CHAR	2	0	Week
31	FIDAY			FIDAY	CHAR	2	0	First day
32	LADAY			LADAY	CHAR	2	0	Last day
33	TPR01			TPROG	CHAR	4	0	Daily Work Schedule
34	TAG01			ABSTP	CHAR	1	0	Absence/attendance category
35	KNZ01			KNINF	CHAR	4	0	Indicator for time infotypes
36	VAR01			VARIA	CHAR	1	0	Daily Work Schedule Variant
37	TPR02			TPROG	CHAR	4	0	Daily Work Schedule
38	TAG02			ABSTP	CHAR	1	0	Absence/attendance category
39	KNZ02			KNINF	CHAR	4	0	Indicator for time infotypes
40	VAR02			VARIA	CHAR	1	0	Daily Work Schedule Variant
41	TPR03			TPROG	CHAR	4	0	Daily Work Schedule
42	TAG03			ABSTP	CHAR	1	0	Absence/attendance category
43	KNZ03			KNINF	CHAR	4	0	Indicator for time infotypes
44	VAR03			VARIA	CHAR	1	0	Daily Work Schedule Variant

Figure A.61 Infotype 2051 — Monthly Calendar, continued

Ref	Field	Key Field	Initial Values	Data Element	Data Type	Length	Decimals	Description
45	TPR04			TPROG	CHAR	4	0	Daily Work Schedule
46	TAG04			ABSTP	CHAR	1	0	Absence/attendance category
47	KNZ04			KNINF	CHAR	4	0	Indicator for time infotypes
48	VAR04			VARIA	CHAR	1	0	Daily Work Schedule Variant
49	TPR05			TPROG	CHAR	4	0	Daily Work Schedule
50	TAG05			ABSTP	CHAR	1	0	Absence/attendance category
51	KNZ05			KNINF	CHAR	4	0	Indicator for time infotypes
52	VAR05			VARIA	CHAR	1	0	Daily Work Schedule Variant
53	TPR06			TPROG	CHAR	4	0	Daily Work Schedule
54	TAG06			ABSTP	CHAR	1	0	Absence/attendance category
55	KNZ06			KNINF	CHAR	4	0	Indicator for time infotypes
56	VAR06			VARIA	CHAR	1	0	Daily Work Schedule Variant
57	TPR07			TPROG	CHAR	4	0	Daily Work Schedule
58	TAG07			ABSTP	CHAR	1	0	Absence/attendance category
59	KNZ07			KNINF	CHAR	4	0	Indicator for time infotypes
60	VAR07			VARIA	CHAR	1	0	Daily Work Schedule Variant

Figure A.62 Infotype 2051 — Monthly Calendar, continued

Ref	Field	Key Field	Initial Values	Data Element	Data Type	Length	Decimals	Description
1	.INCLUDE			PSHDR		0	0	Headers for Infotype Records
2	.INCLUDE			PSKEY		0	0	Keys for HR Master Data
3	PERNR			PERNR_D	NUMC	8	0	Personnel Number
4	INFTY			INFTY	CHAR	4	0	Infotype
5	SUBTY			SUBTY	CHAR	4	0	Subtype
6	OBJPS			OBJPS	CHAR	2	0	Object Identification
7	SPRPS			SPRPS	CHAR	1	0	Lock Indicator for HR Master Data Record
8	ENDDA			ENDDA	DATS	8	0	End Date
9	BEGDA			BEGDA	DATS	8	0	Start Date
10	SEQNR			SEQNR	NUMC	3	0	Number of Infotype Record with Same Key
11	.INCLUDE			PSHD1		0	0	HR Master Record: Control Field
12	AEDTM			AEDAT	DATS	8	0	Changed On
13	UNAME			AENAM	CHAR	12	0	Name of Person Who Changed Object
14	HISTO			HISTO	CHAR	1	0	Historical Record Flag
15	ITXEX			ITXEX	CHAR	1	0	Text Exists for Infotype
16	REFEX			PRFEX	CHAR	1	0	Reference Fields Exist (Primary/Secondary Costs)
17	ORDEX			ORDEX	CHAR	1	0	Confirmation Fields Exist
18	ITBLD			ITBLD	CHAR	2	0	Infotype Screen Control
19	PREAS			PREAS	CHAR	2	0	Reason for Changing Master Data
20	FLAG1			NUSED	CHAR	1	0	Reserved Field/Unused Field
21	FLAG2			NUSED	CHAR	1	0	Reserved Field/Unused Field
22	FLAG3			NUSED	CHAR	1	0	Reserved Field/Unused Field
23	FLAG4			NUSED	CHAR	1	0	Reserved Field/Unused Field
24	RESE1			NUSED2	CHAR	2	0	Reserved Field/Unused Field of Length 2
25	RESE2			NUSED2	CHAR	2	0	Reserved Field/Unused Field of Length 2

Figure A.63 Infotype2052 — Weekly Entry Activity Allocations

Ref	Field	Key Field	Initial Values	Data Element	Data Type	Length	Decimals	Description
26	GRPVL			PCCE_GPVAL	CHAR	4	0	Grouping Value for Personnel Assignments
27	.INCLUDE			PS2052		0	0	HR Time Record: Infotype 2052 (Weekly Calendar)
28	BEGUZ			BEGUZ	TIMS	6	0	Start Time
29	ENDUZ			ENDUZ	TIMS	6	0	End Time
30	VTKEN			VTKEN	CHAR	1	0	Previous Day Indicator
31	AWART			AWART	CHAR	4	0	Attendance or Absence Type
32	ABWTG			ABWTG	DEC	6	2	Attendance and Absence Days
33	ABRTG			ABRTG	DEC	6	2	Payroll days
34	ABRST			ABRST	DEC	7	2	Payroll hours
35	KALTG			KALTG	DEC	6	2	Calendar days
36	STDAZ			ABSTD	DEC	7	2	Absence hours
37	LGART			LGART	CHAR	4	0	Wage Type
38	BWGRL			PTM_VBAS7S	CURR	13	2	Valuation Basis for Different Payment
39	AUFKZ			AUFKN	CHAR	1	0	Extra Pay Indicator
40	VERSL			VRSCH	CHAR	1	0	Overtime Compensation Type
41	TRFGR			TRFGR	CHAR	8	0	Pay Scale Group
42	TRFST			TRFST	CHAR	2	0	Pay Scale Level
43	PRAKN			PRAKN	CHAR	2	0	Premium Number
44	PRAKZ			PRAKZ	NUMC	4	0	Premium Indicator
45	OTYPE			OTYPE	CHAR	2	0	Object Type
46	PLANS			PLANS	NUMC	8	0	Position
47	HRSIF			HRS_INPFL	CHAR	1	0	Set number of hours
48	ALLDF			ALLDF	CHAR	1	0	Record is for Full Day
49	WAERS			WAERS	CUKY	5	0	Currency Key
50	DOCSY			PTM_DOCSY	CHAR	10	0	Logical system for document (personnel time)
51	DOCNR			PTM_DOCNR	NUMC	20	0	Document number for time data
52	ANRTG			ANRTG	DEC	6	2	Days credited for continued pay
53	LFZED			LFZED	DATS	8	0	End of continued pay

Figure A.64 Infotype 2052 — Weekly Entry Activity Allocations, continued

Ref	Field	Key Field	Initial Values	Data Element	Data Type	Length	Decimals	Description
54	KRGED			KRGED	DATS	8	0	End of sick pay
55	KBBEG			KBBEG	DATS	8	0	Certified start of sickness
56	KENN1			KENN1	DEC	2	0	Indicator for Subsequent Illness
57	KENN2			KENN2	DEC	2	0	Indicator for repeated illness
58	RMDDA			RMDDA	DATS	8	0	Date on which illness was confirmed
59	RMDUZ			RMDUZ	TIMS	6	0	Sickness confirmed at
60	MLDDA			MLDDA	DATS	8	0	Reported on
61	UMSKD			UMSKD	CHAR	6	0	Code for description of illness
62	UMSCH			UMSCH	CHAR	20	0	Description of illness
63	MLDUZ			MLDUZ	TIMS	6	0	Reported at
64	VORGS			VORGS	CHAR	15	0	Superior Out Sick (Illness)
65	REFNR			RFNUM	CHAR	8	0	Reference number
66	UNFAL			UNFAL	CHAR	1	0	Absent due to accident?
67	PSARB			PSARB	DEC	4	2	Work capacity percentage
68	URMAN			URMAN	CHAR	1	0	Indicator for manual leave deduction
69	WTART			WTART	CHAR	4	0	Work tax area
70	FAPRS			FAPRS	CHAR	2	0	Evaluation Type for Attendances/Absences
71	AINFT			AINFT	CHAR	4	0	Infotype that maintains 2001

Figure A.65 Infotype2052 — Weekly Entry Activity Allocations, continued

B   Program Overview

Most of the SAP programs listed here can be called upon via Transaction code SE38 or SA38.

This appendix is divided into the following parts and will list the programs separately.

- Cross-Application Time Sheet (CATS)
- HR Plant Data Collection (PDC)
- Leave Requests
- Concurrent Employment
- Time Events
- Time Infotype Data
- Time Evaluation
- Clusters
- Work Schedules
- Quotas
- Employee Expenditures
- Incentive Wages
- Shift Planning
- Business Warehouse
- Configuration Overview
- Misc.

B.1   Cross-Application Time Sheets (CATS)

Program	Description	Functionality
RCATSRCO	CATS: Check and Reorganize Table CATSCO	Cross-Application Time Sheet
RCATSTCO	CATS: Transfer to Controlling	Cross-Application Time Sheet

Table B.1   List of CATS Programs

Program	Description	Functionality
RCATSTPM	CATS: Transfer to Plant Maintenance/Customer Service	Cross-Application Time Sheet
RCATSTPS	CATS: Transfer to Project System	Cross-Application Time Sheet
CATSGETS	Time Sheet: Submit Report for Reading the Logical Database PCH	Cross-Application Time Sheet
CATSSHOW	Display Time Sheet Data	Cross-Application Time Sheet
RCATSB01	Time Sheet: Approve Times	Cross-Application Time Sheet
RCATSBEL	Time Sheet Documents and Follow-on Documents	Cross-Application Time Sheet
RCATSCHR	Time Sheet: Check Consistency Between CATSDB and HR	Cross-Application Time Sheet
RCATSCMP	Time Sheet: Time Leveling	Cross-Application Time Sheet
RCATSDEL	Time Sheet: Delete Transaction Data	Cross-Application Time Sheet
RCATSP01	Time Sheet: Print Times	Cross-Application Time Sheet
RCATSRIF	Reorganize Time Sheet Interface Tables	Cross-Application Time Sheet
RCATSTMP	Standard Template for the Time Sheet	Cross-Application Time Sheet
RCATSW01	CATS: Released Time Data	Cross-Application Time Sheet
RCATS_ARCH_ARCHIVING	Archiving Time Sheet Data	Cross-Application Time Sheet
RCATS_ARCH_DELETING	Deleting Archived Time Sheet Data	Cross-Application Time Sheet
RCATS_ARCH_INDEXING	Creating an Index for Archived Time Sheet Data	Cross-Application Time Sheet

Table B.1 List of CATS Programs (Cont.)

Program	Description	Functionality
RCATS_ARCH_READING	Display Archived Time Sheet Data	Cross-Application Time Sheet
RCATS_ARCH_RELOADING	Restoring Archived Data to CATSDB	Cross-Application Time Sheet
RCATS_REPLACE_WF_TASK	Replace Workflow Task IDs in CATS Profiles	Cross-Application Time Sheet
RCATS_APPROVE_ACTIVITIES	Approve Working Times	Cross-Application Time Sheet
RCATS_SELECTION_VIEW	Maintain Selection Views	Cross-Application Time Sheet
RCATSXC_CHECK	Check Customizing Settings	Cross-Application Time Sheet
RCATSXC_PROFILE_WHERE_USED	Where-Used List of Entry Profile in CATS for Service Providers	Cross-Application Time Sheet
RCATSXT_CHANGE_USER_DEFAULT	CATSXT: Change User Settings	Cross-Application Time Sheet
RCATSXT_DISPLAY_ACTIVITIES	Display Work Times and Tasks	Cross-Application Time Sheet
RCATSXT_DISPLAY_ACTIVITY_DTL	Working Times and Tasks: Display Details	Cross-Application Time Sheet
RCATSXT_EXT_IF_DEBUGGING	Debugging CATSXT_EXTERNAL_INTERFACE Using Log File	Cross-Application Time Sheet
RCATSXT_START_TRANSACTION	Call Up Time Sheet Using Object CL_TIME_SHEET_CATSXT	Cross-Application Time Sheet
RCATS_DISPLAY_ACTIVITIES	Display Working Times	Cross-Application Time Sheet
R_APPROVE_ACTIVITIES_EXPENSES	Approve Working Times and Travel Expenses	Cross-Application Time Sheet
SAPLCATS	Create/Display Working Time	Cross-Application Time Sheet
SAPLCATSXT	Record Working Times Service Provider	Cross-Application Time Sheet

Table B.1 List of CATS Programs (Cont.)

Program	Description	Functionality
RPTCMP00	Time Leveling	Cross-Application Time Sheet
RPTEXTPT	Transfer Time Data to HR Time Management	Cross-Application Time Sheet
RPTWAO_CMP00	Time Leveling Mini App	Cross-Application Time Sheet
RCATSA01	Time Sheet: Approve Times (Selection by Org. Assignment)	Cross-Application Time Sheet
RCATSC01	Time Sheet: Approve Times (Selection by Master Data)	Cross-Application Time Sheet
RCATSTAL	Time Sheet: Transfer to Target Components	Cross-Application Time Sheet
RCATSTHR	Data Transfer CATS -> HR	Cross-Application Time Sheet

Table B.1   List of CATS Programs (Cont.)

B.2   HR PDC

Program	Description	Functionality
RPTCC101	HR PDC: Download HR Mini-Master	HR PDC
RPTCC102	HR PDC: Download Employee Time Balances	HR PDC
RPTCC103	HR PDC: Download Attendance/Absence Reasons	HR PDC
RPTCC104	HR PDC: Download Permitted Employee Expenditures	HR PDC
RPTCC105	HR PDC: Download Time Event Type Groupings	HR PDC
RPTCC106	HR PDC: Download Upload Request for Time Events	HR PDC
RPTCC107	HR PDC: Download Cost Centers	HR PDC
RPTCC108	HR PDC: Download Projects (WBS Elements)	HR PDC

Table B.2   HR PDC Programs

Program	Description	Functionality
RPTCC109	HR PDC: Download Upload Request for Employee Expenditures	HR PDC
RPTCC110	HR PDC: Download Objects (such as Positions)	HR PDC
RPTCC111	HR PDC: Download Internal Orders	HR PDC
RPTDAN00	Download Absence Reasons to DASS	HR PDC
RPTEDO00	Download Mini-master to Sequential File	HR PDC
RPTEUP00	Upload Time Events from Sequential File	HR PDC
RPTEUP10	Upload Time Events	HR PDC
SAPCDT42	Transfer HR Master Record to PDC System	HR PDC
SAPCDT43	Transfer Master Data to PDC Subsystems	HR PDC
SAPCDT44	Batch Report for Uploading Time Events from Subsystem	HR PDC
SAPCDT45	HR PDC: Post Personnel Time Events	HR PDC
SAPCDT46	Post Work Time Events from PP-PDC	HR PDC
SAPMP51E	Time Management Pool	HR PDC

Table B.2 HR PDC Programs (Cont.)

B.3   Leave Requests

Program	Description	Functionality
RPTARQAPP	Leave Requests: Approve Documents	Leave Requests
RPTARQDBDEL	Delete Leave Requests (Database of Requests)	Leave Requests
RPTARQDBVIEW	Display Leave Requests (Database of Requests)	Leave Requests
RPTARQEMAIL	Leave Requests: Send Emails	Leave Requests
RPTARQERR	Leave Requests: Process Posting Errors	Leave Requests
RPTARQERR_ALL	Leave Requests: Process Posting Errors	Leave Requests
RPTARQLIST	Leave Requests: Check	Leave Requests
RPTARQPOST	Leave Requests: Post	Leave Requests

Table B.3 Leave Request Programs

Program	Description	Functionality
RPTARQSTOPWF	Leave Requests: Complete Current Workflows	Leave Requests
RPUARQDEADLINE	Initialization of Periods for Leave Request	Leave Requests
RPTARQ	Test Environment for Leave Request	Leave Requests
RPTARQAPTEST	Test Report: UIA Area Pages for Leave Requests	Leave Requests
RPTREQAPPRCHK	Determine Approver	Leave Requests
RPTREQWEBMO	Determine Rule Group	Leave Requests

Table B.3 Leave Request Programs (Cont.)

B.4   Concurrent Employment

Program	Description	Functionality
RPTBAL00_CE	Time Balances and Time Wage Types for Concurrent Employment	Concurrent Employment
RPTPSHCE	Personal Work Schedule	Concurrent Employment
RPTQTA10_CE	Absence Quota Information for Concurrent Employment	Concurrent Employment

Table B.4 Concurrent Employment Programs

B.5   Time Events

Program	Description	Functionality
RPAFRV00	Time Events with Errors: Post processing	Time Events
RPTCORAPP	Clock-In/Out Corrections: Approve Documents	Time Events
RPTCORDBDEL	Clock-In/Out Corrections: Delete Obsolete Documents	Time Events
RPTCORDBVIEW	Display Clock-In/Out Corrections (Database)	Time Events

Table B.5 Time Events Programs

Program	Description	Functionality
RPTCOREMAIL	Clock-In/Out Corrections: Emails to Involved Persons	Time Events
RPTCORERR	Clock-In/Out Corrections: Process Errors in Entries	Time Events
RPTCORERR_ALL	Clock-In/Out Corrections: Process Errors in Entries	Time Events
RPTCORLIST	Clock-In/Out Corrections: Check Corrections	Time Events
RPTCORPOST	Clock-In/Out Corrections: Post	Time Events
RPTCORSTOPWF	Clock-In/Out Corrections: End Open Processes	Time Events
RPTCORTMAIL	Clock-In/Out Corrections: Request Correction of Errors	Time Events
RPTCOR	Test Environment for Clock-In/Out Corrections	Time Events
RPTCORAPTEST	Test Report: Area Page for Clock-In/Out Corrections	Time Events
RPTCORUIATEST	Test Report for UIA Interface for Clock-In/Out Corrections	Time Events

Table B.5 Time Events Programs (Cont.)

B.6 Time Infotype Data

Program	Description	Functionality
RPLMUT00	Overview of Maternity Data	Time Infotype Data
RPLTIM00	Time Recording Overview List	Time Infotype Data
RPTABS20	Attendance/Absence Data: Overview	Time Infotype Data
RPTABS50	Attendance/Absence Data: Calendar View	Time Infotype Data
RPTABS60	Attendances/Absences: Multiple Employee View	Time Infotype Data

Table B.6 Time Events Programs

Program	Description	Functionality
RPTAPPU0	Report for Time Leveling	Time Infotype Data
RPTBOD00	Report for BUS2079 with Selection	Time Infotype Data
RPTCCXDBDEL	Delete Time Events	Time Infotype Data
RPTCCXDBVIEW	Complete List of All Time Events	Time Infotype Data
RPTCCXTEST	Test Data Transfer for Time Events	Time Infotype Data
RPTEAB00	Attendance Check	Time Infotype Data
RPTIST00	CC2: Transfer HR Actual Times to Logistics	Time Infotype Data
RPTLEA40	Overview Graphic of Attendances/ Absences	Time Infotype Data
RPTPDOC0	Transfer Additional Data for Activity Allocation to Accounting	Time Infotype Data
RPTUPD00	Revaluation of Attendance/Absence Records using Batch Input	Time Infotype Data
RPTWSR_SET_ WWD	Find and Set Number of Weekly Working Days	Time Infotype Data
RPTX2010	Upload EE Remun.Info	Time Infotype Data
SAPMPTFMLA	FMLA Workbench	Time Infotype Data
RPTTMW00	Time Manager's Workplace	Time Infotype Data
RPTWAO_MA_ REP	RPTWAO_MA_REP Report	Time Infotype Data
RPT_TMW	Time Manager's Workplace	Time Infotype Data
RPT_TMW_ CLEAR_DEFAULT_ SELID	Deletes the defaulted Time Manager's Workplace profile	Time Infotype Data
RPT_TMW_ COMPONENT_ TEST	Test Environment for TMW Components	Time Infotype Data
RPT_TME	Time Manager's Workplace	Time Infotype Data

Table B.6 Time Events Programs (Cont.)

B.7   Time Evaluation

Program	Description	Functionality
RPTIME01	Time Evaluation for Concurrent Employment	Time Evaluation
RPTIME00	Time Evaluation	Time Evaluation
RPTIMEPS	Preselection for Time Evaluation for Concurrent Employment	Time Evaluation
RPTERL00	Time Evaluation Messages Display	Time Evaluation
RPTERR00	Time Management: Error Handling	Time Evaluation
RPTEZL00	PDC Time Evaluation: Supply Third-Party Payroll System (Example)	Time Evaluation

Table B.7   Time Evaluation Programs

B.8   Clusters

Program	Description	Functionality
RPCLSTB1	Display Cluster B1 of DB PCL1	Clusters
RPCLSTB2	Display Time Evaluation Results (Cluster B2)	Clusters
RPCLSTPC	Display Cluster PC: Personal Calendar and COVER	Clusters
RPTBAL00	Accumulated Time Evaluation Results: Time Balances/Wage Types	Clusters
RPTBCH00	Initialization of COVER Table for Absence Refinement	Clusters
RPTBOD20	Display Time Balances	Clusters
RPTBPC00	Generate Personal Calendar: International	Clusters
RPTDOW00	Time Accounts	Clusters
RPTEB200	Example: PU12 Format TIME; Export ZL from Cluster B2	Clusters
RPTEDT00	Time Statement Form	Clusters
RPTLEA10	Display Cluster PC Table PURL of DB PCL1	Clusters
RPCLSTG1	Display Database PCL1, Cluster G1 Incentives	Clusters

Table B.8   Clusters Programs

Program	Description	Functionality
RPCLSTL1	Display Database PCL1, Cluster L1 Incentives	Clusters
RPWUG190	Clean-up Cluster G1 (Tool)	Clusters
RPWUL170	Delete Time Tickets from Cluster L1	Clusters
RPWUL190	Clean-up Cluster L1 (Tool)	Clusters

Table B.8 Clusters Programs (Cont.)

B.9   Work Schedules

Program	Description	Functionality
RPDTGP00	Daily and Period Work Schedules	Work Schedules
RPTPSH10	Personal Work Schedule	Work Schedules
RPTSHF00	Generation of Work Schedules	Work Schedules
RPUTPR00	Revaluate Daily Work Schedules	Work Schedules
RPUWSH00	Revaluation of the Planned Working Time Infotype (0007)	Work Schedules

Table B.9 Work Schedule Programs

B.10   Quotas

Program	Description	Functionality
RPILVA00	Leave Accrual	Quotas
RPTBOD10	Call for BUS3018 Screen Display	Quotas
RPTBPC10	Leave Accrual and Quota Deduction	Quotas
RPTKOK00	Check Leave and Quota Deduction	Quotas
RPTLEA00	Leave Overview	Quotas
RPTLEA30	Batch Input: Annual Leave	Quotas
RPTLEACONV	Transfer of Remaining Leave from Infotype 0005 to Infotype 2006	Quotas
RPTQTA00	Generate Absence Quotas	Quotas
RPTQTA10	Display Absence Quota Information	Quotas
SAPMPT50	Quota Overview	Quotas

Table B.10 Quota Programs

B.11   Employee Expenditures

Program	Description	Functionality
RPIEWT00	Create Batch Input Session for Employee Expenditures	Employee Expenditures
RPIEWT01	List for Table TEXLGA (Employee Expenditures)	Employee Expenditures
RPIEWT02	Reorganize Table TEXLGA (Employee Expenditures)	Employee Expenditures
RPIEWT03	Employee Expenditures: Incorrect Batch Input Sessions Exists	Employee Expenditures
RPIEWT04	Batch Input: Process sessions in batch	Employee Expenditures

Table B.11   Employee Expenditure Programs

B.12   Incentive Wages

Program	Description	Functionality
RPWAZL00	Working Times of Time- and Incentive Wage Earners	Incentive Wages
RPWI0000	Batch Input to Incentive Wages	Incentive Wages
RPWI1000	Integration with Logistics: Read Interface File and Generate Session	Incentive Wages
RPWI1100	Integration with Logistics: Read Interface File and Generate Session	Incentive Wages
RPWI3000	Integration with Logistics: Batch Input Sessions with Errors Exist	Incentive Wages
RPWI4000	Integration with Logistics: Reorganize Interface File	Incentive Wages
RPWI4100	Integration with Logistics: Reorganize Interface File	Incentive Wages
RPWUG100	Recalculate Results and Cumulations for Group Incentive Wages	Incentive Wages
RPWUG170	Delete Time Tickets from Cluster G1	Incentive Wages

Table B.12   Incentive Wage Programs

Program	Description	Functionality
RPWUG180	Update Group Membership After Members Have Left	Incentive Wages
RPWUL100	Recalculate Results and Cumulations for Individual Incentive Wages	Incentive Wages
RPWULL00	Reassignment Proposals for Wage Groups	Incentive Wages

Table B.12 Incentive Wage Programs (Cont.)

B.13 Shift Planning

Program	Description	Functionality
RHDOCCPL	Display Attendance List	Shift Planning
RHDPERSL	Display Personal Shift Plan	Shift Planning
RHDREQDL	Requirements Assignment of Persons	Shift Planning
RHDREQUD	Display Target Requirements in Daily Overview	Shift Planning
RHDREQUW	Display Weekly Overview of Target Requirements	Shift Planning
RHPORDL0	Delete Database PSOLL	Shift Planning
RHPSOLL_DEL	Undo Completed Target Plan	Shift Planning
RHPURGE4	Delete Inconsistent Requirements Objects	Shift Planning
RHSP_ADMIN_IT0439	Create infotype 0439 with Subtype 0005	Shift Planning
RHSP_TEMP_ASSIGNMENT	Display Temporary Assignment List	Shift Planning
RHSP_WFP_APPROVAL	Release Workflow Results for Shift Planning	Shift Planning
RHXLTEST	Installation Test for EXCEL Interface to Shift Planning	Shift Planning
SAPFH5AH	Display Shift Plan	Shift Planning
SAPMH06A	View Cluster for Shift Groups	Shift Planning

Table B.13 Shift Planning Programs

B.14 Business Warehouse

Program	Description	Functionality
RPPTDW01	Create Reporting Time Types Automatically	Business Warehouse
RPPTDW02	Create Reporting Quota Types Automatically	Business Warehouse

Table B.14 Business Warehouse Programs

B.15 Configuration Overview

Program	Description	Functionality
RPT55400	Examine Table T554S	Configuration Overview
RPTBOD30	Displays Absence and Attendances Input Checks	Configuration Overview
RPTDSH20	Daily Work Schedule	Configuration Overview
RPTQUOTA_CHECK	Overview of Customizing Settings for Quota Generation	Configuration Overview
RPT_TMW_CUST_ UPDATE_TCVIEW	TMW Customizing: Report for Generating TCVIEW Entries	Configuration Overview
SAPMP51S	Create a Work Schedule	Configuration Overview

Table B.15 Configuration Overview Programs

B.16 Miscellaneous

Program	Description	Functionality
PREAD_WORK_CENTER	Transfer of Work Center Capacity (Crew Availability) to CSD	Misc.
RPCS0000	Schedules Multiple Background Jobs of the Same Program	Misc.
RPDLGA40	Display Processing Classes, Evaluation Classes.	Misc.

Table B.16 Miscellaneous Programs

Program	Description	Functionality
RPUTRBK0	Update Infotype 0003 Payroll Status	Misc.
RPUFRM00	Copy Forms	Misc.
RPCLSTB2	Displays Employee B2 Clusters	Misc.
RPUP2D00	Delete Time Clusters	Misc.
RPUP2D10	Delete Time Clusters Non Production	Misc.
RPUBTCU0	Test BSI Connection	Misc.
RPUDEL20	Delete Payroll by Individual or Mass Population	Misc.
RHPLDF00	Displays Infotype Detail	Misc.
RPUCYC00	List Personnel Calculation Rule Details	Misc.

Table B.16 Miscellaneous Programs (Cont.)

C   Time Management Features

SAP delivers a variety of Features that can be used for many different reasons. A Feature is a tool in the SAP system that you can use to default information on infotype screens, such as Feature TMSTA, which is used in Infoytpe 0007 to default the Time Management status. Another example is a payroll Feature, such as DTAKT, which defaults banking information when running checks and direct deposit programs.

C.1   Listing of Features

Features allow you to default data (or a report) on an infotype for a given criteria. Features can be accessed via Transaction code PE03. The following are the Time Management Features available within the system. A complete list of Features can be obtained for all countries by running program RPUMKD00 via Transaction code SE38. Figure C.1 shows a list of Time Management–related Features available for Time Management including the Feature name, description, the structure, and the area of Time Management it supports.

The structure is the listing of fields and logic available to a Feature for you to make decisions from. By using the fields, for example, Feature TMSTA, you can default the Time Management status of 9 for salaried employees and a 1 for hourly employees. The values would then help control how they process in Time Evaluation.

Feature	Subfeature	Standard/Modified	Description	Structure	Functionality
27SLE		STD	Sick Leave Entitlement	PME58	Quotas
DATAR		MOD	Default value for date specifications	PME01	Leave accrual
DOKNT		STD	Dynamic screen layout of coding block	PME27	External Services
GRDWT		STD	Feature for grouping of reporting time types	PMTDW	TMW
HRSIF		MOD	Recording atts./absences without clock times	PME44	2001 and 2002
I0005		STD	Set control parameters for infotype 0005	PME03	Leave accrual
LDAYW		MOD	Determine last day of a week	PME06	User Interfaces
LIMIE	X	STD	Hourly limits for day balances	PME51	Reporting
LIMIS	X	STD	Hourly limits for cumulated balances	PME51	Reporting
LIMIT		STD	Hourly limits for cumulated balances (RPTBAL00)	PME51	Reporting
LIMIZ	X	STD	Hourly limits for time wage types	PME51	Reporting
LLREP		MOD	Time Management	PME16	Quotas
LVACC		STD	Determine amount of leave to be accumulated	PME03	Leave Accrual
LVBEG		STD	Specify start of deduction for a leave type	PME03	Leave Accrual
LVCUT		STD	Specify reduction rules for total leave entitleme	PME03	Leave Accrual
LVDEF		STD	Processing remaining leave	PME03	Leave Accrual
LVEND		STD	Set end of deduction for leave type	PME03	Leave Accrual
LVMAX		STD	Set limits for leave entitlement	PME03	Leave Accrual
LVNUM		STD	Defining leave entitlement per leave type	PME03	Leave Accrual
LVRND		STD	Round Calculated Leave Entitlement	PME03	Leave Accrual
LVTYP		STD	Defining leave types	PME03	Leave Accrual
LVZER		STD	Generating a leave record when entitlement is zer	PME03	Leave Accrual
P2001		STD	Screen control for all time infotypes	PME04	Quotas
QUOMO		MOD	Determine quota type selection rule group	PME87	Quotas
SCHKZ		MOD	Default value for shift indicator	PME01	Infotype 7
TIMMO		STD	Defining the modifier for table T569R	PME01	Time Evaluation
TIMTA		STD	Determine daily standard time	PME44	User Interfaces
TIRUG		STD	Group Personnel Assignments	PME96	Concurrent Employment
TMSTA		MOD	DEFAULT VALUE FOR TIME MANAGEMENT STATUS	PME01	Infotype 7
TRVCO		MOD	Dynamic screen layout of account assignment block	PME27	External Services
UABEG		STD	Determine start of deduction	PME03	Leave accrual
UAEND		STD	Determine end of deduction	PME03	Leave accrual
VACBE		STD	VACBE Determining the start month/day	PME03	Leave accrual
VTART		STD	VTART Defining substitution type on infotype 2003	PME06	Infotype 2003
WEBMO		MOD	Define Rule Group for Customizing Tables in Web E	PME95	Leave Request
WRKHR		MOD	Input control for working hour fields/weekly work	PME01	Infotype 7
WWEEK		MOD	Default value for working week	PME01	Infotype 7

Figure C.1 Listing of Features

C.2 Sample Feature TMSTA

Figure C.2 shows an example of the Feature TMSTA.

Edit Feature TMSTA: Decision Tree

Error text

Command

Line	Variable key	F	C	Operations
000010			D	MOLGA
000020	* *			&TMSTA=,
000030	10		D	PERSK
000040	10 * *			&TMSTA=9,
000050	10 01			&TMSTA=9,
000060	10 02			&TMSTA=9,
000070	10 03			&TMSTA=1,

Field	Description
Line	Each row of a feature represents 1 line. The lines increments in counts of 10
Variable Key	Represents the response to the decision being asked in the Operations field. If there happens to be more than 1 decision in the feature, a space must exist between responses to the questions being asked.
F	Continuation Indicator determining further table access. This is utilized in Reduced Hours Compensation functionality only.
C	There are two possible entries for this field. 'D'represents decision and an operation must be used with applicable responses available in the Variable Key. '*' is also allowed and when used, the row is deemed a comment
Operations	An Operation with a 'D' is the decision. Once a response is located in the Variable Key, the operation becomes the value that will be used in processing. The &XXXX= is a required format, followed by the values you would like to default

Figure C.2 Feature TMSA

C.3   Features

Feature maintenance can take place in one of two ways:

▶ Tree Maintenance — the new way of doing things
▶ Table Maintenance — the old way of doing things

Both methods work just fine, it really just depends on your preference.

Figure C.3 shows both methods side by side.

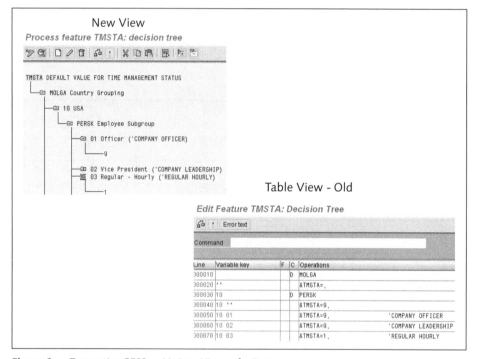

Figure C.3   Transaction PE03 — Various Views of a Feature

D   Work Schedule Combinations

The following figures list all statistical combinations based on the days of the week the employee is to work. This assumes just working day shift combinations. Second and third shifts and rotating period schedules, if applicable, would increase the amount of schedules required. Introduction of specific part-time schedules would further increase the amount of actual Work Schedules required unless the planned working time part-time check box functionality is utilized. The total count of this illustration is equal to 127 Work Schedules. Figures D.1 through D.7 show the various combinations.

Figure D.1 provides a list of five-day work week combinations.

1	Regularly Scheduled 5 Day Work Weeks						
Saturday	Sunday	Monday	Tuesday	Wednesday	Thursday	Friday	Work Schedule ID
Scheduled	Scheduled	Scheduled	Scheduled	Scheduled	OFF	OFF	1
Scheduled	Scheduled	Scheduled	Scheduled	OFF	OFF	Scheduled	2
Scheduled	Scheduled	Scheduled	OFF	OFF	Scheduled	Scheduled	3
Scheduled	Scheduled	OFF	OFF	Scheduled	Scheduled	Scheduled	4
Scheduled	OFF	OFF	Scheduled	Scheduled	Scheduled	Scheduled	5
Scheduled	OFF	Scheduled	OFF	Scheduled	Scheduled	Scheduled	6
Scheduled	OFF	Scheduled	Scheduled	OFF	Scheduled	Scheduled	7
Scheduled	OFF	Scheduled	Scheduled	Scheduled	OFF	Scheduled	8
Scheduled	OFF	Scheduled	Scheduled	Scheduled	Scheduled	OFF	9
Scheduled	Scheduled	OFF	Scheduled	Scheduled	Scheduled	OFF	10
Scheduled	Scheduled	OFF	Scheduled	Scheduled	OFF	Scheduled	11
Scheduled	Scheduled	OFF	Scheduled	OFF	Scheduled	Scheduled	12
Scheduled	Scheduled	Scheduled	OFF	Scheduled	Scheduled	OFF	13
Scheduled	Scheduled	Scheduled	OFF	Scheduled	OFF	Scheduled	14
Scheduled	Scheduled	Scheduled	Scheduled	OFF	Scheduled	OFF	15
OFF	Scheduled	Scheduled	Scheduled	Scheduled	Scheduled	OFF	16
OFF	Scheduled	Scheduled	Scheduled	Scheduled	OFF	Scheduled	17
OFF	Scheduled	Scheduled	Scheduled	OFF	Scheduled	Scheduled	18
OFF	Scheduled	Scheduled	OFF	Scheduled	Scheduled	Scheduled	19
OFF	Scheduled	OFF	Scheduled	Scheduled	Scheduled	Scheduled	20
OFF	OFF	Scheduled	Scheduled	Scheduled	Scheduled	Scheduled	21
6	6	6	6	6	6	6	Off
15	15	15	15	15	15	15	Scheduled

Figure D.1   Combinations for an Employee Working Five Days a Week

Figured D.2 provides a list of four-day work week combinations.

2 Regularly Scheduled 4 Day Work Weeks

Saturday	Sunday	Monday	Tuesday	Wednesday	Thursday	Friday	Work Schedule ID
Scheduled	Scheduled	Scheduled	Scheduled	OFF	OFF	OFF	22
Scheduled	Scheduled	Scheduled	OFF	Scheduled	OFF	OFF	23
Scheduled	Scheduled	OFF	Scheduled	Scheduled	OFF	OFF	24
Scheduled	OFF	Scheduled	Scheduled	Scheduled	OFF	OFF	25
OFF	Scheduled	Scheduled	Scheduled	Scheduled	OFF	OFF	26
OFF	OFF	Scheduled	Scheduled	Scheduled	Scheduled	OFF	27
OFF	OFF	Scheduled	Scheduled	Scheduled	OFF	Scheduled	28
OFF	OFF	Scheduled	Scheduled	OFF	Scheduled	Scheduled	29
OFF	OFF	Scheduled	OFF	Scheduled	Scheduled	Scheduled	30
OFF	OFF	OFF	Scheduled	Scheduled	Scheduled	Scheduled	31
OFF	Scheduled	OFF	Scheduled	Scheduled	Scheduled	OFF	32
OFF	Scheduled	OFF	Scheduled	Scheduled	OFF	Scheduled	33
OFF	Scheduled	OFF	Scheduled	OFF	Scheduled	Scheduled	34
OFF	Scheduled	OFF	OFF	Scheduled	Scheduled	Scheduled	35
OFF	Scheduled	Scheduled	OFF	Scheduled	Scheduled	OFF	36
OFF	Scheduled	Scheduled	OFF	Scheduled	OFF	Scheduled	37
OFF	Scheduled	Scheduled	OFF	OFF	Scheduled	Scheduled	38
OFF	Scheduled	Scheduled	Scheduled	OFF	Scheduled	OFF	39
OFF	Scheduled	Scheduled	Scheduled	OFF	OFF	Scheduled	40
Scheduled	OFF	OFF	Scheduled	Scheduled	Scheduled	OFF	41
Scheduled	OFF	OFF	Scheduled	Scheduled	OFF	Scheduled	42
Scheduled	OFF	OFF	Scheduled	OFF	Scheduled	Scheduled	43
Scheduled	OFF	OFF	OFF	Scheduled	Scheduled	Scheduled	44
Scheduled	Scheduled	OFF	OFF	Scheduled	Scheduled	OFF	45
Scheduled	Scheduled	OFF	OFF	Scheduled	OFF	Scheduled	46
Scheduled	Scheduled	OFF	OFF	OFF	Scheduled	Scheduled	47
Scheduled	off	Scheduled	OFF	Scheduled	OFF	Scheduled	48
Scheduled	OFF	Scheduled	OFF	OFF	Scheduled	Scheduled	49
Scheduled	Scheduled	Scheduled	OFF	OFF	OFF	Scheduled	50
Scheduled	Scheduled	Scheduled	OFF	OFF	Scheduled	OFF	51
Scheduled	OFF	Scheduled	Scheduled	OFF	OFF	Scheduled	52
Scheduled	Scheduled	OFF	Scheduled	OFF	OFF	Scheduled	53
Scheduled	Scheduled	OFF	Scheduled	OFF	Scheduled	OFF	54
Scheduled	OFF	Scheduled	Scheduled	OFF	Scheduled	OFF	55
Scheduled	OFF	Scheduled	OFF	Scheduled	Scheduled	OFF	56
15	15	15	15	15	15	15	Off
20	20	20	20	20	20	20	Scheduled

Figure D.2 Combinations for an Employee Working Four Days a Week

Figure D.3 provides a list of seven-day work week combinations.

3	Scheduled 7 Day Work Week							
Saturday	**Sunday**	**Monday**	**Tuesday**	**Wednesday**	**Thursday**	**Friday**	**Work Schedule ID**	
Scheduled	Scheduled	Scheduled	Scheduled	Scheduled	Scheduled	Scheduled	57	
1 possible combination								

Figure D.3   Combinations for an Employee Working Seven Days a Week

Figure D.4 provides a list of six-day work week combinations.

4	Scheduled 6 Day Work Week							
Saturday	**Sunday**	**Monday**	**Tuesday**	**Wednesday**	**Thursday**	**Friday**	**Work Schedule ID**	
Scheduled	Scheduled	Scheduled	Scheduled	Scheduled	Scheduled	OFF	58	
Scheduled	Scheduled	Scheduled	Scheduled	Scheduled	OFF	Scheduled	59	
Scheduled	Scheduled	Scheduled	Scheduled	OFF	Scheduled	Scheduled	60	
Scheduled	Scheduled	Scheduled	OFF	Scheduled	Scheduled	Scheduled	61	
Scheduled	Scheduled	Off	Scheduled	Scheduled	Scheduled	Scheduled	62	
Scheduled	Off	Scheduled	Scheduled	Scheduled	Scheduled	Scheduled	63	
Off	Scheduled	Scheduled	Scheduled	Scheduled	Scheduled	Scheduled	64	
7 possible combinations								

Figure D.4   Combinations for an Employee Working Six Days a Week

Figure D.5 provides a list of three-day work week combinations.

5 | Scheduled 3 Day Work Week

Saturday	Sunday	Monday	Tuesday	Wednesday	Thursday	Friday	Work Schedule ID
Scheduled	Scheduled	Scheduled	Off	OFF	OFF	OFF	65
Scheduled	scheduled	Off	Scheduled	OFF	OFF	OFF	66
Scheduled	Scheduled	Off	Off	Scheduled	OFF	OFF	67
Scheduled	Scheduled	Off	Off	OFF	scheduled	OFF	68
Scheduled	Scheduled	Off	Off	OFF	OFF	Scheduled	69
Off	Scheduled	Scheduled	Scheduled	OFF	OFF	OFF	70
Off	Scheduled	Scheduled	Off	Scheduled	OFF	OFF	71
Off	Scheduled	Scheduled	Off	OFF	scheduled	OFF	72
Off	Scheduled	Scheduled	Off	OFF	OFF	Scheduled	73
Off	Off	Scheduled	Scheduled	Scheduled	OFF	OFF	74
Off	Off	Scheduled	Scheduled	OFF	scheduled	OFF	75
Off	Off	Scheduled	Scheduled	OFF	OFF	Scheduled	76
Scheduled	Off	Scheduled	Scheduled	OFF	OFF	OFF	77
Off	Off	Off	Scheduled	Scheduled	scheduled	OFF	78
Off	Off	Off	Scheduled	Scheduled	OFF	Scheduled	79
Scheduled	Off	Off	Scheduled	Scheduled	OFF	OFF	80
Off	Scheduled	Off	Scheduled	Scheduled	OFF	OFF	81
Off	Off	Off	Off	Scheduled	scheduled	Scheduled	82
Scheduled	Off	Off	Off	Scheduled	scheduled	OFF	83
Off	Scheduled	Off	Off	Scheduled	scheduled	OFF	84
Off	Off	Scheduled	Off	Scheduled	scheduled	OFF	85
Scheduled	Off	Scheduled	Off	Scheduled	OFF	OFF	86
Scheduled	Off	Scheduled	Off	OFF	Scheduled	OFF	87
Scheduled	Off	Scheduled	Off	OFF	OFF	Scheduled	88
Scheduled	Off	Off	Scheduled	OFF	Scheduled	OFF	89
Scheduled	Off	Off	Scheduled	OFF	OFF	Scheduled	90
Scheduled	Off	Off	Off	Scheduled	OFF	Scheduled	91
Off	Scheduled	Off	Scheduled	OFF	scheduled	OFF	92
Off	Scheduled	Off	Scheduled	OFF	OFF	Scheduled	93
Off	Scheduled	Off	Off	Scheduled	OFF	Scheduled	94
Off	Off	Scheduled	Off	Scheduled	OFF	Scheduled	95
Off	Off	Scheduled	Off	OFF	scheduled	Scheduled	96
Scheduled	Off	Off	Off	OFF	scheduled	Scheduled	97
Off	Scheduled	Off	Off	OFF	scheduled	Scheduled	98
OFF	Off	Off	Scheduled	OFF	scheduled	Scheduled	99
20	20	20	20	20	20	20	Off
15	15	15	15	15	15	15	Scheduled
35 Possible Combinations							

Figure D.5   Combinations for an Employee Working Three Days a Week

Figure D.6 provides a list of two-day work week combinations.

6   Scheduled 2 Day Work Week

Saturday	Sunday	Monday	Tuesday	Wednesday	Thursday	Friday	Work Schedule ID
Scheduled	Scheduled	OFF	OFF	OFF	OFF	OFF	100
Scheduled	OFF	Scheduled	OFF	OFF	OFF	OFF	101
Scheduled	OFF	OFF	Scheduled	OFF	OFF	OFF	102
Scheduled	OFF	OFF	OFF	Scheduled	OFF	OFF	103
Scheduled	OFF	OFF	OFF	OFF	Scheduled	OFF	104
Scheduled	OFF	OFF	OFF	OFF	OFF	Scheduled	105
Off	Scheduled	Scheduled	OFF	OFF	OFF	OFF	106
Off	Scheduled	OFF	Scheduled	OFF	OFF	OFF	107
Off	Scheduled	OFF	OFF	Scheduled	OFF	OFF	108
Off	Scheduled	OFF	OFF	OFF	Scheduled	OFF	109
Off	Scheduled	OFF	OFF	OFF	OFF	Scheduled	110
Off	OFF	Scheduled	Scheduled	OFF	OFF	OFF	111
Off	OFF	Scheduled	OFF	Scheduled	OFF	OFF	112
Off	OFF	Scheduled	OFF	OFF	Scheduled	OFF	113
Off	OFF	Scheduled	OFF	OFF	OFF	Scheduled	114
Off	OFF	OFF	Scheduled	Scheduled	OFF	OFF	115
Off	OFF	OFF	Scheduled	OFF	Scheduled	OFF	116
Off	OFF	OFF	Scheduled	OFF	OFF	Scheduled	117
Off	OFF	OFF	OFF	Scheduled	Scheduled	OFF	118
Off	OFF	OFF	OFF	Scheduled	OFF	Scheduled	119
Off	OFF	OFF	OFF	OFF	Scheduled	Scheduled	120
15	15	15	15	15	15	15	Off
6	6	6	6	6	6	6	Scheduled

21 possible combinations

Figure D.6   Combinations for an Employee Working Two Days a Week

Figure D.7 provides a list of one-day work week combinations.

7   Scheduled 1 Day Work Week

Saturday	Sunday	Monday	Tuesday	Wednesday	Thursday	Friday	Work Schedule ID
Scheduled	OFF	OFF	OFF	OFF	OFF	OFF	121
OFF	Scheduled	OFF	OFF	OFF	OFF	OFF	122
OFF	OFF	Scheduled	OFF	OFF	OFF	OFF	123
OFF	OFF	OFF	Scheduled	OFF	OFF	OFF	124
OFF	OFF	OFF	OFF	Scheduled	OFF	OFF	125
OFF	OFF	OFF	OFF	OFF	Scheduled	OFF	126
OFF	OFF	OFF	OFF	OFF	OFF	Scheduled	127

7 possible combinations

Figure D.7   Combinations for an Employee Working One Day a Week

D.1 Summary

These combinations of Work Schedules have been provided to give you a jump start on determining how many Work Schedules you might need. During the blueprinting and the actual configuration, they may provide a valuable tool when determining how many schedules you might actually need to set up. In addition to these schedules, you may need to double or triple the amount if you also have second and third shift schedules with the combinations listed in each of the figures.

E   Time Evaluation Storage Tables

When Time Evaluation processes, the temporary and permanent results have to be stored somewhere. Time Management utilizes the storage tables we'll discuss in this appendix.

The following sections of tables are a breakdown of the B2 Time Evaluation cluster. This includes the structures that make up the clusters, and the fields within each cluster. The structures can be viewed in the SAP system via Transaction code SE11, or by selecting the radio button for data type for structures. Why is this important? When setting up Time Evaluation, personnel calculation rules determine what should or should not process. Based on the attributes of a field in a table, the system is configured to react differently. Your awareness of these tables, the attributes of the particular fields, and how you can influence them will help you in understanding how Time Evaluation works, and how you can customize the processing and troubleshoot issues when they arise. The fields are populated by either system configuration or processing that you have customized in the system.

E.1   WPBP—Basic Data

The Work Pay Basic Pay information is stored on structure PC205. This information pertains to the employee's master data, such as Personnel Areas and Employee Groups. This table also stores information related to Infotype 0007, Planned Working Time, and Infotype 0008, Basic Pay. Table E.1 shows the fields that are stored during processing.

Field	Notes
Assignment number (APZNR)	
Start Date	
End Date	
Action Type	
Reason for Action	

Table E.1 WPBP Fields

Field	Notes
Company Code	
Personnel area	
Personnel subarea	
Cust.-specific stat.	
Employment status	
Spec.payment status	
Active	
Cost Center	
Employee group	
Employee subgroup	
ES grouping for PCR	
Position	
Business Area	
Organizational key	
Work contract	
Organizational unit	
Job key	
Time Mgmt status	
Work schedule rule	
Employment percent	
Work hours/period	
Capacity Util. Level	
Pay scale type	
Pay Scale Area	
Pay Scale Group	
Pay scale level	
Dyn.daily work schedule	
Daily working hours	
Weekly workdays	

Table E.1 WPBP Fields (Cont.)

Field	Notes
Funds Center	
Fund	
Functional Area	
Grant	
Segment	

Table E.1 WPBP Fields (Cont.)

E.2   PSP — Personal Shift Plan

The personal Work Schedule information is stored on structure PC2BA. The PSP helps drive which days are work days for month-end accruals processing. Table E.2 shows the fields that are stored during processing.

Field	Notes
Date	
Personnel Subarea Grouping for Daily Work Schedules	
Daily Work Schedule	
Day Type	
Public holiday class	
Daily Work Schedule Variant	
Daily Work Schedule Class	
Period Work Schedule	
Number of hours	
Checkbox	
National indicator 1	
National indicator 2	
Work Break Schedule	

Table E.2 PSP Fields

E.3   ZES — Time Balances for Each Day

The daily time balance information is stored on structure PC2B6. This table stores any daily balances created during the Time Evaluation process. Storage for this table is dictated by the configuration in table T555A. Table E.3 shows the fields that are stored during processing.

Field	Notes
Relative day	
Time Type	Time types can be generated via custom calculation rules or table driven.
Number of day balance	This field can be updated

Table E.3   Time Balance Fields

E.4   SALDO — Cumulated Time Balances

The cumulated time balance information is stored on structure PC2B5. This table stores any monthly balances created during the Time Evaluation process. Storage for this table is dictated by the configuration in table T555A. Table E.4 shows the fields that are stored during the processing.

Field	Notes
Time Type	
Number of time balance in period	It is best to update the daily balance of a time type and use table T555A to cumulate the monthly balance.

Table E.4   Cumulated Time Balance Fields

E.5   ZKO — Time Quotas

The time quota information is stored on structure PC2B7. This information is related to Infotypes 2006 and 2007. Table E.5 shows the fields that are stored during processing.

Field	Notes
Relative day	
Quota type	
Infotype	
Subtype	
Object Identification	
Number of Infotype Record with Same Key	
End Date	
Start Date	
Number of Employee Time Quota	

Table E.5 Time Quota Fields

E.6   ZL — Time Wage Types

The time wage type information is stored on structure PC2BF.

The ZL table is a key integration point between the Time Management component and the Payroll component in that wage types that are stored in this table are pulled into Payroll to be evaluated. Table E.6 shows the fields that are stored during processing.

Field	Notes
Date	
Start time	
End time	
Assignment for alternative payment	
Pointer to cost accounting	
Pointer to absences	
Wage Type	
Information type (S/M/A)	
Number of hours per wage type	
Pointer to attendances	
Start Before 00:00	

Table E.6 Time Wage Type Fields

E.7 ALP — Different Payment

The different payment information is stored on structure PC20E. If, for example, on the attendance infotype, you elect to use a different valuation basis for a record, the overwrite will be flagged in this table during processing. Table E.7 shows the fields that are stored during processing.

Field	Notes
Start Date	
End Date	
Start Time	
End Time	
Number	
Time/Measurement Unit	
Wage Type Amount for Payments	
Object Type	
Position	
Premium Number	
Premium Indicator	
Extra Pay Indicator	
Amount	
Pay Scale Group	
Pay Scale Level	
Overtime Compensation Type	
Currency Key	
Work tax area	
Start Before 00:00	

Table E.7 Alternative Payment Fields

E.8 C1 — Cost Distribution

The cost distribution information is stored on structure PC25X. This table stores any cost override that is placed on an infotype. Table E.8 shows the fields that are stored during processing.

Field	Notes
Pointer to cost accounting	
Assignment Values for HR Objects	
Company Code	
Business Area	
Controlling Area	
Cost Center	
Order Number	
Cost Object	
Work Breakdown Structure Element (WBS Element)	
Network Number for Account Assignment	
Operation/Activity Number	
Sales Order Number	
Item Number in Sales Order	
Profitability Segment Number (CO-PA)	
Business Process	
Funds Center	
Commitment Item	
Fund	
Purchasing Document Number	
Item Number of Purchasing Document	
Activity Number	
Activity Type	
Company Code	

Table E.8 Cost Distribution Fields

Field	Notes
Business Area	
Cost Center	
Activity Type	
Assignment number	
Sales Tax Code	
Object Type	
Job	
Number of Hours for Activity Allocation/ External Services	
Service Type (Public Service Germany)	
Service Category (Public Service Germany)	
Item Text	
Tax Jurisdiction	
Commitment Item	
Functional Area	
Grant	
Sender fund	
Sending Functional Area	
Sender Grant	
Segment for Segmental Reporting	
Segment for Segmental Reporting	

Table E.8 Cost Distribution Fields (Cont.)

E.9   VS — Variable Balances

The variable balances information is stored on structure PC2BH. If, during the personnel calculation rules, you utilize variable balance to store time-related data to support one of your calculations, that data is stored in this table. Table E.9 shows the fields that are stored during processing.

Field	Notes
Date	
Comment	
Number of day balance	
Identifier for variable balances	

Table E.9 Variable Balance Fields

E.10 CVS — Accrued Variable Balances

The accrued variable balances information is stored on structure PC2BI. Table E.10 shows the fields that are stored during processing.

Field	Notes
Comment	
Number of time balance in period	
Identifier for variable balances	

Table E.10 Accrued Variable Balance Fields

E.11 FEHLER — Messages

The Time Evaluation–generated message information is stored on structure PC2B8. This table stores the messages that you have instructed Time Evaluation to generate. This table is where the Time Management Pool and the Time Manager's Workplace obtain the messages for the administrator to process. Table E.11 shows the fields that are stored during processing.

Field	Notes
Logical Date	
Logical time	
Category of Message Type	
Number of Message Type	

Table E.11 Message Fields

Field	Notes
Message type (E=Error; A=Cancel; ' '=Note)	
Historical Record Flag	
Message Supplement	
Sequential number for PDC messages	
Message Processing: Processing Status	
Message Processing: Last Processing Date	
Message Processing: Last User	
Origin of Message	

Table E.11 Message Fields (Cont.)

E.12 KNTAG — Work Bridging Two Calendar Days

This table is utilized for German processing only.

E.13 QTACC — Absence Quota Generation

The absence quota generation information is stored on structure PC2BJ. If you utilize Time Evaluation to generate quotas, then this table stores the quota information related to your specific setup. Table E.12 shows the fields that are stored during processing.

Field	Notes
Date Generated	
Absence Quota Type	
Operation Indicators for Automatic Accrual of Absence Quotas	
Number of a Time Quota (Currently Generated)	

Table E.12 Absence Quota Generation Fields

Field	Notes
Number of a Time Quota (Currently Accrued)	
Transfer Accrued Entitlement	
Number of Employee Time Quota	
Number of Employee Time Quota	
Number of Employee Time Quota	
Number of Employee Time Quota	
Accrual point for leave entitlement	
Period parameter	
Earliest accrual point	
Time of transfer to leave entitlement	
Period parameter	
Date type	
Size of transfer packages for absence quotas	
Maximum accrual entitlement	
Rounding rule	
Reduction rule for quota entitlements	
Maximum total entitlement	
Rounding rule	
Start Date	
End Date	
Start Date for Quota Deduction	
Quota Deduction to	
Checkbox	
Pointer to base entitlement for quota generation	
Quota Generation: Rule for Transfer Times	

Table E.12 Absence Quota Generation Fields (Cont.)

E.14   QTBASE — Base Entitlement

The base entitlement information is stored on structure PC2BK. This is an additional table used to store the amount of quota an employee is entitled as determined by the Time Evaluation processing. Table E.13 shows the fields that are stored during processing.

Field	Notes
Pointer to base entitlement for quota generation	
Start Date	
End Date	
Constant value of base entitlement for leave accrual	
Base entitlement period for quota generation	
Period parameter	
Start Date	
End Date	
Date type	
Relative position	
Time/Measurement Unit	

Table E.13   Quota Base Entitlement Fields

E.15   QTTRANS — Transfer Pool

The quota transfer pool information is stored on structure PC2BL. This is another quota table related to the transfer of the quota to Infotypes 2006 and 2007. Table E.14 shows the fields that are stored during processing.

Field	Notes
Date Generated	
Absence Quota Type	
Operation Indicators for Automatic Accrual of Absence Quotas	
Time of transfer to leave entitlement	
Period parameter	

Table E.14   Transfer Pool Fields

Field	Notes
Date type	
Quota number in transfer pool	
Size of transfer packages for absence quotas	
Maximum total entitlement	
Rounding rule	
Start Date	
End Date	
Start Date for Quota Deduction	
Quota Deduction to	
Quota Generation: Rule for Transfer Times	

Table E.14 Transfer Pool Fields (Cont.)

E.16   URLAN — Leave Accrual

The leave accrual information is stored on structure PC2BG. This table is related to data in Infotype 0005 — Leave Entitlement. Table E.15 shows the fields that are stored during processing.

Field	Notes
Infotype	
Subtype	
Object Identification	
End Date	
Start Date	
Number of Infotype Record with Same Key	
Date	
Leave type	
Leave entitlement	
Indicator for update	

Table E.15 Leave Accrual Fields

E.17 PT — Time Pairs

Time pairs information is stored on structure PDCPT. This table stores the information related to Infotype 2011. Table E.16 shows the fields that are stored during processing.

Field	Notes
Logical Date	
Start time	
End time	
Attendance/absence reason for begin entry	
Attendance/absence reason for end entry	
Terminal ID of start entry	
Terminal ID of end entry	
Time event pair start	
Time event pair end	
Status from pair formation	
Status from time evaluation	
Attendance or absence status in pair formation	
Change status	
Multi-purpose field for begin entry	
Multi-purpose field for end entry	
Sequential number for PDC messages	
Sequential number for PDC messages	
Start Before 00:00	

Table E.16 Time Pair Fields

E.18 WST — Time Tickets and Other Documents

The time tickets and other document information are stored on structure PDCWST.

Table E.17 shows the fields that are stored during processing.

Field	Notes
Logical Date	
Completion confirmation number for the operation	
Time ticket counter per confirmation no. and day	
Time ticket counter per day	
Logical system	
Start time	
End time	
Time event number with account assignment	
Number of last time event for this time ticket	
Destination indicator for external applications	
Destination within HR	
Indicator for single/multi operation processing	
External update: yes/no	
PDC Time Tickets: Times and Quantity	
Incentive Wages: Activities	
Standard value of processing time	
Measurement unit for standard value	
Target value of processing time	
Measurement unit for target value	
Confirmed value of processing time	
Measurement unit of confirmed value	
Start of processing time	
End of processing time	

Table E.17 Time Tickets and Other Document Fields

Field	Notes
Standard value of setup time	
Measurement unit for standard value	
Target value of setup time	
Measurement unit for target value	
Confirmed value of setup time	
Measurement unit of confirmed value	
Start of setup time	
End of setup time	
Standard value of machine time	
Measurement unit for standard value	
Target value of machine time	
Measurement unit for target value	
Confirmed value of machine time	
Measurement unit of confirmed value	
Start machine time	
End of machine time	
Standard value of variable activity	
Measurement unit for standard value	
Target value of variable activity	
Measurement unit for target value	
Confirmed value of variable activity	
Measurement unit of confirmed value	
Start of variable activity	
End of variable activity	
Standard value of teardown time	
Measurement unit for standard value	
Target value of teardown time	
Measurement unit for target value	
Confirmed value of teardown time	

Table E.17 Time Tickets and Other Document Fields (Cont.)

Field	Notes
Measurement unit of confirmed value	
Start of teardown time	
End of teardown time	
Standard value of variable activity	
Measurement unit for standard value	
Target value of variable activity	
Measurement unit for target value	
Confirmed value of variable activity	
Measurement unit of confirmed value	
Start of variable activity	
End of variable activity	
Incentive Wages: Quantities	
Unit of Measure	
Yield	
Scrap	
Scrap reason	
Base quantity	
Confirmed value of processing time from Logistics	
Measurement unit of confirmed value	
Confirmed value of setup time from Logistics	
Measurement unit of confirmed value	
Confirmed value of machine time from Logistics	
Measurement unit of confirmed value	
Confirmed value of variable activity from Logistics	
Measurement unit of confirmed value	

Table E.17 Time Tickets and Other Document Fields (Cont.)

Field	Notes
Confirmed Value of Teardown Time for Logistics	
Measurement unit of confirmed value	
Confirmed value of variable activity from Logistics	
Measurement unit of confirmed value	
Malfunction or interruption reason	
Accumulation rule for activity type	
Wage Type	
Pay Scale Group	
Pay scale level	
Time ticket type	
Transfer lock indicator for time ticket	
Group number	
Group name	
Customer-Specific Field	
Customer-Specific Field	
FI Assignment Sizes for HR Objects (for Time Tickets)	
Company Code	
Business Area	
Cost Center	
Activity Type	
Order Number	
Cost Object	
Work Breakdown Structure Element (WBS Element)	
Network Number for Account Assignment	
Operation/Activity Number	

Table E.17 Time Tickets and Other Document Fields (Cont.)

Field	Notes
Sales Order Number	
Item Number in Sales Order	
Business Process	
Funds Center	
Fund	
Cost Center	
Company Code	
Business Area	
Item Text	
Service Type (Public Service Germany)	
Service Category (Public Service Germany)	
Different Payment (for Time Tickets)	
Premium Number	
Premium Indicator	
Object Type	
Position	
Extra Pay Indicator	
Valuation Basis for Different Payment	
Currency Key	
Time Ticket Status	
End Date	
Interface Assignment	
Fund Accounting	
Functional Area	
Grant	
Commitment Item	
Commitment Item	

Table E.17 Time Tickets and Other Document Fields (Cont.)

E.19   AB — Absences

The absences information is stored on structure PC20I. Table E.18 shows the fields that are stored during processing.

Field	Notes
Pointer to absences	
Settlement Type	
PC205 assignment	
National split	
National split	
National split	
End Date	
Start Date	
Previous Day Indicator	
Start time	
End time	
Attendance or Absence Type	
Attendance and Absence Days	
Absence hours	
Attendance and Absence Days	
Payroll hours	
Calendar days	
Indicator for Subsequent Illness	
Indicator for repeated illness	
Absence valuation rule	
Work capacity percentage	
Old start date	
Old end date	
Reference Fields Exist (Primary/Secondary Costs)	

Table E.18   Absence Fields

Field	Notes
Confirmation Fields Exist	
Subtype	
Object Identification	
Lock Indicator for HR Master Data Record	
Number of Infotype Record with Same Key	
Record is for Full Day	
Set number of hours	
Indicator for absence valuation in off-cycle payroll	
Document number for time data	
Assignment for alternative payment	
Next Day Indicator	
Start Before 00:00	

Table E.18 Absence Fields (Cont.)

E.20 ANWES — Attendances

The attendances information is stored on structure PC2BD. This table stores Infotype 2002–related information and the fields that were set during Time Evaluation processing. Table E.19 shows the fields that are stored during processing.

Field	Notes
Pointer to attendances	
End Date	
Start Date	
Start time	
End time	

Table E.19 Attendance Fields

Field	Notes
Previous Day Indicator	
Attendance or Absence Type	
Attendance and Absence Days	
Absence hours	
Payroll days	
Payroll hours	
Calendar days	
Overtime Compensation Type	
Wage Type	
Record is for Full Day	
Set number of hours	
Reference Fields Exist (Primary/Secondary Costs)	
Confirmation Fields Exist	
Subtype	
Object Identification	
Lock Indicator for HR Master Data Record	
Number of Infotype Record with Same Key	
Evaluation Type for Attendances/ Absences	
Breaks During Attendances	
No break	
Breaks Specified Explicitly	
Breaks	
Start of Break	
End of Break	
Paid Break Period	
Unpaid Break Period	

Table E.19 Attendance Fields (Cont.)

Field	Notes
Start of Break	
End of Break	
Paid Break Period	
Unpaid Break Period	
Next Day Indicator	

Table E.19 Attendance Fields (Cont.)

E.21 VERT — Substitutions

The substitutions information is stored on structure PC2B4. This table stores all data related to Infotype 2003 — Substitutions. Table E.20 shows the fields that are stored during processing.

Field	Notes
Start Date	
End Date	
Previous Day Indicator	
Start time	
End time	
Substitution Type	
Daily Work Schedule Class	
Day Type	
Employee Subgroup Grouping for Work Schedules	
Public Holiday Calendar	
Personnel Subarea Grouping for Work Schedules	
Work Schedule Rule	
Personnel Subarea Grouping for Daily Work Schedules	

Table E.20 Substiution Fields

Field	Notes
Daily Work Schedule Variant	
Daily Work Schedule	
Company Code	
Personnel Area	
Position	
Start of break	
End of break	
Paid Break Period	
Unpaid Break Period	
Start of break	
End of break	
Paid Break Period	
Unpaid Break Period	
Object Identification	
Number of Infotype Record with Same Key	
Next Day Indicator	

Table E.20 Substiution Fields (Cont.)

E.22 RUFB — On-Call Duty

The on-call duty information is stored on structure PC2BE. Table E.21 shows the fields that are stored during processing.

Field	Notes
End Date	
Start Date	
Previous Day Indicator	

Table E.21 On-Call Duty Fields

Field	Notes
Start time	
End time	
Availability Subtype	
Employee Subgroup Grouping for Work Schedules	
Public Holiday Calendar	
Personnel Subarea Grouping for Work Schedules	
Work Schedule Rule	
Personnel Subarea Grouping for Daily Work Schedules	
Daily Work Schedule Variant	
Daily Work Schedule	
Object Identification	
Number of Infotype Record with Same Key	

Table E.21 On-Call Duty Fields (Cont.)

E.23 MEHR — Overtime

The overtime information is stored on structure PC2BC. Table E.22 shows the fields that are stored during processing.

Field	Notes
End Date	
Start Date	
Previous Day Indicator	
Start time	
End time	

Table E.22 Overtime Fields

Field	Notes
Overtime Compensation Type	
Start of break	
End of break	
Paid Break Period	
Unpaid Break Period	
Start of break	
End of break	
Paid Break Period	
Unpaid Break Period	
Start of break	
End of break	
Paid Break Period	
Paid Break Period	
Unpaid Break Period	
Start of break	
End of break	
Paid Break Period	
Unpaid Break Period	
Object Identification	
Number of Infotype Record with Same Key	

Table E.22 Overtime Fields (Cont.)

E.24   ABWKONTI — Absence Quotas

The absence quotas information is stored on structure PC2B9. This information stores Infotype 2006 — Absence Quotas — related information. Table E.23 shows the fields that are stored during processing.

Field	Notes
Infotype	
Subtype	
Object Identification	
Number of Infotype Record with Same Key	
End Date	
Start Date	
Previous Day Indicator	
Start time	
End time	
Absence Quota Type	
Number of Employee Time Quota	
Time/Measurement Unit	
Deduction of Employee Time Quota	
Indicator for update	
Start Date for Quota Deduction	
Quota Deduction to	

Table E.23 Absence Quota Fields

E.25 ANWKONTI — Attendance Quotas

The attendance quota information is stored on structure PC2BB. This table stores Infotype 2007 — Attendance Quotas — related information. Table E.24 shows the fields that are stored during processing.

Field	Notes
Infotype	
Subtype	
Object Identification	

Table E.24 Attendance Quota Fields

Field	Notes
Number of Infotype Record with Same Key	
End Date	
Start Date	
Start time	
End time	
Attendance Quota Type	
Number of Employee Time Quota	
Time/Measurement Unit	
Overtime Compensation Type	
Deduction of Employee Time Quota	
Indicator for update	
Approval only before working time	
Approval only after working time	
Full-day approval	
Start Date for Quota Deduction	
Quota Deduction to	

Table E.24 Attendance Quota Fields (Cont.)

E.26 SKO — Time Transfer Specifications

The time transfer specification information is stored on structure PC2B3. This information is obtained from Infotype 2012 — Time Transfer Specifications. Table E.25 shows the fields that are stored during processing.

Field	Notes
End Date	
Start Date	
Employee Time Transfer Type	
Number of hours in a time type	

Table E.25 Time Transfer Specification Fields

Field	Notes
Time point for time evaluation	
Object Identification	
Number of Infotype Record with Same Key	

Table E.25   Time Transfer Specification Fields (Cont.)

E.27   BEZUG — Recalculation Data

The recalculation data information is stored so that the system knows the last day that was evaluated for future processing. Table E.26 shows the fields that are stored during processing.

Field	Notes
Last Day Evaluated	
Recalculation period for Time Statement	
Recalculation period for third-party payroll	

Table E.26   Recalculation Fields

E.28   VERSION — B2 Version

The version table provides data regarding information about when the cluster was created. Table E.27 shows the fields that are stored during processing.

Field	Notes
Release	Version of SAP
Version Number	
Created by	
Created on	
Created at	
Created using	

Table E.27   B2 Cluster Version Fields

E.29 TIP/TOP

The time input table and time output table information is stored on structure PZI01. This is a table that you will see throughout Time Evaluation processing. The TIP table becomes the TOP table for a particular rule. The TOP table then becomes the next personnel calculation rules TIP table. For example, you have an absence that flows through a personnel calculation rule. The absence starts the rule as part of the TIP table. The rule conducts its calculations, and writes it to the TOP table. The TIP table is the input, and the TOP table is the output. This is one table in which you can directly influence the various values for a time type. Table E.28 shows the fields that are stored during processing.

Field	Notes
Start time (Header From)	
End Time (Header To)	
Status from pair formation (Header = 1)	A = Pair is delimited
	E = Missing order confirmation
	Blank or 0 = Error free
	1 — Interim entries
	2 — No clock-in
	3 — No clock-out
	4 — No break end time
	5 — No break start time
	7 — No off-site work start time
	9 — No off-site work end time
Attendance status of pair in time evaluation (Header P)	0 = Non recorded time
	1 = At Work
	2 = Recorded Absence
	3 = Off-Site Work or Attendance

Table E.28 TIP/TOP Fields

Field	Notes
Time identifier for daily work schedule (Header ID)	01 — Overtime unapproved outside of planned working time
	02 — Fill time during the planned working time
	03 — Core time
	04 — Core time break
	05 — Fill time break
	06 — Paid break
	07 — Overtime break unpaid
	08 — Overtime break paid
	09 — Overtime break
Processing type/time type class (Header CT)	Assigned in table V_T555Y
Processing type for Time Evaluation (Header P)	A = Absence
	S = Planned working time
	M = Overtime
	X = Public holiday attendance
	Table V_T510V
Time Type (Header TTyp)	Time types associate with the record from T555Y, T555Z, or through a custom rule
Number of hours	
Time event pair start (Header BR)	
Time event pair end (Header ER)	
Overtime Compensation Type (Header C)	Driven from the assignment of table entries T555R to an infotype record
Pointer to time pairs from time events (Header PT)	
Assignment for alternative payment (Header ALP)	
Pointer to cost accounting (Header C1)	

Table E.28 TIP/TOP Fields (Cont.)

Field	Notes
Pointer to attendances	
Pointer to absences (Header AB)	
Pointer to attendance quotas	
Origin indicator for time pairs (Header O)	A = Absence Infotype 2001
	C = Attendance and absence reasons
	D = Generated planned pair ex public holiday
	E = Time Event
	O = Overtime Infoytpe 2005
	P = Attendance Infotype 2002
	R = Availability Infotype 2004
Internal key for availability duty (Header I)	
Attendance/absence reason for begin entry (Header BPin)	
Attendance/absence reason for end entry (Header EPin)	
Terminal ID of start entry	
Terminal ID of end entry	
Change status	
Common sort field	
Arbitrary indicator (1)	
Arbitrary indicator (2)	

Table E.28 TIP/TOP Fields (Cont.)

E.30 TZP

The planned work schedule specification information is stored on structure PZIO9. Table E.29 shows the fields that are stored during processing.

Field	Notes
Point in time	
Time identifier for daily work schedule	
Paid break period, 4 decimals	
Unpaid break period, 4 decimals	
Break type 1	
Break type 2	
Single-Character Indicator	

Table E.29 TZP Fields

E.31   DZL

The generated wage types in Time Evaluation information is stored on structure PTM_DZL. Table E.30 shows the fields that are stored during processing.

Field	Notes
Date	
Start time	
End time	
Assignment for alternative payment	
Pointer to cost accounting	
Pointer to absences	
Wage Type	
Information type (S/M/A)	
Number of hours per wage type	
Pointer to attendances	
Start Before 00:00	

Table E.30 DZL Fields

E.32 TES

The time types in Time Evaluation information are temporarily stored on structure PZIO2. The TES table is the temporary table during Time Evaluation that stores the daily and monthly balances during processing. Once Time Evaluation exports the results, the various buckets of time are then moved to the ZES and SALDO tables. Table E.31 shows the fields that are stored during processing.

Field	Notes
Time Type	
Number of hours	

Table E.31 Daily Balance Fields

E.33 ZML

The time types in Time Evaluation information is temporarily stored on structure PZIO8. Table E.32 shows the fields that are stored during processing.

Field	Notes
Wage type	
Overtime Compensation Type	
Information Type (S/M/A)	
Start Time	
End Time	
Number of hours per wage type	
Assignment for alternative payment	
Pointer to cost accounting	
Pointer to absence	
Pointer to attendances	
Start Before 00:00	

Table E.32 ZML Fields

F   Time Functions

The standard delivered system offers various time functions that enable Time Evaluation processing. Each of these functions has various parameters that can determine how the system should process. These functions have Advanced Business Application Programming (ABAP) coding behind the scenes that is called to process Time Management data. For further help, and to review the options for each function, use Transaction code PE04 to access the function setup.

If your business requirements cannot be handled by the delivered functions, you can also create a custom function.

Figure F.1 shows the first list of functions.

Function	Description	Details
A2003	Process Work Center Substitutions	Used to process positions involving a different rate by means of the ALP split indicator on the TIP entry
ACTIO	Rule Controlled Execution of an action	Used to process a personnel calculation rule regardless of whether or not a TIP entry exists
ADJAB	Absence Record	Used to count the time of all of the TIP entries
AUL2	Base Entitlement Calculation	Used in Australia for base entitlement calculations
AUQUO	Generate Absence Quotas Australia	Used in Australia for generating absences quotas
BDAY	Initiate Block in Day Processing	Used to define processing blocks of information within a time schema
BEND	Processing Block After Day Processing	Used to define the end of a certain processing block
BINI	Initiate Processing Block	Used to define certain employee dependent settings prior to a processing block
BLOCK	Log Structure	Used to make the output log of the time evaluation schema cleaner to review
BREAK	Set Break Point	Used to interrupt processing and branches to the break mode
CHECK	General Checks Before Evaluations/Determine Status	Used to establish program statues controlling basic function of the time evaluation
COLLI	Collision Check for Multiple Personnel Assignments	Used to validate time collisions between all personnel assignment records
COM	Comment Lines in a Schema	Used to entry documentation into the schema log
COPY	Copies Front-End Subschema	Used to execute a subschemas processing steps
CUMBT	Cumulate Interim Results	Used to cumulate the interim results calculated at that point of the processing
DAYMO	Set Selection of Time Wage Types for Day Grouping	Used to establish groupings for wage type selections
DEFTP	Determine Planned Working Time Pairs	Used to determine the planned working time pairs in the TIP table
DKG	Reduced Hours Infotype (0049)	Used to reference data from infotype 0049
DODMO	Set Selection Rule Group for Time Wage Types	Used to set the time wage type selection group for the time wage type selection rule table

Figure F.1 Time Functions

Figure F.2 shows the second list of functions.

Function	Description	Details
DPTOL	Daily Work Schedule Tolerances	Used to processes time pairs according to the tolerance configured in the daily work schedule
DYNBR	Set Dynamic Breaks	Used to determine how many dynamic break are distributed within the daily work schedule
DYNWS	Dynamic Daily Work Schedule Assignment: Planned & Actual Overlap	Used to assign a new daily work schedule within time evaluation
EDAY	Exit Block in Day Processing	Used to define the end of processing blocks of information within a time schema
EEND	Processing Block After Day Processing	Used to mark the end of the day processing for the employee
EINI	Exit Initialization of Processing Block	Used to determine the end of a processing block
ELSE	Perform an Function If a Condition Does Not Apply	Used during an IF statement to provide other processing options
ENDIF	End Function of a Condition	Used to close the IF function processing
EXPRT	Export Results of Payroll	Used to store the results to the clusters
GOT	Generation of Overtime Time Pairs	Used to compare TIP entries with the overtime approvals of infotype 2007
GOU	Generation of Overtime Time Pairs Without Quota Deductions	Used to generate overtime without impacting quotas
GWT	Generate Wage Types From Time Pairs	Used to generate time wage types from the existing time pairs per rules established in the time wage type selection rules
IF	Execute Function if a Condition is Fulfilled	Used to process certain functionality under particular conditions
KNTAG	Fill KNTAG String for Core Night Work	Used to review time pairs to determine if the employee is working core night work
LIMIT	Value Limits for Time Balances	Used to validate time balance limits
MMSRV	Set Switch for External Services Accounting	Used to instruct SAP to provide employees infotype 2002 data to the SAP External Service Management component
MOD	Set Groupings	Used to call personnel calculation rules in which groupings have been established by the operation MODIF
OPTT	Set Program Parameters	Used to set program features
P2000	Import Daily Work Schedule/Create Time Pairs from Daily Work Schedule	Used to import the daily work schedule to create TIP entries

Figure F.2 Time Functions, continued

Figure F.3 shows the third list of functions.

Function	Description	Details
P2001	Import Absences to Table TIP	Used to import absences from infotype 2001 to the TIP table
P2002	Import Attendances to Table TIP	Used to import attendances from infotype 2002 to the TIP table
P2004	Import Availability Data to Table TIP	Used to import the availability information from infotype 2004 to the TIP table
P2005	Import Overtime Data to Table TIP	Used to import overtime information from infotype 2005 to the TIP table
P2006	Process Absence Quotas	Used to process the quota information from infotype 2006
P2007	Request Personnel Calculation Rule via ANWKONTI	Used to process attendance quota information
P2011	Import Daily WE/Enter Recorded Time Pairs in TIP	Used to import the daily work schedule to the TZP table and create TIP entries
P2012	Process Time Transfer Specifications	Used to import the time transfer information from infotype 2012 for processing
P2013	Processing of Quota Corrections	Used to process quota corrections entered on infotype 2013
PBRKS	Process Break Specifications	Used to evaluate all breaks according to the daily work schedule
PDB	Process Daily Balances Table TES	Used to process a calculation rule for the TES table day balances
PERT	Process Error Table PERT	Used to process the input table ERT
PMB	Process Daily Balances Table SALDO	Used to process the period balance table SALDO
POVT	Process Table ZML (Overtime Wage Types)	Used to process the overtime wages from table ZML
PRINT	Print Request	Used to display time evaluation values during the log
PROTO	Processing Log	Obsolete as of release 4.0
PTIP	Process Time Data Table TIP	Used to process all input table TIP entries
PTIPA	Process Time Data Table TIP if Absence Exists	Used to process input table entries for absences
PZL	Processing Time Wage Type Table ZL	Used to process the time wage type table DZL or ZL

Figure F.3 Time Functions, continued

Figure F.4 shows the final list of functions.

Function	Description	Details
QUOTA	Generate Absence Quotas	Used to generate absence quota per the rules configured
RTIP	Read Pairs Table TIP	Used to read the table TIP
RTIPA	Read Pairs Table TIP if Absences Exists	Used to read the table TIP for absences
SORT	Sort Internal Tables	Used to sort the sequence of the internal tables
TIMTP	Assign Time Types to Time Pairs	Used to create time pairs by comparing the time pairs with the daily work schedule
TYPES	Assign Processing Type and Time Type	Used to assign processing types and time types to the TIP entry based on table T555Y
UPAAP	Time Management Function for Checking PAAP Integration	Used for non-profit checking the PAAP integration

Figure F.4 Time Functions, continued

G   Time Management Operations

The standard delivered system offers various time operations that are used in conjunction with the functions that enable Time Evaluation processing. Each of these operations has various parameters that can determine how the system should process. Each of the operations has Advanced Business Application Programming (ABAP) coding behind the scenes. For further help, and to review the options for each operation, use Transaction code PE04 to access the function setup. The key thing to remember is that these operations have a variety of standard delivered processing functions, which can be completely researched via the SAP help on Transaction code PE04, or by hitting the F1 button if you are within a rule and you would like additional information on a particular operation.

If your business requirements cannot be handled by the delivered operations, you can also create a custom operation.

Figure G.1 shows the first list of operations.

Operations	Description	Details
ADDDB	Cumulate in day balance table	Adds the number of hours field to a time type of the internal table of a day balance
ADDMB	Cumulate in monthly balance table	Adds the number of hours field to the time type in the internal table of the period balances (Saldo)
ADDOT	Transfer to Table ZMO	Used to enter the wage types into table ZML
ADDVS	Cumulate in variable balances table	Used to add the number of hours field into the variable balances internal table
ADDZL	Cumulate in time wage types table	Used to add the number of hours field into the ZL table used by payroll
ALLDT	check 24-Hour coverage from start period	Used to determine shift and rotating shift bonuses
BITQU	Generate batch input session for attendances quotas	Used to create the attendance quotas on infotype 2007
BREAK	Set a break point	Used to interrupt the schema processing at any point
COLER	Transfer to error table	Used to transfer errors to internal table FEHLER
COLOP	Transfer data to internal table TOP	Used to transfer data from the TIP internal table to the TOP internal table
COLPA	Transfer to pair table	Used to change the values of a generated time pair
COLTQ	Increase amount of quota taken	Used to increate the amount of attendance quota used by the current number of hours field
COMOT	Overtime Pairs Analysis	Used to compare TIP pairs according to their processing Type. One new time pair is created based on the overlapping time pairs in the TIP table
DAYPG	Replace Daily Work Schedule	Used to override the employee's Daily Work Schedule
DELIM	Delimit Time Pair	Used to delimit time pairs with times from the daily work schedule
DYNDP	Dynamic Daily Work Schedule	Used to assign a new daily work schedule dynamically
FILLP	Change Time Pair Information	Used to enter a status and time data for a time pair
FILLW	Fill Wage Type Data	Used to assign additional information to internal wage type tables
GCY	Branch to Other Personnel Calculation Rule	Used to terminate the current rule processing and branch to a new rule

Figure G.1 Time Operations

Figure G.2 shows the second list of operations.

Operations	Description	Details
GENOT	Generate Time Pairs for Overtime	Used to flag time wage types as overtime given sufficient overtime quota
GENOW	Generate Wage Type in ZML	Used to split out a portion of the time wage type into the overtime table ZML
GENTG	Generate a TIP Entry	Used to enter a new entry into the TIP table
GENTP	Split TIP Entry	Used to split out a portion of the TIP entry into a new TIP entry
GENTW	Generate Wage Types	Used to split out a portion of the time wage type into the time wage type table ZL
GOTC	Request Internal Recalculation Run for Time Evaluation	Used to analyze overtime for a given period of time
HRS	Edit Number of Hours Field	Used to change the number of hours field
INSLR	Insert Locked Record in Table TIP	Used to automatically generate absences and attendances that have not yet been locked in theTIP table
INSTP	Correctly Setup Pair	Used to adjust time pairs in the TIP table based information of previous and subsequent pairs
LDPAY	Query End of Continued Pay	Used to query against the end of the continued pay of an absence record
LEAVE	Exit Processing of Personnel Calculation Rule	Used to exist the current personnel calculation rule and continue with the next rule
MESSG	Message Output	Used to output a particular message containing the employee number
MNPAS	Determine Main Personnel Assignment	Used to determine whether or not the personnel assignment is the main one associated with the employee
MODIF	Set Groupings	Used to set grouping for table access
NEXTR	Process a Continuation Line	Used to continue processing within the rule to the next line
OUTAL	Provide Data for Different Payment	Used to call data from the alternative payment table for decisions
OUTAQ	Retrieve Information From Absence Quotas	Used to call data from the absence quota table ABWKONTI for decisions
OUTER	Error Information	Used to enter the data on the error to the variable key
OUTOT	Provide Data on Overtime Wage Types	Used to entry overtime related data into the variable key

Figure G.2 Time Operations, continued

Figure G.3 shows the third list of operations.

Operations	Description	Details
OUTPQ	Retrieve Information from Attendances Quotas	Used to call data from the attendance quota table ANWKONTI for decisions
OUTTI	Retrieve Fields from the Time Recording Infotype	Used to read data from infotype 0050
OUTTP	Providing Time Pair Data	Used to enter data on the current time pair into the variable key
OUTWP	Providing Work Center Data	Used to enter various data into the variable key
OUTZL	Provide Information from Time Wage Types	Used to enter data from the ZL table into the variable key
PAYTP	Setting Employee Subgroup Grouping for Personnel Calculation Rule	Used to reclassify the employee subgroup grouping for personnel calculation rules during the processing
PCY	Go to a Personnel Calculation Subrule	Used to call a different personnel calculation rule. The original rule then continues to process
PLOOP	Nth Execution of Command Sequence	Used to process a set of date a certain amount of times
PPINC	Process Attendance/ Absence Reasons (PIN Codes)	Used to process the reason associated with the attendance or absence
R555D	Read Absence and Attendance Reasons for Subsystem	Used to read the reason codes for subsystem table entries
RETCD	Query Return Code	Used to enter the return code value into the variable key
RJCT	Rejection of employee	Used to cancel the processing of a personnel calculation rule
RNDOT	Round Time Pairs	Used to round time pairs to a particular value
ROUND	Round Clock Times or Number of Hours Field	Used to round start and end times, durations or the number of hours in a time pair
SCOND	Set Validity of Condition	Used to set conditions true or false
SORTP	Sort Daily Input Table TIP	Used to sort the time pairs in the daily input table TIP

Figure G.3 Time Operations, continued

Figure G.4 shows the fourth list of operations.

Operations	Description	Details
SUBST	Substitutions	Used to validate if there is a substitution
SUM	Cumulation of a Time Type Over a Particular Period	Used to summarize the daily balances over a given period of time
TABLE	Prepare Access to Table Fields	Used to access other customization tables
TEXIT	Exit Schema Processing	Used to exit the current schema block based on BIBI/EINI, BDAY/EDAY, or BEND/EEND
TFLAG	Change Status Data of a Day	Used to set various indicators controlling the way the day is processed
TIMAP	Have the Infotypes Imported by Time Evaluation Been Checked	Used to check the infotypes processed for a release date based on infotype 0130
TIPOS	Determine Relative Position of a Time Pair	Used to validate whether or not the current time pair is in relation to the previous and subsequent time pairs
TKUZR	Query Reduced Work Hours (RWH) Period	Used to validate the day being processed against the reduced working hours period
TMBRE	Generate Break Time	Used to make breaks paid, unpaid or working time
TSNDB	Determine Time Type and Add to TES (Student Nurses)	Used to determine temporary assignment is related to a practical training subject
TSNDC	Decision Operation for Time Statement for Student Nurses	Used to query student nurses data in Germany
TSORT	Sort Internal Tables	Used to sort internal tables in time evaluation
UPDLE	Absence Quota Accrual	Used to automatically accrue entitlement to specific leave types on infotype 0005
UPDTQ	Accrue Absence Quota	Used to automatically update entitlement to specific absence quotas on infotype 2006

Figure G.4 Time Operations, continued

Figure G.5 shows the final list of operations.

Operations	Description	Details
VALEN	Length of Variable Key	Used to vary the length of the variable key response to the decision to the Nth position
VAOFF	Offsetting Variable Key	Used to check a field as of the Nth position
VARAB	Provide Information on Absences	Used to enter data on the current absence into the variable key
VARPR	Provide Data on Current Attendance	Used to enter data on the current attendance into the variable key
VARST	Provide General Fields	Used to query a variety of general fields
VSTRG	Provide Strings in Variable Key	Used to enter strings into the variable key
VWTCL	Provide Processing Class of Wage Type	Used to query against the processing class associated with a wage type from table T512W

Figure G.5 Time Operations, continued

H Personnel Calculation Rules

Personnel calculation rules provide the functionality for you to customize your Time Evaluation schema so that your specific business requirements can be met by various calculations in the system. Appendix G provides a list of all of the delivered SAP operations available to Time Evaluation. This appendix explains a few of those operations.

H.1 Sample Operations in Personnel Calculation Rules

The following figures display samples of various operations within a personnel calculation rule. Let's have a look at Figure H.1, which shows how the operation HRS can be used to set a time type to the previous day's balance. Each of the examples show the rule, and are then broken down into the components of the rule and described in the table.

Set Hours Of Time Type Equal Previous Days Balance of Another Time Type

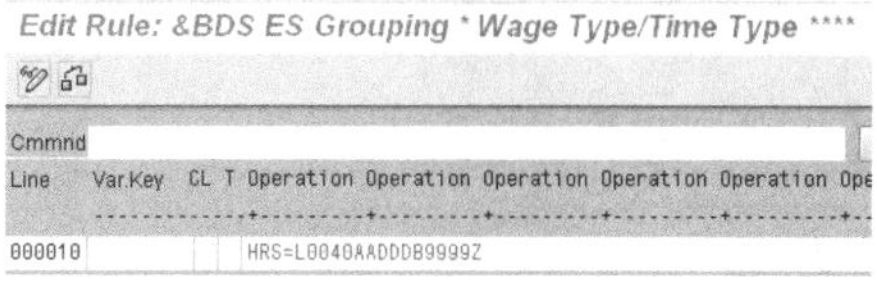

Operation	Description
HRS=L	Set the hours to the previous day's balance of a time type
0040	This is the time type that will have the previous day's balance selected
ADDDB	Add the previous days balance to the daily balance of a time type
9999	This is the time type the balance will be added to
Z	Replace any current daily balance of time type 9999 with the new balance

Figure H.1 Operation HRS

The next example also utilizes the operation HRS; however, this time the value is defaulted from a constant in table T511P. The amount is multiple by 1.5 and then added to time type 9999. Let's have a look at Figure H.2.

Set Hours Of Time Type Equal a Constant Value in Table V_T511K
and Add to Time Type 9999

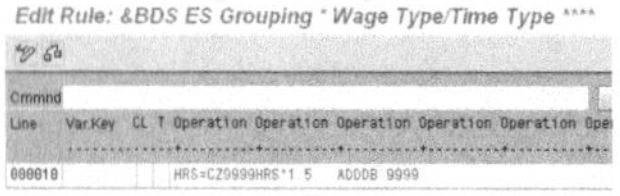

Operation	Description
HRS=C	Set the hours to equal a constant value in table V_T511K
Z9999	This is the constant in table V_T511K. You can set any value necessary
Hrs*1.5	Multiple the value of the constants time 1.5
ADDDB	Add the amount to the daily balance table
9999	Time type 9999 that will hold the final value

Figure H.2 Operation HRS

The next sample operation also utilizes the HRS operation. This example determines how long the employee has been employed based on Infotype 0041 date specifications. If the employee has been employed for at least four weeks, then time type 9999 is set to 1. Figure H.3 shows this example.

Set Hours Of Time Type Equal to the amount of time passed from a date type on infotype 41 until the date of processing. This example looks at full weeks worked at the date of entry and sets a counter time type to 1 if greater or equal to 4 full weeks work from date type B1.

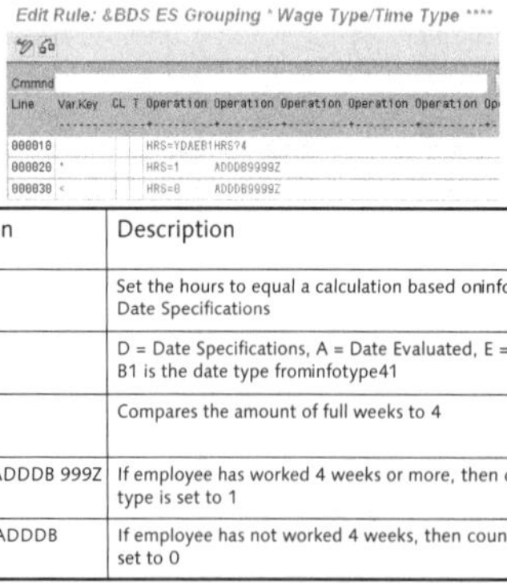

Operation	Description
HRS=Y	Set the hours to equal a calculation based oninfotype0041 Date Specifications
DAEB1	D = Date Specifications, A = Date Evaluated, E = Full Weeks, B1 is the date type frominfotype41
HRS?4	Compares the amount of full weeks to 4
* Hrs=1 ADDDB 999Z	If employee has worked 4 weeks or more, then counter time type is set to 1
< Hrs=1 ADDDB 999Z	If employee has not worked 4 weeks, then counter time type is set to 0

Figure H.3 Operation HRS

The next example in Figure H.4 shows the operation FILLP. This example set the current time type processing type to M, which is normally used for overtime.

Change the pair type to M or overtime and add to overtime time type 0040

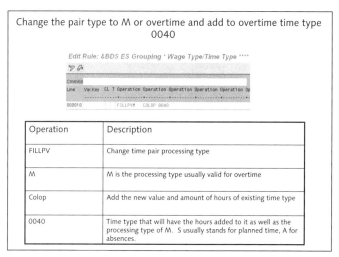

Operation	Description
FILLPV	Change time pair processing type
M	M is the processing type usually valid for overtime
Colop	Add the new value and amount of hours of existing time type
0040	Time type that will have the hours added to it as well as the processing type of M. S usually stands for planned time, A for absences.

Figure H.4 Operation FILLP

The next example in Figure H.5 is for operation OUTTP, which is used to make decisions based on the type of attendance that is processed. The various attendances types are added to time types XXXX and XXXZ.

Accumulate values from attendance types to various time types

Operation	Description
OUTTPPRTYP	Determine the attendance type being processed
0001	Attendance type 0001 will add to time type XXXX and then be passed to the next personnel calculation rule
0002	Attendance type 0002 will add to time type XXXX and XXXZZ. XXXZ will have any current balance replaced. The attendance is then be passed to the next personnel calculation rule

Figure H.5 Operation OUTTP

The following operation in Figure H.6 shows OUTWP, which is used to make decisions based on employee master data. In this example, we make a decision based on company code and set the condition to true or false. If the statement is true, the subsequent rule within an IF statement would be processed.

Set If statement True or False to determine if subsequent rules should process

*Edit Rule: &BDS ES Grouping * Wage Type/Time Type *****

Line	VarKey	CL	T	Operation	Operation	Operation	Operation	Operation	Op
000010			D	OUTWPCOMPY					
000020	1000			SCOND=T IF					
000030	2000			SCOND=F IF					

Operation	Description
OUTWPCOMPY	Determine the company code
1000	If the employee is in company 1000, then subsequent rules of the if statement in the schema will process
2000	If the employee is in company 2000, then subsequent rules of the if statement in the schema will not process

Figure H.6 Operation OUTWP

Figure H.7 shows operation VARST. This example shows a decision based on the day of the week and then a second decision is made based on the day type of the Work Schedule rule.

Determine if it is the first day of the period, if so then set the counter time type XXXX to value 1 for day type 0 or a 5 for day type 1. The counter can be called in subsequent rules to make decisions.

*Edit Rule: &BDS ES Grouping * Wage Type/Time Type *****

Line	VarKey	CL	T	Operation	Operation	Operation	Operation	Operation	Op
000010			D	VARSTFDYWW					
000020	N			COLOP *					
000030	Y		D	VARSTDAYTY					
000040	Y	*		COLOP *					
000050	Y	0		HRS=1	ADDDBXXXX				
000060	Y	1		HRS=5	ADDDBXXXX				

Operation	Description
VARSTFDYWW	Determine if it is the first day of the work week
Y = Yes N = No	If no, then just pass the time type through for the next personnel calculation rule.
Y	If yes, the determine the day type based on the daily work schedule. If *, the pass the time type through. If 0 or 1 then build a time type XXXX
0 or 1	If 0, then set the hours field to 1 and add to time type XXXX. If 1, then set the hours field to 5 and add to time type XXXX.

Figure H.7 Operation VARST

Figure H.8 shows operation HRS and operation GENTPB. In this example, we determine if any overtime has occurred for hours greater than eight. If there are, then those hours greater than eight are moved to time type 0040.

Generate an overtime time type by separating the overtime hours from the regular hours.

Operation	Description
HRS?8	Checks the time type that entered the rule to determine if the hours are greater than 8. If the hours are not greater than 8, the time type is added through to the next rule
*	If the hours are equal or greater than 8, then the rule continues processing
Hrs-8	The rule takes the hours from the time type and subtracts 8
GENTPB S	The 8 hours that are subtracted are removed with the processing type set to S for planned time.
ADDDB0010	The 8 hours are added to time type 0010 for planned time
FILLLPVM COLOP 0040	The remaining hours greater than 8 have the pair type set to M for overtime. The hours are then added to time type 0040 for overtime

Figure H.8   Operation HRS

The final example in Figure H.9 shows the operation ROUND, which is used to round the value of the time type. In this example, we used Z1, which is stored in table T559R. Table T559R is a rounding configuration table used to specify the rules regarding the rounding procedures.

Operation	Description
Round R	Rounds the time type XXXX hours according to table V_T559R
Z1	This is the rounding rule in table V_T559R

Figure H.9   Operation ROUND

Index

Provides a complete guide to
Organizational Management (OM)
with SAP ERP HCM

Teaches all functions of OM from a
global perspective

Includes practical integration and
customizing tips and techniques

Sylvia Chaudoir

Mastering SAP ERP HCM
Organizational Management

This book teaches the HCM team how to maximize the organizational management (OM)
component of SAP ERP HCM. It takes readers beyond the basics, by delving into all aspects
of the component as well as the little-known concepts. It teaches all of the key OM
functions, their purpose, and how to use and customize them. Numerous examples from
customers are used to provide context for decisions and to explain the benefits of the choices
that can be made. And in-depth explanations and practical examples are used to help readers
leverage the many available organizational objects to get the most out of their SAP HR
implementation.

348 pp., 2008, 69,95 Euro / US$ 69.95
ISBN 978-1-59229-208-0

>> www.sap-press.de/1796

Provides an overview of ESS and MSS

Covers the fundamentals of implementing SAP ESS/MSS

Provides an overview of Duet™ focusing on key areas, and provides a roadmap of future releases/functionality.

Uses ECC 6.0 and SAP NetWeaver Portal 7.0

Jeremy Masters, Christos Kotsakis

Implementing Employee and Manager Self-Services in SAP ERP HCM

Written for HR managers, power users, IT professionals, and consultants, this is the first comprehensive guide to what Employee and Manager self services (ESS & MSS) are all about. Not only does it explain ESS & MSS, but it also teaches how to implement an effective strategy in SAP ERP HCM.   The book details the baseline ESS/MSS functionality in SAP's latest release (ECC 6.0) using NetWeaver Portal (EP 7.0. It also covers more advanced topics like developing self-service applications with the Floor Plan Manager, authorization management (i.e., security), workflow, and delegation. In addition, Duet™ is used as the example of an intuitive (and familiar) user interface. The book concludes with real-world case studies as examples of effective ESS/MSS applications currently in use.

approx. 431 pp., 69,95 Euro / US$ 69.95
ISBN 978-1-59229-188-5

>> www.sap-press.de/1682

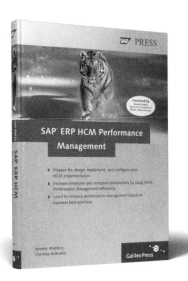

Prepare for, design, implement, and configure your HCM implementation

Increase employee and company productivity by using HCM Performance Management efficiently

Learn to enhance performance management based on business best practices

Jeremy Masters, Christos Kotsakis

SAP ERP HCM Performance Management

From Design to Implementation

This comprehensive book is an indispensable reference for HR professionals, analysts, and consultants learning how to implement SAP ERP HCM Performance Management. The book teaches you everything you need to know about the Objective Setting and Appraisal (OSA) module within SAP so that you can identify and retain key talent within your organization. You'll take a step-by-step journey through the design and implementation of your own performance management application that will help you improve your companies' performance and talent management processes. The book covers all the latest releases, including the R/3 Enterprise Release (4.7), SAP ERP 2004 (ECC 5.0) and SAP ERP 2005 (ECC 6.0).

302 pp., 2008, 69,95 Euro / US$ 69.95
ISBN 978-1-59229-124-3

>> www.sap-press.de/1421

Provides a complete guide to
the functionality of E-Recruiting

Teaches how to configure and
use E-Recruiting with other
HCM components

Uses a real-world workflow
approach

Ben Hayes

E-Recruiting with SAP ERP HCM

This book provides a practical guide to configuring and using SAP E-Recruitment effectively in the real-world. It is written to teach SAP ERP HCM users and the implementation team what the E-Recruiting tool is so that they can use it effectively in their recruitment process and integrate it easily with other HCM components. Beginning with an overview, the book progresses through the configuration process from a real workflow perspective. And all of the processes are covered in the order in which they are used in a real recruiting project. The book also details how to integrate E-Recruiting with other SAP components, and, as applicable, examples of companies using E-Recruiting successfully will be integrated throughout.

approx. 320 pp., 69,90 Euro / US$ 69.95
ISBN 978-1-59229-243-1, Jan 2009

>> www.sap-press.de/1957

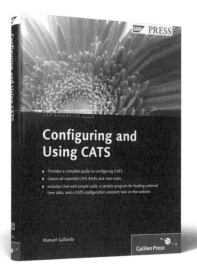

Provides a complete guide to configuring CATS

Covers all essential CATS enhancements and User-Exits

Includes user-exit sample code, a sample program for loading external CATS data, and a configuration assistant tool on the website

Manuel Gallardo

Configuring and Using CATS

SAP PRESS Essentials 51

This Essentials is a complete guide to effectively configuring CATS to meet your business needs. It provides detailed explanations of items to consider before beginning an implementation, along with steps for setting up CATS to fulfill the many complex configuration requirements. It also includes details about each CATS user-exit and tips on what functionality can or cannot be accomplished with particular user-exits. In addition, explanations for how to prevent and correct performance problems, answers to frequently asked questions, and tips for audit report development are provided.

approx. 160 pp., 68,– Euro / US$ 85
ISBN 978-1-59229-232-5

>> www.sap-press.de/1864